AF605394
Indented Head
Queenscliff
Clifton Springs
Point Richards

FISHING ATLAS FOR

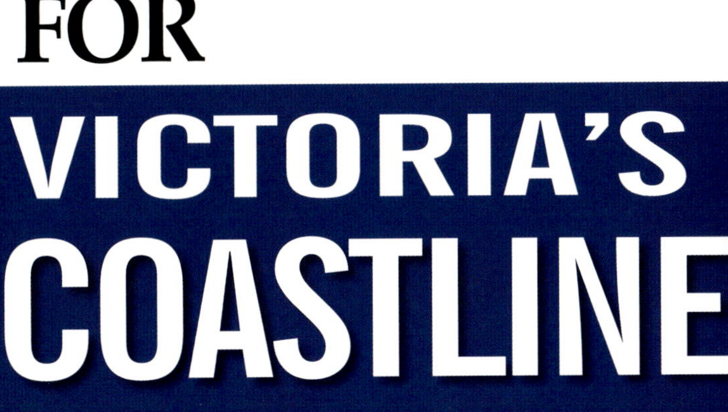

VICTORIA'S COASTLINE

JARROD DAY • BILL CLASSON

SCOTT GRAY • WILL THOMPSON • JUSTIN FELIX • LEE RAYNER • GEOFF WILSON

ACKNOWLEDGEMENTS

To the authors and editors who set the groundwork to make this revised and updated edition possible, thank you.

The contributing authors to this edition would like to thank all of those involved in the research and production of this fishing guide. Without the help of many, a book containing such a wealth of information could not be possible. To everyone that imparted their knowledge and experience, it is greatly appreciated—please excuse us for not listing you all individually.

To our friends and family for understanding that fishing plays a major role in our lives and quite honestly, we just can't get enough—thank you.

Lastly, we would like to acknowledge all of those directly or indirectly involved in recreational fishing not only in Victoria but Australia-wide, for without you all, this great sport would be lost.

First published 2012
Revised and updated 2016
Reprinted 2025

Published and distributed by
AFN Fishing & Outdoors
PO Box 544 Croydon, Victoria 3136
Telephone: (03) 9729 8788
Email: sales@afn.com.au
www.afn.com.au

ISBN: 9781 8651 3215 0

Printed in China

FOREWORD

It doesn't matter where you have previously fished along the Victorian coastline, there is always somewhere new to explore. This book has been updated numerous times over the years and with talented anglers exploring the coastline at every chance they get, more and more information has come to fruition. Better yet, some of these talented anglers have passed on this information and as you'll find within the pages of this book, this information is invaluable. The *Fishing Atlas for Victoria's Coastline* is not just a book but a bible that needs to be read from cover to cover. Just skipping through to the pages you are interested in doesn't do it justice and the more you dive in, the more information you'll pull to aid you in finding fish at your chosen location.

Changes in the environment have changed Victoria's fishing somewhat dramatically in recent times. Increased rainfall in the Spring in 2016 saw immense flooding state wide. This filled the dams and lakes with some overcapacity. This in turn saw a boom in redfin, Murray cod, trout and yellow belly throughout the state.

Then again for the saltwater, the large amount of freshwater spilling out into Port Phillip Bay and Western Port saw the snapper fishery slow down due to cooler water temperatures.

The world has cycles and no matter the season or the waterway things change, we just have to ride the wave and get out to explore more areas, more locations off the beaten track where there might be that slight chance, that one bream you can see holding under a fallen tree trunk hasn't see the lure you're about to toss at him.

With over 2000 km of coastline to fish, this book is jam packed with as much information that you could possibly fit in to it. So, now that you have this book in your hand, don't put it down. Each page has much information that will help you along your way to a successful day's fishing.

JARROD DAY

SAFETY DISCLAIMER

Information published in this book should be used as a guide only. Maps and GPS coordinates should not be used for navigational purposes. Water depths shown on maps have been thoroughly reviewed at the time of publication but cannot be guaranteed. The changing nature of the marine environment suggests that some structures are likely to change in response to the forces of nature. Mariners should use the latest information available to plan safe passage through the waters described in this book. Published GPS coordinates have been obtained from reliable sources and although every effort was made, not all were able to be verified. These marks cannot be guaranteed.

CONTENTS

NAVIGATION AIDS FOR MAPS

Port When lighted exhibits Starboard When lighted exhibits

Beacons, Bouys

CARDINAL MARKS Indicate navigable water for the area beyond the mark in the direction depicted.

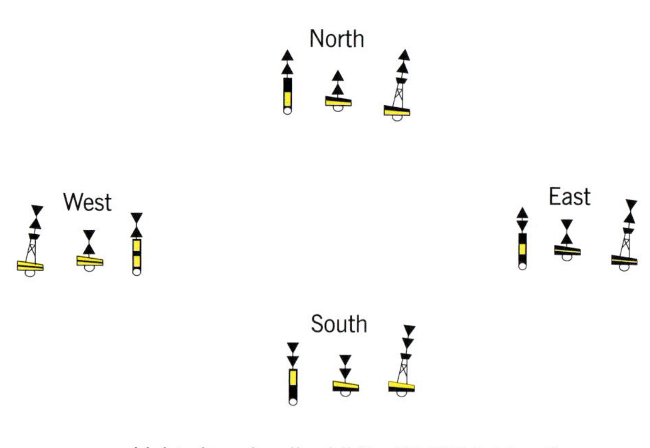

Lighted marks all exhibit a WHITE light.

SPECIAL MARKS Indicate several features (eg: pipe outfall) where navigable water is usually evident from the map.

When lighted exhibits

ISOLATED DANGER MARKS Are stationed over a submerged hazard. KEEP CLEAR.

When lighted exhibits

SAFE WATER MARKS

When lighted exhibits

MARINE PARK BUOYS

INTRODUCTION

The Fishing Atlas of Victoria's Coastline was last revised in 2007 and since then the fishing across the State has continued to hold and in many cases improve! The Port Phillip Bay and Western Port fisheries have sustained their recreational fisheries year after year. The snapper fishing in both areas, especially Port Phillip Bay has had a series of great years from 2008 right through until the 2012 season and the expectations are that this will continue well into the future under the watchful management of Fisheries Victoria.

Yellowtail kingfish have also been a target for many anglers and there have been serious fisheries explored around our coastline at places like Portland, Warnambool, Western Port, Cape Liptrap and Cliffy and Rabbit Islands.

The southern bluefin tuna have continued to be the mainstay of our offshore game fishery. On the surf fishing front our Australian salmon have been the mainstay and all the western and eastern surf beaches have experienced consistent fishing each year.

In our estuaries the bream fishery has a very bright future, with a series of solid breeding seasons associated with recent rains and floods. Mallacoota has been a standout, but there are literally dozens of waters that are producing quality bream. These are big and small from places as wise as the Glenelg River to local waters like the Werribee River and Patterson Lakes.

The Marine Parks have now been fully gazetted along Victoria's coast and the boundaries and restrictions have been completely updated marked and noted on the fishing maps contained in this book.

We have over 12 new maps in this atlas and have extensively updated all the maps in the previous edition.

Enjoy our coastline and the diverse range of locations, fish and types of fishing that you can pursue.

I hope this guide will give you the information required to enjoy a successful fishing day.

Bill Classon

Fishing Atlas for Victoria's Coastline Key for map positioning

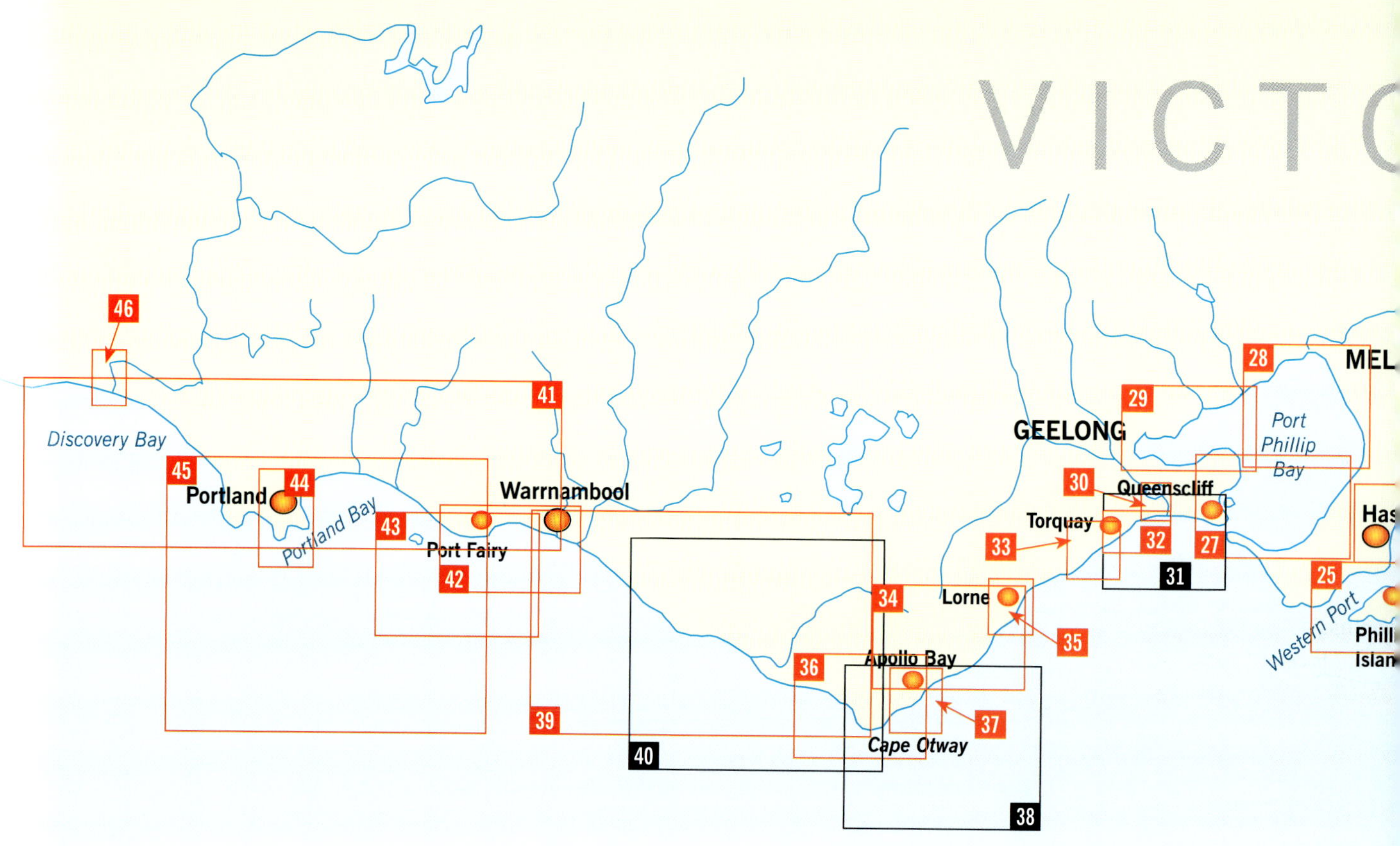

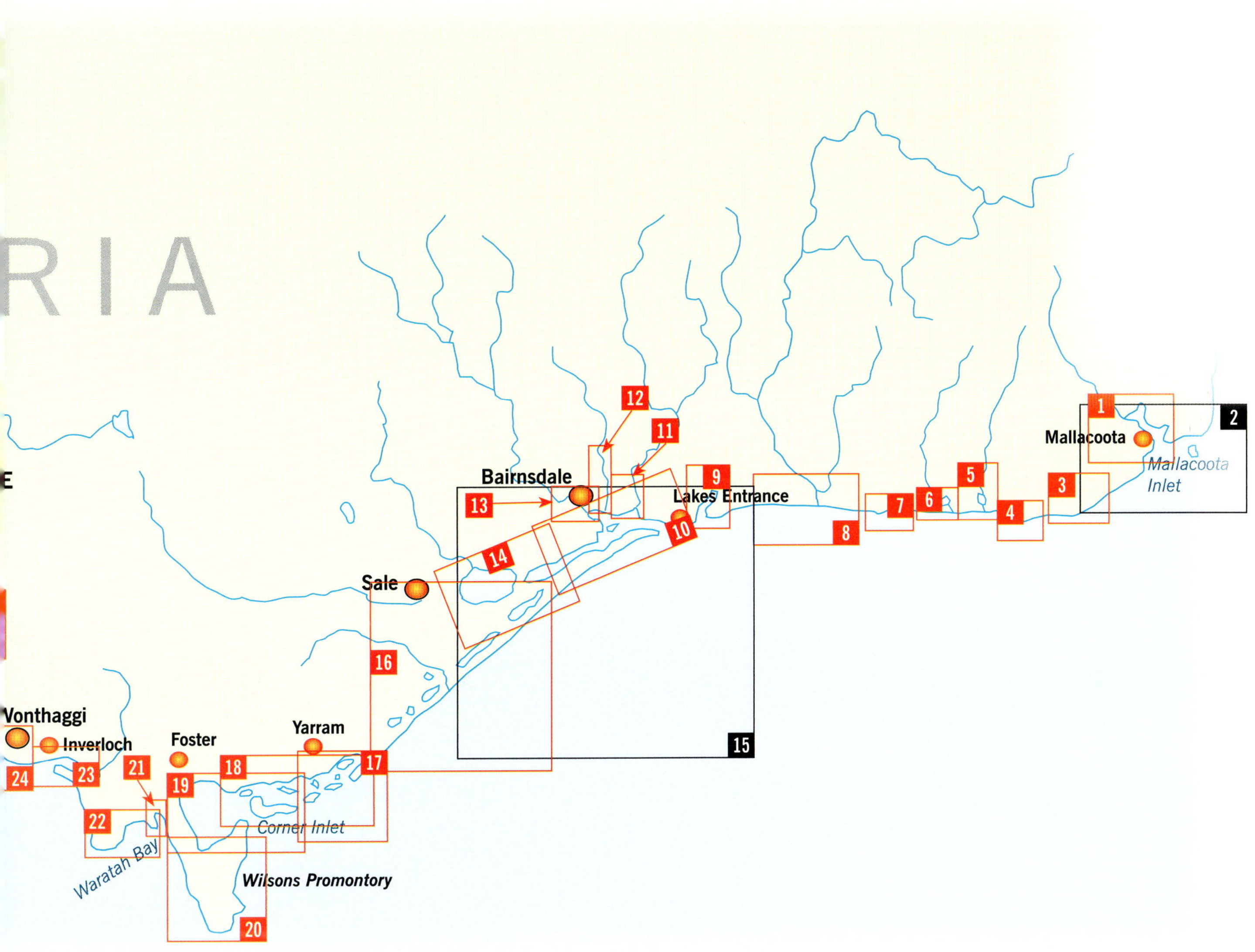
RIA
Mallacoota
Mallacoota Inlet
Bairnsdale
Lakes Entrance
Sale
Vonthaggi
Inverloch
Foster
Yarram
Corner Inlet
Waratah Bay
Wilsons Promontory
1
2
3
4
5
6
7
8
9
10
11
12
13
14
15
16
17
18
19
20
21
22
23
24

CHAPTER 1
MALLACOOTA

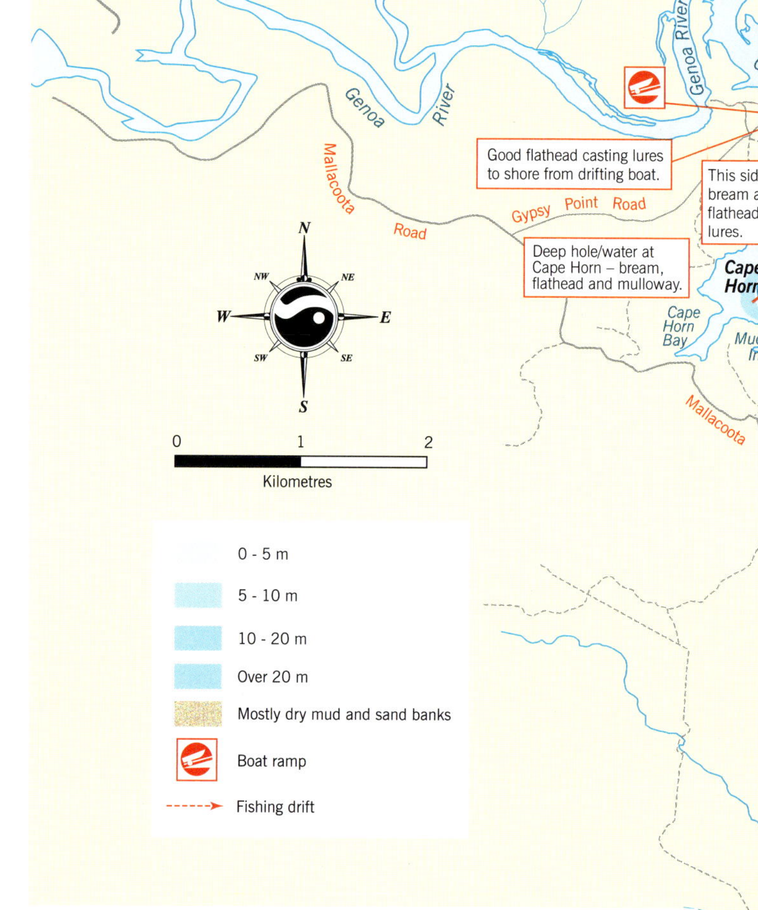

The township of Mallacoota is located at the entrance of Mallacoota Inlet, some 23 km by winding road from Genoa on the Princes Highway. The journey by road from Melbourne takes approximately six hours, longer if towing a boat or caravan. A favoured destination for many Victorian anglers, Mallacoota and its surrounding waters offer a wide variety of exceptional fishing opportunities. These range from the surf beaches and offshore, to the huge estuary system that is Mallacoota Inlet. Each year, this waterway produces good numbers of monster flathead and bream. Thankfully, with the soaring popularity of lure fishing, nowadays many anglers prefer to carefully photograph and release these fish to continue breeding and rejuvenating the system.

Mallacoota Inlet is the combined estuary of the Genoa and Wallagaraugh rivers. They join, then open out into a huge tidal lagoon downstream, before running to sea through a comparatively narrow and shallow entrance which periodically closes.

Mallacoota Inlet is divided into two bodies of water known as the Top Lake and Bottom Lake. A deep channel, approximately 1.5 km in length and known as 'The Narrows', connects the two lakes. The Bottom Lake is the largest body of water in the system by far and bears the brunt of the fishing pressure.

While there are plenty of great locations for land based fishing within the estuary system, the majority of anglers fish from boats, either bringing their own craft, or using the hire boats which are available. Public boat ramps are at Bastion Point, Mallacoota, Karbethong and Gypsy Point.

BOAT RAMPS

LOCATION	BOAT SIZE	PARKING	BUILD
Bemm River	5 m	Excellent	Concrete
Marlo	6 m	Excellent	Concrete
Brodribb River	5 m	Average	Concrete
Tyers	5.5 m	Good	Concrete
Cape Conran	5.5 m	Good	Concrete

Bastion Point Boat Ramp

In previous editions of this book, Bastion Point Boat Ramp was always referred to as a single lane ramp.

Recently the ramp has been gone through an upgrade whereby is it now a duel lane concrete ramp with fixed pontoon. A break wall has also been installed to keep ocean swells at bay while launching. Like all break walls created where ramps access the ocean, great care when launching must still be taken.

Mallacoota Ramp

A double lane ramp adjacent to the main wharf, Mallacoota boat ramp gives access to the entire inlet via the Bottom Lake and the Narrows. However, the passage to the ocean should never be attempted without an experienced hand in charge of the vessel.

Karbethong Ramp

Karbethong is on the Bottom Lake just north of Mallacoota. The water surrounding the boat ramp is shallow, limiting the size of craft being launched here to around 5.5 metres. This ramp is convenient to The Narrows, Top Lake and the Goodwin Sands, a favoured flathead fishing and bait pumping location, in the Bottom Lake.

Gypsy Point Ramp

The settlement of Gypsy Point boasts a hotel, wharf, boat ramp and a few houses. To reach Gypsy Point, take the Mallacoota turn-off from the Princes Highway at Genoa and travel for 8 km to the Gypsy Point turn-off.

The gravel boat ramp at Gypsy Point drops sharply into deep water, thus enabling boats of up to 6m or more to be launched with ease. Even though parking space is usually quite adequate, difficulties can be encountered during the Christmas holidays.

BOTTOM LAKE

The Bottom Lake is relatively deep except for the Goodwin Sands, Robertsons Bank, the sand spit marked by the structure known as 'John Bull', and the shallow bank surrounding the two islands just inside the entrance.

These shallow water hazards are obvious and the main channels are clearly marked with pylons. This makes navigating the Bottom Lake reasonably easy provided due care is taken.

The shallow banks provide good bait pumping grounds and are popular with anglers using bait or lures to fish for big flathead. Long-tailed estuarine stingrays are common on the shallow banks and are sometimes reluctant to move aside for a wading angler, so be careful not to step on one.

These shallow waters are also favoured areas for trapping mullet that are baited live to tempt large flathead. A clear plastic cordial bottle with a rectangular slot about 4cm wide is quite effective for trapping these mullet. The trap is baited with

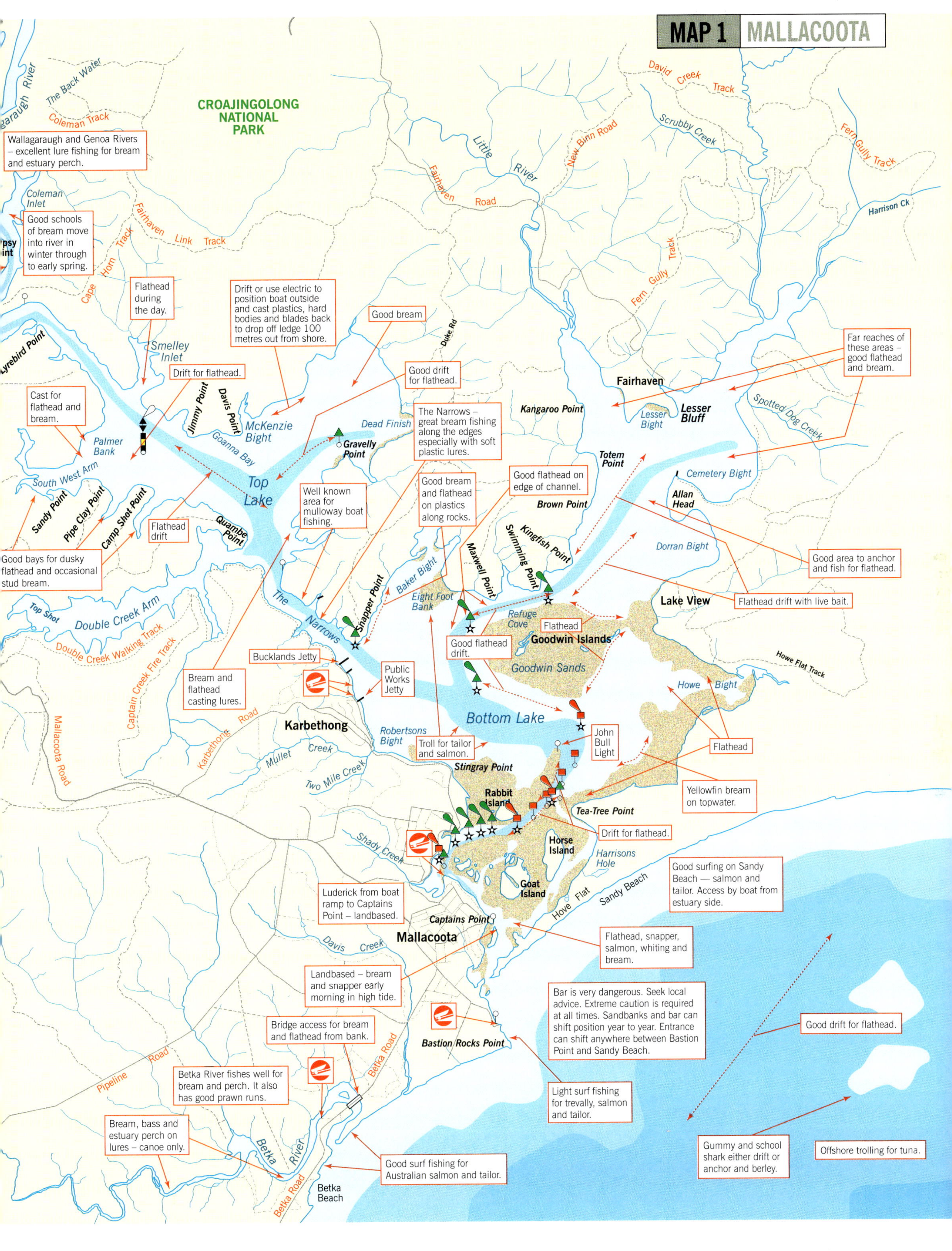
MAP 1 MALLACOOTA
CROAJINGOLONG NATIONAL PARK
Wallagaraugh and Genoa Rivers – excellent lure fishing for bream and estuary perch.
Good schools of bream move into river in winter through to early spring.
Flathead during the day.
Drift or use electric to position boat outside and cast plastics, hard bodies and blades back to drop off ledge 100 metres out from shore.
Good bream
Drift for flathead.
Cast for flathead and bream.
Good drift for flathead.
The Narrows – great bream fishing along the edges especially with soft plastic lures.
Far reaches of these areas – good flathead and bream.
Good bream and flathead on plastics along rocks.
Good flathead on edge of channel.
Well known area for mulloway boat fishing.
Flathead drift
Good bays for dusky flathead and occasional stud bream.
Good area to anchor and fish for flathead.
Flathead drift with live bait.
Flathead
Good flathead drift.
Bucklands Jetty
Public Works Jetty
Bream and flathead casting lures.
Troll for tailor and salmon.
John Bull Light
Flathead
Yellowfin bream on topwater.
Drift for flathead.
Good surfing on Sandy Beach — salmon and tailor. Access by boat from estuary side.
Luderick from boat ramp to Captains Point – landbased.
Flathead, snapper, salmon, whiting and bream.
Landbased – bream and snapper early morning in high tide.
Bar is very dangerous. Seek local advice. Extreme caution is required at all times. Sandbanks and bar can shift position year to year. Entrance can shift anywhere between Bastion Point and Sandy Beach.
Bridge access for bream and flathead from bank.
Good drift for flathead.
Betka River fishes well for bream and perch. It also has good prawn runs.
Light surf fishing for trevally, salmon and tailor.
Bream, bass and estuary perch on lures – canoe only.
Good surf fishing for Australian salmon and tailor.
Gummy and school shark either drift or anchor and berley.
Offshore trolling for tuna.
Top Lake
Bottom Lake
Karbethong
Mallacoota
Lake View
Fairhaven
Goodwin Islands
Goodwin Sands
Rabbit Island
Horse Island
Goat Island
Captains Point
Bastion Rocks Point
Stingray Point
Tea-Tree Point
Betka Beach
Sandy Beach
Howe Flat
Harrisons Hole
Howe Bight
Robertsons Bight
Eight Foot Bank
Refuge Cove
Snapper Point
Baker Bight
Maxwell Point
Swimming Point
Kingfish Point
Brown Point
Totem Point
Allan Head
Cemetery Bight
Dorran Bight
Lesser Bight
Lesser Bluff
Kangaroo Point
Dead Finish
Gravelly Point
McKenzie Bight
Goanna Bay
Davis Point
Jimmy Point
Smelley Inlet
Palmer Bank
South West Arm
Sandy Point
Pipe Clay Point
Camp Shot Point
Quambe Point
Lyrebird Point
Coleman Inlet
Double Creek Arm
Top Shot
The Narrows
Mullet Creek
Two Mile Creek
Shady Creek
Davis Creek
Betka River
The Back Water
Little River
Scrubby Creek
Spotted Dog Creek
Harrison Ck
Coleman Track
Fairhaven Link Track
Cape Horn Track
Fairhaven Road
New Binn Road
David Creek Track
Fern Gully Track
Duke Rd
Howe Flat Track
Double Creek Walking Track
Captain Creek Fire Track
Karbethong Road
Mallacoota Road
Pipeline Road
Betka Road

breadcrumbs, weighted with a heavy sinker or stone, and placed on the bottom, hole uppermost, in water just deep enough to cover the trap. If you put the trap out in water that is too deep, the mullet will not go inside.

Goodwin Sands

Probably one of the most famous spots in Mallacoota and for good reason, the Goodwin Sands is a perfect spot for anglers to chase flathead and other estuary species such as bream and whiting. Accessible only by boat or Kayak, the large expanse of sand flats allows anglers to either leave their vessel and wade the flats casting lures or baits, or fish while boat drifting. Boats setup with electric motors can easily manoeuvre around thoroughly working every inch of the bank. Whichever method you choose this area is a great producer of big flathead. Look for areas where the sand flat drops off into deeper water or along the edges of weed beds as these are places where flathead will lie in ambush. The backside of Goodwin Sands is particularly productive for flathead in the summer months where they sun themselves. This is a top spot to flick soft plastics and hard body lures but it is imperative that anglers hold off the bank within casting distance so not to spook the fish.

The deeper water around the Goodwin Sands also holds silver trevally, small snapper, small flathead and the occasional mulloway; the latter have been caught just off the spit on the north side.

Howe Bight

This deep water location is a perfect area for anglers to look for large predatory fish. Accessible by boat, Howe Bight is surrounded by shallow sandbanks that drop abruptly into quite deep water. Anglers can either wade the shallows, casting out over the deep drop-offs, or nowadays many anglers have bow or transom mounted electric motors on their boats, allowing them to silently move along these edges, casting lures as they go. Working the edges of the shallows from Howe Bight to Tea Tree Point is particularly productive for yellowfin bream. Yellow fin are more aggressive than black bream and respond exceptionally well to small surface stick baits and poppers. This area also provides a chance of hooking a mulloway, which like to patrol the deep drop-offs.

Baker Bight

Access to Baker Bight is by boat or kayak. There are some deep edges suitable for anglers seeking mulloway and large flathead, but tailor can be a problem when using live bait. If this is the case, try catching a smallish tailor and use this for a live bait—if a mulloway eats it hang on as it's a fair bet it will be big.

This area is also home to some flathead that live on its shallow banks. These banks are best suited to lure fishing and there is quite a bit of weed you will need to work your lures around.

Following the bank back towards Snapper Point, the banks edge is quite rocky. This area is very popular with anglers flicking soft plastics and hard body lures for large flathead and bream.

Captains Point

Captains Point is accessible through the main caravan park and drops away sharply into deep water. This area is a favourite haunt of luderick specialists. When the entrance is open, the tide runs strongly through here, but bottom fishing is possible either side of the change of tide. A variety of fish, including mulloway, have been caught here. However, the bottom is snaggy, so unfortunately some tackle losses can be expected.

Just around the corner from Captains Point, the rocks in the large, shallow backwater provide plenty of weed suitable for catching luderick.

Mallacoota Wharf

When the entrance is open the tidal flow can be quite strong at the wharf making it an ideal location for many species. Every year some great fish are taken here, everything from bream, trevally, whiting, luderick, flathead and even mulloway frequent the area. However the most common catches would be good sized flathead. It is worth fishing from the wharf with live baits and fresh fish fillets for mulloway although clumps of floating weed and other boats can make landing them difficult.

Slipway Jetty

The Slipway Jetty is near the wharf and offers the same sort of fishing, as it protrudes into deep water. Unfortunately, there is only room for a couple of people to fish here comfortably at any one time.

Prawns can sometimes be taken in good numbers under the lights of the Slipway Jetty using a dip net on an outgoing tide, particularly during the late summer and autumn.

Cow Paddock

The Cow Paddock is the section of bank between Coull's Inlet (where the private jetties are, just to the left of the Slipway Jetty) and the Fisheries Jetty upstream. The water is very deep right in close along here and luderick can be caught in good numbers by anglers skilled in targeting them.

The Narrows

Made up of snags and rock walls that drop into deep water, The Narrows is a 1.5 km channel that joins the top and bottom lake at Mallacoota. The average depth through here is about 8 to 9 metres.

The main species on offer here are bream and estuary perch, both of which love to sit close to the rock walls and in the snags that line The Narrows. Many anglers target them with baits such as prawns but it is also a favourite location for anglers casting small soft plastic, metal vibe or hard bodied lures.

When working this area, losing lures is just part and parcel of it. Stay within casting range from the bank and work lures right down along the rock wall. Always let the soft plastic or Metal Vibe to rest on the bottom for 1-2 seconds before twitching it back up into the water column.

Aside from the bream and perch The Narrows is a favoured haunt for mulloway, which like to cruise and hunt in this area. Most are taken at night by anglers using freshly caught bait such as octopus, tailor fillets or live mullet, although many are taken on soft plastic lures—both intentionally and by anglers chasing bream

OVERVIEW

Whiting are sometimes taken in the Bottom Lake during summer. School whiting predominate, but King George whiting are also occasionally taken in good numbers.

Bream, both yellowfin and black bream, are prolific in the Bottom Lake during summer and may be caught in good numbers by anglers prepared to prospect in likely areas. This is especially so when the entrance is open and the prawns are around. At these times the bream become very active in the tidal waters towards the entrance.

Tailor are also prolific in the Bottom Lake during summer and may be readily caught by trolling lures behind the boat. The majority of these fish are relatively small. However, licensed netters in the lake have taken some huge specimens and these would be a possibility on suitable rigs baited with live mullet.

Mulloway are taken in the Bottom Lake both accidentally and also by anglers specifically targeting them. Should the entrance be open and tidal, the deep water passages, both to the north and the south of the Goodwin Sands, are well worth trying particularly around a change of tide on evening or just after dark, make sure you use the freshest of baits either live or dead or another option is to fish with large soft plastic lures.

Landbased Fishing

Without a boat, land based anglers are limited to a handful of locations, but the more capable anglers do well.

TOP LAKE

The shallower banks within the Top Lake, particularly the Palmer Bank, are a haven for lure and bait anglers chasing flathead. However, some of the better areas can be weeded up quite badly, which makes lure fishing difficult. Stingrays are also abundant on the shallow banks in the Top Lake so take care when wading.

Obvious snags within the Top Lake support good populations of bream, and sometimes luderick and estuary perch as well. These snags are hard on tackle but they provide excellent fishing.

The moderately shallow waters of the east arm of the Top Lake, all the way up to what is known as 'Dead Finish', are well worth prospecting with live mullet, particularly on evening. Big flathead are the main chance up here, along with the real prospect of hooking a good sized mulloway.

DOUBLE CREEK ARM

The narrow west arm of the Top Lake, Double Creek Arm, supports good populations of large flathead and bream but is heavily weeded and difficult to fish. To combat the weed use either unweighted live prawns or lightly weighted soft plastics. Surface poppers are also a good option as well.

CAPE HORN

Cape Horn is the spit of land projecting into the sharp bend made by the Genoa River above the Top Lake. Here, the steeply shelving bank drops away into an average depth of some 12m making it the deepest stretch of water in the system.

Bream, estuary perch and luderick may all be taken from the obvious snags and submerged timber on either side of the river here. Mulloway are also taken here at times by anglers patient enough to put in the necessary time to be successful.

GYPSY POINT

The wharf at Gypsy Point is just upstream from the boat ramp and is well worth trying for a bream or flathead, particularly on evening or just after dark.

The sandbanks and submerged trees, both upstream and downstream from Gypsy Point, are great places to begin prospecting for flathead and bream either with lures or bait. Luderick may also be taken in good numbers from the obvious snags, along with the occasional estuary perch. Amongst the snags, soft plastics and sinking hard body lures work exceptionally well. Unfortunately you will lose some tackle so be prepared and take a good selection of options.

GENOA RIVER

The Genoa River upstream from Gypsy Point, particularly above the Gypsy Point Lodge and private launching ramp, becomes shallower and sandbars and snags become more numerous—navigation needs to be undertaken with care.

The extensive shallow sandbars in the Genoa River are well populated with sandworms and enough for a day's fishing can be pumped in a short space of time.

Although almost fresh, this upstream reach of the Genoa is well worth fishing in winter after the action has slowed in the larger bodies of water. Flathead, bream, estuary perch and luderick are all numerous in this section of river well into winter, along with the long-tailed estuarine stingrays usually found further downstream in summer.

WALLAGARAUGH RIVER

The Wallagaraugh River branches to the right of the Genoa River several hundred metres above Gypsy Point. Although shallow and gravelly, the Wallagaraugh is navigable for several kilometres to the section known as the 'Bull Ring'.

Cape Horn

It's hard to say precisely how the Bull Ring got its name, but it used to be the scene of an annual massacre of black bream during their spring spawning run. Year after year, from September through until the end of November, it would be impossible to estimate the tonnage of bream slaughtered in this section of the river. It's been some years since there has been a large spawning run of bream in this section of the Wallagaraugh. Hopefully the bream have somehow become aware of how vulnerable they are during their seasonal, up-river spawning migration.

While the bream fishing may not be quite as good as it used to be, the river still produces excellent bream, especially for anglers fishing with lures, and thankfully these days most prefer to release all of the bigger fish into the system to continue breeding.

The Wallagaraugh once had a good population of Australian bass. That population is in decline, not so much from angling pressure but from river improvement trusts that removed submerged timber from the river to speed the flow.

However, despite man's greed and stupidity, both the Wallagaraugh and Genoa rivers still produce excellent fish to anglers who enjoy the challenge of fishing in the unrivalled grandeur of the Croajingalong National Park.

BOAT RAMPS

LOCATION	BOAT SIZE	PARKING	BUILD
Bastion Point	6 m	Good	Concrete
Mallacoota	8 m	Excellent	Concrete
Lakeside Drive	5 m	Very Good	Crushed Rock
Gipsy Point	6 m	Very Good	Concrete

Gypsy Point

MAP 2 MALLACOOTA OFFSHORE

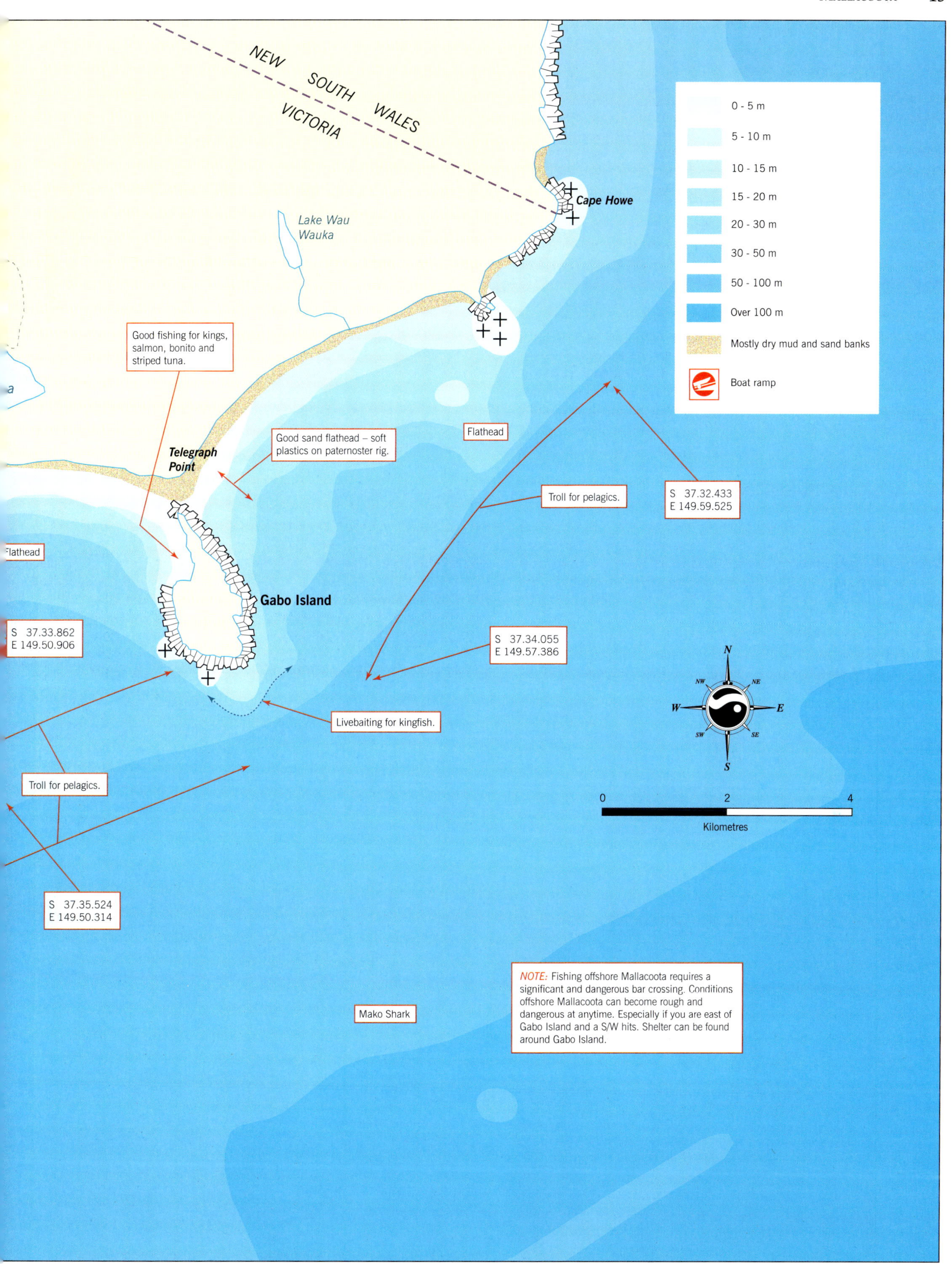
NEW SOUTH WALES
VICTORIA
Lake Wau Wauka
Cape Howe
0 - 5 m
5 - 10 m
10 - 15 m
15 - 20 m
20 - 30 m
30 - 50 m
50 - 100 m
Over 100 m
Mostly dry mud and sand banks
Boat ramp
Good fishing for kings, salmon, bonito and striped tuna.
Flathead
Good sand flathead – soft plastics on paternoster rig.
Telegraph Point
Troll for pelagics.
S 37.32.433
E 149.59.525
Flathead
Gabo Island
S 37.33.862
E 149.50.906
S 37.34.055
E 149.57.386
Livebaiting for kingfish.
N
NW
NE
W
E
SW
SE
S
0
2
4
Kilometres
Troll for pelagics.
S 37.35.524
E 149.50.314
Mako Shark
NOTE: Fishing offshore Mallacoota requires a significant and dangerous bar crossing. Conditions offshore Mallacoota can become rough and dangerous at anytime. Especially if you are east of Gabo Island and a S/W hits. Shelter can be found around Gabo Island.

OFFSHORE AND SURF

Offshore Fishing

When the entrance is open and navigable the offshore waters around Mallacoota have a wide variety of species on offer to anglers. There are excellent flathead and gummy shark grounds, and reef systems that hold snapper and other reef species. However it's the bluewater fishing potential off here that gets the blood pumping and heart racing.

Seven and 13 km to the north-east respectively, Tallaberga and Gabo islands attract pelagic species including tuna.

Twenty kilometres to the south and rising out of 100m of water to just 30m are the Star banks. Aside from being a great spot to target reef fish, this large reef system creates upwellings and holds large numbers of baitfish. When warm summer currents flow over it, many predators such as kingfish, sharks, tuna and at times marlin frequent the area. In recent times, Marlin fishing has become much more popular with anglers heading out to the oil rigs to find success. Kingfish are also more abundant now than ever with anglers using live baits, trolling and jigging methods to catch them.

Forty kilometres to the east, the 300m line is within range of suitably equipped trailer boats. Out anglers fish the edge of the continental shelf for the same species that are targeted just up the coast at places such as Eden and Merimbula.

It really is a shame that there isn't safe, permanent access to the offshore waters of Mallacoota; if there was it would have great potential to become a game fishing port. .

Surf Fishing

The coastline either side of Mallacoota offers great surf fishing for those who enjoy getting sand between their toes—or donning waders in the cooler weather.

Many of the beaches have long deep gutters that run close to shore, but as with all beaches they can and do change with the weather and time.

Early morning and late afternoon will see anglers chasing tailor and salmon while through the day mullet, bream and more salmon are the rewards. Bait fishing is the standard technique used with a paternoster rig serving well. Blue bait and white bait are best offered. When salmon and tailor are in good numbers, spinning with metal slugs can be very rewarding. However once darkness falls many of the beaches in the area are known for good gummy shark fishing, and at times school and bronze whaler sharks.

Strangely enough, while the inlet itself produces good mulloway, very few are ever taken from the surf.

Entrance Beach

Taking the road to Bastion Point, the Entrance Beach is on the left. This beach is situated on the ocean side of a large sand spit which divides the ocean from the estuary. The beach slopes away quickly thus providing deep water well within modest casting range.

Bait may be pumped on the sand flats at low tide on the estuary side of the spit.

Tip Beach

Take the road to Bastion Point, then the Golf Club turn-off to the right. Continue on past the Golf Club to where you can park your car and walk down to the beach.

TACKLE & GENERAL INFORMATION

Pelican Pete's Bait & Tackle (Caltex)
42 – 44 Maurice Ave, Mallacoota Vic 3892
Phone: (03) 5158 0354

WEST MALLACOOTA

Betka Beach

Take the road to the aerodrome for approximately 3 km and look for the sign indicating the track to the beach as you descend toward the bridge over the Betka River.

Betka River

The Betka River is usually open to the sea and salmon, mullet and small silver trevally move back and forth with the tide, providing anglers with good sport on light tackle downstream from the bridge.

Sandworms and yabbies may be pumped in the vicinity of the bridge and shrimp may be dip-netted amongst the prolific weed growth in the lower reaches. Prawns may also be netted in the shallows and backwaters at night with the aid of a light.

The area just downstream from the bridge provides good fishing for bream, particularly during the first hour or two of the incoming tide. Luderick are also present here in good numbers at times and can be seen from the bridge.

Upstream access is virtually impossible for land based anglers, but there is a small boat ramp on the Betka some 500 or 600m past the Betka Bridge on the right, heading toward the aerodrome.

The Betka is navigable for several kilometres upstream by small boat, and these reaches produces luderick, bream, estuary perch, flathead, garfish, mullet, small salmon and some very large eels.

left: Stuart Hindson displays a lovely Mallacoota flathead.

CHAPTER 2

FAR EAST GIPPSLAND

Cape Howe to Tamboon Inlet

Although the majority of the far East Gippsland estuaries are very small in comparison to Mallacoota, they can at times offer some of the finest bream and estuary perch fishing in the country. This is especially so in the two better known inlets of Wingan Inlet and Tamboon Inlet.

Access to Wingan Inlet is via the West Wingan Road, between Cann River and Genoa. The inlet itself is a tidal estuary system and offers great bream fishing for both lure and bait fishers. The inlet also has several other species on offer such as mullet, along with good numbers of estuary perch and flathead, some of which are monsters. The surf beach which heads south west from the entrance offers some fantastic fishing for good sized salmon, plenty of mullet, and around the full moon it is definitely worth fishing of a night for gummy sharks.

Tamboon Inlet is fed by the Cann River. While this system is not always open to the sea, it has become a very popular fishing and holidaying location over the past few years, and for good reason. The inlet holds great numbers of flathead, many of which are large, as well as a good population of bream and estuary perch. Aside from these species the inlet has good prawning on offer over the warmer months when the entrance is open to the sea. Tamboon Inlet is best fished from a small boat or canoe and is especially suited to lure fishing enthusiasts, who like to slowly fish along the edges casting to likely looking areas.

MALLACOOTA TO PT HICKS

Shipwreck Creek

Only a small waterway that is often closed to the sea, it does hold a population of bream. It is a location best suited to keen anglers who like to get away from the crowds and find their own small piece of water to fish. Bait fishing methods prevail here with prawns rigged on running sinker rigs best offered.

Benedore River

The Benedore River is accessible from Mallacoota on the Betka River Road, then the Old Coast Road past the Mallacoota Aerodrome. The track into the Benedore deteriorates to 4WD status past Shipwreck Creek.

The estuary of the Benedore River is tea coloured and usually closed to the sea but holds excellent populations of mullet and bream and probably flathead, estuary perch and Australian bass as well. Bank access is limited to the mouth, but the estuary of the Benedore is quite deep and navigable by rowing boat or canoe for at least 1.5 kilometres.

If approaching the river from the Princes Highway, take the Peak Road turn-off to the right, coming from Genoa. The road deteriorates to 4WD status after crossing the Wingan Road and winds down to the coast over a distance of approximately 18 km before reaching the track from Betka River. Turn to the right here and proceed to the coast and mouth of the Benedore River.

Sandpatch Point

Sandpatch Point is located between the Benedore River estuary and the Red River estuary. It is so named because large patches of vegetation have been covered by sand. Access is from the Red River Track or the Sand Patch Track off the East Wingan Track.

Sandpatch Point is worth describing because the broken rock shelf on the east side of Sandpatch Point drops into deep water, and is sheltered from the prevailing south-westerly swells. This rock platform offers up a variety of species from salmon to wrasse, sweep and trevally as well as the occasional drummer. Paternoster rigs work well for all species.

Red River and Easby Creek

Both these rivers are best suited to keen anglers, especially those that enjoy getting to locations that don't see too many people. The long and bumpy journey in is worth it, especially if you are equipped with a canoe or small boat that can be launched from the bank.

Access is by 4WD. After leaving the Princes Highway on the East Wingan Road, proceed some 9 km or so to where the East Wingan Track turns right, winding a slow and painfully rough path to the coast where the road forks. The right fork is to Easby Creek and the left fork is to Red River.

To explore the whole Red River a boat is advised because bank access is limited to the narrow sand strip inside the entrance spit. The water is the colour of tea, which makes visual observation of fish difficult. Red River holds a regular population of bream perch and mullet. If the entrance is open to the sea, the waterway becomes tidal for almost two kilometres upstream until it hits the rock barrier where the road crosses it. At these times it is also known to hold luderick, tailor and some very large King George whiting

Easby Creek is a small, discoloured, shallow estuary with abundant rocky outcrops, situated approximately 1 km east of Wingan Inlet. The Easby Track branches left from the Red River Track to the entrance of the Easby Creek estuary. It is within walking distance of Wingan Inlet.

For anglers who like to wade along the shoreline there is some good fishing on offer casting small baits or lures at any likely looking rocky outcrops in search of some big bream.

Surf fishers will usually find good action along the beach between Easby Creek and Red River with the main targets being mullet, salmon and gummy sharks.

Wingan Inlet

The West Wingan Road is clearly marked off the Princes Highway between Cann River and Genoa. The 30 km or so of unmade road are very rough and corrugated in places so drive with care, particularly when towing, If possible try to cover the boat before travelling along this road—the cover will save the boat and everything in it being covered in dust. There are no shops at Wingan Inlet and camping facilities are basic with pit toilets and spring water. These sites may be booked through the DSE office at Cann River.

Wingan Inlet is the estuary of the Wingan River and one of the most beautiful areas along the coast. The entrance remains open to the sea and many fish move back and forth with the tide. Fishing for bream is excellent here but you do need a small boat or kayak.

There are no boat launching ramps at Wingan Inlet and very

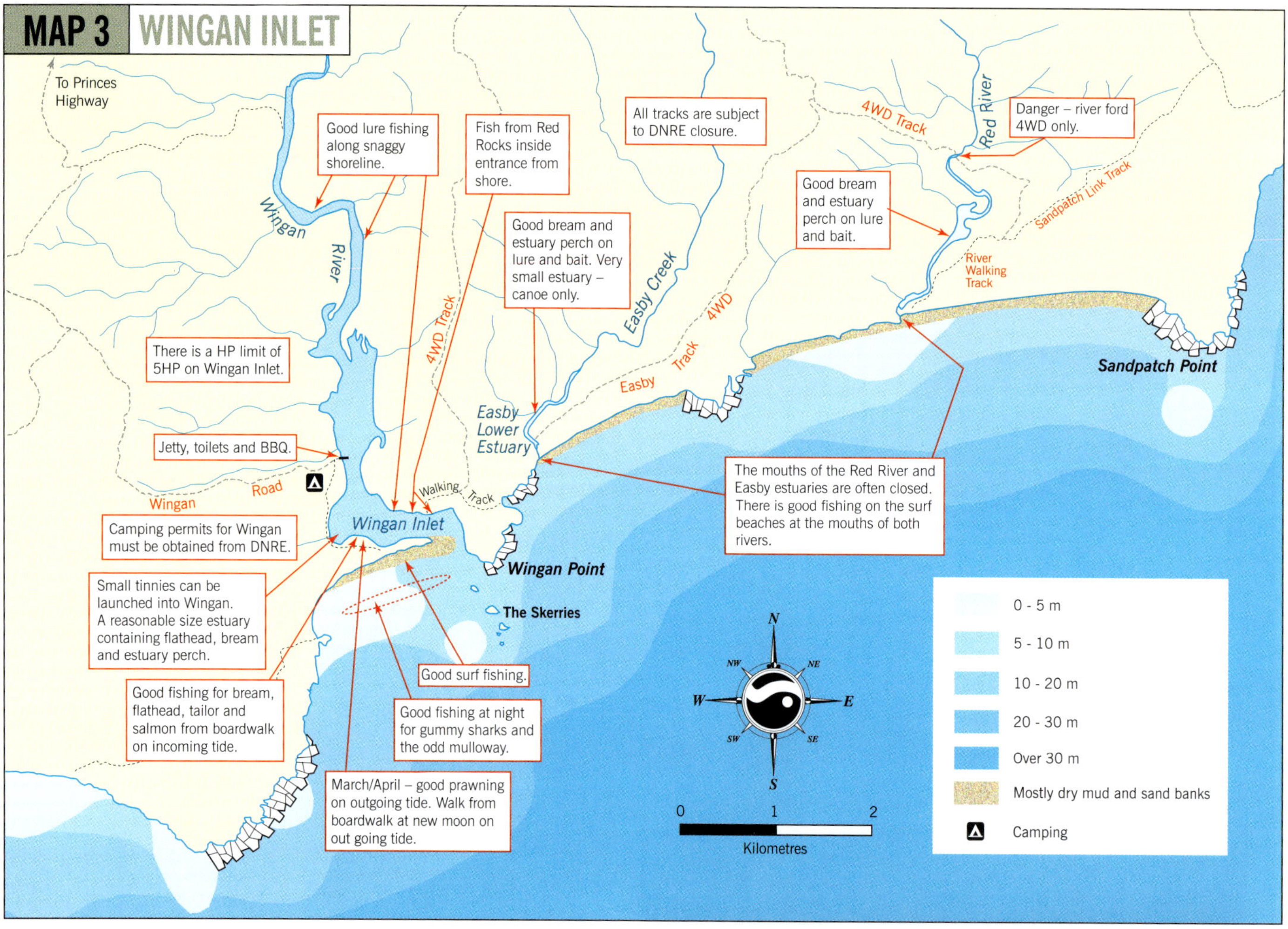

MAP 3 WINGAN INLET

To Princes Highway

Good lure fishing along snaggy shoreline.

Fish from Red Rocks inside entrance from shore.

All tracks are subject to DNRE closure.

4WD Track

Red River

Danger – river ford 4WD only.

Good bream and estuary perch on lure and bait.

Sandpatch Link Track

Wingan River

Good bream and estuary perch on lure and bait. Very small estuary – canoe only.

Easby Creek

River Walking Track

4WD Track

Easby 4WD Track

There is a HP limit of 5HP on Wingan Inlet.

Easby Lower Estuary

Sandpatch Point

Jetty, toilets and BBQ.

Wingan Road

Walking Track

The mouths of the Red River and Easby estuaries are often closed. There is good fishing on the surf beaches at the mouths of both rivers.

Camping permits for Wingan must be obtained from DNRE.

Wingan Inlet

Wingan Point

Small tinnies can be launched into Wingan. A reasonable size estuary containing flathead, bream and estuary perch.

The Skerries

Good surf fishing.

Good fishing for bream, flathead, tailor and salmon from boardwalk on incoming tide.

Good fishing at night for gummy sharks and the odd mulloway.

March/April – good prawning on outgoing tide. Walk from boardwalk at new moon on out going tide.

N NE E SE S SW W NW

0 1 2 Kilometres

0 - 5 m
5 - 10 m
10 - 20 m
20 - 30 m
Over 30 m
Mostly dry mud and sand banks
Camping

little bank access because of tussocks and other bankside foliage. But, in places you can launch a small boat or canoe from the bank.

The inlet itself offers anglers some excellent bream fishing both in size and numbers, however it's not just bream that call this waterway home. Tailor, garfish, leatherjacket and mullet, as well as a solid population of estuary perch and good numbers of flathead, are reasons this location is popular with lure fishers especially.

While those that like to soak a bait can do so by tying up to the bank and casting back into the deeper waters is a popular technique, sporting anglers prefer to cast soft plastics and hard body lures about the bank edges, weed beds and snags.

Beach fishing at Wingan Inlet is superb with better-than-average salmon and tailor usually on the bite during the day, and sharks at night. From the car parking area, it is approximately 30minutes' walk to the beach through magnificently wild country inhabited by abundant animals and reptiles, including venomous snakes, so take reasonable care.

Wingan Rocks

The rocks on the east side of the Wingan entrance drop into fairly deep water. Here, a variety of fish including salmon, snook and sweep may be taken on bait and lures. Other species that can be caught from time to time off the rocks here are gummy sharks and trevally. The rock platform faces east and is protected by the Wingan Headland and offshore formations known as 'The Skerries'.

BOAT RAMPS

There are no boat launching ramps at Wingan Inlet and very little bank access because of tussocks and other bankside foliage. However, you can launch a small boat or canoe from the bank.

ABOVE: The rivers, creeks and smaller estuaries around the coast are full of bream.

Thurra and Mueller Rivers

The Mueller and Thurra estuaries are reached by taking the Tamboon Road from the township of Cann River on the Princes Highway, and turning left on the Point Hicks (Cape Everard) Road. After approximately 22 km, you will reach the Thurra River at the bridge near the coast. The Thurra River is a small stream barely trickling out to sea. However, small mullet and bream are usually present in the lower reaches.

The Thurra is shallow for 2 km upstream from the mouth to the sand dune, making navigation difficult. However, from the dune upstream the Thurra becomes much deeper, perhaps as much as 10m deep in places, and navigable for perhaps another 2 kilometres. Here the river contains good populations of estuary perch and Australian bass.

Fishing for them requires a stealth approach; fishing from a kayak is very productive. Bass and Perch respond well to small suspending hard body lures and soft plastics.

To reach the Mueller River by vehicle, take the very last track to your left before the Thurra River Bridge. The track should be signposted, but in case it is not, you may have to proceed to the bridge, make a U-turn and proceed back up the hill to the first track to your right. This track leads to the mouth of the Mueller River and descends steeply over loose stones then soft sand, so take care.

There is a good open parking area along the river where the track finishes and you can fish within sight, and easy walking distance, of your car with the expectation of catching enough fish for a meal each time you try. Although usually closed to the sea, the Mueller River has healthy populations of mullet, estuary perch, flathead and bream. Small mullet are abundant and easily caught in bait traps for flathead baits. Rig your mullet on a running sinker rig with small circle hook for best results. There is no launching ramp, so you'll have to launch from the banks edge.

Camp Creek

A substantial tributary of the Mueller River entering on the east side of the entrance spit, Camp Creek is reasonably deep and navigable by canoe or rowing boat for approximately 1 km upstream. Fisheries surveys have shown Camp Creek to contain similar populations of fish to the Mueller.

Thurra and Mueller Surf Beaches

The surf beach is reached by crossing the Thurra bridge then proceeding along the unmade road for about 400 m to where you can park your car and walk to the beach, a distance of only a few hundred metres. There is usually a deep inshore gutter running parallel to the beach close to the mouths of both the Thurra and Mueller rivers, well within casting range. Mullet and small salmon dominate daytime fishing, but its well worth saving the fillets off a few for bait to be used once it is dark, as the deep gutters hold good gummy sharks. It pays to beef up your tackle as some of the gummies are of exceptional size.

Point Hicks (Cape Everard)

Continuing along the unmade road over the Thurra Bridge you will pass many walking tracks giving access to the beach where fishing is excellent. (DSE have made some track closures). The road leads to Point Hicks lighthouse where there is access for rock anglers in good weather, particularly on the east side which has a small bay sheltered from prevailing south-westerly swells. The rocks drop into deep water with excellent fishing potential if using lures and bait for salmon, snook and sweep.

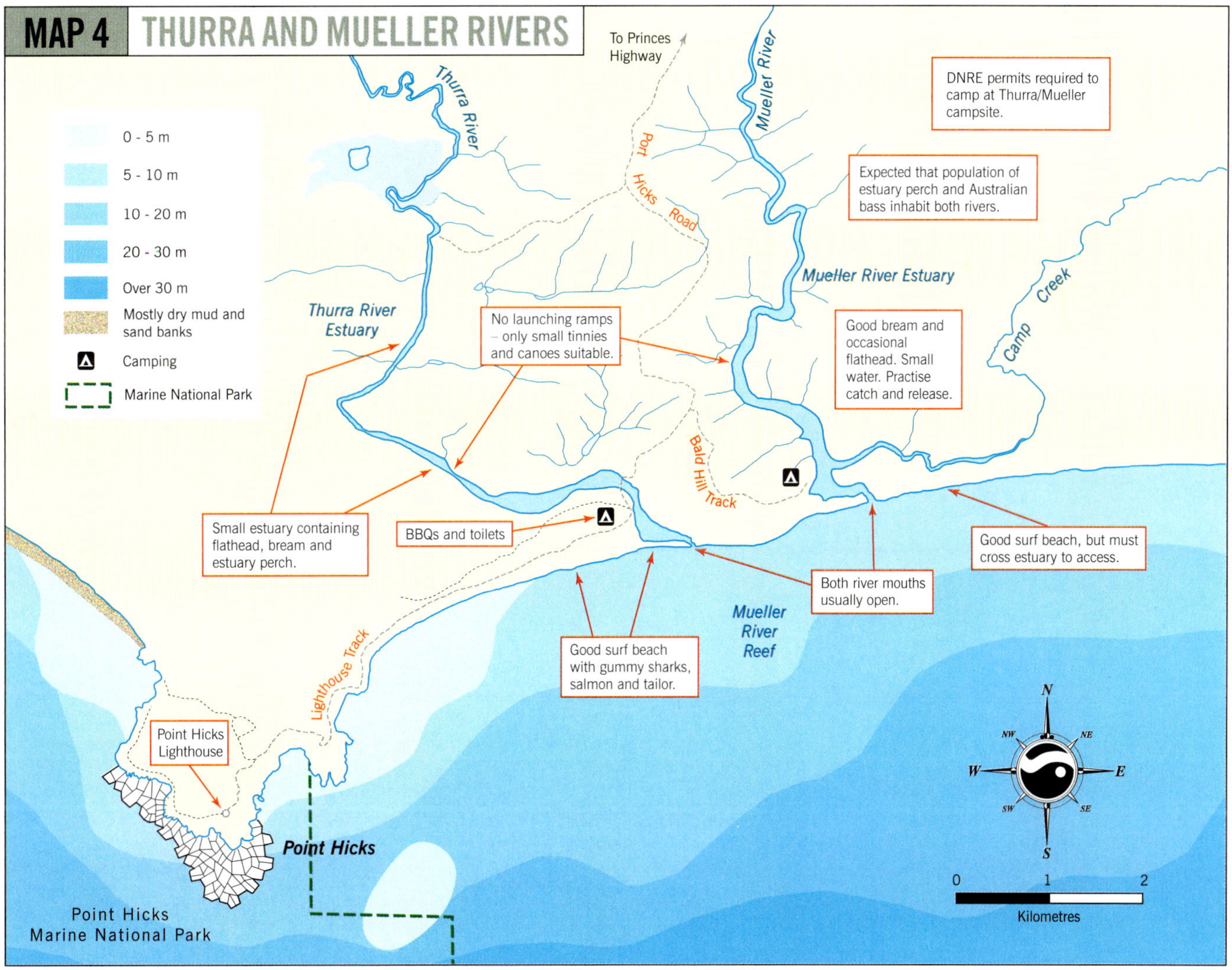

CANN RIVER AND TAMBOON INLET

FURNELLS LANDING

There is no boat ramp at Tamboon Inlet and no road access around the inlet. However, there is a ramp at Furnells Landing some 22 km by road from the township of Cann River. From here you can launch a boat with your supplies and gear, and proceed down the Cann River itself to Tamboon Inlet. The actual road to Tamboon Inlet ends at the mouth of the Cann River above the inlet. Camping sites can be booked through the Cann River DSE office.

The camp ground is very good with drop toilets provided. The ramp itself has a small jetty but when the mouth is closed and excess rain from the mountains above flow into the system, the water can easily be covering the jetty providing no walking access.

TAMBOON INLET

Having accesses Tamboon Inlet from Furnells Landing, boat operators will find that when the entrance is open and the level of the river is low, rocky shoals pose a considerable danger to navigation so take care. However when the entrance is closed, the level of the river is usually high enough to give clearance to most trailer boats.

Although not always open to the sea, Tamboon Inlet has good populations of bream, estuary perch, big flathead, and Australian bass. There is also a healthy population of huge long-finned eels in the Cann River.

Tamboon has become increasingly popular over the past few years, especially so with the boom in the use of soft plastics lures. Big flathead are a challenging quarry at Tamboon Inlet and flathead specialist, Freddy Bayes, has caught them here to more than 7kg,

When searching for flathead cast to the sand holes and edges of the weed beds.

Bream are lure eating machines. Flicking hard body lures amongst the snags will bring results.

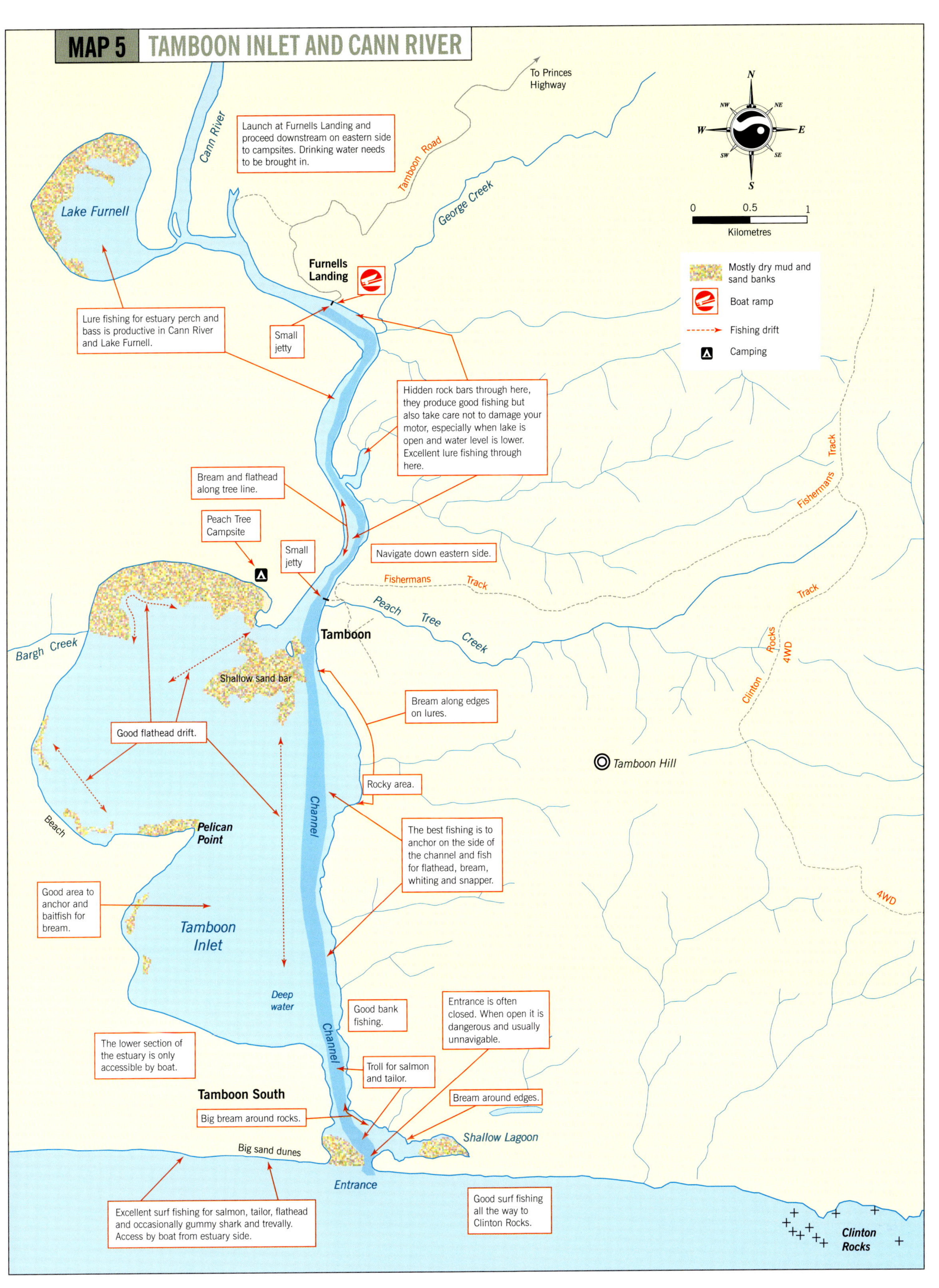
MAP 5 TAMBOON INLET AND CANN RIVER
To Princes Highway
N
NW
NE
W
E
SW
SE
S
0
0.5
1
Kilometres
Mostly dry mud and sand banks
Boat ramp
Fishing drift
Camping
Cann River
Lake Furnell
Launch at Furnells Landing and proceed downstream on eastern side to campsites. Drinking water needs to be brought in.
Tamboon Road
George Creek
Furnells Landing
Lure fishing for estuary perch and bass is productive in Cann River and Lake Furnell.
Small jetty
Hidden rock bars through here, they produce good fishing but also take care not to damage your motor, especially when lake is open and water level is lower. Excellent lure fishing through here.
Bream and flathead along tree line.
Peach Tree Campsite
Small jetty
Navigate down eastern side.
Fishermans Track
Fishermans Track
Track
Peach Tree Creek
Tamboon
Bargh Creek
Shallow sand bar
Clinton Rocks 4WD
Bream along edges on lures.
Good flathead drift.
Tamboon Hill
Rocky area.
Beach
Pelican Point
Channel
The best fishing is to anchor on the side of the channel and fish for flathead, bream, whiting and snapper.
Good area to anchor and baitfish for bream.
Tamboon Inlet
4WD
Deep water
Good bank fishing.
Entrance is often closed. When open it is dangerous and usually unnavigable.
The lower section of the estuary is only accessible by boat.
Channel
Troll for salmon and tailor.
Tamboon South
Bream around edges.
Big bream around rocks.
Shallow Lagoon
Big sand dunes
Entrance
Excellent surf fishing for salmon, tailor, flathead and occasionally gummy shark and trevally. Access by boat from estuary side.
Good surf fishing all the way to Clinton Rocks.
Clinton Rocks

ABOVE: The Tamboon Inlet holds good populations of bream.

BOAT RAMPS

There is no boat launching ramp at Tamboon Inlet and no road access around the inlet. However there is a ramp at Furnells Landing some 22 km by road from Cann River.

LOCATION	BOAT SIZE	PARKING	BUILD
Furnells Landing	5.5 m	Very Good	Concrete

both on lures and on live bait. Fred says increased weed growth has made fishing difficult though. While not every flathead is a monster Tamboon has great numbers of them for anglers to chase.

When the entrance is open to the sea it often attracts schools of salmon and tailor which like to harass the baitfish there. Trolling or casting with a variety of lures such as metal slices, diving minnows and soft plastics will see you locked in battle with both species. Aside from this it is worth fishing with either live baits or fresh fish fillets at night as local professional netters catch large mulloway there in nets.

Once the sun disappears further fun can be provided by prawns, abundant in the inlet from late summer through autumn. These can be caught with a net at night. During the day they hide in the sand but can be flushed out with a garden rake and caught in a dip net, one at a time.

The Cann River is navigable by small boat from Furnell's Landing, both downstream to Tamboon Inlet and upstream to the falls. Fisheries netting surveys reveal estuary perch are the most common species in the Cann River followed by bream, trevally and luderick. Dusky flathead have been netted in the shallow waters of Furnell Lake along with immature bream, estuary perch and large long-finned eels.

Tamboon Beach

The beach at the entrance to Tamboon inlet has a deep gutter that runs along close to shore, offering fantastic surf fishing for salmon, tailor and mullet of a day. Once the sun sets it is well worth using fresh fillet baits obtained from these species to target gummy sharks and the possible mulloway.

Clinton Rock

Approximately an hour's walk toward Point Hicks, Clinton Rock stands alone, flanked on either side by sandy beaches. The main dome is difficult to fish from but usually remains dry in a reasonable sea. As with all rock locations care needs to be taken, especially as it is a long way to get help. While it is a decent walk, the fishing here is well worth it. The inner ledge on the Tamboon side of the rock drops into deep water, and with the use of a bit of berley there are large sweep and rock blackfish to be caught using baits such as cunjevoi and peeled prawn. At times this ledge also holds good numbers of silver trevally and several people mention seeing large blue groper cruising the edges in calm weather. To target these blue bulldozers you will need heavy tackle and baits of crab gathered from the rocks.

Aside from Clinton Rock, the beach on either side of it offers good surf fishing. As with all beaches, look for the deep fish-holding gutters.

TACKLE & GENERAL INFORMATION

Pelican Petes – Bait & Tackle
42 – 44 Maurice Avenue
Mallacoota Vic 3892
Phone: (03) 5158 0354

CHAPTER 3

EAST GIPPSLAND

Sydenham Inlet to Lake Tyers

Cape Conran, Marlo, Lake Tyers and Bemm River/ Sydenham Inlet are the hubs of this region. The latter is one of the most popular and best-known destinations, and this is for one simple reason. It just continues to produce big bream, estuary perch and flathead year after year. The inlet itself is very shallow and weedy around the edges in most places so fishing from a boat is best. The nearby surf beaches offer great fishing for salmon and gummy sharks which like to hunt in the deep gutters that run close to shore.

Cape Conran provides access to the inshore reefs. Regular target species include snapper and gummy sharks as well as plenty of flathead. Trolling lures around the headland of Cape Conran produces good catches of salmon and tailor while kingfish are also a chance close to the headland. The rocks in this area offer marginal rock fishing in good weather.

Marlo has several shops and two nearby boat ramps. Most of the inlet, including the Snowy and Brodribb Rivers, are navigable by boat. Fishing is excellent for bream, luderick, estuary perch, big flathead and other species. Beach fishing is also very good, but a boat is required to cross the inlet.

The Lake Tyers system consists of two arms—Toorloo Arm and Nowa Nowa Arm. The area is full of small bream, snapper and trevally, however big fish can still be caught. Lake Tyers is also known for its huge prawn runs. Visitors are catered for with accommodation, food, fuel and bait and there are also several boat hire services.

BEMM RIVER AND SYDENHAM INLET

The turn-off to Bemm River is clearly marked from the Princes Highway between Cann River and Orbost.

The settlement of Bemm River is on Sydenham Inlet, the lagoon estuary of the river itself. Bemm River caters for anglers with basic, comfortable accommodation and boat hire. Bait and some basic fishing tackle are available.

Sydenham Inlet is very shallow with limited bank access. When the entrance is open the boat ramp is almost useless at low tide, so you will need to time your arrival and departure with the tides. Otherwise, fishing within the inlet is excellent, especially for the large bream that are common in the lake, along with other species such as estuary perch, tailor, mullet and big luderick. During the warmer months anglers chase some very large flathead down towards the entrance with soft plastic lures. When the mouth is open, at times schools of big salmon will come into the lake giving anglers great sport in calm water.

With the inlet being so shallow with a soft mud bottom, the favoured method for anchoring is to use two poles which are driven into the mud at the front and back of the boat. This works better than using an anchor as it holds the boat steady.

BEMM RIVER

Once you have accessed the river it is considerably deeper than Sydenham Inlet which it runs into. There are several places you can fish from the bank. The majority of anglers access the river by boat, although the entrance can be very shallow when the inlet is open to the sea and can require you to actually get out of the boat to drag it across shallow sand bars. Once you cross the sand bar, the river drops in deeper water quite quickly. Flicking along the edges of the sand bar is productive for bream and flathead. Anglers with an electric motor fitted to the boat can do very well holding and flicking the area.

The river is full of great fishy-looking structure in the form of thick snags that line the river bank for several kilometres. Most of these snags are home to species such as bream, estuary perch, bass and even the very occasional brown trout.

While many anglers still like to fish the snags with live prawns and sandworms, it is the lure fishermen who really excel as they move from snag to snag to find the fish. Occasionally the fish can be quite finicky which may require you to flick a range of lures from sinking, suspending and floating models until you find what they favour.

SWAN LAKE

Swan Lake is a substantial lake adjacent to Sydenham Inlet, averaging approximately 2 m in depth. The water in the lower part of the lake remains brackish from marginal tidal influence when Sydenham Inlet is open to the sea. Although difficult to get into it can at times hold great numbers of bream and estuary perch. It also carries large numbers of mullet, and at times blackfish or luderick.

Due to its shallow nature this lake is a great location for lure and fly fishing, as it enables you to fish around and over the abundant weed. Access by road is from the Swan Lake Track which in turn joins the Princes Highway west of Cann River.

SURF BEACH

You can only get to this beach by taking a boat towards the entrance and then anchoring it to the shore, before walking over a large sand dune. However the effort is worth it with exceptional fishing at times for big salmon which regularly move through the gutters. At night time there is excellent gummy shark fishing for keen anglers. Gummy sharks will take a variety of baits but if you can use fresh mullet and salmon fillet you'll certainly increase your success rate.

PEARL POINT

The beach at Pearl Point is sheltered from prevailing south-westerly swells and is particularly noted for good catches of gummy shark, and salmon of 3 and 4 kg are not uncommon. Access is by 4WD track from the settlement of Bemm River.

DOCK INLET

Dock Inlet is a shallow, twin coastal lake system with a maximum depth of two metres. Although once a tidal system, there is no longer any connection to the sea. The two main bodies of water are linked by a narrow passage around a central sand spit protruding from the southern shoreline. Dock Inlet shows no evidence of reopening to the sea in recent times and Fisheries surveys have discovered no estuarine fish. Dock Creek flows into the west end of Dock Inlet and retains a maximum depth of about five metres. Access to Dock Inlet is by 4WD track from Bemm River via Pearl Point.

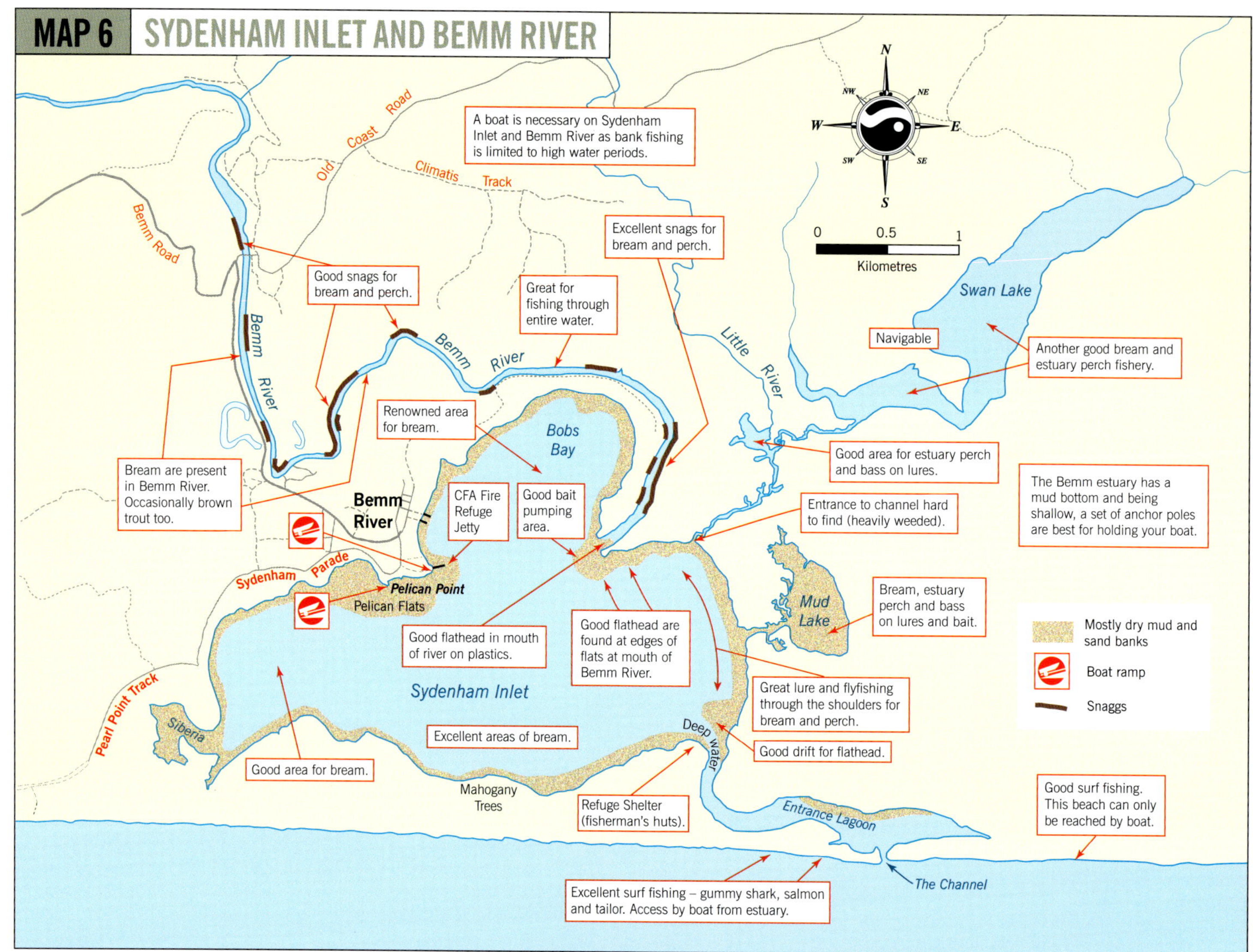

MARLO

Yeerung River

The Yeerung River is a remote stream near Cape Conran, receiving little attention from anglers. It is best reached by turning east past the ranger station from Conran Road.

The Yeerung River is usually closed to the sea and the water is the colour of tea and full of snags and timber—ideal estuary perch habitat. Bream are also abundant in the Yeerung River with some big specimens among them. With such heavy timber this small waterway is best suited to lure fishing, especially so with small diving minnows that can be twitched through and over the snags to entice the local perch into striking. Soft plastics are also very effective in here but are easily snagged on the timber.

Although there is little bank access and no launching facilities on the Yeerung River, you can launch a small boat or canoe from the bank. A pair of oars or paddles is all you will need to explore some almost-virgin water.

Cape Conran

The turn-off to Cape Conran is on the Princes Highway at Cabbage Tree, although most approach Cape Conran from Marlo to the west. A sheltered concrete boat ramp gives access to offshore anglers who take snapper and a variety of other fish from inshore reefs. Flathead are abundant on the flat rubble and sand bottom, and drifting is very productive indeed when the weather permits. These same areas also produce more than a few gummy sharks for those who target them.

Trolling small, skirted lures such as pink squids and a range of smallish diving minnows produces good catches of salmon and at times tailor. Another bonus over the past few years has been increased numbers of kingfish—these are targeted by anglers who know the water and who are able to get there lures close to the headland when weather permits. Aside from trolling these inshore waters in good weather, anglers trolling offshore sometimes find striped tuna. Bluefin tuna used to be prolific until commercial fishing almost wiped them out. Thankfully with stricter regulations over the past few seasons, anglers have once again reported seeing the odd school of bluefin moving through the area.

The rocks of Cape Conran and East Cape offer marginal rock fishing in good weather and should produce snapper. Lure casting enthusiasts will have little trouble taking large snook, and some big salmon as well as the occasional kingfish when conditions permit.

Snowy River

Although a long river and still quite large, the mighty Snowy is a shadow of its former glory. It was once a deep water, but it has suffered the effects of siltation and lack of water flow due to the huge dams and diversions in its headwaters.

This said the Snowy still produces good fishing and offers many great land based fishing opportunities. Many tracks run down and along the river, enabling anglers to fish close to their car.

Major target species are bream, mullet and estuary perch, all of which can be taken in good numbers with bait, however many

ABOVE: Lakes Entrance fishing guide Frank Milito spends a lot of time at Bemm River because of its productivity year round.

anglers are now finding success by walking slowly along the river casting lures at likely looking snags and structure.

Higher up the river, Australian Bass are also caught by anglers flicking amongst the snag with lures and soft plastics. A big challenge, some models caught have exceeded 50 cm in length

Brodribb River

The journey to Marlo, the main community on the system, will take you across the Brodribb River where there is excellent bream and estuary perch fishing. Bank access is limited however, and a small boat is helpful. This stretch of water has become a favourite for lure fishermen who find great success moving along the river casting lures at any likely looking places.

There is access both downstream to the main body of water at Marlo and upstream to Cabbage Tree Lake, and Lake Curlip, a shallow lake supporting a small population of estuary perch.

Cabbage Tree Lake

Cabbage Tree Lake is a small but highly productive lagoon on Cabbage Tree Creek just prior to its confluence with the Brodribb River. It is an open drainage system with fresh water flowing into it from Cabbage Tree Creek to the east and leaving the lake to the west. It is also exposed to marginal tidal influence from the Brodribb River.

Fisheries netting surveys show it to contain estuary perch, bream, mullet, trevally, flathead and luderick.

Lake Corringle

Lake Corringle is the north-west extremity of the combined estuarine system of the Snowy and Brodribb rivers. The lake is shallow—less than 2m deep—but supports a good population of luderick. Surveys show that luderick averaging 850g are the dominant species in Lake Corringle, followed by estuary perch, large yellow eye mullet and black bream.

Marlo

Marlo has a hotel and several shops from which you can buy supplies and bait. A small jetty produces good catches of mullet, but

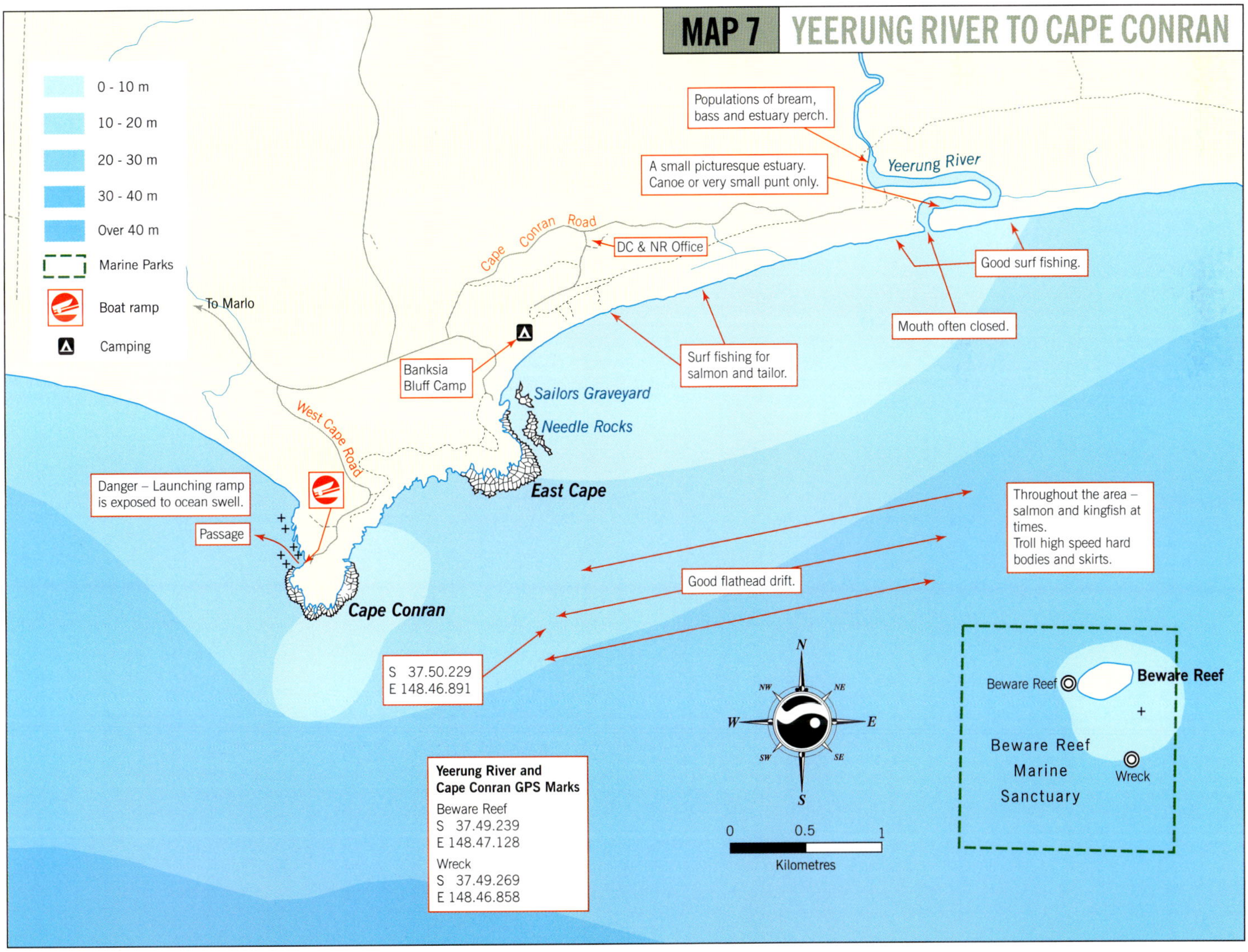

MAP 7 YEERUNG RIVER TO CAPE CONRAN

0 - 10 m
10 - 20 m
20 - 30 m
30 - 40 m
Over 40 m
Marine Parks
Boat ramp
Camping

Populations of bream, bass and estuary perch.
A small picturesque estuary. Canoe or very small punt only.
Yeerung River
Cape Conran Road
DC & NR Office
Good surf fishing.
Mouth often closed.
Surf fishing for salmon and tailor.
To Marlo
Banksia Bluff Camp
Sailors Graveyard
Needle Rocks
West Cape Road
East Cape
Danger – Launching ramp is exposed to ocean swell.
Passage
Cape Conran
Throughout the area – salmon and kingfish at times.
Troll high speed hard bodies and skirts.
Good flathead drift.
S 37.50.229
E 148.46.891
Beware Reef
Beware Reef
Beware Reef Marine Sanctuary
Wreck
N
NE
E
SE
S
SW
W
NW
0 0.5 1
Kilometres

Yeerung River and Cape Conran GPS Marks
Beware Reef
S 37.49.239
E 148.47.128
Wreck
S 37.49.269
E 148.46.858

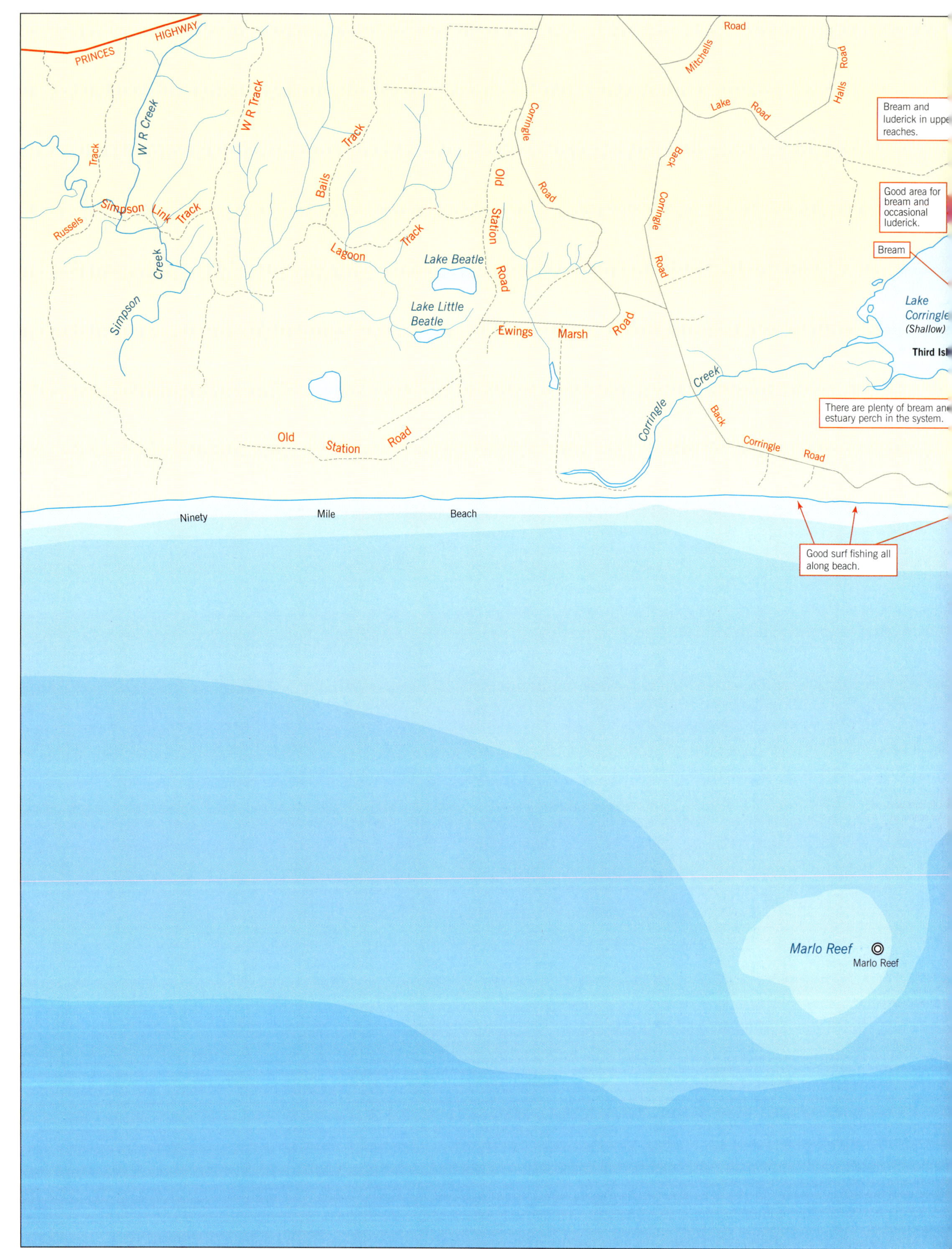

PRINCES HIGHWAY
W R Creek
Track
Russels
Simpson Link Track
Creek
Simpson
W R Track
Bails Track
Lagoon Track
Lake Beatle
Lake Little Beatle
Old Station Road
Corringle Road
Ewings Marsh Road
Old Station Road
Mitchells Road
Lake Road
Halls Road
Back Corringle Road
Corringle Creek
Back Corringle Road
Bream and luderick in uppe reaches.
Good area for bream and occasional luderick.
Bream
Lake Corringle (Shallow)
Third Isl
There are plenty of bream an estuary perch in the system.
Ninety Mile Beach
Good surf fishing all along beach.
Marlo Reef
Marlo Reef

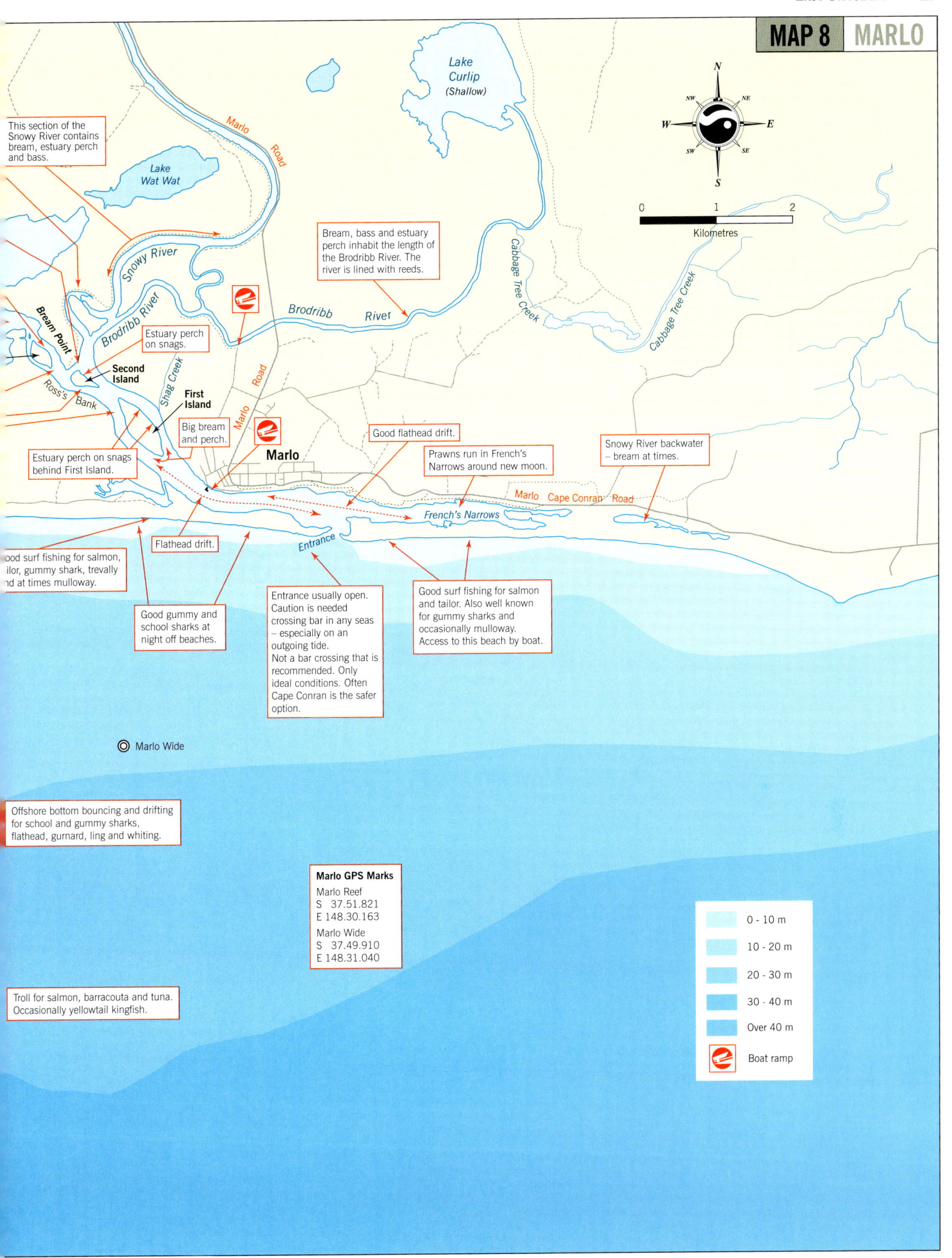
MAP 8 MARLO
Lake Curlip (Shallow)
Lake Wat Wat
This section of the Snowy River contains bream, estuary perch and bass.
Marlo Road
Snowy River
Brodribb River
Bream Point
Bream, bass and estuary perch inhabit the length of the Brodribb River. The river is lined with reeds.
Brodribb River
Cabbage Tree Creek
Cabbage Tree Creek
Estuary perch on snags.
Second Island
Shag Creek
First Island
Ross's Bank
Marlo Road
Big bream and perch.
Estuary perch on snags behind First Island.
Marlo
Good flathead drift.
Prawns run in French's Narrows around new moon.
Snowy River backwater – bream at times.
Marlo Cape Conran Road
French's Narrows
Entrance
Flathead drift.
ood surf fishing for salmon, ilor, gummy shark, trevally nd at times mulloway.
Good gummy and school sharks at night off beaches.
Entrance usually open. Caution is needed crossing bar in any seas – especially on an outgoing tide. Not a bar crossing that is recommended. Only ideal conditions. Often Cape Conran is the safer option.
Good surf fishing for salmon and tailor. Also well known for gummy sharks and occasionally mulloway. Access to this beach by boat.
N
S
E
W
NE
NW
SE
SW
0
1
2
Kilometres
Marlo Wide
Offshore bottom bouncing and drifting for school and gummy sharks, flathead, gurnard, ling and whiting.
Marlo GPS Marks
Marlo Reef
S 37.51.821
E 148.30.163
Marlo Wide
S 37.49.910
E 148.31.040
Troll for salmon, barracouta and tuna. Occasionally yellowtail kingfish.
0 - 10 m
10 - 20 m
20 - 30 m
30 - 40 m
Over 40 m
Boat ramp

the tide runs fairly strongly here at times making fishing difficult.

There are two boat ramps close to Marlo: an excellent concrete ramp right at the town, and a modest ramp on the Brodribb River. Most of the inlet, and both the Snowy and Brodribb rivers are navigable throughout.

The waters surrounding Marlo not only offer good numbers of fish but also regularly in large sizes especially for those anglers chasing bream and estuary perch. As well as the bream, luderick and estuary perch, big flathead, mullet, garfish and tailor are all caught here. Mulloway are also present at Marlo but few anglers fish for them.

The premier bait for most fish species at Marlo is live or fresh prawns. These can be netted throughout the system during late summer and autumn. One productive place is along the bank of French's Narrows below the Cape Conran Road.

Beach Fishing

Just as the estuary offers great fishing for several species so do the local surf beaches. Access is by either crossing the inlet by boat, or by car taking the Cape Conran Road which reveals a number of access tracks to the beach at intervals between Marlo and Cape Conran.

Major target species in the surf are big Australian salmon and the odd tailor, while at night large gummy sharks move into the gutters in good numbers. It is worth using freshly caught bait if possible whenever fishing at night, as some large mulloway frequent the deep surf gutters.

LAKE TYERS

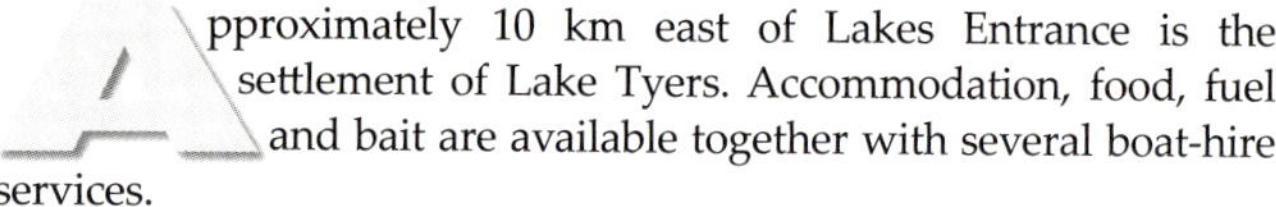

Approximately 10 km east of Lakes Entrance is the settlement of Lake Tyers. Accommodation, food, fuel and bait are available together with several boat-hire services.

Lake Tyers teems with fish, mostly small bream, silver trevally, tailor and snapper, and this vast population of juveniles can frustrate the serious angler seeking worthwhile fish like big flathead and bream. Garfish and mullet are also in abundance.

The Lake Tyers system consists of two arms, the Toorloo and Nowa Nowa. The Toorloo Arm is navigable for some 5 or 6 km upstream but gets very shallow quick, while the Nowa Nowa Arm is more than 20 km long. This location is not marked on GPS systems and care must be taken when boating.

The peninsula between the two arms belongs to The Lake Tyers Aboriginal Trust and access above high tide mark is prohibited. The rocky bank between the two produces flathead and bream by those flicking lures into the shallows.

There are many different fishing techniques that can be used in Lake Tyers. Bait fishing, trolling and lure fishing are all extremely successful.

Anchoring on the edges of the lake allows anglers to cast baits back into the deeper water where bream and flathead are the target. Prawns, blue bait and whitebait are best offered. These baits can be rigged on a running sinker rig which allows the bait to sit on the bottom.

Lure fishing is an extremely popular fishing style. Trolling is mostly conducted in the main lake where small 70 to 100 mm minnow style hard bodies catch the attention of schooling tailor. If schools of tailor are sighted busting the surface, metal slugs can be thrown and are highly deadly. The best location to troll in along the bank between the Toorloo and Nowa Nowa arms in 5 meters of water.

Bream respond well to soft plastics, hard body lures and metal vibes. On the flats, shallow diving hard bodies that reach a maximum of 1 to 2 ft are recommended. Proven soft plastics are the DOA prawn along with 2″ and 3″ grubs or bass minnows. The sand flats around the islands are also worth flicking a soft plastic around. There are some very big flathead which hold around here. Few anglers paddle kayaks from boat ramp no.2 then hop out and wade the shallows.

Bream can also be caught in the snags so expect to lose a few lures. In this situation both floating and sinking hard bodies work well. Stick with lures in the 50 to 70 mm range, natural life-like colours work very well.

If the bream are in the deep water, metal vibes will secure a good catch. Simply drop to the bottom and lift the rod tip to get the desired action. Schooling bream will set upon the vibe quickly.

If you're after big flathead then stick to using soft plastics. These should be rigged on a 1/8th ounce jig head with at least a 2/0–3/0 hook size. There are many soft plastics available but the 3″ DOA prawn, squidgy 100 mm wriggler and fish are proven flathead food.

Flathead can be found right throughout the system but popular locations are the shallow flats fished at dawn and on dusk. If you are fishing during the middle of the day, try working the banks of the deeper channels and along the edges of the weed beds.

During the warmer months, prawning in Lake Tyers is a popular affair. Catches of several kilograms a night are not uncommon. Although they are very good to eat, fresh prawns make excellent baits for both flathead and bream.

Fisherman's Arm

The turn-off to Fisherman's Arm is clearly signposted approximately 1 km down the road to Lake Tyers after turning off the Princes Highway. Here there is a boat ramp and jetty, boat hire and other facilities for anglers. These days the ramp is very shallow and launching can prove difficult at times.

The Entrance

The entrance to Lake Tyers is open to the sea spasmodically, every second year or so; but for most of the time the system is closed. However, when it does open, some of the locals are quickly on the scene with dip nets to catch prawns and fish as they run out to sea. Fishing from the sand is effective here for land based anglers and bait fishing is the preferred method. Lure fishing is possible but the area is quite shallow. Flathead and tailor will be the main catch when using lures. During the summer months and on the lead up to a new moon, prawning is very popular at Lake Tyers. Anglers armed with a good prawning light and net, wade the shallows and net countless numbers of prawns. Though they are scattered throughout the system, the most profitable areas are around Boat Ramp no.1 and the entrance.

Toorloo Arm

Road access to Toorloo Arm above Mill Point is from Peterson Road that runs off the Princes Highway to the right about 3 km past the Lake Tyers turn off.

Travelling down Peterson Road past the Burnt Bridge turn-off, Byrnes Track branches left to Long Point; a favourite picnic area and a good fishing spot for big flathead in particular. Bream are a common catch but tend to be on the smaller size.

Depending on boat size, access to the Toorloo Arm is also made possible by the single lane concrete ramp at Boat Ramp number 2. This is a great launching facility that gives you access to the bottom lake, Toorloo and Nowa Nowa arms. The boat ramp also has a floating pontoon and excellent fish cleaning facilities as well as a well maintained toilet block.

Two nearby jetties also offer excellent fishing for flathead, tailor and bream.

The Toorloo arm is quite shallow so care must be taken when travelling. The top end of the arm is very popular for large flathead

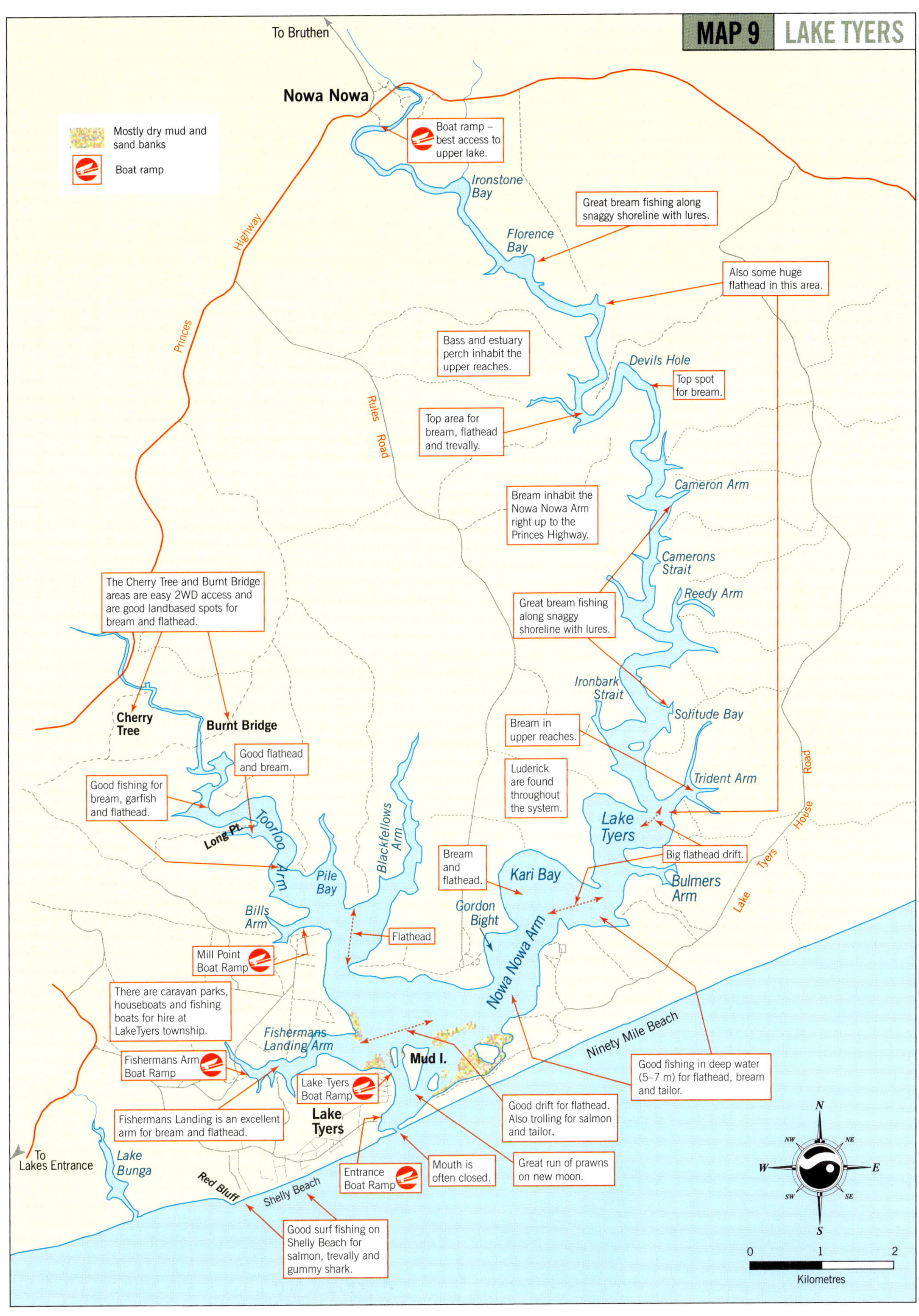
MAP 9 LAKE TYERS
Mostly dry mud and sand banks
Boat ramp
To Bruthen
Nowa Nowa
Boat ramp – best access to upper lake.
Ironstone Bay
Florence Bay
Great bream fishing along snaggy shoreline with lures.
Also some huge flathead in this area.
Princes Highway
Bass and estuary perch inhabit the upper reaches.
Devils Hole
Top spot for bream.
Top area for bream, flathead and trevally.
Rules Road
Cameron Arm
Bream inhabit the Nowa Nowa Arm right up to the Princes Highway.
Camerons Strait
Reedy Arm
The Cherry Tree and Burnt Bridge areas are easy 2WD access and are good landbased spots for bream and flathead.
Great bream fishing along snaggy shoreline with lures.
Ironbark Strait
Solitude Bay
Cherry Tree
Burnt Bridge
Good flathead and bream.
Bream in upper reaches.
Luderick are found throughout the system.
Trident Arm
Lake Tyers House Road
Good fishing for bream, garfish and flathead.
Long Pt.
Toorloo Arm
Blackfellows Arm
Lake Tyers
Big flathead drift.
Bream and flathead.
Kari Bay
Bulmers Arm
Pile Bay
Bills Arm
Gordon Bight
Flathead
Mill Point Boat Ramp
Nowa Nowa Arm
There are caravan parks, houseboats and fishing boats for hire at LakeTyers township.
Fishermans Landing Arm
Mud I.
Ninety Mile Beach
Fishermans Arm Boat Ramp
Lake Tyers Boat Ramp
Good fishing in deep water (5–7 m) for flathead, bream and tailor.
Lake Tyers
Good drift for flathead. Also trolling for salmon and tailor.
Fishermans Landing is an excellent arm for bream and flathead.
To Lakes Entrance
Lake Bunga
Red Bluff
Shelly Beach
Entrance Boat Ramp
Mouth is often closed.
Great run of prawns on new moon.
Good surf fishing on Shelly Beach for salmon, trevally and gummy shark.
N
NW
NE
W
E
SW
SE
S
0
1
2
Kilometres

Lake Tyers is the home of big flathead. Ensure you work the edges to find them.

but that are spooked quite easily. The bank the runs adjacent to the Aboriginal Trust is particularly productive for large flathead

Mill Point

There is another boat ramp at Mill Point in the Toorloo Arm. It is reached by continuing on past the Fisherman's Landing, crossing the bridge and proceeding for another 2 kilometres. After launching, to the right of the boat ramp, the arm is short but full of snags. This is a great location to begin searching for bream. In the main body of the arm to the left of the boat ramp, flathead are abundant. Soft plastics worked along the bottom and edges of the channel work very well. There are some big flatties in here so upgrade your leader to 10 or 15 pound.

The next track branching off Peterson Road to the left leads to Ironbark Point; another notable fishing spot for big flathead and bream in the snags. This is a dry weather track recommended for 4WD vehicles only.

Nowa Nowa Arm

The Nowa Nowa Arm seems endless, covering over 20 km through some of the most beautiful scenery imaginable. There is access by boat from Lake Tyers, or downstream from a ramp suitable for small boats at Nowa Nowa on the Princes Highway.

Working small hard body lures and soft plastics along the rock and snag-lined shores is a great way to find bream and estuary perch, while the shallower drop-offs, weed beds and sand patches hold good numbers of flathead with some truly huge fish amongst them.

For anglers who like to troll or cast in the deeper water with bigger lures and pilchards, there are good numbers of tailor with some exceptionally large ones present. There are also some great snapper that live in the lake with fish over 3kg being occasionally caught. Silver trevally are also a common catch but respond mostly to lures. These are of exceptional size with 50 cm models quite common. If it is bream you're after then concentrate on working hard body lures into the snags and along the edges of the banks. The outskirts of the island usually produce some quality flathead on soft plastics and it pays to work this area first thing in the morning.

Bream and flathead are abundant and it pays to cast and work every inch of the banks as you can. Use the lands contour to your advantage also. Steep cliffs mean deep water where they meet the water and slow sloping hills which meet the water also continue on creating shallow banks, the ideal locations to find flathead sunning themselves.

A bank to the eastern as you pass under the electricity wires produces some very nice flathead for those flicking soft plastics.

Lake Tyers House Road

Branching to the right from the Princes Highway past Nowa Nowa, Lake Tyers House Road skirts the Nowa Nowa Arm for approximately 15 kilometres.

Branching off Lake Tyers House Road are a number of designated 4WD tracks giving access to lots of secluded fishing locations including Cameron's Arm and Reedy Arm where small boats or canoes may be launched from the bank. In all of these areas there are good fish to be caught with bream the main species. Some very large flathead live in these bays also—for best results keep quiet as noise travels a long way and can scare the bigger fish in the area. Casts should be made to each point as flathead can be up in the shallows sunning themselves.

Lake Bunga

Clearly signposted from the Princes Highway, Lake Bunga is the lagoon estuary of the Bunga Creek between Lake Tyers and Lakes Entrance.

Like Lake Tyers it is rarely open to the sea, but contains plenty of mullet, small bream and a variety of other fish including small silver trevally and some very respectable flathead.

The surf beach adjacent to the entrance to Lake Bunga offers some exceptional surf fishing for salmon and also consistent catches of gummy shark at night. It's also a favourite spot for local anglers, which is a fair indication of a good location!

BOAT RAMPS

LOCATION	BOAT SIZE	PARKING	BUILD
Bemm River	5 m	Excellent	Concrete
Marlo	6 m	Excellent	Concrete
Brodribb River	5 m	Average	Concrete
Tyers	5.5 m	Good	Concrete
Cape Conran	5.5 m	Good	Concrete

TACKLE & GENERAL INFORMATION

Cosy Nook
Holiday Flats
Sydenham Pde
Bemm River Vic 3889

Mitchell Sports
196 Main St
Bairnsdale Vic 3875
Phone: (03) 5152 4524

Stows Authorised Newsagency
212 Main Street
Bairnsdale Vic 3878
Phone: (03) 5152 4363

Tackle World Sale
82 Macarthur Street
Sale Vic 3850
Phone: (03) 5144 7505

East End Bait & Tackle
577 Esplanade
Lakes Entrance Vic 3909
Phone: (03) 5155 1593

CHAPTER 4

GIPPSLAND LAKES

Lakes Entrance to Seaspray

It was Angus McMillan who discovered the vast system of coastal lagoons now known as the Gippsland Lakes, and most of the lakes, channels and islands bear the names of members of his party.

Initially, the Gippsland Lakes did not have a permanent entrance to the sea. Work began at the site of the present entrance in 1869 with the intention of developing a shipping port. Almost twenty years elapsed before a permanent entrance was established, and then only with the help of a storm that gouged the remaining sand from between the man-made walls to almost4m deep. The port, which took so long to establish, thrived only until the mid-1930s by which time improved rail and road links made sea transport less viable.

The stone sea walls served to maintain the entrance until perhaps the early 1980s. In more recent times, the sand has built up along the beach to the ends of both walls, a situation that has caused the channel to silt up so that constant dredging is required to keep it open.

Nowadays, although the port of Lakes Entrance carries no commercial shipping, it does shelter a huge commercial fishing fleet. However, it is the army of recreational anglers who fish the Gippsland Lakes to which the region owes its prosperity, and the fish sought by most anglers to the exclusion of all others is bream.

Bream, both southern black bream and yellowfin bream, maintain healthy populations throughout the Gippsland Lakes despite immense pressure from commercial fish harvesting within the system. One can only trust that this balance can be maintained through responsible management.

Bream are prolific throughout the whole of the Gippsland Lakes. You can see them under all of the jetties, not only in the port of Lakes Entrance on Cunningham Arm, but under almost every man-made structure in the system including the marinas at Loch Sport, Metung and Paynesville.

Unfortunately these bream you can see, or at least the bigger ones, are like barking dogs—they seldom bite. The small ones are more co-operative, but even the smaller fish don't always seem willing to feed under scrutiny from above.

Besides bream, other targeted species within the Lakes include flathead that are common throughout the whole system, estuary perch that are found in various locations (usually where there are snag-lined banks) and other seasonal species such as King George whiting and tailor through the warmer months.

Prawns are caught within the Gippsland Lakes in late summer and autumn, and can often be obtained with a fine mesh prawn net and a torch or flounder light. Anglers who are short on time organise to buy live prawns for bait, and at times the fishermen's co-operative at Lakes Entrance sells live prawns.

Snapper enter the Gippsland Lakes over summer and can be caught as far into the system as Lake King. Juvenile snapper can be caught in Cunningham Arm from the wharves in front of the town. Unfortunately most are undersize. Reduced catches of bigger snapper within the system over the last twenty or thirty years may well be due to increased numbers of large sand crabs that make bait fishing near the entrance almost impossible.

The waters offshore of the Gippsland Lakes, especially off Lakes Entrance itself, offer great fishing when weather permits for a range of species. The deep reefs hold good snapper along with big gummy and school sharks, and the odd kingfish. The area also boasts great offshore flathead grounds where anglers can drift around catching big sand flathead.

Anglers who like to target sharks will also find good numbers of makos living around the offshore reefs through the summer months, ranging in size from babies to beasts.

Wide of Lakes Entrance and the Gippsland Lakes are several oil rigs. These stand in relatively deep water that has huge potential for game fishing. Unfortunately the weather in the area often stops anglers from getting out there, but workers on the rigs often report seeing marlin and big tuna schools passing by. For those wishing to catch a Victorian marlin, lots of preparation needs to be in place. Correct weather and warm water currents are the most important factors that dictate whether or not the fish will be around.

LAKES ENTRANCE

CUNNINGHAM ARM

The Cunningham Arm runs right beside the highway and is only a short walk across the road from the shops and accommodation. You certainly don't have to go very far to see fish here because they gather in numbers around all of the numerous jetties in the port. Fishing from any of the jetties with sandworms will usually produce whiting, trevally, small bream and small snapper, but undersize fish comprise most of the catch.

For best result try to fish and cast near to where any of the local trawlers are washing their boats down after fishing. This activity attracts any fish in the area as they look for small bits of fish washed overboard.

The footbridge crossing Cunningham Arm gives access to the surf, and the east entrance wall. The surf beach is popular in summer where small salmon, mullet, silver trevally and the odd flathead are caught. During winter, the salmon fishing really fires up with fish as big as 3 kg common. After crossing the bridge, the walk to the wall and adjacent Flagstaff Jetty takes approximately forty minutes. The parapet on the outer wall is uncomfortably high for fishing, but the rest of the wall is easy to fish and luderick anglers regularly do well here.

It is worth heading out this way to see the trawlers crossing the bar especially when there is a bit of a swell running—the bar can be quite dangerous and the skill with which the skippers guide the big boats through is a sight to see.

CUNNINGHAM ARM EAST

Cunningham Arm becomes shallow and narrow east of the footbridge until it finally becomes a narrow channel. Anglers overlook this area, but there are large eels to be caught as well as bream and mullet. Best place to fish is the prominent sand spit at the bottom of Long Street.

McLeod Morass
'Grassy Bank' – easy access by road. Western side good for bream and estuary perch.
Good bream and flatties in 'The Cut' area.
Bream over flats on lures.
Boat fishing – the area at the end of the silt jetties and channel markers is good for bream. Some big flathead at the mouth.
Bolodun Point
Morgate Point
Nugent Bay
Jones Bay
Rickies Point
Lardner Point
Thumb Point
The Cut
Tyers Creek
Forge Creek
De Tracy Creek
Silt Jetties
Eagle Point
Eagle Point Bay
Point Foster
Dawson Point
Good for bream.
Lake King – good for salmon, tailor and barracouta on calm days. Also anchor and fish for bream and salmon.
Banksia Peninsula – great shore based fishing outside of peak times.
Bream, flathead and trevally.
Plenty of bream around and under jetties.
Point Fullerton
Lake King
Tom Roberts Creek
Newland Arm
Great bream fishing when no people around
Good landbased bream in McMillan Strait.
Picnic Arm
Paynesville
Bream
Dawson Cove
Mason Bay
Duck Bay
Bluff Point
Butler Point
McMillan Strait
Raymond Island
King Po
Terrace Point
Wattle Point
James Point
Banksia Peninsula
Lady Bay
Montague Point
Bream and whiting close in.
Lake Victoria
Elbow Point
Point Turner
Resid Jetty
Trouser Point
Walker Point
Campbell Channel
Scott Point
Wilson Point
Emu Bight
Bream, flathead and whiting with silver trevally and snapper in deeper areas.
Carstairs Bank
Lakes National Park
Rotomah Channel
Point Best
Sperm Whale Head
Jones Point
Trapper Point
Rotten Island
Waddy Island
Wollaston
Lake Reeve
Barton Island
Jubilee Head
Rotomah Island
Prawns
Wallaby Island
Bunga Arm
Scattered fishing for flounder and garfish in shallows.
Good flathead and bream form and off Elbow Point to Point Turner.
Good area for prawns.
Bream on lures.
Good surf beach. Acces by boat – Bunga Arm.
Bass Strait

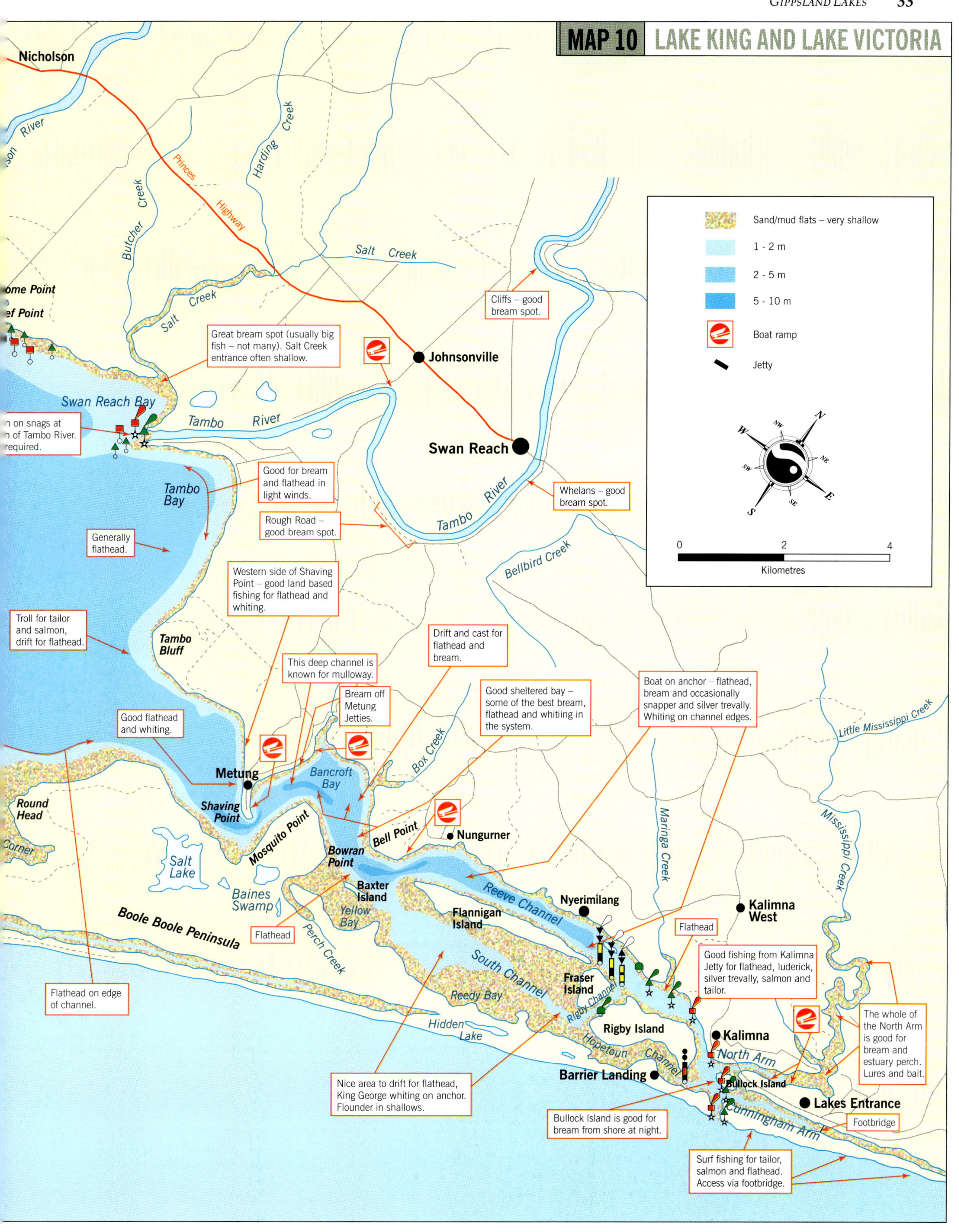
MAP 10 LAKE KING AND LAKE VICTORIA
Sand/mud flats – very shallow
1 - 2 m
2 - 5 m
5 - 10 m
Boat ramp
Jetty
0 2 4
Kilometres
Nicholson
Princes Highway
Harding Creek
Butcher Creek
Salt Creek
Salt Creek
Johnsonville
Swan Reach
Swan Reach Bay
Tambo River
Tambo River
Tambo Bay
Tambo Bluff
Bellbird Creek
Metung
Shaving Point
Bancroft Bay
Box Creek
Mosquito Point
Bell Point
Nungurner
Bowran Point
Baxter Island
Yellow Bay
Flannigan Island
Reeve Channel
South Channel
Nyerimilang
Kalimna West
Fraser Island
Rigby Channel
Rigby Island
Reedy Bay
Hidden Lake
Hopetoun Channel
Barrier Landing
Kalimna
North Arm
Bullock Island
Lakes Entrance
Cunningham Arm
Maringa Creek
Mississippi Creek
Little Mississippi Creek
Round Head
Salt Lake
Baines Swamp
Boole Boole Peninsula
Perch Creek
Great bream spot (usually big fish – not many). Salt Creek entrance often shallow.
Cliffs – good bream spot.
Whelans – good bream spot.
Good for bream and flathead in light winds.
Rough Road – good bream spot.
Generally flathead.
Western side of Shaving Point – good land based fishing for flathead and whiting.
Troll for tailor and salmon, drift for flathead.
This deep channel is known for mulloway.
Drift and cast for flathead and bream.
Bream off Metung Jetties.
Good flathead and whiting.
Good sheltered bay – some of the best bream, flathead and whitiing in the system.
Boat on anchor – flathead, bream and occasionally snapper and silver trevally. Whiting on channel edges.
Flathead
Flathead
Good fishing from Kalimna Jetty for flathead, luderick, silver trevally, salmon and tailor.
The whole of the North Arm is good for bream and estuary perch. Lures and bait.
Flathead on edge of channel.
Nice area to drift for flathead, King George whiting on anchor. Flounder in shallows.
Bullock Island is good for bream from shore at night.
Footbridge
Surf fishing for tailor, salmon and flathead. Access via footbridge.

BULLOCK ISLAND

Bullock Island is on your right hand side as you cross the bridge over the North Arm driving into Lakes Entrance. Bullock Island is at the head of Cunningham Arm and the site of the fish processing plant. This island is connected to Lakes Entrance by Road Bridge and is popular with anglers seeking luderick, mullet, bream and silver trevally.

You can park close enough to the sea wall on Bullock Island to watch your rod from your car. However, crabs are prolific in this area and you will need to check your bait regularly.

More energetic types cast lures from the Bullock Island Light on the corner of the wall, and, should a shoal of salmon or tailor come by, you will soon see many others doing likewise.

The jetty once adjacent to the fish processing plant has been demolished, but you can fish from the sandblasting jetty nearby.

EASTERN BEACH

Eastern Beach is accessible from Eastern Beach Road, which leads to a large car parking area behind the sand dunes. The beach is popular with anglers seeking salmon and tailor. Mullet may also be caught in the shore break on soft baits like pipis and prawns.

For a bit of exercise and easy fishing many local anglers choose to walk the beach with a light surf rod and a few lures, casting them into the likely looking gutters and holes. The best thing about this strategy is you can cover a large portion of water until you find the fish, rather than them finding you.

During evening and night time, anglers use fillet baits such as fresh salmon and tailor to target gummy sharks that move into the gutters.

KALIMNA JETTY

The jetty near the Kalimna Hotel is an excellent spot to fish for bream, flathead, luderick, small tailor and salmon. Large bream may be taken with live or dead prawns or with sandworms fished on the bottom. Small 2 and 3 inch soft plastics are also effective.

KALIMNA WALL

The retaining wall, which extends from the Kalimna Jetty all the way down to Jemmy's Point at the entrance to the North Arm, is popular with anglers seeking luderick and bream. A variety of baits will work here but many anglers do well casting small lures close in along the wall either from a boat or the shore. Mussels may be gathered from the rocks along the Kalimna wall at low tide.

JEMMY'S POINT

At the end of the Kalimna Wall, where the North Arm joins the Reeve Channel, anglers fish for luderick and may supplement their bait supply with weed growing on the rocks.

You can walk to Jemmy's Point from Kalimna, or park at the boat ramp below the bridge at Lakes Entrance, and walk across the bridge and out to the point.

ARINGA CREEK

This small creek runs off the Reeve Channel just west of Kalimna Jetty. There is no realistic land based access, but at night, from a small boat, the shallow creek entrance is well worth fishing for bream.

LAKES ENTRANCE

Crossing the bridge over the North Arm as you drive into Lakes Entrance, you will very likely see people fishing from boats or from the bank because Lakes Entrance is noted for its fishing. Boat ramps, hire boats services and bait suppliers are right in the town.

NORTH ARM

Lakes Entrance caters for anglers with boat hire services and an excellent boat ramp. These are located on the North Arm that runs roughly parallel to the port but behind the town, before running inland to become the estuary of the Lower Mississippi Creek. There is no practical access to the North Arm for land based anglers, but there are a number of areas where land based anglers can fish having gained access by boat.

The North Arm is best noted for prodigious catches of garfish when they are about. However other estuary species gather around the jetty pylons at daybreak and at other times, but are difficult to catch. Due to the fishing pressure in the local area larger sized fish are very wary and timid. For best results fish early morning, late evening and into the night with fresh baits and very light line.

Casting out into the deeper water has produced snapper and even mulloway in the past, but dumping of dredge spoil in the channel over recent years has been deleterious to fishing.

The weed beds adjacent to the jetty are an excellent source of shrimp, and occasionally crab, for bait.

BARRIER LANDING

Barrier Landing is right across the other side of the Hopetoun Channel past Rigby Island from Kalimna and access is by boat. It is of little significance except as a place to stop when cruising the lakes. Bream are often abundant around the pylons of the jetty but shy of baited hooks.

NUNGURNER

There is an excellent jetty situated at Nungurner where you are able to fish, but undersize bream always seem to be in plague proportions there. There is also a modest boat ramp at Nungurner and a sheltered bay where you can fish if the Reeve Channel is rough.

Many anglers now fish this area with lures, as lures seems to sort through the smaller fish and find the bigger ones—being the

BOAT RAMPS

LOCATION	BOAT SIZE	PARKING	BUILD
Eagle Point	4.5 m	Very good	Concrete
Eagle Point (Mitchell River)	6 m	Good	Concrete
Lakes Entrance (Marine Parade)	6 m	Excellent	Concrete
Loch Sport (Charlies Street)	7 m	Good	Concrete
Loch Sport (Seagull Drive)	3 m	Good	Sand
Hollands Landing	6 m	Very good	Concrete
Marley Point	7 m	Excellent	Concrete
Nicholson River	6 m	Good	Concrete
Nungurner	7 m	Good	Concrete
Paynesville (Motel)	6 m	Excellent	Concrete
Paynesville (King Street)	6 m	Good	Concrete
Paynesville (Newlands)	6 m	Good	Concrete
Paynesville (Yacht Club)	6 m	Good	Concrete
Raymond Island	6 m	Average	Concrete
Seacombe	6 m	Average	Concrete
Metung	5 m	Average	Concrete
Shaving Point	5.5 m	Average	Concrete
Tambo River (Swan Reach)	4.5 m	Average	Crushed rock
Tambo River (Johnsonville)	7 m	Excellent	Concrete
Wattle Point	6 m	Excellent	Concrete

above: Lakes Entrance.

fish that normally don't get a chance to get hold of a bait before the tiddlers.

Reeve Channel

The Reeve Channel runs between Flannigan Island and the mainland and provides good fishing throughout its length. It is also the main access channel to Bancroft Bay and Lake King.

On the north side of the channel, between say Kalimna and Nungurner, there are some excellent rock platforms from where you could fish but access is by boat, the descent from Nyerimilang and adjacent areas being virtually impossible.

Perch Creek

Perch Creek is so named because of the abundance of estuary perch here. Adult fish have been recorded by Fisheries surveys here in summer. Access to Perch Creek is limited to small boats because the water is shallow.

Approach Perch Creek from the west end of Flannigan Island, taking a heading between Pelican Island and the mainland. Having reached mid-point, steer for the prominent National Parks sign to the west. The creek entrance is on the left approximately 300m after passing a second National Parks sign on the left.

METUNG AND PAYNESVILLE

Bancroft Bay

Bancroft Bay lies between Bell Point to the east and Shaving Point to the west and includes the estuaries of Chinaman's and Box creeks. The settlement of Metung is on Shaving Point, a substantial spit dividing Bancroft Bay from Lake King. Metung caters for anglers needs with accommodation, fuel, bait and boat hire. There is also an excellent boat ramp at Shaving Point.

With no boat, you may still fish from the tip of Shaving Point and from the Crane Jetty with the expectation of catching bream at least. The deep water off Shaving Point is known for mulloway captures with some exceptionally large fish amongst them. During late summer, fish in the areas where tailor schools are present as they are a favourite prey for mulloway. Use baits such as fresh caught tailor fillets or live tailor and mullet.

Ocean Grange

The tiny settlement of Ocean Grange is located on the narrow coastal strip dividing the lakes from Bass Strait and lies adjacent to where the Gippsland Lakes periodically opened to the sea prior to the present entrance being built.

At Ocean Grange anglers have the choice of being able to fish in the surf, or from the sheltered water of Bunga Arm. The most popular access to Ocean Grange is by ferry from Paynesville.

Navigation to Ocean Grange by private craft from Paynesville requires specific knowledge because the passage between the Gergon and Radford banks divides into two smaller channels—the Aurora and Bunga channels. The number of channel markers, all of which seem to be in close proximity to one another, are confusing. However, once inside the Bunga Arm, the narrow and shallow channel behind the coastal strip, which is locally known as the 'Back Lake', provides sheltered fishing for a variety of species including bream, luderick, mullet and garfish.

Paynesville

The town of Paynesville is on a peninsula enclosing the sheltered anchorage of Newland Arm, with the mainland to the south-west and McMillan Strait with Raymond Island to the east. Paynesville caters for anglers and boating enthusiasts with five boat ramps within close proximity to the town. The large double ramp on McMillan Strait gives access to any size trailer boat at all times.

These days, the area is a favoured location for anglers chasing bream with lures, especially those who like to fish around jetties and moored boats. While these bream are often difficult to catch they are of a good size and offer excellent sport.

McMillan Strait

From 100 to 300 m wide, 3 km long, and several metres deep, McMillan Strait divides Paynesville on the mainland from Raymond Island.

On either side of McMillan Strait there are a number of structures where you may fish with the expectation of catching bream, luderick and a several species, but the Fisherman's Wharf at Paynesville would be the pick of these.

Newland Arm

Newland Arm is an elongated lagoon about 3.5 km in length, with a sand spit (Butler Point) restricting the entrance to about 150 m adjacent to the southern entrance of McMillan Strait.

Boat moorings dominate the north side, while the south side is dominated by residential development with little bank access. The bank shelves steeply into 3 m or more of water holding excellent bream. Most of these bream are caught by anglers in small boats using a variety of soft plastics and small hard bodied lures. Moving around the area using an electric motor helps to find patches of active fish.

Lady Bay

Lady Bay on Lake Victoria extends from Point Turner on the Banksia Peninsula, north-east to Bluff Head and includes the entrance to Duck Arm.

This area of the Gippsland Lakes holds good numbers of tailor, which can be caught trolling small diving lures or using a paravane. Otherwise, drifting along the edge of the deeper water with either baits or casting soft plastic lures should see you in action with the local flathead.

For lure fishing anglers the Duck Arm holds good bream around the jetties and moored boats, although the fishing can slow during the school holidays as it is a popular location for school camps.

Raymond Island

Access to Raymond Island, across McMillan Strait, is by ferry from Paynesville. Narrow, unmade roads give access to banksia and manna gum forests sustaining one of our country's few remaining healthy koala populations. With a couple of exceptions, the fishing opportunities are limited.

Raymond Island Jetty

One of the best places to fish on Raymond Island is from the jetty just north of the ferry terminal. There are some big bream around the pylons but you do need to be crafty to catch one. A bait cast out into McMillan Strait is likely to tempt a good size flathead.

Montague Point

Montague Point is a sandy promontory dropping away sharply into deep water where you can take the family fishing with the expectation of catching bream and the occasional good size flathead. Weed can be a problem. Take the first street to the right from the ferry terminal, turn right at the T-intersection, park your car at the end of the street and walk out onto the point.

Mick's Spit

At night the shallow sandy spit extending out from Point Harrington is popular with anglers seeking flounder with light and spear. Fishing during the day is best with soft plastic lures, cast along the edge of the edge of the sand spit for flathead. Although they're not plentiful there are some very nice fish in the area.

Point Scott

Point Scott is the most easterly tip of Raymond Island and is popular with flounder spearing enthusiasts. Take care because dark patches of weed sometimes disguise the drop-off into deeper water.

Resides Jetty

About 1 km north of Point Scott, accessible from a track running parallel to the beach and beginning just before Gravely Point Road turns south to the beach, Resides Jetty gives access to just over 2 m of water over a weedy bottom.

Garfish are the main species and best targeted with a float, but it is also worth fishing a bait such as live prawn under a float for some of the big bream and flathead that also live in and near the weed.

LAKE KING

Lake King sustains a healthy population of fish with virtually all species recorded from the Gippsland Lakes represented. However, during floods or periods of heavy rainfall, the fish populations of Lake King soar because it is where three major rivers—the Mitchell, Nicholson, and Tambo—all flow into the Gippsland Lakes.

Eagle Point Bay

Partially enclosed by the silt jetties at the mouth of the Mitchell River and the sand spit that extends out from Point Fullarton at Paynesville, Eagle Point Bay is noted for good catches of tailor during autumn and winter, and whiting and flathead in the summer.

Fish populations swell in Eagle Point Bay following heavy rain and flooding. Should the flooding be severe, the fish move out into Lake King, then move back into the rivers again when the flooding subsides.

There is a public boat ramp just north of the Lake King Caravan Park and another ramp in the park itself for park residents. However, others may use this ramp for a fee.

There is a jetty in Eagle Point Bay giving access to about 1.5m of water, but the bottom tends to be very weedy so baits need to be suspended from floats.

Swan Reach Bay

Immediately west of the Tambo River mouth, Salt Creek empties into Swan Reach Bay. Although shallow, Swan Reach Bay has good populations of mullet and some good size flathead.

Tambo Bay

Immediately east of the Tambo River, this shallow bay has good populations of mullet, flounder, flathead and sometimes prawns.

When the prawns move into this area, anglers can experience some great fishing for bream with small popper-style lures

Jones Bay

A shallow lagoon, partly enclosed by the silt jetties of the Mitchell River, it is an area rich in sandworms and a favourite location for pumping bait. The area has great numbers of bream, plus occasional mulloway which make off with bream baits never to be seen again!

At the onset of flooding, fish populations explode in Jones Bay until the fish are pushed further out into Lake King. When flooding subsides, fish populations rise once more until conditions become favourable for their migration back up the Mitchell and Nicholson rivers. The most effective technique is to flick shallow running hard body lures and small soft plastics over the flats.

SALT CREEK

Salt Creek flows into Lake King approximately 1 km north of the Tambo entrance and the deep estuarine section extends some 5 km upstream, almost to the Princes Highway. However, the entrance to Lake King is very shallow, preventing navigation by any but the smallest craft.

This body of water holds good populations of mullet, bream, estuary perch and probably other species as well, but it receives very little attention from anglers.

Following heavy rain, Salt Creek becomes a holding area for fish populations flushed out of the Tambo, and the number of fish in Salt Creek, especially mullet, increases exponentially.

MAJOR RIVERS

The Tambo, Nicholson and Mitchell rivers that run into Lake King determine the estuarine nature of the Gippsland Lakes. Many anglers never fish anywhere else but on one or more of these three rivers, and accommodation and other requirements are well catered for at places like Johnsonville, Swan Reach, Nicholson and Bairnsdale.

TAMBO RIVER

Undoubtedly the most famous and popular river in the Gippsland Lakes, and for good reason—the Tambo is a bream fishing mecca. The river many not be quite as good as it once was, but it still produces great bream fishing. Aside from bream the river also holds good numbers of mullet, estuary perch, luderick, flathead and a few mulloway

Perhaps part of the Tambo's appeal is that it offers so many great land based locations, where shore based anglers can catch as many fish as those with boats.

While the Tambo has been and always will be popular with bait fishers, it is growing more popular with lure fishers who catch good numbers of huge bream in this system from the mouth to well

upstream. Thankfully in line with this style of fishing the majority of the fish—and especially large fish—are released.

The Tambo is accessible to land based anglers both below the Princes Highway Bridge via the road to Metung, and above the bridge via the Upper Tambo Road. Downstream access from Johnsonville is from McFarlanes Road. Anglers with boats launch from the Johnsonville Ramp, which is reached by turning south from the Princes Highway at Johnsonville.

Tambo Mouth

The Tambo runs into Lake King and is accessible on the south-side from Reynolds Road, which runs off Punt Road. In turn, Punt Road branches right from the road to Metung from Swan Reach. The number of snags and dead trees in the water restricts bank fishing somewhat. These snags however can offer some fine lure fishing for big bream that like to sit in the cover of the twisted timber. Fishing this area requires fast reflexes and a strong leader to pull the bream from cover before they cut you off. Twitching hard body lures, metal vibes and soft plastics are all effective techniques. The rock walls hold excellent numbers of bream but can be finicky at times. The prime time to fish for bream is a few days after heavy rain when they school up in the mouth. Winter is the prime time to be fishing the rock walls on the north western wide.

Marshall's Flat

Marshall's Flat is a wide, exposed expanse of bank on the north side accessible from Johnsonville by McFarlane's Road, an unmade road best avoided following heavy rain. Although a productive area for bream, this spot's exposed nature does not endear it to most anglers.

Three Gums

The stretch of river on the north bank of the Tambo known as 'Three Gums' is off McFarlane's Road between Marshall's Flat and Clues Bluff. Access depends on the condition of the track.

Clues Bluff

Only a few hundred metres downstream from the Johnsonville boat ramp, Clues Bluff is an escarpment on the north side of the river, dropping into a deep hole of around eight metres. This is an excellent spot to look for bream after heavy rains have reduced the salinity of the river. Soft plastics and metal vibe lures work exceptionally well here.

Punt House Point

The old punt house site is on the opposite side of the river to the Johnsonville boat ramp at the end of Punt Road, which in turn runs off the Metung Swan Reach Road. There is good bank access here and it is a favourite area for anglers staying the weekend.

Rough Road

Rough Road is an unmade road following the river downstream past the junction of Metung and Rosherville roads. Although unmade, occasional upgrades allow access by standard vehicles.

Sandys Bluff

Sandys Bluff is a minor escarpment dropping into deep water and providing shelter from prevailing winds. Bank access does not extend to Sandys Bluff but it is a favourite area for anglers seeking bream and other species.

Howletts Flat

Beginning on the north side of the river opposite Sandys Bluff, Howletts Flat is on a wide bend of the river extending almost to the Princes Highway. Access in dry weather is from a rough track from the Johnsonville boat ramp.

The Poplars

Beginning at Howletts Flat on the north side of the river, and extending for several hundred metres along the river opposite Rough Road, is the stretch of river known as 'The Poplars'.

Sardine Flat

Sardine Flat is right on the bend immediately upstream from The Poplars as the river changes course and heads towards the Princes Highway.

Bennetts Brook

Bennetts Brook is a small creek joining the river opposite Sardine Flat. Near Bennetts Brook is a warm artesian spring, a legacy of an early and misguided attempt at drilling for oil, virtually on the bank of the magnificent Tambo River. Access is from the Metung Swan Reach Road.

above: Frank Milito (East Gippsland Charters) with black bream caught from the Tambo River.

Whelans

The stretch of river in front of Whelans Nursery offers comfortable bank fishing with few snags. Access is from the Swan Reach Metung Road.

Swan Reach

The settlement of Swan Reach is right on the Princes Highway. Just upstream, at the site of the old bridge, anglers sometimes hook the occasional mulloway, although few are landed on the light tackle usually used for bream.

Burns Flat

Access is by boat from Swan Reach on the west side of the river. Burns Flat is a comfortable spot to fish that is seldom crowded, even in holiday periods

The Lucerne Paddock

Taking the Upper Tambo Road north, it follows the bank for almost a kilometre giving easy access to a picturesque and productive stretch of river before turning inland to skirt the bankside strip known as 'The Lucerne Paddock'. Access to this area is by boat only.

The Willows

On the upstream end of the Lucerne Paddock, the Willows is a favoured fishing area for anglers in boats.

The Timber

So called because of the big trees growing along the west bank of the river opposite and upstream from The Willows. Access is by boat.Casting hardbody lures and soft plastics into the snags here is highly effective.

The Blue Hole

The area known as the Blue Hole is where the river turns sharply to the right immediately upstream from The Timber. There is no blue colouring anywhere here, nor is there any hole, except perhaps in the imagination of the person who named it.

The Cliffs

The Upper Tambo Road swings back alongside the river at The Cliffs after skirting the Lucerne Paddock. The Cliffs is a steep escarpment where the water is deeper than most other areas, but the bottom is very snaggy.

The Cliff is a significant area because it is a holding area for just about every species found in the Tambo during periods of low rainfall and high salinity. Occasionally good size mulloway are hooked in this area but few have ever been landed because of the snaggy nature of the bottom.

NICHOLSON RIVER

andbased access to the Nicholson is limited but includes the boat ramp and adjacent area near the Princes Highway, and upstream near the Omeo Highway from School Road (a continuation of the Nicholson-Sarsfield Road). However, the angler with a boat will find many more areas to fish.

'The Nicko' as it is referred to is a great fishery and just as the Tambo has become popular with lure fishermen so too has this river, as anglers find good bream fishing while casting lures towards the snags and rock walls

The Mouth

The Nicholson runs into Jones Bay off Lake King near the entrance of the Mitchell. The entrance is marked with pylons but is only about 1.5m deep. These poles at times hold good bream for anglers that sit back from them and cast lures and baits close by. Upstream the depth increases to around 4m and is safely navigable upstream past the Princes Highway.

The Pear Tree

The Pear Tree is the name given to the first slow bend below the Princes Highway and is renowned for bream and most other species found within the Gippsland Lakes.

The Boat Ramp

The boat ramp and adjacent jetties are on the Melbourne side of the river just downstream from the highway bridge. The jetty is quite a productive place to fish at times, especially so in the evening.

The Railway Bridge

Just upstream from the highway bridge, bream and estuary perch may be caught at the concrete bridge pylons. Estuary perch are particularly active here in the warmer weather.

The Reeds

Upstream from the railway bridge the area known as 'the reeds' is well worth fishing for bream, estuary perch and luderick. You may need to suspend your baits above the bottom because of heavy weed growth here.

The Tyres

The Tyres are along the bank as you round the sweeping bend upstream from the railway bridge. The bottom is heavily weeded so you may need to suspend your baits from a float.

The Cliffs

There are some noticeably deeper sections as you approach the escarpment on the next bend known as The Cliffs. Tailor are plentiful in this section of the river during the warmer months of the year, along with a variety of other species including mulloway.

The Six Furlong Strait (Strait Six)

Having rounded the bend upstream from The Cliffs, the river runs straight for approximately six furlongs by imperial measurement. Anglers troll for tailor along this section but other species like bream and flathead are to be caught here as well.

The Junction

Approximately 1 km upstream from the Strait Six, a substantial creek joins the Nicholson on the left-hand side, while the Nicholson (right fork) continues up past the Omeo Highway. However, upstream access is difficult because of the number of dead trees in the river.

School Road

Some 3km upstream from the junction, School Road, which runs off the Omeo Highway, offers limited bank access to anglers. Fish populations depend on salinity, but good fishing is generally experienced here during the warmer months of the year.

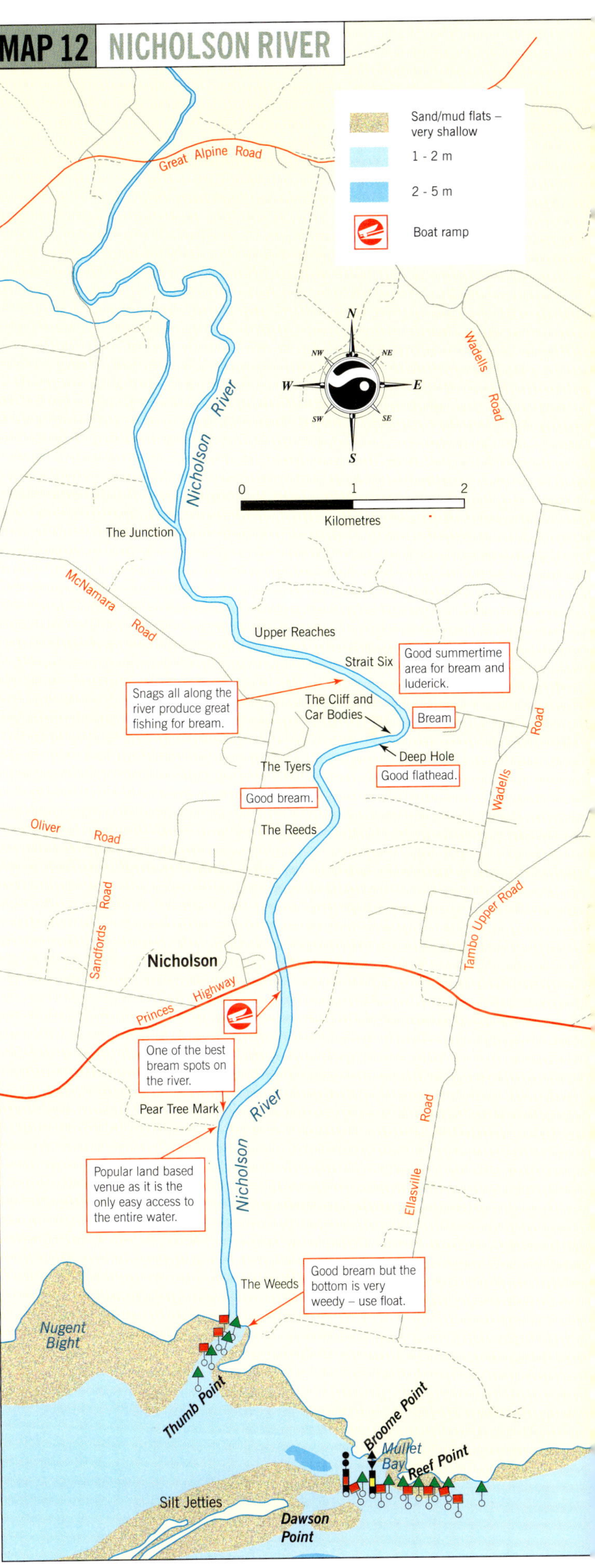

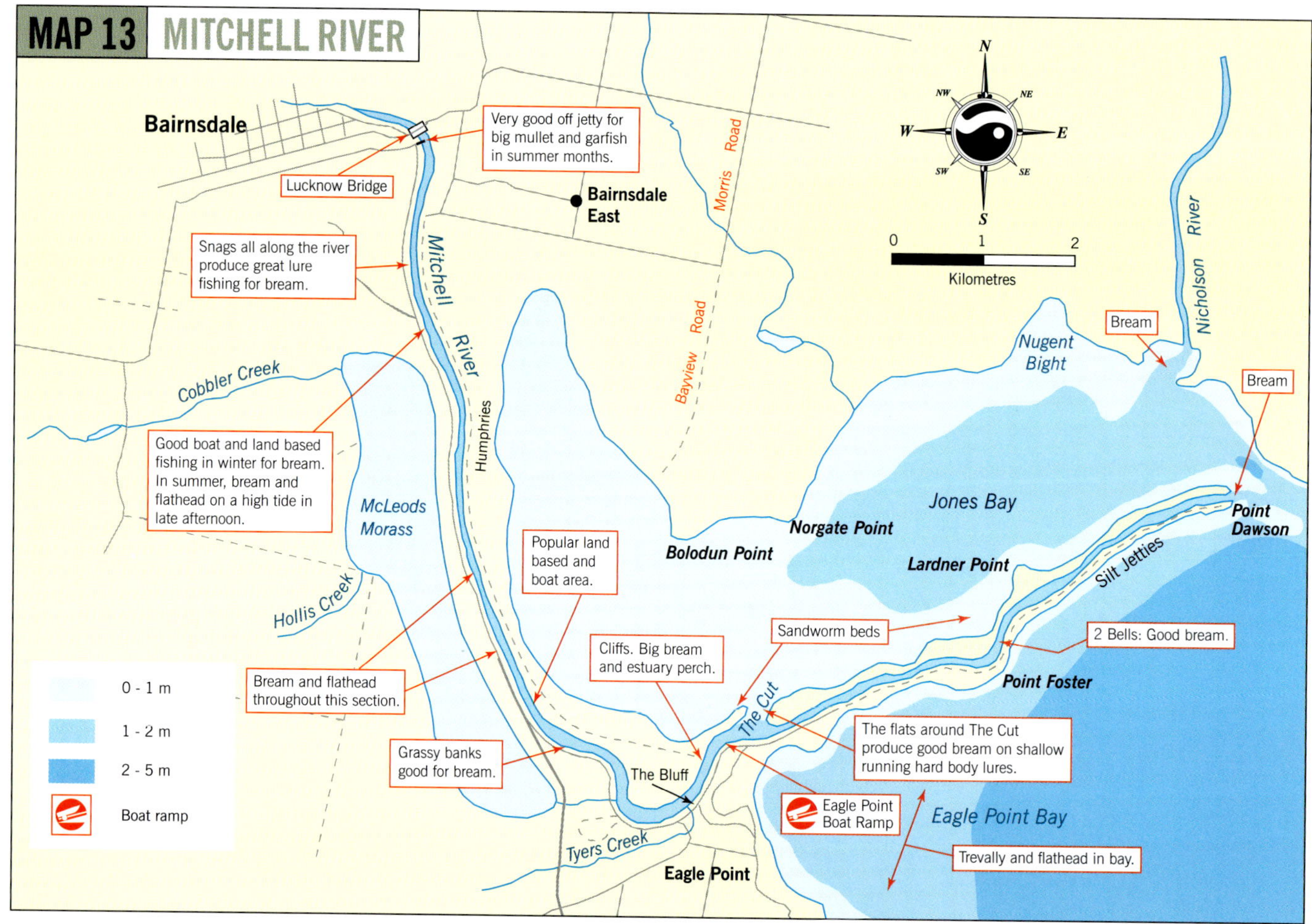

MITCHELL RIVER

The Mitchell River runs into Lake King between two roughly parallel silt banks some 5km in length. These silt banks enclose a shallow body of water known as Jones Bay, which is popular with amateur and licensed bait collectors alike.

The Silt Jetties

A unique feature of the Mitchell River is that it runs into Lake King through two, roughly parallel silt jetties or banks, which extend almost completely across the lake. The northern silt jetty terminates at Stevensons Point, the southern silt jetty at Point Dawson.

The entrance channel from the north-east side of Lake King into the Mitchell River is clearly marked by red pylons to port and green pylons to starboard. There is a public jetty just inside the mouth on the left-hand side as you proceed upstream.

The southern silt jetty is accessible from Rivermouth Road, an unmade road that goes all the way out to Point Dawson. Anglers will usually be fishing at intervals along here because there are good populations of bream, along with estuary perch, luderick and many other species as well.

Eagle Point Boat Ramp

Eagle Point boat ramp is off Rivermouth Road and gives access to the river downstream from the prominent feature known as 'The Bluff'. It is opposite and a little downstream from the break in the north silt jetty known as 'The Cut'. A row of pylons indicates the south side of the upstream passage. Fresh bait may be obtained from the Eagle Point Bait Supply nearby.

The Cut

Situated more or less at the base of the northern silt jetty, The Cut is a wide and shallow break through the silt jetty into Jones Bay. The fishing potential of The Cut is excellent because it has numerous snags that support fish and it is a passage between the Mitchell River and Jones Bay.

The Bluff

The escarpment on Mason's Bend, just upstream from the boat ramp is a favoured fishing area for bream but there are also good populations of luderick that regularly move along the river below the steep bank. Access is by boat, but you can walk in from the Old Paynesville Road.

Humphries

Named after the adjacent property, Humphries is about 2 km upstream from The Cut on the east side of the river. Access is by boat or from East Riverbank Road. Humphries has a reputation for producing good size bream but large eels can be a nuisance after dark.

Clifton Creek

Sometimes known as 'The Backwater', Clifton Creek joins the Mitchell as a narrow stream above the Lucknow Bridge at Bairnsdale and increases in size after taking a bend to follow the Mitchell upstream.

Access is from the Princes Highway about 150m past the Lucknow Bridge at Howitt Park. There is bank access and a small makeshift ramp suitable for small rowing boats.

Most fish species found in the Mitchell are also represented in Clifton Creek, along with a minor population of Australian bass.

Paynesville Road

Paynesville Road gives land based anglers access to a great deal of the Mitchell River. The jetty in front of the old butter factory is a very popular fishing spot for mullet during the warmer months.

Coming from Bairnsdale, the road divides with the left fork becoming the Old Paynesville Road, which extends river access almost to The Bluff.

Lucknow Bridge Downstream

Vehicle access to the east side of the Mitchell River is from the highway, just over the Lucknow Bridge from Bairnsdale.

After crossing the Lucknow Bridge coming from Bairnsdale, turn right from McEachern Street, right again into Broadlands Road, and left into East Riverbank Road, which follows the river almost to The Cut.

LAKE VICTORIA

Approximately 25 km long and with an average width of 2.5 km, Lake Victoria is second in size to Lake Wellington. The average depth is in excess of 5 m but the lake is shallow at the western end and channel markers should be observed when approaching McLennan Strait.

Loch Sport

The township of Loch Sport has all the facilities required by anglers and is situated on the southern shore of Lake Victoria. Loch Sport may be reached by boat from Lake Victoria, or by road from Sale or Rosedale on the Princes Highway, then from Longford via Collier Hill from the South Gippsland Highway.

Anglers launching from the Loch Sport boat ramp have access to Lake Victoria where bream, garfish, mullet and flathead are the dominant species. Tailor may also be taken on lures.

Mullet, bream and garfish may also be caught from the Loch Sport Jetty with evening and early mornings being the best times. Flounder spearing enthusiasts will find their quarry at Loch Sport.

Access to the beach from Loch Sport is via the Causeway over Lake Reeve, which is about half an hour's walk after entering the Gippsland Lake Coastal Park. Additional information may be obtained from the local ranger's office.

Duck Arm

Duck Arm is a sheltered lagoon about 2.5 km long and several hundred metres wide at its widest point. It has an average depth of around 4m and is partially enclosed by Banksia Peninsula, which juts out from the east headland of Mason Bay on the northern shoreline of Lake Victoria.

There is limited vehicle access to Banksia Peninsula from Lake Victoria Road and the shoreline accommodates a number of school and church holiday camps. At the bottom of the descent from Lake Victoria Road, there is a cleared area when small boats may be launched in Duck Arm but there is virtually no other bank access except for perhaps the sand spit at the entrance.

Duck Bay and the adjacent Picnic Arm are known to contain good populations of tailor during the cooler months of the year, along with bream and the other species found within the system. Mulloway captures have been reported from the sheltered water of Duck Arm as well.

At times, Duck Arm can produce great lure fishing for bream around the moorings and jetties, although it does fish best when there are no school camps on.

Wattle Point

Access is from Goon Nure Road off Bengworden Road. Facilities include toilets and a picnic area. There is a small boat ramp at Wattle Point and a jetty where anglers may fish with the expectation of catching bream, flathead, and tailor. The Wattle Point Retreat, right beside the lake, caters for families seeking comfort in a bush setting.

Tom's Creek

A small creek, which can produce some great bream fishing, Tom's Creek is at the west end of Lake Victoria on the north side. Access is by boat after launching at Hollands Landing and proceeding east along McLennan Strait. Observe the channel markers at the entrance to Lake Victoria, before turning left at the third red pylon, then heading NNW some 2 km to Jones Bay. There, the remains of an old wooden duck hide precede a number of sticks marking the shallow entrance to Tom's Creek.

Once inside the entrance, Tom's Creek becomes a good deal deeper and is navigable for another 1.5 kilometres. The bream fishing here is excellent in unspoiled surroundings. Due to it only being a small piece of water and quite narrow it does pay to keep noise to a minimum as the bream in here can be quite timid.

McLennan Strait

McLennan Strait is the 9 km channel joining Lake Victoria and Lake Wellington. It averages about 100m wide with an average depth of around four metres. Approaches to the strait at either end are well marked. At times there is a strong current in the channel. This is mainly due to the disparate water levels in the two lakes caused by the effects of the wind. The tide has little influence on the water levels of either lake.

Fishing in the Strait can be great anywhere—due to the water flow the fish can be quite mobile with the best spots changing daily. At times of high water some of the best fishing can be found in the shallow backwaters most anglers would never think of heading into.

The Strait holds good numbers of bream and estuary perch, which frequent the snags; other species on offer include flathead, mullet and luderick. There is also a large hole at the top of the Strait just before Lake Wellington that is known to be a good spot to chase the elusive mulloway.

Bait fishing is very productive for anglers who fish close to the shore with baits such as sandworm, crab and prawns. The Strait is also a favoured location for lure fishermen, with big bream and perch present that are only too keen to test anglers out in the heavy snags.

Hollands Landing

Hollands Landing is on the north side of McLennan Strait, not far from where it enters Lake Victoria, and caters specifically for anglers. Vehicle access is from Bengworden Road from the Princes Highway near Stratford via Meerlieu.

Hollands Landing consists of a caravan park and a small licensed liquor store that sells freshly caught bait and other necessities. There is an excellent boat ramp at Hollands Landing and ample parking for cars and boat trailers.

There is a retaining wall and wharf at Hollands Landing where anglers may tie up for short periods while loading or unloading, and from which land based anglers may fish with the expectation of catching a bream or two.

Seacombe Landing

Situated about 1.5 km from the western entrance to McLennan Strait, where it joins Lake Wellington, Seacombe Landing has a caravan park, toilet block and a modest boat ramp with limited parking for cars and boat trailers.

Road access to Seacombe Landing is from Longford on the South Gippsland Highway via Collier Hill, then the Loch Sport Road to the Seacombe Landing turn-off. Access from the Princes Highway is from Sale or Rosedale.

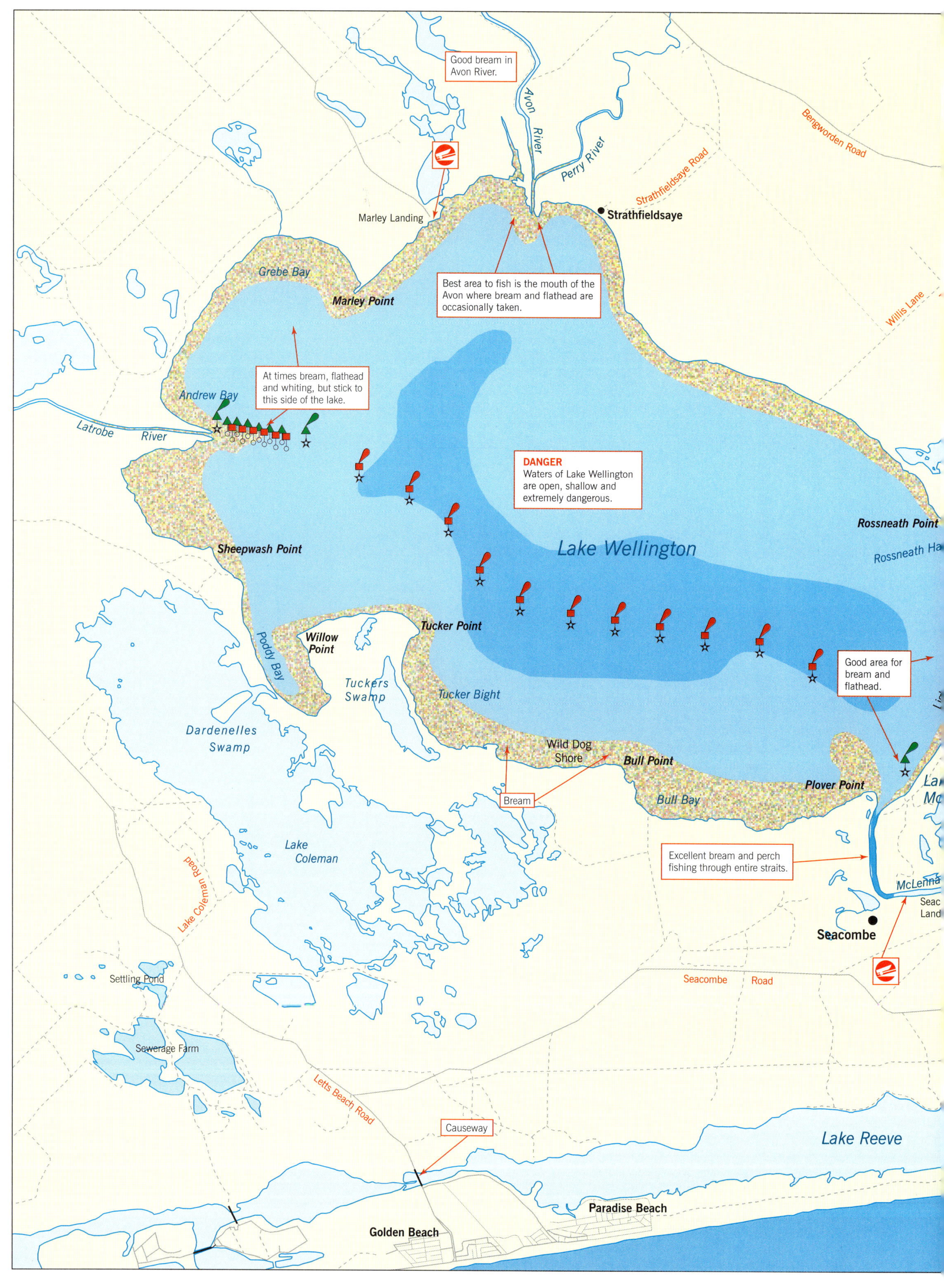

Good bream in Avon River.
Avon River
Perry River
Bengworden Road
Strathfieldsaye Road
Strathfieldsaye
Marley Landing
Grebe Bay
Marley Point
Best area to fish is the mouth of the Avon where bream and flathead are occasionally taken.
Willis Lane
At times bream, flathead and whiting, but stick to this side of the lake.
Andrew Bay
Latrobe River
DANGER
Waters of Lake Wellington are open, shallow and extremely dangerous.
Rossneath Point
Lake Wellington
Sheepwash Point
Willow Point
Poddy Bay
Tucker Point
Tuckers Swamp
Tucker Bight
Good area for bream and flathead.
Dardenelles Swamp
Wild Dog Shore
Bull Point
Plover Point
Bull Bay
Bream
Excellent bream and perch fishing through entire straits.
Lake Coleman
Lake Coleman Road
Seacombe
Seacombe Road
Settling Pond
Sewerage Farm
Letts Beach Road
Causeway
Lake Reeve
Paradise Beach
Golden Beach

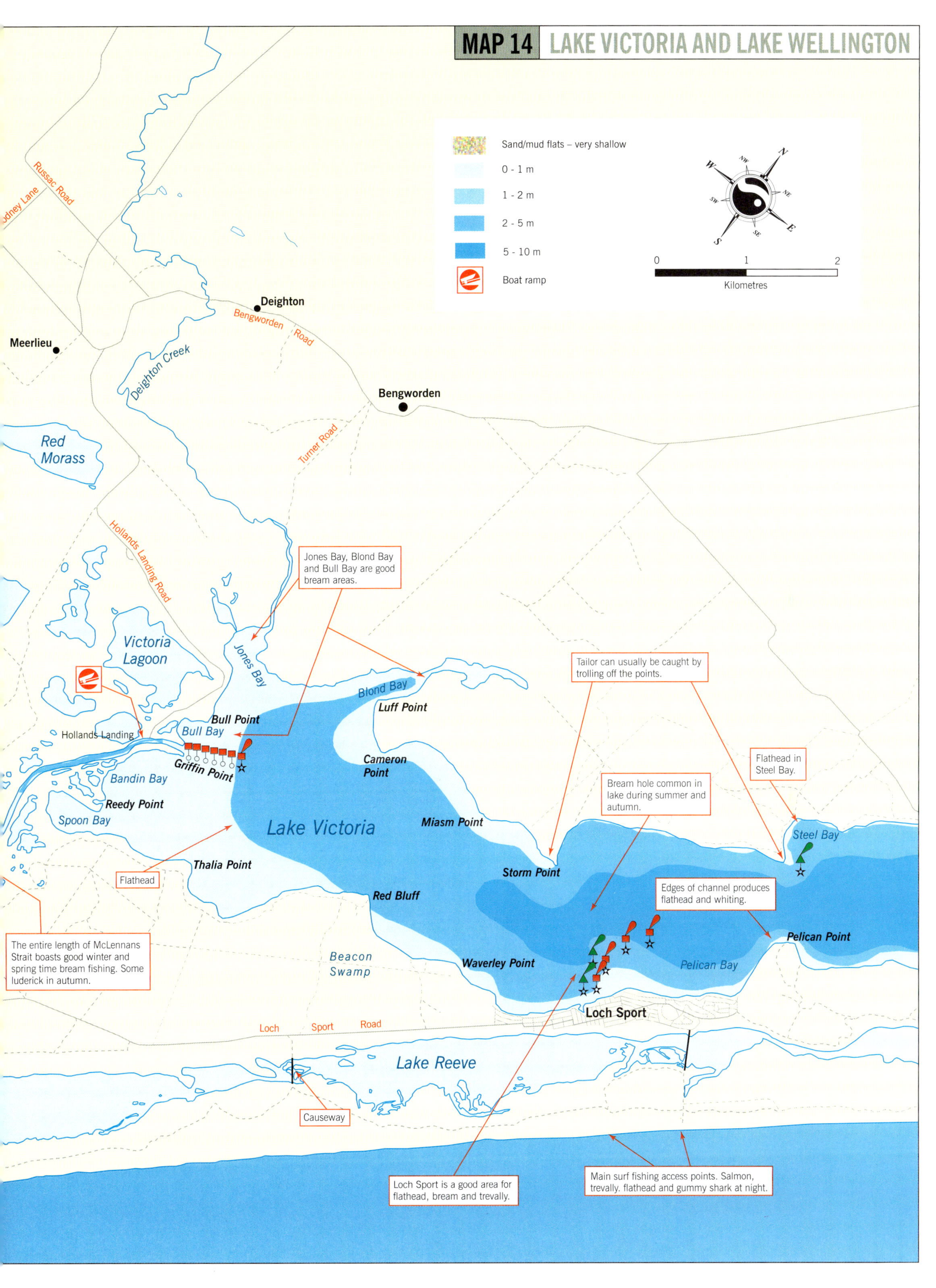
MAP 14 LAKE VICTORIA AND LAKE WELLINGTON
Sand/mud flats – very shallow
0 - 1 m
1 - 2 m
2 - 5 m
5 - 10 m
Boat ramp
0
1
2
Kilometres
Russac Road
Deighton
Bengworden Road
Meerlieu
Deighton Creek
Bengworden
Red Morass
Turner Road
Hollands Landing Road
Jones Bay, Blond Bay and Bull Bay are good bream areas.
Victoria Lagoon
Jones Bay
Tailor can usually be caught by trolling off the points.
Blond Bay
Luff Point
Bull Point
Bull Bay
Hollands Landing
Griffin Point
Cameron Point
Flathead in Steel Bay.
Bandin Bay
Bream hole common in lake during summer and autumn.
Reedy Point
Spoon Bay
Lake Victoria
Miasm Point
Steel Bay
Thalia Point
Storm Point
Flathead
Red Bluff
Edges of channel produces flathead and whiting.
Pelican Point
The entire length of McLennans Strait boasts good winter and spring time bream fishing. Some luderick in autumn.
Beacon Swamp
Waverley Point
Pelican Bay
Loch Sport
Loch Sport Road
Lake Reeve
Causeway
Loch Sport is a good area for flathead, bream and trevally.
Main surf fishing access points. Salmon, trevally, flathead and gummy shark at night.

MAP 15 OFFSHORE LAKES ENTRANCE – OIL RIGS

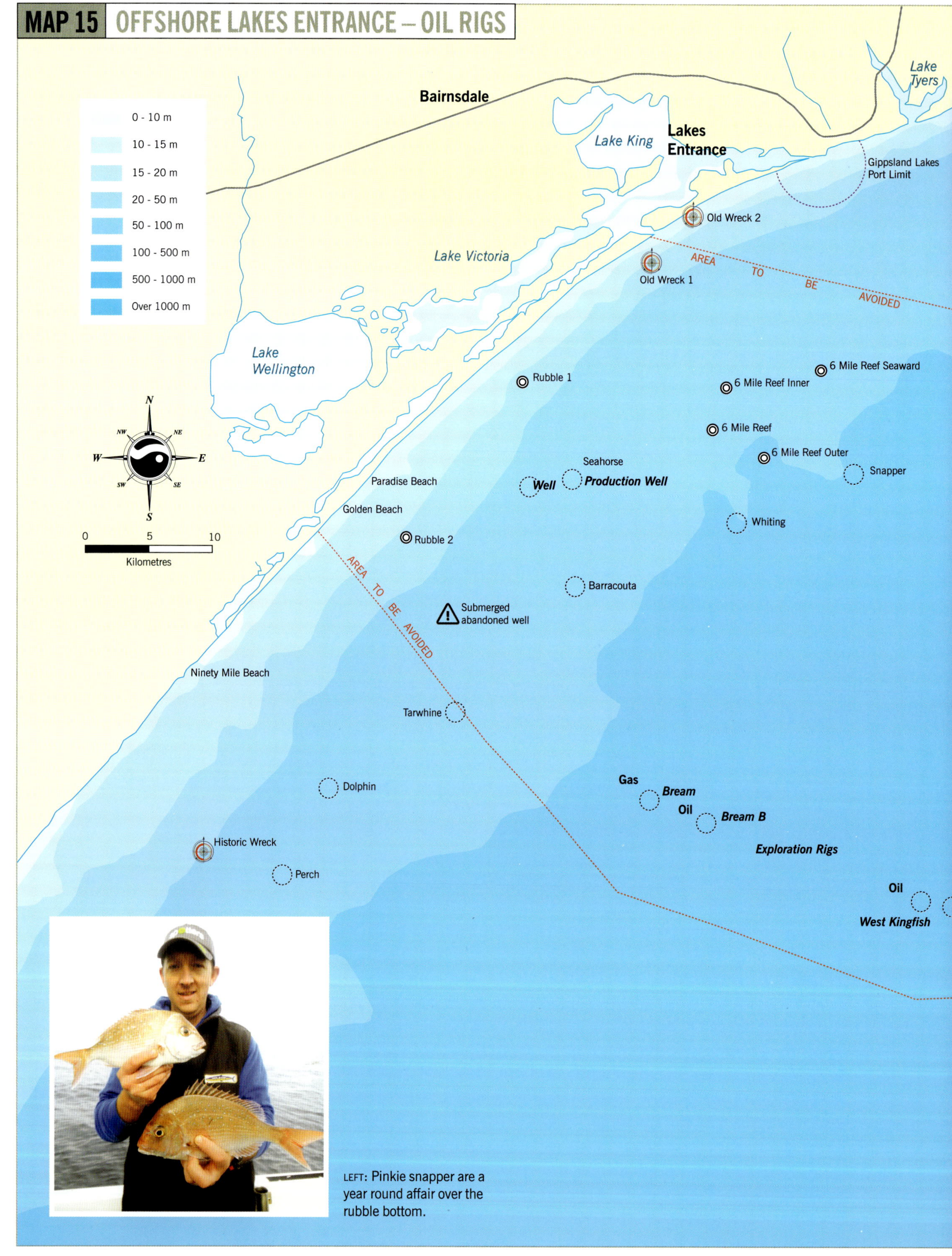

LEFT: Pinkie snapper are a year round affair over the rubble bottom.

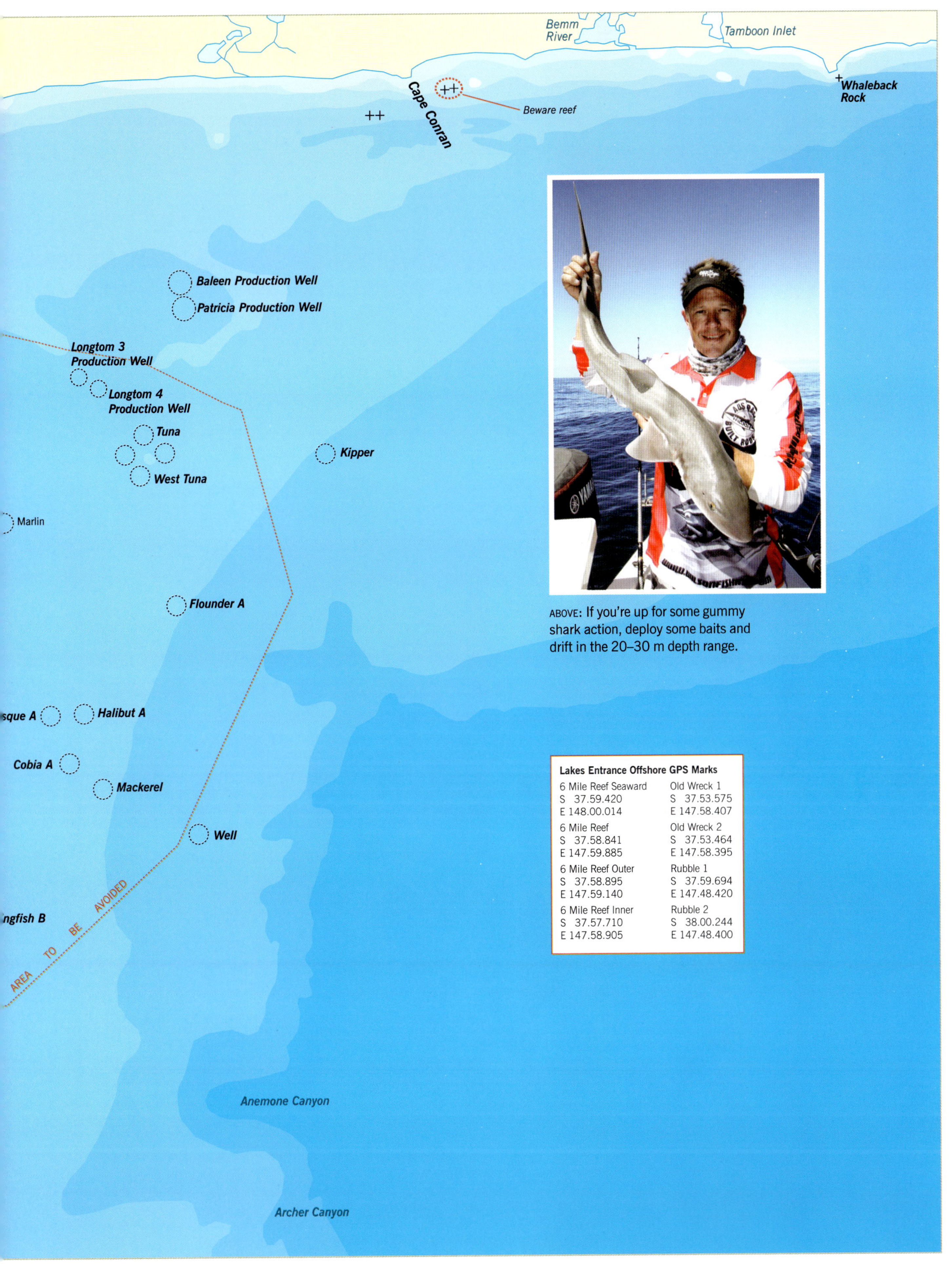

ABOVE: If you're up for some gummy shark action, deploy some baits and drift in the 20–30 m depth range.

Lakes Entrance Offshore GPS Marks

6 Mile Reef Seaward S 37.59.420 E 148.00.014	Old Wreck 1 S 37.53.575 E 147.58.407
6 Mile Reef S 37.58.841 E 147.59.885	Old Wreck 2 S 37.53.464 E 147.58.395
6 Mile Reef Outer S 37.58.895 E 147.59.140	Rubble 1 S 37.59.694 E 147.48.420
6 Mile Reef Inner S 37.57.710 E 147.58.905	Rubble 2 S 38.00.244 E 147.48.400

LAKE WELLINGTON

Lake Wellington is the most westerly body of water within the Gippsland Lakes and the most expansive, being approximately 17 km long and 8 km wide. The average depth of the lake is only about 2.5 m and this contributes to the treacherous nature of this water during windy conditions, which cause a nasty, short chop capable of capsizing small craft.

Most, if not all species found in the Gippsland Lakes, are represented in Lake Wellington along with freshwater species including European carp, trout and eels. Lake Wellington is also considered a nursery area because it usually contains large numbers of juvenile fish.

Boat Ramps

A public boat ramp with loading jetty and sheltering breakwater is about 2 km north of Marley Point adjacent to the Marley Point Yacht Club, giving access to around half a metre of water. Access from Sale is on the Clydebank Road, or via the Bengworden Road.

Small boats may also be launched at Spooners Landing in Bull Bay near the jetty on the south side the lake in the lee of Bull Point. Access to Spooners Landing is via a dry weather track branching off Seacombe Road.

Avon and Perry Rivers

The combined estuary of the Avon and Perry rivers runs into Lake Wellington in Disher Bay, about 2 km north of the Marley Point boat ramp.

The bay on the west side of the entrance has a small quantity of snags that at times hold good bream for anglers who can quietly sneak up on them in a boat.

The entrance is fairly shallow and flanked by silt jetties extending some 200 m out into the lake, but once inside the estuary the Avon River is navigable for about three kilometres. There is a small dirt boat ramp on the east side of the river about 1.5 km inside the river mouth, although for the most part anglers fish land based around the ramp.

The Perry River joins the Avon some 700 m upstream from the entrance and is navigable for almost three kilometres. This estuary system has mullet, bream, estuary perch and several other species.

La Trobe River

Anglers with boats have access to the Thompson and La Trobe rivers from the boat ramp in the Port of Sale where there is a wharf, parking area and toilets.

Downstream access to the La Trobe River from Sale is past the RAAF Air Base down Lower Heart Road. Then, turning right into Fresh Waterhole Road (opposite the Heart Morass Sign) there is a dirt ramp suitable for small boats at the Heart Landing after travelling about a kilometre.

Continuing past the sign, a dry weather track known as Bay Road takes you to the shore of Lake Wellington where there is another dirt ramp near the jetty ruins. However, be aware that the Bay Road track is recommended for 4WD vehicles only.

From Lake Wellington the La Trobe River is navigable all the way to Sale once the shallow entrance, which is marked with pylons, has been negotiated. Proceeding from Lake Wellington, the La Trobe River varies from 4 to 6 m deep all the way to the swing bridge, which has some 4 m clearance.

To reach the Port of Sale, take the right fork, which is the Thompson River, and continue for about 1.5 km until you reach the canal leading into the Port of Sale.

Although there are bream and mullet, along with freshwater eels and European carp in this river system, most anglers prefer to fish elsewhere.

above: Small hard body lures flicked along the tree lined edges is where you'll encounter some good perch.

left: Surface lures are particularly productive for bream in the summer months.

TACKLE & GENERAL INFORMATION

Alpine Country
82 Mac Arthur Street
Sale Vic 3850
Phone: (03) 5144 7505

Eastend Bait & Tackle
577 Esplanade
Lakes Entrance Vic 3909
Phone: (03) 5155 1593

Mitchell Sports Depot
196 Main Street
Bairnsdale Vic 3875
Phone: (03) 5152 4524

Stows Authorised Newsagency Pty Ltd
212 Main Street
Bairnsdale Vic 3878
Phone: (03) 5152 4363

CHAPTER 5
NINETY MILE BEACH

Myriad surf fishing opportunities exist along the Ninety Mile Beach, which extends from east of Lakes Entrance west to McLoughlins Beach in South Gippsland. During the summer months, the main target species are sharks, flathead, snapper and salmon, as well as mullet, elephant fish and the odd trevally. The gummy sharks are the main target species in these parts and are predominantly caught at night time and early mornings, however the odd gummy does get caught during the day. The gummy sharks start to get caught as early as late August; however they are at their peak between September and April. In the October/November period, a few of the beaches are renowned for their run of snapper; however they can be caught all throughout summer. The flathead last all summer too although the numbers dwindle to a minimum in winter.

The western end of the Ninety Mile Beach is renowned for the run of big southern bluespot flathead during spring and early summer. Over the recent years, paddling out large baits with surf skis, kayaks or small dinghies has become increasingly popular with anglers whom target bigger sharks. This is best done during the warmest months when the bigger sharks are most prevalent. The winter period is best fished for large amounts of Australian salmon. The run of these fish generally starts in April and can last all the way up until October. The biggest salmon are most prevalent between April and June and fish have been caught exceeding 5 kg in recent years. Spinning the shoreline is an extremely productive method as it eliminates the unwanted common winter species such as the poorly regarded draughtboard shark. Experienced anglers launch small aluminium craft from some of the beaches, Delray Beach and McGauran's Beach being the two most common locations to do so. This is extremely weather dependent and much care should be taken as this can be quite dangerous if there is a swell around. Snapper and gummy sharks are the main target species here, as there are numerous reefs scattered with 10 km of distance from the shore.

Along this massive stretch of coast, some of the more popular beaches include Golden Beach, Paradise Beach, Delray Beach, Seaspray and Woodside.

Best baits are generally blue bait, squid, whitebait, pipi, pilchard and fresh cut flesh baits, depending on the species being targeted. Service stations and other small shops in this area have a ready supply. However, for those anglers who wish to target the large sharks, snapper and mulloway that live along this coast, fresh bait is best with fillets of fresh salmon, tailor, trevally and mullet being ideal.

ABOVE: Salmon are often more plentiful on first and last light.

GOLDEN BEACH

Golden Beach is approximately 28 km from Longford after leaving the South Gippsland Highway, 7 km south of Sale. Taking the right-hand fork in the road for approximately 6 km past Collier Hill you will reach the settlement of Golden Beach after crossing the causeway over Lake Reeve.

Golden Beach is possibly best known for having the deepest gutters and strongest currents along the Ninety Mile. This makes the beach excellent for nearly every species available in South Gippsland. The summer months are best fished for gummy sharks and other sharks such as school sharks and bronze whalers. This can be done land based with long surf rods, 12 ft. to 16 ft. rods being optimum for the big swells and lines of weed in the shore break. For your best chance of catching a shark, the evening and night time session is by far the most productive time. The freshest baits such as salmon, trevally and tailor will catch more sharks than other baits, but in saying that, plenty of gummy sharks get caught on blue bait, squid and even surf poppers. The flathead are highly prolific here during the warmer months and average 35 cm but can be caught up to 55 centimetres. Blue bait, surf poppers and white Mister Twister grubs fished on a paternoster rig is ideal for the flathead. The big salmon arrive here as early as March however May/June is usually the most productive time. Golden Beach has a main beach in the heart of the town opposite the roundabout. Here there is a shelter and BBQ area as well as a good car park.

Also, while it's not really talked about and is very rare, the beach does produce the occasional large mulloway—particularly when anglers use fresh bait when the surf is discoloured from local flooding.

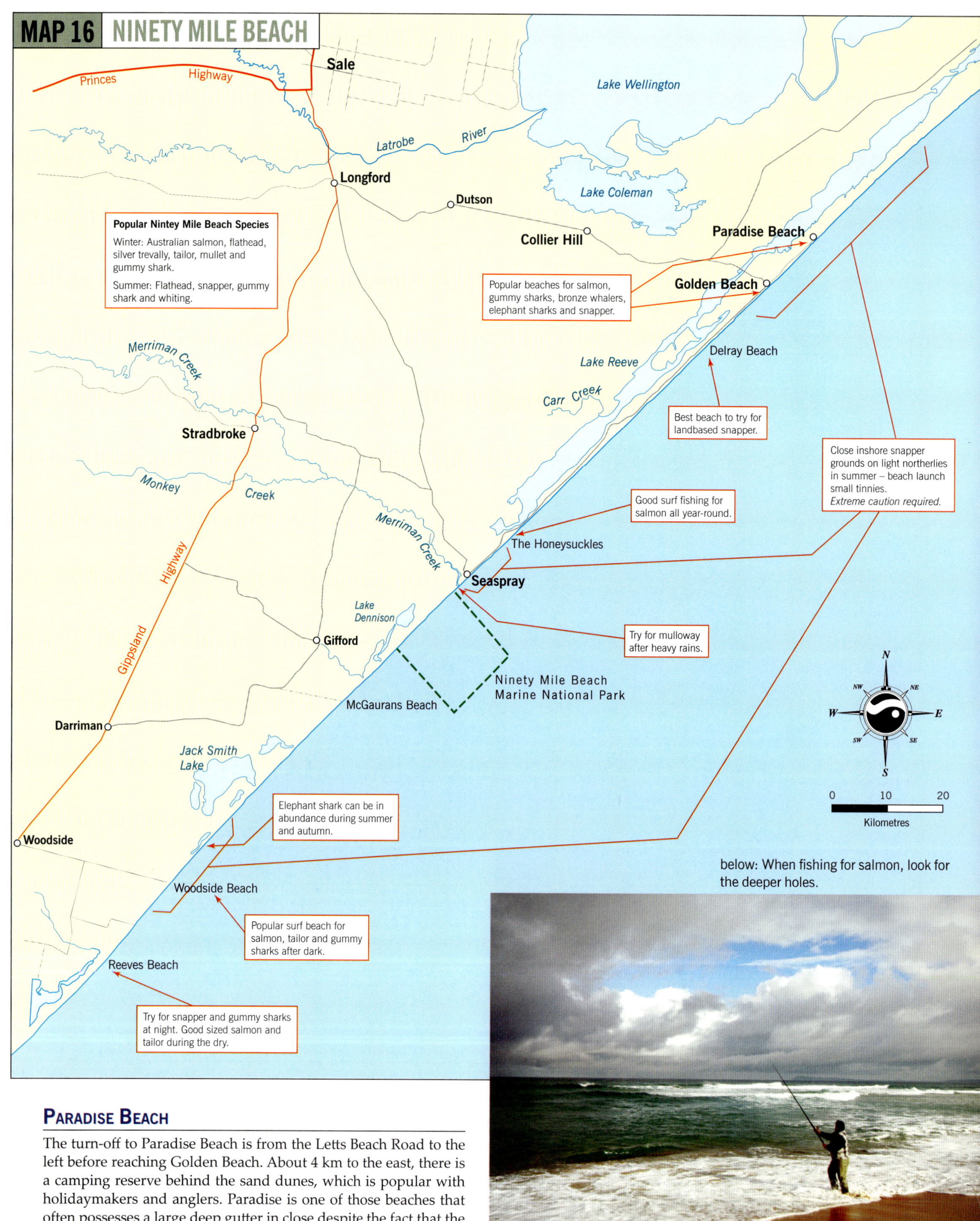

below: When fishing for salmon, look for the deeper holes.

PARADISE BEACH

The turn-off to Paradise Beach is from the Letts Beach Road to the left before reaching Golden Beach. About 4 km to the east, there is a camping reserve behind the sand dunes, which is popular with holidaymakers and anglers. Paradise is one of those beaches that often possesses a large deep gutter in close despite the fact that the beach is always changing with the winds and tides.

Like Golden Beach, the most common species include sharks,

snapper and flathead over summer and salmon, tailor and even the odd trevally over winter. Many anglers complain of too many crabs but the crabs can be bad at any of the beaches along the length of the Ninety Mile and no beach has more crabs than the next, it just depends on the day.

Delray Beach

Follow Shoreline Drive past Golden Beach to the west and you will eventually reach Delray Beach. Delray Beach has gained a measure of popularity due to the position of the car park and the sand ramp that can be used for boat launching. This 'sand ramp' is so-called in the broadest of terms. The severe weather and storms that are common here always wash this makeshift sand/concrete ramp away so don't expect to arrive here and see a beautiful useable boat ramp. You need to know what you're doing here! In saying this, it's used a lot for launching small aluminium boats. There is access to some very productive reef systems that are in quiet close. Here you will catch good bags of snapper between October and April. Landbased, it's not uncommon to catch snapper from the shore here and it's actually one of the more common beaches to accomplish this. It's also a fantastic beach to prospect for gummy sharks. It's not uncommon to see land based game fishermen paddling out large baits for big sharks over summer. Doing so will put you in with a chance of catching bronze whalers, school sharks and hammerheads. For the most part, flathead are the most common species here and it's usually quite easy to get a good feed over spring and summer. During autumn and winter, the Australian salmon call this beach home. It's another good beach to spin with metal lures and light fishing rods, but bait fishing with surf rods and paternoster rigs is just as productive for nearly all species.

Seaspray

The road to Seaspray is clearly signposted from the South Gippsland Highway, approximately 2 km south of Longford. You may also reach Seaspray, or any part of the Ninety Mile Beach along the 28 km stretch of beach road between Golden Beach and Seaspray. Here, the surf can be reached in multiple locations like at Golden Beach as there are numerous tracks over the dunes which can be accessed by parking in the multiple parking bays along the foreshore road heading towards Golden Beach. Further along, the area known as the 'Honeysuckles' resides. This stretch can be very good due to the number of gutter formations and rips. Big schools of salmon congregate here all year round; the bigger fish being more prevalent in autumn and winter. These fish can be caught on blue bait and surf poppers fished on a paternoster rig. This method will also catch tailor and trevally during certain times of the year. It's also a fantastic beach for spinning. In the summer it's a popular beach for land based shark fishing. You will often see kayakers paddling out large baits here for gummy sharks and bronze whalers.

The night fishing is renowned for producing good catches of gummy sharks, seven gill sharks and flathead. Due to the close proximity of Merrimans Creek, the beach will get dirty after large rains and minor flooding. It's at this time that there is the potential to catch a mulloway near the river mouth.

Shark fishing enthusiasts have had success at Seaspray, and some have even been known to paddle generous baits out past the surge on surf skis!

Excellent gutter formations at Seaspray ensure that good populations of salmon, and sometimes tailor, move inshore during the day and there is more than a chance of gummy shark at night.

The beach which is known as 'Honeysuckles' is most popular with anglers and has occasionally produced very large mulloway.

McGaurans Beach

McGaurans Beach is accessible from Four Mile Creek Road off the South Gippsland Highway and is between Woodside Beach and Seaspray.

It is generally acknowledged that beaches like Woodside and Seaspray are credited with the better catches actually taken from McGaurans Beach. This is because it is a favourite with local anglers who are quite happy to leave the better-known beaches to tourists and weekend anglers. There is plenty of room to accommodate large numbers of anglers as there are numerous tracks leading through the sand dunes to the beach. This beach is the number one hot spot for snapper. Fresh squid will definitely give you the best chances of catching a big red.

Jack Smith Lake

Jack Smith Lake is a shallow coastal lagoon between McGaurans Beach and Woodside, which is rarely open to the sea and of little interest to anglers. Access is from the South Gippsland Highway at Darriman.

Woodside Beach

Woodside Beach is signposted from Woodside on the South Gippsland Highway. It has camping facilities and a small kiosk where you can buy basic commodities.

Woodside Beach is popular with swimmers during summer and there is a Surf Life Saving Club at the bottom of Ben Rendell Drive. However, Woodside Beach is also popular with anglers who catch all varieties of fish. This beach is one of the better beaches to catch large bluespot flathead in the spring and summer months. They can be caught easily with blue bait, however it's also one of the most popular beaches to use the white Mister Twister grubs, especially on the large flathead. Gummy sharks also frequent this beach of a night time; however it is usually a little shallower than the eastern end which makes it very good for salmon fishing. During late summer and autumn, Woodside usually gets a large run of elephant fish which can at times become a pest due to their large numbers.

Reeves Beach

Reeves Beach is between Woodside Beach and McLoughlins Beach, accessible from Reeves Beach Road. This runs off Balloong Road that connects Woodside Beach Road with McLoughlins Beach Road. Once, 4WD vehicles could access the McLoughlins Entrance from Reeves Beach, but a barrier has now been erected across the track along with a sign prohibiting such access.

Reeves Beach carries a good deal of flotsam including dead trees, probably resulting from flooding in the nearby river systems. It is a beach that is almost forgotten during the quieter months due to the more popular ones further along the coast. However it can be a hidden treasure as it consistently produces good-sized salmon, tailor and mullet, along with gummy sharks and some big snapper at night. There's also more than the occasional mulloway to be caught for those prepared to put in the hours, especially when there is dirty water on the beach from flooding. The beach is very popular during the holidays, and it can often be almost impossible to get a camp site despite the massive camping area here.

TACKLE & GENERAL INFORMATION

Allways Angling
Shop 13/58 Hotham Arc
Traralgon Vic 3844
Phone: (03) 5174 8544

Alpine Country
82 MacArthur Street
Sale Vic 3850
Phone: (03) 5144 7505

Alpine Country
6 Saskia Way
Morwell Vic 3840
Phone: (03) 5134 1380

Mitchell Sports Depot
196 Main Street
Bairnsdale Vic 3875
Phone: (03) 5152 4524

"In Season Hunting & Fishing"
2/12 June Court
Warragul Vic 3820
Phone: (03) 5623 1944

CHAPTER 6

SOUTH GIPPSLAND

McLoughlins Beach to Venus Bay

South Gippsland is arguably one of the best inshore and offshore fishing locations in Victoria. This large region encompasses several popular areas, including McLoughlins and Manns Beaches, Port Albert, Port Welshpool, Wilson's Promontory, Shallow Inlet, Waratah Bay, Anderson's Inlet, Cape Patterson and Kilcunda. Given the large area, fishing opportunities are diverse, ranging from river and estuary fishing, pier/wharf fishing, beach and rock fishing, through to boat fishing over the shallows and inshore and offshore fishing around the many island groups and reefs. Species range from estuary perch, whiting, salmon and flathead, through to large snapper, kingfish and sharks—and almost everything in between.

Being only a few hours' drive from Melbourne's CBD, the offshore waters are very popular with anglers. In fact, anglers travel from around Victoria to South Gippsland, as the size of the snapper and gummy sharks in these parts often outweigh and outnumber the fish caught in their local waters. Perhaps the only downside to this part of the coast is the often unfavourable weather, which can keep anglers confined to the more protected inshore waters.

Good launching ramps and other facilities are common throughout this region, particularly in larger holiday destinations such as Port Albert and Inverloch (Anderson's Inlet).

Boat access to offshore fishing grounds is possible via the various entrances and passages through island groups, but make sure you are familiar with the local conditions. Note that conditions on the eastern side of Wilson's Promontory are often quite different to those experienced on the western side.

McLOUGHLINS BEACH TO TARRA RIVER

McLoughlins Beach, Manns Beach and Robertsons Beach are all clearly signposted from the township of Yarram on the South Gippsland Highway.

McLoughlins Beach

The boat ramp at McLoughlins Beach is on the extreme east arm of the complex system of tidal lagoons extending west to Corner Inlet near Wilsons Promontory. Crossing McLoughlins Entrance should only be attempted in a seaworthy craft and in the hands of an experienced boat handler, or following another boat whose skipper knows the area. This entrance is renowned for being smooth at one stage and extremely rough a few hours later so care needs to be taken.

The waters off McLoughlins offer anglers some of the best snapper and gummy shark fishing available. These waters are known not only for good numbers of fish, but also huge specimens, with 10 kg snapper and 20 kg gummy sharks being a serious possibility.

Aside from the snapper and gummies there are also great flathead, thumping whiting, and over the past few years' anglers have also been finding themselves in battle with the occasional school of yellowtail kingfish.

These waters also hold all sorts of offshore predators with everything from mako sharks to great white sharks. During summer schools of striped tuna are common around the numerous reef systems out here, and even extremely rare captures of cobia have been documented more than once. The bottom bashing scene is definitely the most popular fishing method offshore, and as mentioned earlier, the reef systems out wide are home to large schools of big snapper. The snapper can start as early as October and last through till May; however, summer is by far the most popular time to fish the offshore reefs. For snapper, a running sinker rig is extremely useful and you usually can't go past the humble pilchard as bait. To catch large numbers of flathead, a paternoster rig is best and drifting for flathead can be a good way to get a feed.

For land based anglers, there is a substantial jetty near the boat ramp that produces good numbers of trevally, mullet, flathead and the odd estuary perch on the rising tide. Should you be of athletic

Above: No captions supplied for McLoughlins Beach

disposition, you can walk the 3 km or so to McLoughlins Entrance. Some care is needed when fishing the entrance because the banks are steep, dropping into around 5m of water and the tide runs very fast. In the colder months, this can be a great land based option to catch big salmon on lures and during summer, you might just get yourself a snapper during an early morning tide change. Next to the boat ramp there is a foot bridge crossing the estuary which eventually leads to the surf beach via a 1.2 km walk. Anglers can be seen fishing off the footbridge for trevally, mullet and flathead. The end of the run in tide and start of the run out is definitely the most productive times to fish here.

Opposite the boat ramp over the foot bridge the shallow mud flat that winds down the channel is a popular area to catch prawns in the summer months. Flounder are also caught.

For the boat anglers, the estuary produces endless possibilities, especially for lure fishermen. This estuary really is built for soft plastics due to the large numbers of gutters, run offs and weed beds. Hard bodied lures can be good at times, however conditions must be perfect as the large amounts of floating weed that seems to appear during big tides and strong winds can make using hard bodies almost impossible. Casting hard body lures and soft plastics into the mangroves usually sees some nice estuary perch being caught. These are a high tide only affair. Flathead is the main target species here, and it's not uncommon to get blue spot flathead measuring up to and over 70 centimetres. The bait fishermen love this estuary because of its large expanses of weed beds which are home to large numbers of King George whiting, garfish and mullet. In autumn and winter, McLoughlins Beach becomes a sport fishing haven for Australian salmon, tailor and trevally. The salmon can get very big and school up in large numbers in the deeper channels in the entrance.

No captions supplied for McLoughlins Beach

Manns Beach

The settlement of Manns Beach is made up of holiday shacks and a handful of permanent inhabitants, mainly keen anglers. The boat ramp is high and dry for around half the tide cycle and local anglers launch their boats using tractors or older four wheel drives. The boat ramp is normally only used for small aluminium craft.

Like McLoughlins Beach, Manns Entrance provides access to great offshore snapper grounds but you do need local knowledge to negotiate the entrance. Bar crossings here should not be taken lightly and like McLoughlins, great care and respect needs to be taken! Inside the estuary, the channel system and shallow flats inside the entrance provide excellent fishing for whiting, large flathead and at times, gummy shark. Yet there is nearly every species here available to Victorians including, massive garfish, mullet, trevally, salmon, tailor and snook. Like McLoughlins, the channel systems and gutters provide excellent lure fishing for large flathead in summer and big salmon in the winter. The bait fishermen can pump Bass yabbies here and even the odd beach worm when the tide is out. This is the prime bait for whiting. The channel system between McLoughlins Beach and Manns Beach (Shoal Inlet) is also productive for some good estuary perch and even the odd black bream at times. The Bass yabbies would unarguably be the best baits for doing this, but lures are also extremely successful for these fish in the right areas. The jetty at Manns Beach produces small fish like mullet and silver trevally, and occasionally a good flathead, but apart from that there are no other land based fishing options.

Robertsons Beach and Tarra River

The road to Robertsons Beach, from Yarram crosses the Tarra River then runs alongside its lower reaches where you can fish for estuary perch, bream, mullet and silver trevally with some expectation of success. Upstream from the bridge, there are good populations of estuary perch which can be caught with hard bodied lures and saltwater flies.

The road ends at Robertsons Beach where there are a few houses and shacks, but you can launch a small boat from the hard-packed sand on the bank of the deep canal draining the lagoon near where the Tarra River empties. This is beach launching and it recommended a 4WD is used. Having launched your boat in the canal, you will eventually reach the channels that lead to Kate Kearney entrance, the third entrance in the system. Don't attempt the crossing to the ocean without an experienced hand in charge of the vessel.

The canal can be fished from the bank at low tide with a view to catching a variety of fish including monster sized flathead, King George whiting and some of the biggest garfish you are ever likely to come across. Fishing here at night can also yield nice gummy sharks, the odd bronze whaler and even perhaps the elusive mulloway.

Boat Ramps

LOCATION	BOAT SIZE	PARKING	BUILD
McLoughlins Beach	6	V Good	Double Concrete
Port Albert	6	Excellent	Double Concrete
Port Welshpool	6	Excellent	Double Concrete
Toora	5.5	V Good	Concrete
Yanakie (Duck Pt)	4.5	Good	Concrete
Sandy Point	4.5	Good	Packed Sand
Tarwin Lower	6	V Good	Double Concrete
Inverloch	6	Excellent	Double Concrete
Fishermans Landing	5	V Good	Double Concrete
Mahers Landing	5	V Good	Double Concrete
Cape Paterson	4.5	Poor	Bitumen/Sand
Manns Beach	4.5	Good	Concrete

MAP 17 McLOUGHLINS BEACH AND OFFSHORE

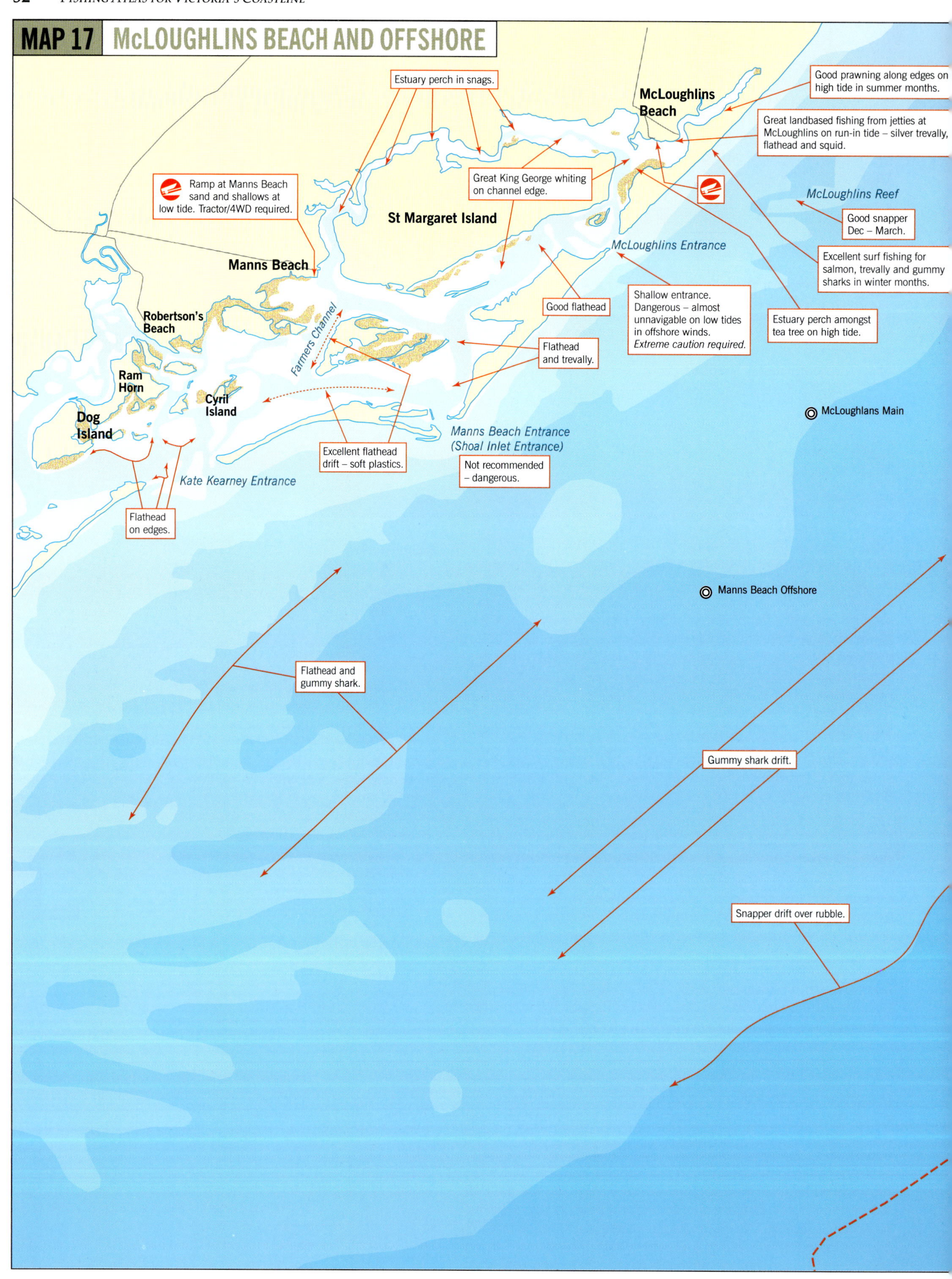

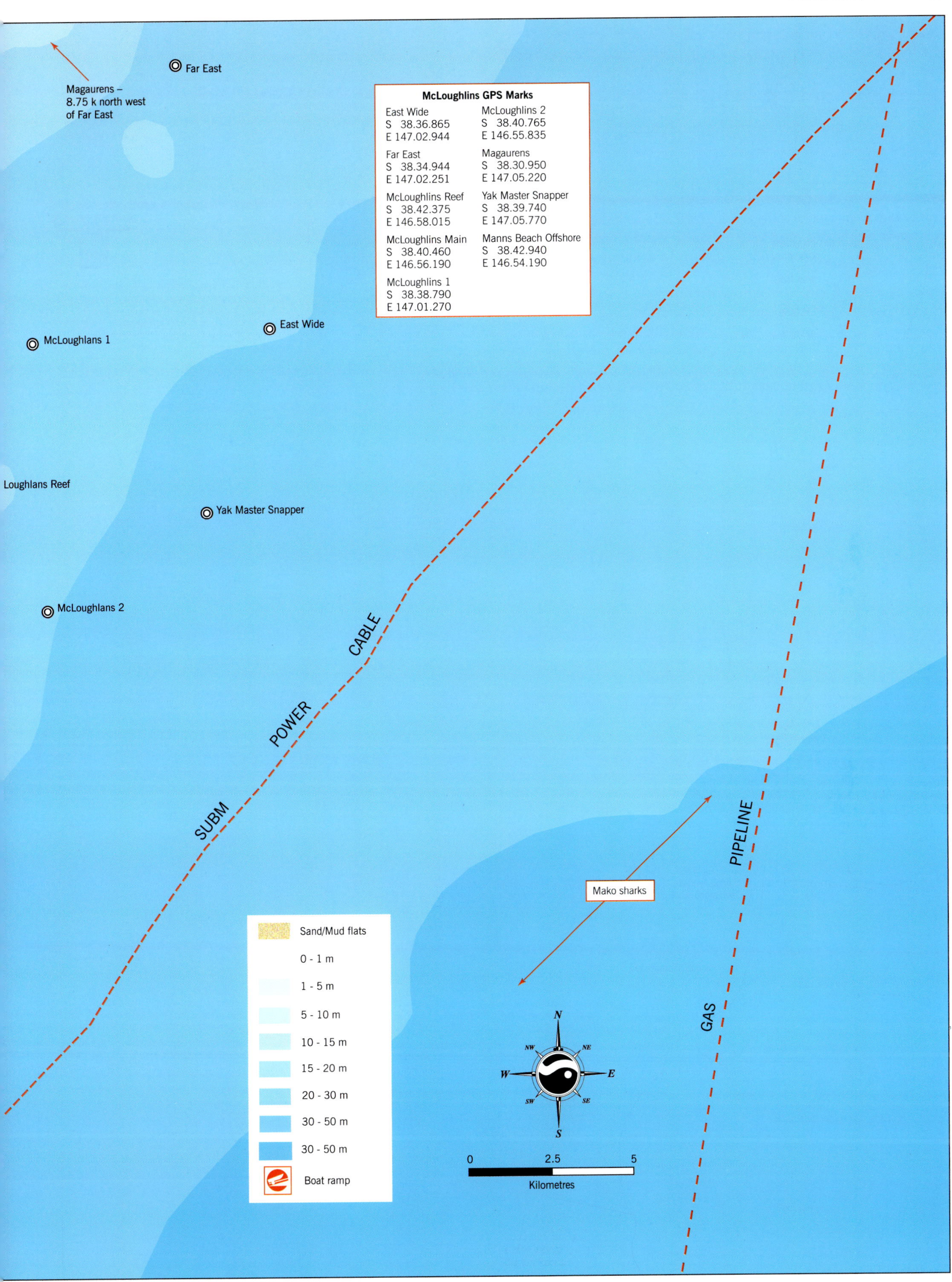

Far East
Magaurens –
8.75 k north west
of Far East
McLoughlins GPS Marks
East Wide
S 38.36.865
E 147.02.944
Far East
S 38.34.944
E 147.02.251
McLoughlins Reef
S 38.42.375
E 146.58.015
McLoughlins Main
S 38.40.460
E 146.56.190
McLoughlins 1
S 38.38.790
E 147.01.270
McLoughlins 2
S 38.40.765
E 146.55.835
Magaurens
S 38.30.950
E 147.05.220
Yak Master Snapper
S 38.39.740
E 147.05.770
Manns Beach Offshore
S 38.42.940
E 146.54.190
East Wide
McLoughlans 1
Loughlans Reef
Yak Master Snapper
McLoughlans 2
SUBM POWER CABLE
GAS PIPELINE
Mako sharks
Sand/Mud flats
0 - 1 m
1 - 5 m
5 - 10 m
10 - 15 m
15 - 20 m
20 - 30 m
30 - 50 m
30 - 50 m
Boat ramp
N
NE
E
SE
S
SW
W
NW
0
2.5
5
Kilometres

MAP 18 PORT ALBERT, PORT WELSHPOOL AND MCLOUGHLINS

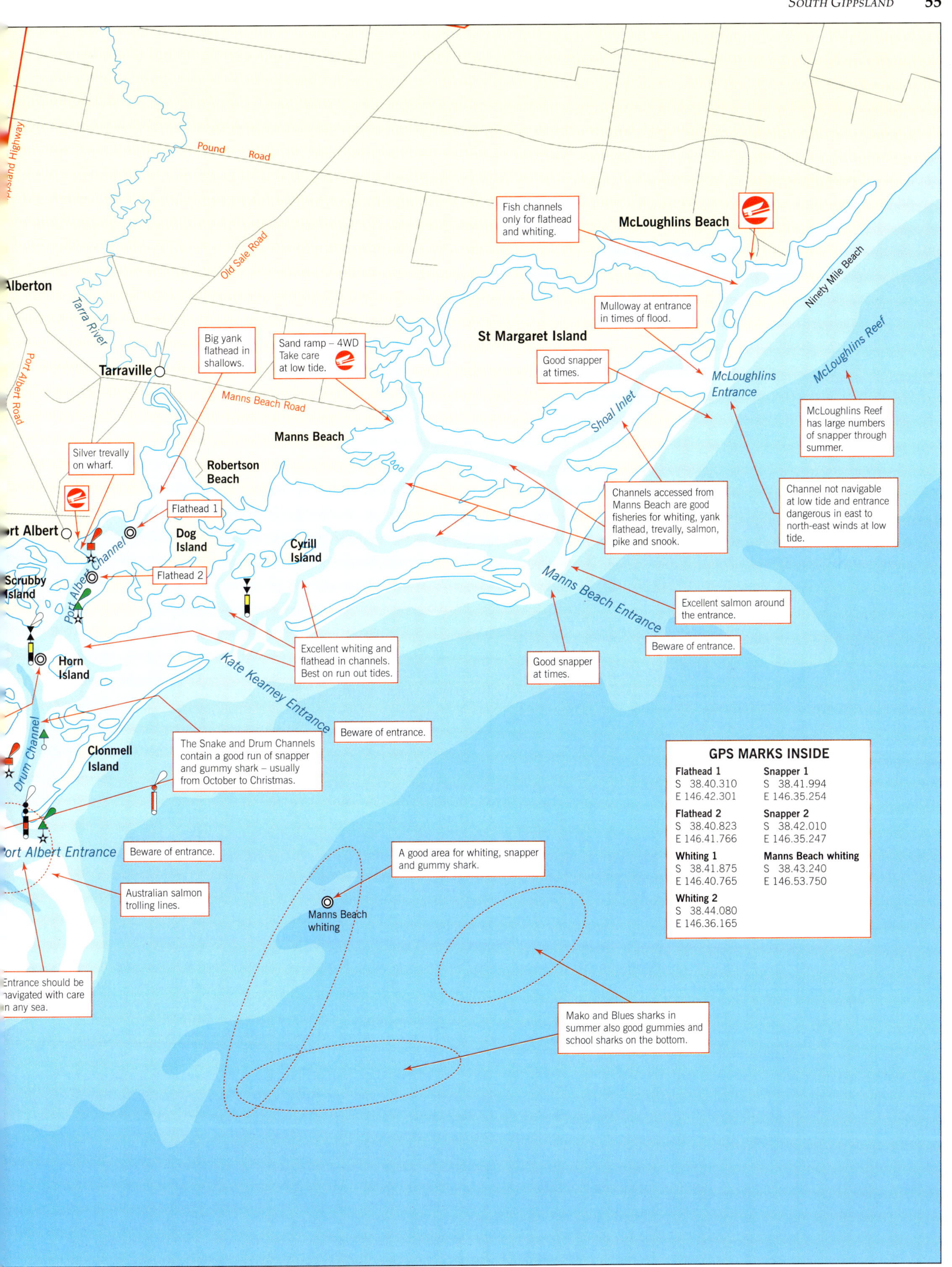

Pound Road
Old Sale Road
Alberton
Tarra River
Tarraville
Port Albert Road
Manns Beach Road
Manns Beach
Robertson Beach
McLoughlins Beach
St Margaret Island
Ninety Mile Beach
McLoughlins Reef
McLoughlins Entrance
Shoal Inlet
Dog Island
Cyrill Island
Scrubby Island
Horn Island
Clonmell Island
Port Albert Channel
Drum Channel
Kate Kearney Entrance
Manns Beach Entrance
Port Albert Entrance
Flathead 1
Flathead 2
Manns Beach whiting
Fish channels only for flathead and whiting.
Mulloway at entrance in times of flood.
Good snapper at times.
McLoughlins Reef has large numbers of snapper through summer.
Channel not navigable at low tide and entrance dangerous in east to north-east winds at low tide.
Big yank flathead in shallows.
Sand ramp – 4WD Take care at low tide.
Silver trevally on wharf.
Channels accessed from Manns Beach are good fisheries for whiting, yank flathead, trevally, salmon, pike and snook.
Excellent salmon around the entrance.
Beware of entrance.
Good snapper at times.
Excellent whiting and flathead in channels. Best on run out tides.
Beware of entrance.
The Snake and Drum Channels contain a good run of snapper and gummy shark – usually from October to Christmas.
Beware of entrance.
Australian salmon trolling lines.
A good area for whiting, snapper and gummy shark.
Entrance should be navigated with care in any sea.
Mako and Blues sharks in summer also good gummies and school sharks on the bottom.
GPS MARKS INSIDE
Flathead 1 S 38.40.310 E 146.42.301
Flathead 2 S 38.40.823 E 146.41.766
Whiting 1 S 38.41.875 E 146.40.765
Whiting 2 S 38.44.080 E 146.36.165
Snapper 1 S 38.41.994 E 146.35.254
Snapper 2 S 38.42.010 E 146.35.247
Manns Beach whiting S 38.43.240 E 146.53.750

PORT ALBERT

The turn-off to Port Albert from the South Gippsland Highway is clearly marked a few hundred metres east of the Albert River at Alberton.

The whole area is made up of a myriad of sand channels that are host to a range of species from juvenile whiting and mullet, to big flathead and at times snapper and gummy sharks.

For the land based angler, working the edges of the channels with soft plastic lures is sure to see some action with the local flathead, some of which are monsters. Some of the slightly deeper channels are also home to some nice snapper and gummy sharks, often surprising anglers by venturing into the small channels and the shallower water. The beginning of October to the end of April appears to be the best time to catch all three species.

PORT ALBERT BOAT RAMP

The boat ramp at Port Albert is a three bay large boat ramp with a floating pontoon. It's a great facility with a large car park and toilets. Port Albert can be so popular in summer that the car park fills by 7am and cars and trailers can be seen parked all the way up the main road. The boat ramp will grant anglers access to the myriad of channels expanding around Sunday Island. It also leads to the main entrance which gives access to the open ocean around the islands of Wilson's Promontory. The area around Port Albert is part of the Nooramunga Marine and Coastal Park. Although fishing is not prohibited in this park, there are rules and regulations in regards to the flora and fauna within the areas. Normal Victorian fishing regulations apply here just as in all Victorian marine waters and anglers should adhere to the current size and bag limits of marine species. Unfortunately, this inlet is still heavily fished by commercial fishermen and it is one of the only locations left in Victoria where commercial netting is still legal and practiced. The commercial licences possessed by fishermen here actually give them access to legally net the whole system up to and expanding to McLoughlins Beach and Corner Inlet as these waters are all connected. Unfortunately Port Albert seems to get more commercial pressure than the rest of the system.

Aside from the commercial pressure the area receives, it still can still produce some fine fish for those who are prepared to put in the time and effort to learn about the area. Good whiting can be found along the edges of the banks, and a bonus is that most of the banks have a plentiful supply of Bass yabbies, which are excellent bait.

Some of the deeper holes can hold good snapper and gummy sharks, while for the lure angler, there are great flathead on offer, especially if in a small boat which enables access to some of the small runoffs and channels that hold water during the lower tides.

PORT ALBERT JETTIES

A number of jetties exist between the boat ramp and the wharves. Some of these may be private jetties, so obey any signs. The main wharf is also popular for land based anglers. These man-made structures provide ready access to the channel and are also havens for myriad species at different times of the year. Best fishing is on the run in and at high tides. Expect to catch flathead, King George whiting, trevally, mullet and other species. Some good fish have been taken here over the years including yellowtail kingfish. A great 'family fishing' destination, these jetties and wharves have also been the site of many an angler's first fish. Blue bait, whitebait and pipi are the best for most species close to the jetties; but, many anglers can be seen casting squid jigs around boats and pylons for squid at certain times of the year. Soft plastics can be dynamite on large populations of trevally hanging around the structure at times.

ALBERT RIVER/OLD PORT

The Albert River holds excellent estuary perch populations and is navigable for some distance in a small boat, but launching is limited here. Anglers staying at the Sea Bank Caravan Park have high tide access for small boats via a bitumen ramp on the Old Port lagoon, which itself provides reasonable fishing. The Old Port itself can be accessed via the midge channel if you launch at the main ramp. This area was once renowned for producing the biggest snapper in the area. It doesn't live up to its expectations as much now, but plenty of pinkie snapper get caught in this area as well as the odd monster snapper as well. The shallower flats and weed banks provide exceptional whiting grounds and also some of the biggest yank flathead you will ever see. Small bronze whalers have been known to have been caught in the shallows here and it's not uncommon to get a gummy shark or two as well.

BASKET BEACON

The No 3 starboard marker of the Port Albert Channel now marks the site of the old basket beacon. The area surrounding the basket beacon is a productive snapper mark in late September and early October. Best results are to be had at night and very early in the morning, with the high tide running off. WA Pilchards are favoured bait for both snapper and the large gummy sharks—which are often encountered while targeting the former. On a calm night during the peak of the snapper season many boats will be anchored in this area, and you will certainly know if people are catching fish!

MIDGE CHANNEL

The main Port Albert Channel divides around the basket beacon, with one arm going around Sunday Island to the right (Midge Channel) and past the Old Port; the other going to the left, past the entrance and connecting with the other channel behind Sunday Island. Midge Channel is a popular place for big flathead, as well as whiting and the occasional snapper.

PORT ALBERT ENTRANCE

The Port Albert entrance is wide and deep, but the passage from the entrance to Bass Strait is a tortuous 3 km gauntlet of shallow water and uncomfortable chop. While it is perhaps not as dangerous as the McLoughlins Entrance, it does require extreme care as there is a far greater distance to get through than the few waves at McLoughlins. It is also worth getting local information on the best lead to take when heading out as the channel does move with sand build up. This area produces quite a lot of snapper during October and November and gummy sharks are always a welcomed by-catch here as well. Pilchards are probably the most reliable baits here, but don't look past squid either.

SNAKE CHANNEL

The Snake Channel extends due west for 8 km from the Port Albert entrance beacon to One Tree Island. It is the largest and deepest body of water within Port Albert and is the best place to catch a big snapper and gummy sharks. While it does produce massive snapper each season, best results still come to those who put in the time and especially if they use fresh-caught bait such as whiting heads, salmon fillets and squid, although WA pilchards are also dynamite.

Your best chance of catching a big snapper here is from first light until mid-morning, particularly if there is a tide change. Snapper are caught from late September to late April, with October and March probably being the best months.

A deep area at the western end of the Snake Channel known as the 'Blue Hole' is another popular area for big snapper. It also produces good gummy shark fishing in between snapper bites.

For those anglers who like to get their arms stretched during the warmer months, a solid berley trail and some large bait on the bottom should see you tangling with some big bronze whaler sharks. The shallower edges are home to good drop-offs and gutters and here you will have excellent flathead fishing with lures such as soft plastics. It's not uncommon to catch flathead at an average length of 60 cm and you might just catch a monster weighing in at double figures in the old scale. The strong tide often means you will need slightly heavier jig heads such as ¼ oz and heavier hard bodied lures and vibes can therefore be very productive as well. The run off tide is definitely the most productive when doing this sort of fishing.

Middle Ground

The Middle Ground refers to the shallow stretch of water between One Tree Island and Port Welshpool. Barely navigable even at high tide, if you time the tides right this area provides excellent lure, fly and live bait fishing for big flathead in the shallows. Whiting are regularly caught where the water deepens as you get closer to Port Welshpool.

PORT WELSHPOOL & CORNER INLET

Port Welshpool boasts an excellent boat ramp on the Lewis Channel, giving access to both the extensive waters of Corner Inlet, and to the ocean itself through the largest and deepest entrance in the system.

Once through the Port Welshpool entrance, anglers are out in some prime fishing grounds with snapper, gummy sharks and big sand flathead being the major targets. While for the adventurous, a 30 km run will see them on the very productive fishing grounds of the Seal Islands group, which includes the famous Cliffy Island group. Through the warmer months these islands hold a good population of kingfish that range in size from rats to monsters. The area also features huge snook and plenty of wrasse species. It's worth keeping an eye out for birds diving on bait as the area is known for yellowfin and bluefin tuna, and in the last few years there has also been the odd report of free jumping marlin—let's hope it's only a matter of time until one is caught here.

For the angler who prefers to stay closer to the shore, the coastline down towards the southern tip of the Prom holds great salmon, whiting, and some of the best thresher shark fishing on offer, especially around Sealers Cove.

Inside Port Welshpool there are plenty of fishing opportunities for both the boat and land based angler. In the summer months, snapper migrate into the system and are mainly caught in Singapore Deep and the Franklin channel. Gummy sharks are also plentiful along with some toothies that follow in the snapper schools. Kingfish make regular appearances throughout the system right up to and out the front of the long jetty in the Lewis Channel but can be challenging to catch; trolling squid strips is most effective. Whiting and calamari are also abundant along the weed bank lined edges especially where the Lewis channel meets possum creek. The bank running along here between red channel marker 12 and 8 is particularly productive for flathead and whiting.

The bank nearing the west cardinal market no.7 is heavily weeded and a calamari hotspot. Drifting the edge of the bank is very productive year round. Another hot spot is up on the bank between green channel marker no.3 and no.1 just before Singapore Deep.

Lewis Channel

The Lewis Channel is well marked. However, several large channels feed into the entrance of Corner Inlet so it pays to spend some time familiarising yourself with the markers.

Snapper and gummy shark are the main target species within the deeper channels of Corner Inlet, and whiting are caught on the shallower banks along with the occasional big flathead.

The best whiting spot close to Port Welshpool is an area known as 'Possum Creek', a channel draining the mud flats near the No 10 pile on the west side of the Lewis Channel. Possum Creek begins between two obvious small islands on the west bank of the channel known as Possum North and Possum South. This location also holds good numbers of calamari which respond well to artificial jigs. Baited jigs are also effective but the most productive method is to drift along the bank while casting and retrieving.

During the summer months and in particular from January throughout to March, Kingfish frequently visit this area. Often, anglers trolling 100mm to 130mm diving jerk baits do quite well but the best success comes from those trolling lead lines with strips of calamari. In calm weather, it is common to have the kingfish busting baitfish on the surface and angler's equip with surface poppers and stick baits can experience some mind blowing top water action.

Long Jetty

Landbased anglers are well catered for with the long jetty that ends in the deep water of the Lewis Channel. The Long Jetty is still in a current state of disrepair and as much as we can only hope it will be repair, the near outlook is look grim. Fire destroyed the end of the pier and it is currently fenced off, limiting access to the deeper water. However anglers can still fish from the jetty accessing the shallow flats where flathead and whiting are a popular catch. A high tide just beginning to run off at daybreak is a good time to fish here. The channel can also be accessed at low tide by walking across the exposed sand flats. Anglers can fish directly into the deep water, opposite the end of the long jetty. The tide rises quickly so be wary as it can come around behind you. The flats provide good fishing for flathead as the water begins to cover them.

Boat anglers can also fish around the jetty which is very productive for whiting, garfish, salmon, silver trevally and kingfish in season. Whiting are often caught when anglers anchor on the edge of the channel and set a berley trail. Using a paternoster rig with size #4 Mustad Demon Circle hook is ideal for catching whiting. Don't be surprised if you hook into some big flathead either as they are a common catch when berley is used.

Little Snake and Snake Islands

The channel in between Little Snake and Snake Islands provides great shallow water fishing for some big flathead. Anglers keen for sport fishing often arm themselves with a selection of soft plastics and work the sandy edges. Some flathead can exceed 70cm. Whiting are also caught a little further out in the deeper water as are some good size calamari. Calamari tend to be caught while drifting over the weed beds but due to the height of the weed, jigs in the 2.0 and 2.5 size are best offered. When searching for good locations to target whiting, look for areas where there are sand patches free from weed. Set anchor within casting distance and berley casting your baits onto the sand holes. Anglers fishing out the front of Snake Island in the deep water either side of the Singapore Deep Channel regularly catch good snapper and gummy shark from October to March. While on the easiest location to fish, setting anchor along the edge of the drop off and setting a berley trail of cubed pilchard will bring success.

In the past few years, increasing numbers of kingfish make it worth casting poppers or dropping jigs near the channel markers around the entrance to Port Welshpool, especially early in the morning during favourable weather.

Toora

The township of Toora has an excellent boat ramp at the top of the Toora Channel. There doesn't appear to be any signpost pointing to the boat ramp, but access is via Harriet Street, which runs off the South Gippsland Highway in the township of Toora.

Like the Lewis Channel, the Toora Channel is deep, well-marked, and gives access to the main entrance in the system.

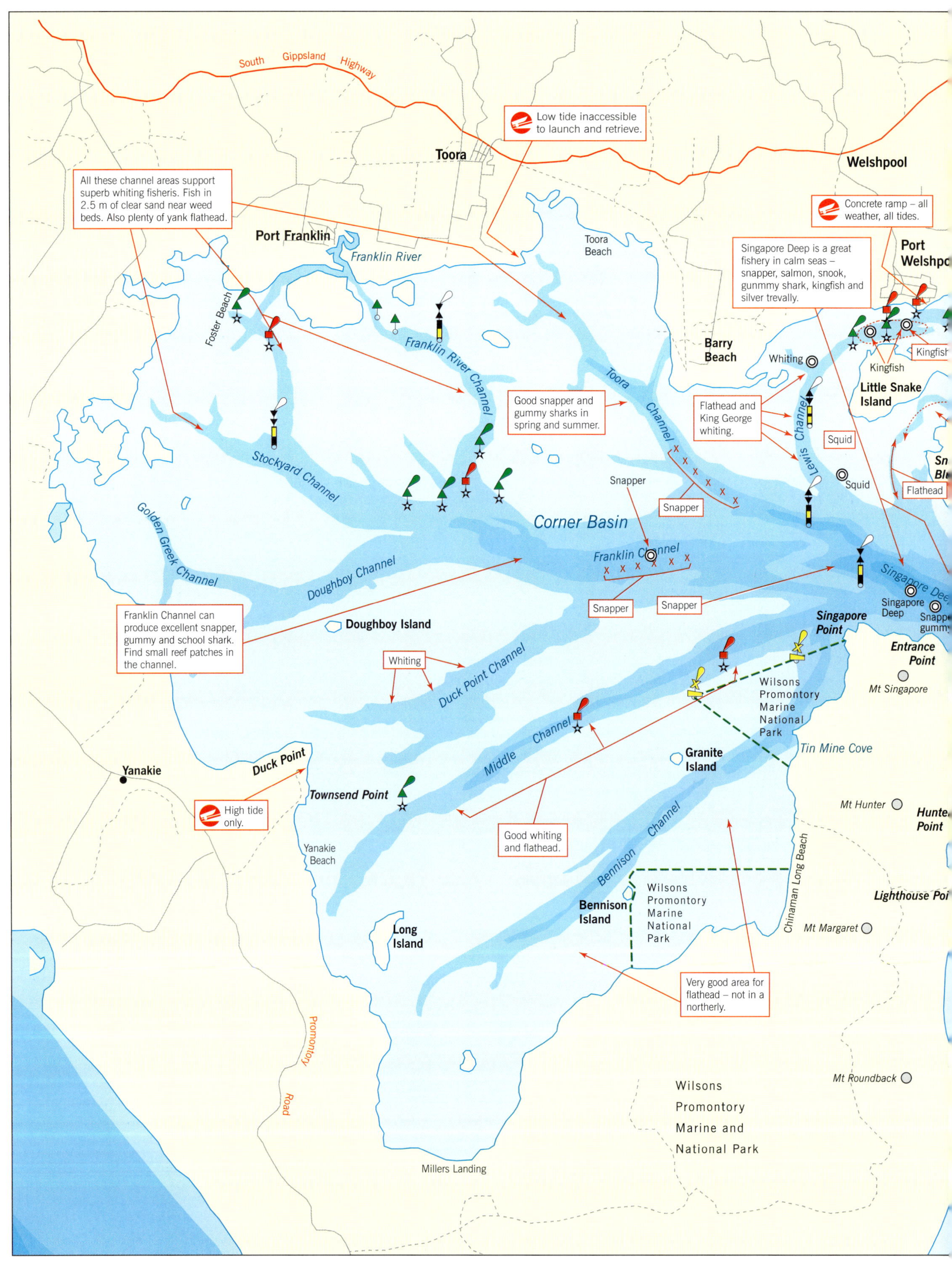

South Gippsland Highway
Low tide inaccessible to launch and retrieve.
Toora
Welshpool
All these channel areas support superb whiting fisheris. Fish in 2.5 m of clear sand near weed beds. Also plenty of yank flathead.
Concrete ramp – all weather, all tides.
Port Franklin
Franklin River
Toora Beach
Singapore Deep is a great fishery in calm seas – snapper, salmon, snook, gunmmy shark, kingfish and silver trevally.
Port Welshpo
Foster Beach
Franklin River Channel
Barry Beach
Whiting
Kingfish
Little Snake Island
Toora Channel
Good snapper and gummy sharks in spring and summer.
Flathead and King George whiting.
Squid
Lewis Channel
Stockyard Channel
Snapper
Squid
Flathead
Snapper
Corner Basin
Golden Greek Channel
Franklin Channel
Doughboy Channel
Snapper
Snapper
Singapore Deep
Singapore Deep
Franklin Channel can produce excellent snapper, gummy and school shark. Find small reef patches in the channel.
Doughboy Island
Singapore Point
Entrance Point
Whiting
Duck Point Channel
Mt Singapore
Wilsons Promontory Marine National Park
Middle Channel
Tin Mine Cove
Granite Island
Yanakie
Duck Point
High tide only.
Townsend Point
Mt Hunter
Good whiting and flathead.
Yanakie Beach
Bennison Channel
Chinaman Long Beach
Lighthouse Poi
Bennison Island
Wilsons Promontory Marine National Park
Mt Margaret
Long Island
Very good area for flathead – not in a northerly.
Promontory Road
Mt Roundback
Wilsons Promontory Marine and National Park
Millers Landing

MAP 19 PORT WELSHPOOL AND CORNER INLET

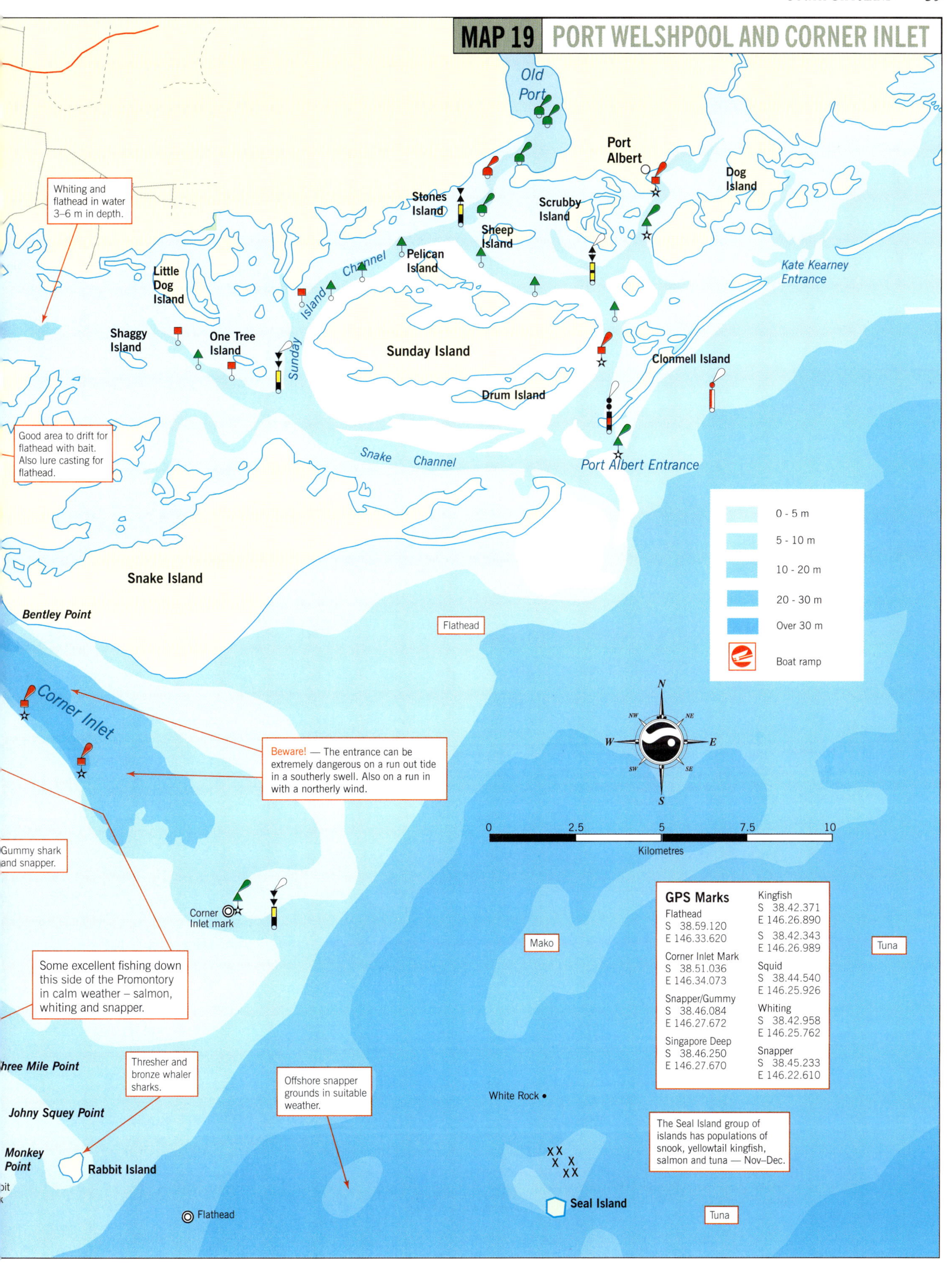

Promontory Road
Millers Landing
Wilsons Promontory Marine and National Park
Mt Roundback
Three Mile Point
Johny Squey Poin
Monkey Point
Five Mile Beach
Good flathead drift area.
Wilsons Promontory Marine and National Park
No Fishing
Darby River
Landbased rock fishing allowed.
Darby Bay
Tongue Point
Whisky Bay
Tidal River
Sealers Cove
Leonard Point
Norman Island
Kingfish
Refuge
Norman Bay
Flathead
Norman Point
Oberon Bay
Cape Wellington
Kingfish
Waterloo Bay
Oberon Point
Waterloo Point
Glennie Island
Glennie Group
Wilsons Promontory Marine National Park
South West Point
South East Point
Wattle Island
Anser Group

MAP 20 WILSONS PROMONTORY

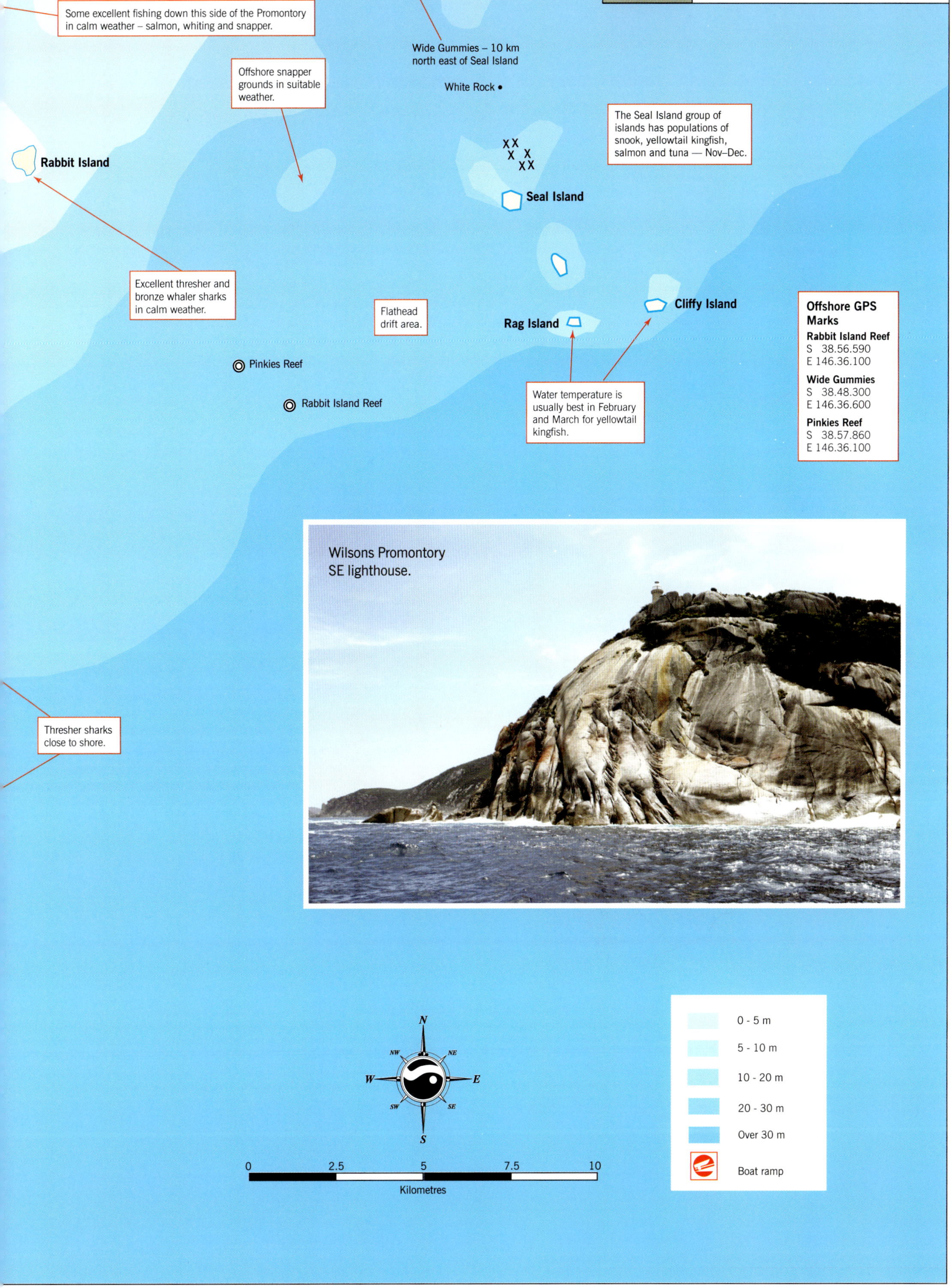

Some excellent fishing down this side of the Promontory in calm weather – salmon, whiting and snapper.

Wide Gummies – 10 km north east of Seal Island

White Rock

Offshore snapper grounds in suitable weather.

The Seal Island group of islands has populations of snook, yellowtail kingfish, salmon and tuna — Nov–Dec.

Rabbit Island

Seal Island

Excellent thresher and bronze whaler sharks in calm weather.

Flathead drift area.

Rag Island

Cliffy Island

Pinkies Reef

Rabbit Island Reef

Water temperature is usually best in February and March for yellowtail kingfish.

Offshore GPS Marks

Rabbit Island Reef
S 38.56.590
E 146.36.100

Wide Gummies
S 38.48.300
E 146.36.600

Pinkies Reef
S 38.57.860
E 146.36.100

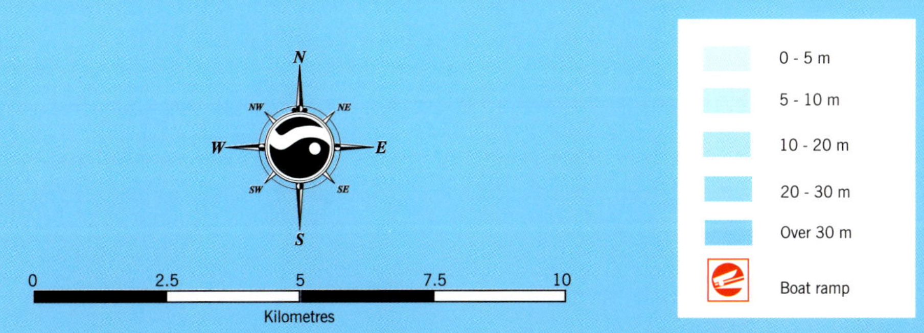

Wilsons Promontory SE lighthouse.

Thresher sharks close to shore.

N, NE, E, SE, S, SW, W, NW

0 2.5 5 7.5 10
Kilometres

	0 - 5 m
	5 - 10 m
	10 - 20 m
	20 - 30 m
	Over 30 m
	Boat ramp

However the approach to the boat ramp is shallow, and for this reason the ramp is unusable at low tide. Toora Channel produces snapper and gummy sharks, along with the usual stingrays, gurnard, slimy cod and small flathead. The shallower banks produce whiting and the occasional good size flathead. Some parts of the channel drop so steeply into deep water it is possible to be fishing with whiting baits on one side of the boat in 3m of water and larger gummy and snapper baits in 15m on the other side. For best results anglers should spend some time using their sounder to locate small patches of reef that are to be found lower in the channel: these provide the best fishing, especially if snapper are the target. A running sinker rig tied from 60lb trace is recommended with a 5/0-6/0 hook ideal for gummy shark and snapper. Sinker weight will vary depending on the stage of the tide.

The extensive sandflats in the area hold great numbers of bass yabbies that make superb whiting bait, and on the high tide flounder are plentiful.

There is little opportunity for land based anglers at Toora Beach, but at low tide some anglers drive their cars out on the exposed bank near the ruins of the Toora Jetty and fish into the channel. They catch mainly silver trevally and flathead, but driving out on the bank is not a recommended practice. During summer when the kingfish frequent that area, the mouth of the Toora is a popular hangout. Trolling calamari strips or throwing surface poppers if they're on the surface works well.

Singapore Deep

Singapore deep is a very well-known deep hole located in the entrance into Corner Inlet. Up to 34m in depth, Singapore Deep is popular with anglers targeting snapper and gummy sharks. With the possibility of capturing a genuine 20 lb snapper or gummy shark over 20 kg, it is worth fishing if conditions allow. The area is quite tidal and not recommended for smaller vessels. That is unless the conditions are seaworthy for smaller craft. If they are and it is a so called "sheet of glass" the snapper might not come on the bite because it is too calm. Once you have a set anchor, ensure you let out a little anchor rope more than normal. Due to the force of the tide, the anchor can often become dislodged causing you to drag off the mark.

Once in position, set a berley trail of cubed pilchards and keep it constant. Over use of berley will attract as variety of unwanted species, but with the right amount and a consistent trail, snapper, gummy shark and other pelagic sharks will be a possible catch.

When fishing this location, a variety of rigs can be used depending on species targeted. For snapper and gummy shark, a running sinker rig is ideal when fishing such deep waters. Drifting is also a popular technique whereby anglers are best to use paternoster rigs or pre-rigged paternoster rigs utilising Mustad's 39935NPBN Octopus Circle Hook so the fish hook themselves on taking the bait. When tying rigs, it is recommended, the either the rig be tied from 60lb or 80lb Fluorocarbon leader for its abrasion resistance capabilities.

Snapper and gummy sharks respond to a variety of baits including pilchards, tuna and salmon fillets. For best results fresh calamari rings, strips and heads reap the rewards.

During the warmer months when the snapper arrive, large sharks are usually not far behind. It is common to lose fish to great whites so be on the lookout.

Bronze whalers and thresher sharks are also common catches in the area. Live baiting with salmon, calamari or mullet under a balloon is effective. Just make sure your using a wire trace otherwise you'll be bitten off.

Port Franklin

There is no public boat ramp at Port Franklin so local boat operators launch into the Franklin River using a crane on the dock.

The Franklin River produces small trevally, mullet, flathead and a good many other species including bream. Good populations of estuary perch are to be found a short distance above the town and these have not been educated by excessive fishing pressure. There are a lot of smaller creeks and rivers the run into Corner Inlet, many which are inaccessible by boat. However, kayak anglers and those on foot that can find a way in, tend to be very surprised at some of the fish encountered. Bait fishing is effective but those flicking lures will see great results.

Foster Beach

Foster Beach is reached by turning off the South Gippsland Highway just a few kilometres west of the Point Franklin turn-off. There is a small launching ramp on Stockyard Creek suitable for small boats at high tide. With this in mind there are excellent whiting to be caught in the obvious channel a few hundred metres out from shore.

Yanakie

The settlement of Yanakie is on the road to Wilsons Promontory, the turn-off from the Gippsland Highway being well marked at either Meeniyan or Foster. To reach the Yanakie boat ramp, and Yanakie Caravan Park which is on Corner Inlet, take Foley Road to the left after passing Millar Road on the right for the second time.

Yanakie boat ramp is high and dry for nearly half the tide cycle so boats can only be launched from half flood to half ebb. Trailer boats larger than 4.5 m should launch even closer to the top of the tide.

The Yanakie area is shallow, but there is excellent fishing for whiting and big flathead. Heading north toward Doughboy Island, after rounding Duck Point you will cross the Duck Point Channel, and should you continue on the same course passing to the right (east) of Doughboy Island to locate the Doughboy Channel.

Excellent fishing for big flathead is to be found in the shallow water (less than a metre deep) between Duck Point and Doughboy Island.

Heading east from the ramp you will come to the Middle Channel, midway between Benison and Granite islands, after approximately four kilometres. Here, there is the likelihood of taking whiting, snapper, large flathead and gummy shark. However, rays are a nuisance when using large baits

WILSONS PROMONTORY

You may reach Wilsons Promontory by turning south from the South Gippsland Highway at either Foster or Meeniyan. There is a toll gate at the park boundary where a fee is charged to enter the park. Should you intend to stay and fish overnight, a sticker for your windscreen may be obtained from the collection window of the ticket box. Wilson's Promontory itself is a national park, and part of it is surrounded by marine national park, so fishing is reasonably limited—estuary fishing is restricted, and no sea fishing is permitted in much of the water around the Prom's southern half.

Several beaches are accessible from the road to Tidal River on Wilson's Promontory including Darby River, Picnic Bay, Squeaky Bay and Norman Bay at Tidal River. All are exposed to prevailing winds from the south-west and accumulate a good deal of weed. However, mullet, silver trevally and salmon are plentiful and easily caught on small hooks without having to cast too far out.

Beware of the large dome-shaped boulders on the points of many of the beaches. They can be very slippery and dangerous.

Darby River

Heading toward Tidal River on Wilsons Promontory, the first spot of note is Darby River. There is a parking area just south of the bridge where you can stop and have a look about.

Darby River is usually closed to the sea but contains mullet, bream, and there are populations of estuary perch upstream. Fishing from the bank is usually done with a float setup and prawns used for bait. Soft plastics can be flicked about the weeded banks where the perch like to hide.

Tongue Point

From Darby River it is a long walk (almost 5km) to Tongue Point, a rocky promontory giving landbased access to deep water where lure casting enthusiasts take big salmon, snook and the very occasionally yellowtail kingfish.

Anglers fishing with bait on the sandy bottom take snapper, large King George whiting and a variety of less highly esteemed species including wrasse and leatherjackets.

Thresher sharks are regular visitors to Tongue Point and have occasionally been hooked by anglers fishing from the rocks with bait. Possibly this area provides yet another opportunity for landbased game anglers to try their skill in Victorian waters.

Perhaps one of the things that has stopped this location becoming more popular is the danger involved in fishing the rocks around the Prom area. Tongue Point is no different. It is very exposed to the prevailing south-westerly wind, the rocks you stand on are round and don't provide good footholds, and the adjacent water is quite deep so large swells can come from nowhere, hitting the lower areas very hard.

Tidal River

Tidal River is a small settlement with a post office, petrol filling station, a store and café which swells to a tent city during holiday periods. Tidal River is more popular with tourists and bush walkers than anglers. Accommodation is available at Tidal River, and flats can be booked through the Tidal River Office 03 5680 9500.

There is also a ranger station at Tidal River from where you may gain additional information about the many fishing, camping and access restrictions that apply to Wilsons Promontory.

Tidal River itself contains mullet in the lower reaches and good populations of estuary perch and luderick upstream. These can be caught on soft plastics and baits including prawns fished under a float. A running sinker rig is effective but also a float setup as you can water and see when a fish takes the bait more clearly.

Tidal River runs into Norman Bay, a shallow bight enclosed by two headlands. You are permitted to fish from Pillar Point, which is the north headland running out into deep water from Tidal River. Take great care should you do so because the rocks are domed and very dangerous, particularly with a south-westerly swell running. Salmon and silver trevally are most popular along here. Small long shank hooks tied onto a paternoster rig works exceptionally well. The most effective baits are pipi and prawn.

Fishing is not permitted between Norman Bay on the west side of the Promontory and all the way around to near Refuge Cove on the east side of the Promontory—make sure you consult Parks Victoria maps for exact details.

On the Prom's eastern side, there is deep water access from the rocks between Sealers Cove and Refuge Cove where you can fish legally. Anglers who make the journey here have the potential to experience some great fishing. Divers have reported seeing kingfish, thresher sharks and occasionally tuna in very close. One of the other bonuses of this area is the shelter it offers from the prevailing winds. Any of these spot would be a prize for most land based anglers, however the walk in takes many hours.

Norman Island

Boat anglers fishing out wide from Wilsons Prom can access Normal Island. The nearest boat ramp is Port Welshpool, Toora or Duck Point but you are looking at around a 150km round trip. In saying that, smaller craft can be launched off the beach at Tidal River or for those experienced at beach launching with larger vessels, Waratah Bay.

Norman Island and the surrounding area offers excellent drift fishing for flathead while in the summer months, kingfish are a popular target. Though they can be caught using numerous techniques, live baiting and jigging are the most favoured and effective.

SHALLOW INLET

Shallow Inlet is a medium sized tidal lagoon between Waratah Bay and Wilson's Promontory. Despite its name, it encloses a system of reasonably deep channels and the fishing is good for King George whiting in particular. Flathead are also a common catch as are Australian salmon.

Shallow Inlet is reached from the Wilsons Promontory Road near Yanakie, after turning off the South Gippsland Highway at Foster, or from the Fish Creek-Yanakie Road.

Continuing toward Waratah Bay before taking the Sandy Point turn-off accesses both Shallow Inlet and Sandy Point. Take care during summer holidays because you will be sharing the roadway with pedestrians, cyclists, equestrians and others.

Whiting are the most sought after species in Shallow Inlet followed by salmon, flathead, garfish, and snapper when they enter the inlet—usually in November. Standard whiting techniques apply but increase your leader to 15lb fluorocarbon when the snapper are about. It isn't uncommon to catch a snapper on a pipi. Salmon can be seen busting the surface and respond well to cast and retrieve techniques with soft plastics and metal slugs. Trolling lures is also effective.

While the inlet is popular with holidaymakers, most of whom aren't serious anglers, it does offer some great lure and fly fishing opportunities. With large sandflats, drains and channels mixed with weed beds, it is the perfect location to wade the shallows or use a boat to chase some very large flathead that live in the area, along with mullet and snapper in the deeper water. If you're in a boat chasing flathead over the flats, take care not to become stranded when the tide goes out. Anglers fishing from Kayaks can navigate the area more easily and access the shallower banks where large flathead perch themselves in the mid-day sun.

Yanakie Side

Access to this side of the inlet is from Hourigan Camp Road, off Millar Road, which runs off the Wilsons Promontory Road at Yanakie; then by foot across the boardwalk to the beach, followed by about 2 km along the beach to the entrance. Remember, beach access is only possible when the tide is out.

Around the entrance to Shallow Inlet, where a deep water channel runs very close to the eastern shoreline, is possibly one of the best land based locations in the whole area. The only downside is that it's a low tide spot only, so it doesn't allow anglers to fish there for an extended period. For best results and the most fishing time, be there two hours before low tide as this will allow you around four hours of solid fishing time. Smaller baits fished close to the drop-off will see you in action with whiting, mullet, the occasional trevally and small salmon, while a lure cast out into deeper water often finds the better salmon.

For those chasing other big fish, larger baits such as pilchard and squid cast into the deep water offer a very good chance of gummy sharks and snapper. Switched-on anglers also use fresh fillets of salmon and mullet (or even live mullet) to target some of the large mulloway that hunt in this area.

Sandy Point

The settlement of Sandy Point is on the west side of Shallow Inlet. Boats are launched from the hard packed sand at the designated

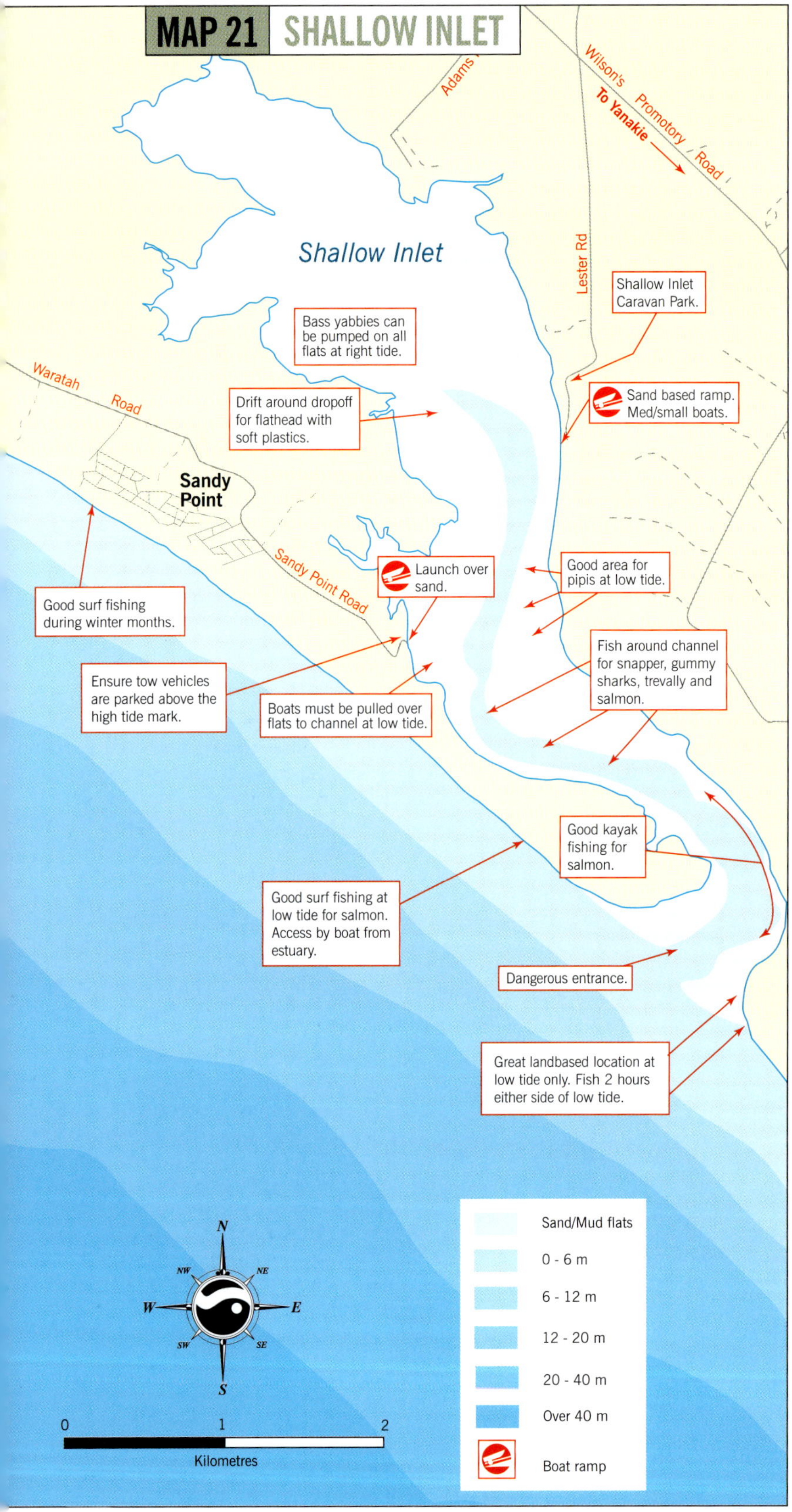

MAP 21 SHALLOW INLET

Shallow Inlet
Adams
Wilson's Promotory Road
To Yanakie
Lester Rd
Shallow Inlet Caravan Park.
Bass yabbies can be pumped on all flats at right tide.
Waratah Road
Drift around dropoff for flathead with soft plastics.
Sand based ramp. Med/small boats.
Sandy Point
Sandy Point Road
Launch over sand.
Good area for pipis at low tide.
Good surf fishing during winter months.
Ensure tow vehicles are parked above the high tide mark.
Boats must be pulled over flats to channel at low tide.
Fish around channel for snapper, gummy sharks, trevally and salmon.
Good kayak fishing for salmon.
Good surf fishing at low tide for salmon. Access by boat from estuary.
Dangerous entrance.
Great landbased location at low tide only. Fish 2 hours either side of low tide.
N
NE
E
SE
S
SW
W
NW
Sand/Mud flats
0 - 6 m
6 - 12 m
12 - 20 m
20 - 40 m
Over 40 m
Boat ramp
0
1
2
Kilometres

launching area in the reserve off Sandy Point Road. Anglers catch whiting in the inlet along with the occasional good size flathead. Snapper and gummy sharks are taken in the channel during the warmer months. Make sure you leave your launch vehicle and trailer above the high tide mark! When launching and retrieving boats from the beach ramp at Sandy Point, newcomers are advised to approach and leave the ramp at an angle rather than straight to and from the water. This avoids the risk of 'drowning' your vehicle should you lose traction on the sand.

Anglers also fish from the bank at Sandy Point in the vicinity of the boat launching area. Theoretically you could walk out and fish anywhere along the point into the inlet but the sand is treacherously soft on this side of the inlet and walking any distance is difficult.

Salmon are regular visitors to the inlet and anglers trolling lures in the entrance channel have made extraordinarily large catches. Landbased anglers may fish from the beach parking area, from where they can cast into the deep channel that's some 50 m out at high tide, and a good deal closer at low tide. Alternatively you can walk further along towards the entrance.

Sandy Point itself extends for at least 3 km to inlet's deep entrance to the sea, through which the tide flows strongly. The sand is soft though, making the walk tough.

Although the noticeably deep channel running around the inside of Sandy Point then out to sea is the most likely place to hook a large gummy shark or even a snapper, there is a limited period of slack water when you can fish and large sand crabs can be voracious on bait.

WARATAH BAY TO CAPE LIPTRAP

Waratah Bay

Waratah Bay is reached by turning off the South Gippsland Highway at Meeniyan and proceeding via Fish Creek. There is no launching ramp at Waratah Bay, but many anglers launch small boats from the beach below the concrete access ramp.

While it doesn't have the best launching facilities in the area, Waratah Bay is known for catches of big whiting. Most are taken from the boats but at times some anglers get good numbers of big fish from the shore. Most of the land based catch is made up of salmon and mullet.

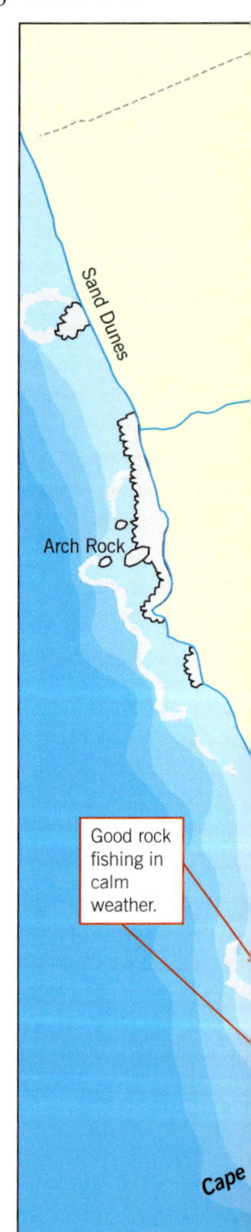

Anglers fishing for whiting over the prominent broken weed and sand patches also find themselves in great squid territory, especially in the area of Cape Liptrap, which has abundant sea-grass beds. While good numbers of squid can be taken year round, during autumn large squid move into the area to spawn. Spawners respond very well to large jigs in the 3.0 and 3.5 sizes.

The squid are possibly one reason why this area also holds good numbers of kingfish through summer and autumn. The kingfish are best targeted by trolling squid strips around Bear Gully, which lies between Walkerville Sth and Cape Liptrap. Many anglers also do very well by casting soft plastics over the reefs, or even anchoring up and berleying to attract the kingfish. If you can catch small live baits such as yakkas, they are dynamite when trolled slowly.

The size of the kings in the area can vary, and landing larger fish can prove difficult due to the shallow water and the rugged bottom they like to live around.

Walkerville

West of Waratah Bay are the settlements of Walkerville North and Walkerville South, sheltered from prevailing south-westerly winds by Cape

Liptrap. There are beach launching sites for small boats which give access to superb inshore whiting fishing, as well as to deeper water around Cape Liptrap to the south-west in good weather. There is a camping area with all facilities adjacent to the beach and a shop selling basic items including food and fuel.

Launching from the beach is best accomplished by uncoupling the boat trailer, and securing the trailer to the vehicle with a long rope, permitting the boat to be floated from the trailer while the vehicle is high and dry on firm sand.

This area is very productive with big whiting for those willing to put in the effort. Salmon are also fun to target when busting on the surface.

Launching from Walkerville also provides access to Cape Liptrap if the conditions allow.

Cape Liptrap

Considering its prominent position, Cape Liptrap is disappointing for land based anglers because the rock formations are uncomfortable to fish from and give only limited access to deep water. Baits fished on the bottom may catch wrasse and leatherjackets, and lure casting early in the morning and on evening will usually produce snook and the occasional barracouta or salmon. Access to the best fishing areas are from the track to the left of the lighthouse descending to the rocks below. Rock fishing can be dangerous so special care is of upmost importance.

Boat anglers can access this area by beach launching at Walkerville. While mako sharks are a prime target, it is the kingfish schools that arrive during the warmer months of the year that become highly sought. Those fishing for kingfish can do so by trolling lures, live baits and tossing surface poppers. There are some very big fish around here and it is recommended that 50 lb tackle is used.

Andersons Inlet

Andersons Inlet is the tidal lagoon estuary of the Tarwin River. It runs to the sea through a split channel system between the sand spit at Point Smythe and the beach at Inverloch. Although Andersons Inlet provides access to the ocean, the bar is dangerous and crossing to the ocean should not be attempted without an experienced hand in charge of the vessel. Navigating the Inlet itself should be undertaken with caution. At low tide the Inlet virtually drains, apart from the deep channels. Andersons Inlet supports a wide variety of species including salmon, whiting, mullet, estuary perch and silver trevally.

Tarwin River

The lower Tarwin River is accessible from Inverloch along the Inverloch–Lower Tarwin Road, from Meeniyan and several other places both on, and adjacent to, the South Gippsland Highway. The estuary of the Tarwin, and the upper reaches of the inlet, produce excellent estuary perch fishing and some bream. Anglers casting lures and flies to the rock walls, reeds and snags from boats take many good perch.

Scattered along its length, are purpose built fishing platforms situated in or around areas where perch and bream frequent. Anglers choosing to fish with bait tend to do quite well using a running sinker rig. Top baits are pipi, prawn and live bass yabbies.

The town of Tarwin Lower, not far from where the Tarwin flows into Andersons Inlet, has a history of catering for anglers. Road access to the riverbank begins above the town and continues to the inlet where many obvious access points to the river can be seen.

Tarwin Lower has a boat ramp providing access to both the river and inlet, and a jetty beside it. The traditional quarry from this

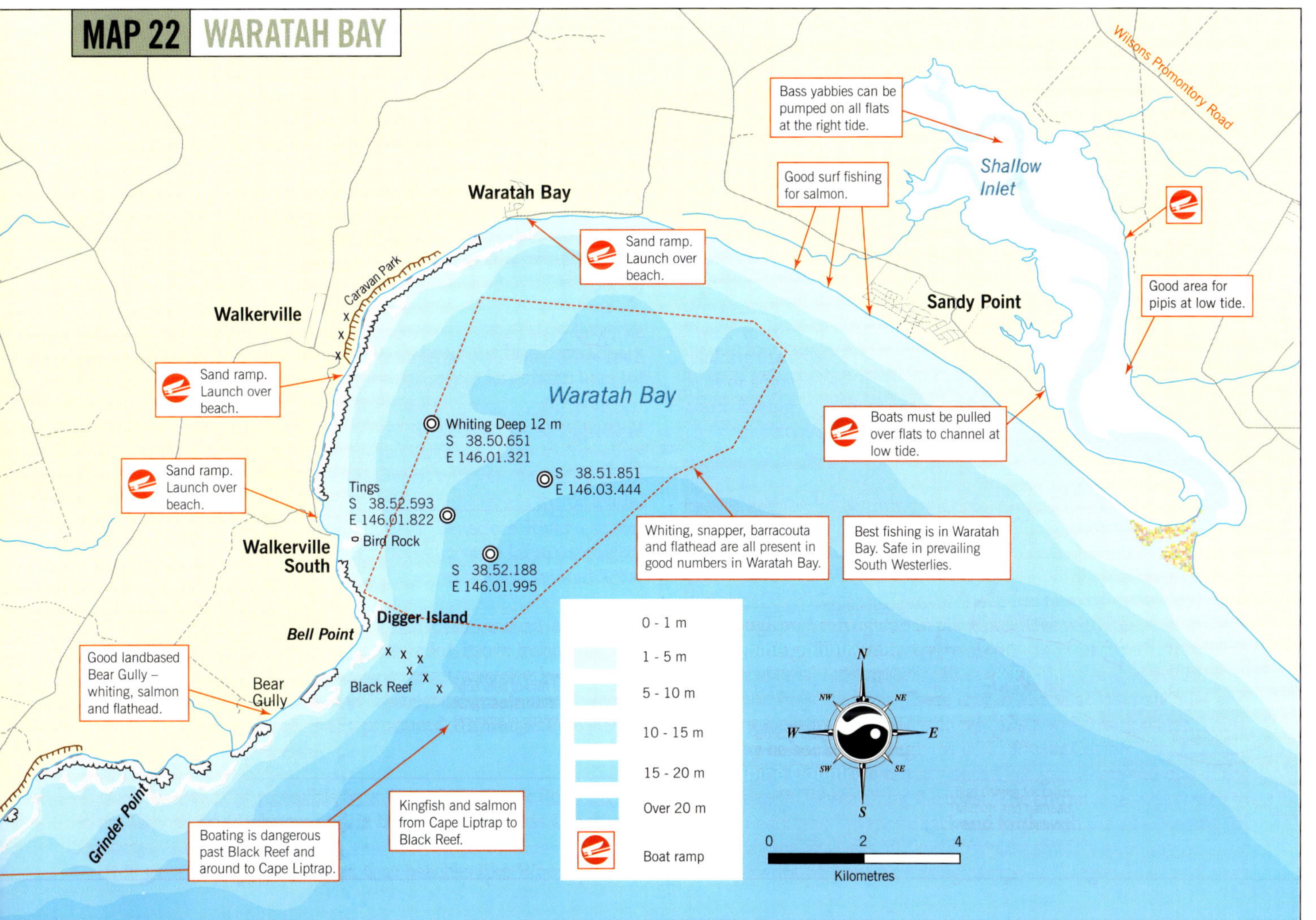

section of river has been estuary perch, but during holiday periods, most anglers can be seen amusing themselves taking small trevally, salmon and mullet.

Mulloway have also been taken from the estuary of the Tarwin River—most are small but there is always the chance of a bigger specimen. Mulloway have been sighted as far upstream as the Stewart and Dunlops Road Bridge over the Tarwin River at Woorayl. Specialised fishing techniques are required for mulloway. Most productive baits are fresh calamari strips or live baits.

BOAT RAMPS

Anglers fishing the Andersons Inlet can launch at the ramp at Tarwin Lower, or use one of the three other boat ramps located around the inlet. The Inverloch ramp is just inside the entrance and will handle boats to 6 m, however, it does accumulate a layer of sand from time to time.

There is a modest boat ramp at Mahers Landing, which is signposted from the Inverloch–Tarwin Lower Road. There is another ramp on the other side of the inlet, at Fisherman's Landing.

TACKLE & GENERAL INFORMATION

Rod Bendings World of Fishing
Shop 1
8 Williams Street
Inverloch Vic 3996
Phone: (03) 5674 3322

Surf-n-fish
Shop 6/7
157 Great Ocean Road
Apollo Bay Vic 3233
Phone: (03) 5237 6426

The inlet itself is well signposted, so be sure to stay within to the channels to avoid running aground onto the sand.

Fishing within the Inlet

As well as being prominent in the Tarwin River itself, estuary perch are also abundant around the weed beds and among the numerous snags within the inlet. Soft plastics work exceptionally well with 80 mm Squidgy Wrigglers in the bloodworm colour a proven performer. Large flathead inhabit the shallows while the deeper channels produce gummy sharks along with the occasional snapper or mulloway. Best results are experienced in the deeper channels within the inlet by fishing either side of the low tide change with large baits of freshly caught squid or fish fillets. Salmon are also taken by anglers trolling the channels with lures. Setting anchor and using berley is a great way to attract them. Anglers can then cast soft plastics or throw metal slugs into the schools. Some very nice catches are taken at times.

The lower reaches of the inlet produce good whiting over the summer months as well as decent gummy sharks and flathead in some of the deeper channels. Whiting respond well to pipi baits fished on paternoster rigs. A berley trail will attract them to your general area. Flathead will also steal any offerings. Gummy sharks respond well to fresh calamari or salmon fillets fished on the bottom.

Bass yabbies (nippers) can be pumped at many locations throughout the inlet at low tide, and are good bait for perch and whiting. While pumping bait, the lies of flathead can often be seen. Fishing these areas as the tide starts to rise will often produce good-sized specimens—using lures and flies is very productive.

Venus Bay

Venus Bay is a tiny township situated on the large sand spit dividing Andersons Inlet from the ocean. There are 5 main beaches that make up Venus Bay which have long been popular with anglers seeking salmon, particularly during winter when the fishing is best. These beaches are relatively flat with few gutters, ensuring the most productive fishing occurs on a high tide.

The most productive fishing for large salmon and gummy shark is at night. Other species to be taken here include yellow-eye mullet and tailor. The surf beaches at Venus Bay are numbered from 1–5 and signposted. Pipis are prolific and at the time of writing anglers are permitted to take a 5 litre bucketful on any one day—check your Recreational Fishing Guide for the latest limits.

Salmon respond well to pipi, blue bait, whitebait and pilchards while gummy shark can't resist a fresh fillet of salmon. Spinning for salmon with metal slugs is very effective if you can locate a school of fish in a gutter. Berley is essential to attract salmon. The Venus Bay Beaches are odd locations whereby if the salmon are running, one beach in particular will fish at its best while the others perform poorly. The next day, one of the other beaches will fish well and the beach fished the previous day won't produce at all. Finding where the fish are on a particular day is pot luck but you can always get the latest info from Rod Bendings Tackle Store at Inverloch.

Fishermen's Landing

Fishermen's Landing consists of a jetty and boat ramp clearly signposted from Lees Road at the settlement of Venus Bay.

Boat access is from half flood tide to half ebb—while the ramp itself is fine at all stages of the tide, the channel to and from the ramp is very shallow on the low tide, and there are several sandbars located at each end of the sand islands. This is a top location for anglers fishing from kayaks to launch and fish for estuary perch around the Double Islands where they can be prolific at times.

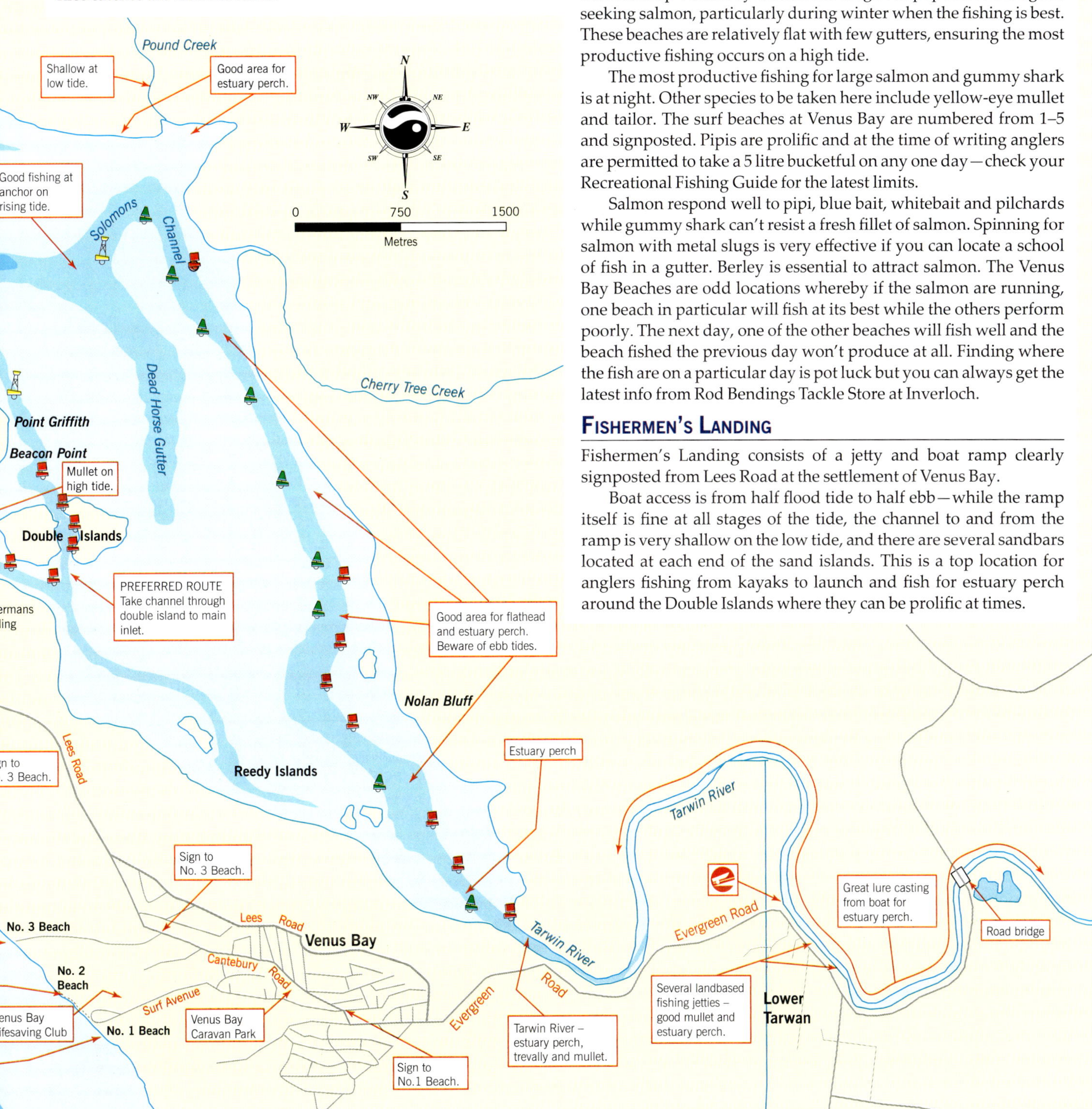

Access to the main basin can be reached by travelling right from the boat ramp, between the two islands and out into the main Inlet channel. This is the preferred route, as the water between the island and Beacon Point is generally too shallow to navigate in a boat. The water off Beacon Point (Point Griffith on some maps) slopes into a reasonably deep channel on the bend and this area produces perch, silver trevally and some very large luderick. Bait fishing is popular but for those targeting flathead and perch, soft plastics are best.

Maher's Landing

Maher's Landing is clearly signposted off the Inverloch-Tarwin Lower Road. This is a particularly good area to pump bait. There is also a modest boat ramp and trailer parking area at Mahers Landing. The launching area has been dredged, and the channel marked to provide trouble-free access to the main body of the inlet. Anglers take good salmon trolling lures just out from the ramp at the right time of year.

Screw Creek

Screw Creek is a beautiful stream with good populations of bream and estuary perch. It may be reached either from the Inverloch-Lower Tarwin Road, or from The Esplanade through the Inverloch Foreshore Caravan Park and Camping Area. Take it easy driving through here because there are eight speed humps in the space of a few hundred metres to the car park. Screw Creek is a5 minute walk away on a scenic bush track.

The mouth of Screw Creek fishes well as the tide is rising. Mullet, flathead and salmon are taken regularly. Other creeks running into the system, like Cherry Tree Creek and Pound Creek, also have potential.

To see and experience the best of Screw Creek, a small canoe or kayak is best—especially if you are interested in chasing bream and perch in pristine surroundings. Casting at some of the snags in this waterway may leave you with a broken line as perch tend to bust you off. Often you're left in awe with an open mouth and a huge smile if you manage to extract one from its timber home. Perch are fond of shallow diving hard body lures but during the warmer months, try surface lures on dusk for some truly memorable fishing. Land based fishing Screw Creek is also a possibility by parking near the road bridge along Inverloch-Venus Bay Rd or the foot bridge along the Screw Creek Nature Walk Path. Access is limited but some good fish can be caught.

The Snags

On the other side of the Inlet, land based anglers not averse to walking may park their cars at the bottom of Lees Road at Point Smythe and walk through the Fauna Reserve to the area known as The Snags.

Here, the bank shelves steeply into 8m of water and the tide runs strongly, so you must fish the change of tide to have any realistic expectation of being able to fish effectively. A wide variety of fish may be taken here, but fishing time from the bank is short, say an hour each side of any tide change.

Some anglers fish this location with lures for estuary perch and trevally that like to sit in the flowing water. The bonus is that lures don't get snagged up as often as baits do on the timber-covered bottom.

Inverloch

The township of Inverloch is reached from Wonthaggi on the Bass Highway or by turning off the South Gippsland Highway at either Lang Lang (on Western Port), or from Leongatha. Inverloch is a popular holiday destination during peak holiday periods and has a range of amenities. There is a jetty near the mouth of the Inlet that can be fished fairly comfortably when the tide is not running too strongly. Good sized salmon can be caught by either casting lures or fishing with bait. Trevally, whiting and flathead are also regularly caught on bait.

The Entrance Channel

The beach in front of Ayr Creek offers anglers the best opportunity to cast into the entrance channel, but again only at low tide and within an hour or so of the low slack water, which does not occur until well after the nominal time of low tide.

Throughout winter, salmon are a common catch for anglers spinning from the bank of the inlet at Inverloch.

Landbased anglers may fish from the jetty and Wyethers Beach, which is between the jetty and the rocks in front of the central camping area. Salmon, whiting, and silver trevally are regularly caught at these locations during the day, and anglers fishing large baits on evening and after dark, could easily tempt a gummy shark. Elephant sharks have also been caught here over the years, as have snapper and the odd mulloway—particularly when the water is discoloured from mild flooding in the Tarwin River.

Speaking more generally, often the best fishing can be found when the water is discoloured from rain. At these times, schools of large salmon move into the inlet providing great fishing. While land based anglers catch plenty when casting metal slugs from the rocks in the entrance, boat anglers also catch their fair share and it is recommended that berley is used to attract the schools. Whiting are quite common in season and are reasonably easy to catch. Using berley will bring them to your area. A paternoster rig with two long shank or circle hooks works well. Whiting respond well to Bass yabbies, mussel and pipi. Landbased anglers can also catch whiting from the shore. Known as 'Pensioners Corner', this area fishes very well on both low and high tide. Berleying is a little more challenging from the land, but instead of using a berley cage, opt for an onion bag or scaling bag and attach it to a long rope secured to a beach rod holder. The bag, containing the berley can be tossed out into the water where the current will disperse the contents. When using berley always ensure you cast your baits into the trail as this is where the fish will be schooled up.

Offshore

Fishing offshore is extremely productive and access to Bass Strait is throughout the Inverloch Entrance or bar. Due to storm activity throughout the past few years, heavy rains coupled with battering southerly swells and strong tides, the entrance and channels for the matter have shifted to what they used to be. The entrance should be navigated with great care at all times.

For local anglers in seaworthy boats the offshore grounds from Inverloch have great potential for catching a variety of species, with the most common being snapper and gummy sharks.

Both species can be found around the reef systems, which occur throughout the area. One reef relatively close to Inverloch is known as the Cody Bank. It rises up out of moderately deep water with a steep wall on the outside edge. The whole reef looks very impressive on a fish finder and one would think it would be the number one spot to find snapper, kingfish and sharks. However, for the most part, anglers who have fished it report only catching wrasse, sweep and leatherjackets.

Shark fishermen will find good fishing off Inverloch especially for the mako and thresher sharks that live around the inshore reefs. Drifting over the area while fishing the bottom can lead to some very impressive catches of tiger flathead. Barracouta and arrow squid are also commonly caught. During a drift, it is common to drift across a rubble bed where small pinkie snapper up to a kilo in weight can be caught.

The Rocks

The rocks in front of the central camping area are accessible at low tide giving access to the reasonably deep entrance channel. However, the current is strong here, limiting fishing to within an hour or so each side of slack water. Fishing from the beach is much more comfortable.

The Entrance

Trolling at the entrance to the ocean sometimes yields good catches of salmon, but this activity is definitely not for the inexperienced. Apart from being sloppy, the passage to the ocean is often ill-defined because of moving sand. There is also the hazard of Sheep Rocks off the entrance point. When conditions are safe to do so, trolling diving minnows in a 90 mm to 110 mm length works very well in the main channels. It always pays to have quick access to a hand full of metal slugs as well, just in case you notice any surface activity. In this case, you'll be able to throw them into the bubbling mayhem.

The Sand Spit

The sand spit on the opposite side of the entrance from Inverloch (Point Smythe) gives anglers with boats the opportunity to come ashore and fish from the sand into deep water. Unfortunately for land based anglers, the spit is separated from Point Smythe by another channel. Flathead, salmon and silver trevally are common catches. Aside from fishing, it is a nice spot to beach the boat and have lunch with the family.

BUNURONG, CAPE PATERSON AND KILCUNDA

From Wreck Creek at Inverloch to Coal Point at Harmers Haven is the Bunurong Coastal Reserve. Within the reserve, collection of bait is prohibited in the intertidal zone.

From just east of the striking rock formation, Eagles Nest, to just west of a beach called The Oaks, is Bunurong Marine National Park where no bait gathering or fishing is permitted, either from the shore or within an extensive area out to sea—contact Parks Victoria for details.

Flat Rocks

Traveling west along Ramsay Boulevard from Inverloch, you will pass through the Bunurong Coastal Reserve and Marine Park, eventually reaching Cape Patterson after approximately 13 kilometres. Just past Wreck Creek you will see the Flat Rocks sign and parking area.

There is a sheltered beach inside two rock formations giving anglers relatively calm water to fish for whiting, snapper, silver trevally and a variety of other fish.

Just past the Flat Rocks sign is a parking area and limited vehicle access to the beach for launching small boats. From here, with careful navigation between the rocks and patches of shallow reef, you can reach open water where excellent whiting are to be caught. Garfish can also be in abundance and are taken on a float type setup. A light surface berley is used to attract them.

Bunurong Marine National Park

Situated between Andersons Inlet entrance and Cape Patterson is the Bunurong Marine Park. No fishing is allowed between the GPS marks:

S 38 43.290 E 145 37.54 and S 38 43.310 E 145 40.233

The Caves

Approximately 1.5 km past the Flat Rocks sign is The Caves where there is a car park and access to rocks below. There is a large rock pool opening out to the sea here and the rock platforms provide lure and bottom fishing at low tide, provided the sea is calm. With a variety of species on offer, salmon, barracouta, wrasse and sweep are most common.

Undertow Bay

Undertow Bay is between the rocky promontory sheltering the beach in front of the Royal Wonthaggi Life Saving Club and the rock platform under the first section of the Bunurong Cliffs.

The beach slopes away nicely here so a very long cast is not needed to reach productive water. With a low tide and calm seas, the rock platform under the Bunurong Cliffs allows access to anglers seeking large whiting from the fairly obvious sand holes well within casting range.

CAPE PATERSON BOAT RAMP

A modest boat ramp and parking area is signposted from Surf Beach Parade at the settlement of Cape Patterson. It is about 100 m past the Illawong camping and caravan park. The ramp gives small trailer boats access to the ocean and is reasonably sheltered from all-weather except from the south-east, a direction that should rule out fishing anyway. Make sure you examine the ramp closely before backing your boat down because it does have a sharp kick to the left near the bottom.

To the left or east of the boat ramp, a couple of hundred metres or so, is a sheltered beach in front of the Royal Wonthaggi Life Saving Club. While bathers have preference here, it is worth trying for whiting during the off season or early in the morning.

FIRST BEACH

First Beach at Cape Patterson extends from the Cape Patterson Life Saving Club and the Cape itself for approximately 350 metres. This beach is substantially protected from prevailing westerlies by the exposed reef extending out from the Cape. The beach is shallow and most productive on low tide when you can walk out far enough to cast into deeper water.

CAPE PATERSON ROCKS

With a low tide and calm seas, you can fish from the rocks at the Point southwest of the town, and from any of several rocky promontories accessible from Surf Beach Parade.

Fishing from the rocks with lures, particularly early in the morning, is likely to produce good size snook and perhaps a salmon or two. The bottom is snaggy, but there are decent whiting to be taken from any visible sand holes. Garfish enthusiasts will also find their quarry in this spot should the seas be calm enough.

SECOND BEACH

Second Beach is between the rocky promontory at Cape Patterson and Wilsons Road to the west. Close to a kilometre in length with notable gutter formations, Second Beach bears the brunt of southwest prevailing winds and swells, usually ruling out fishing.

HARMERS HAVEN

Harmers Haven is approximately 8km from Wonthaggi and clearly signposted. The rock platforms at Harmers Haven are accessible at low tide, but exposed to prevailing winds and swells from the southwest. Fish targeted here on bait include whiting and sweep but small wrasse can be a nuisance. Salmon and snook may be taken on lures.

WRECK BEACH

Wreck Beach is accessible from Wonthaggi and is at the mouth of Coal Creek, approximately 1 km east of Harmers Haven. Like other beaches in the area, Wreck Beach is exposed to prevailing winds and swells and collects a fair bit of kelp.

THE BOILERS

The Boilers, sometimes known by local anglers as 'The Pines', is reached from Wonthaggi by first taking the road to Cape Patterson, then by taking the Old Boilers Road to the right after passing the turn off to Cape Patterson to your left.

The rock platforms here are several hundred metres from where you can park your car, and, like those at Harmers Haven, are exposed to prevailing south-westerly winds and swells. Sweep and whiting are the main target species here weather permitting

POWLETT RIVER

Approximately 3km west of Wonthaggi, the Bass Highway crosses the Powlett River near the settlement of Dalyston. A little further on past the township you will see a sign indicating the road to the mouth of the Powlett.

The mouth of the Powlett usually remains open although it is

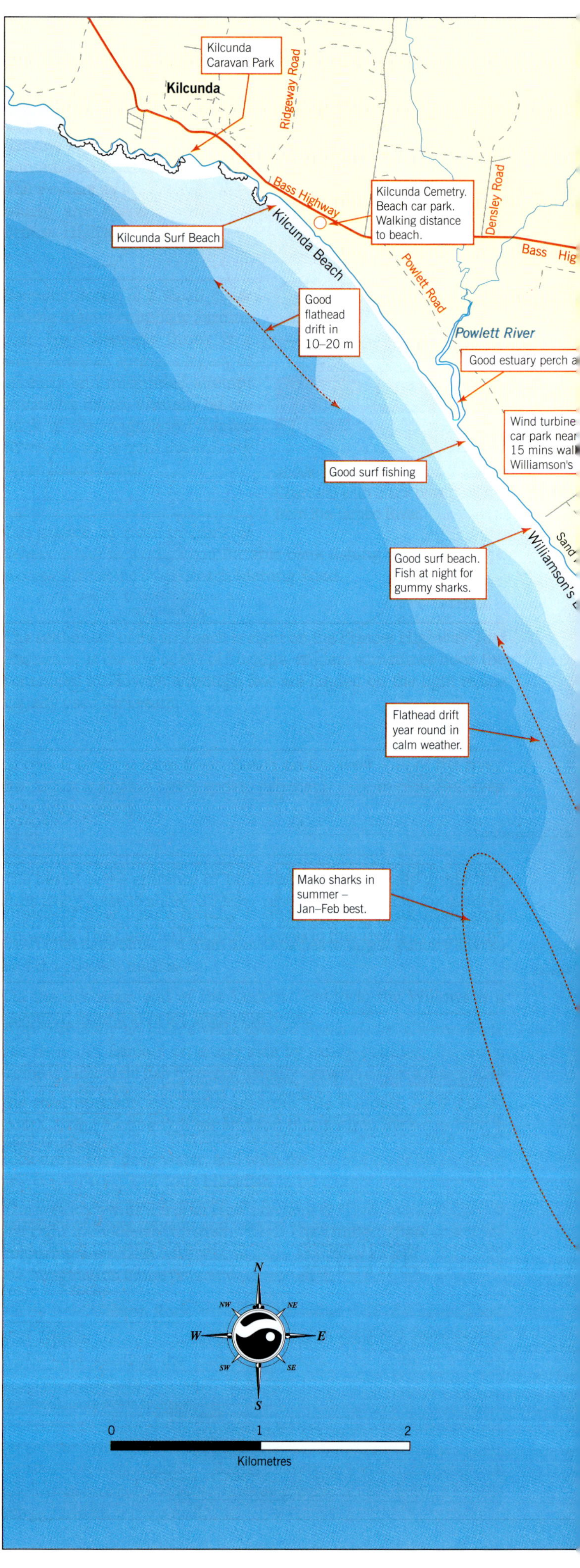

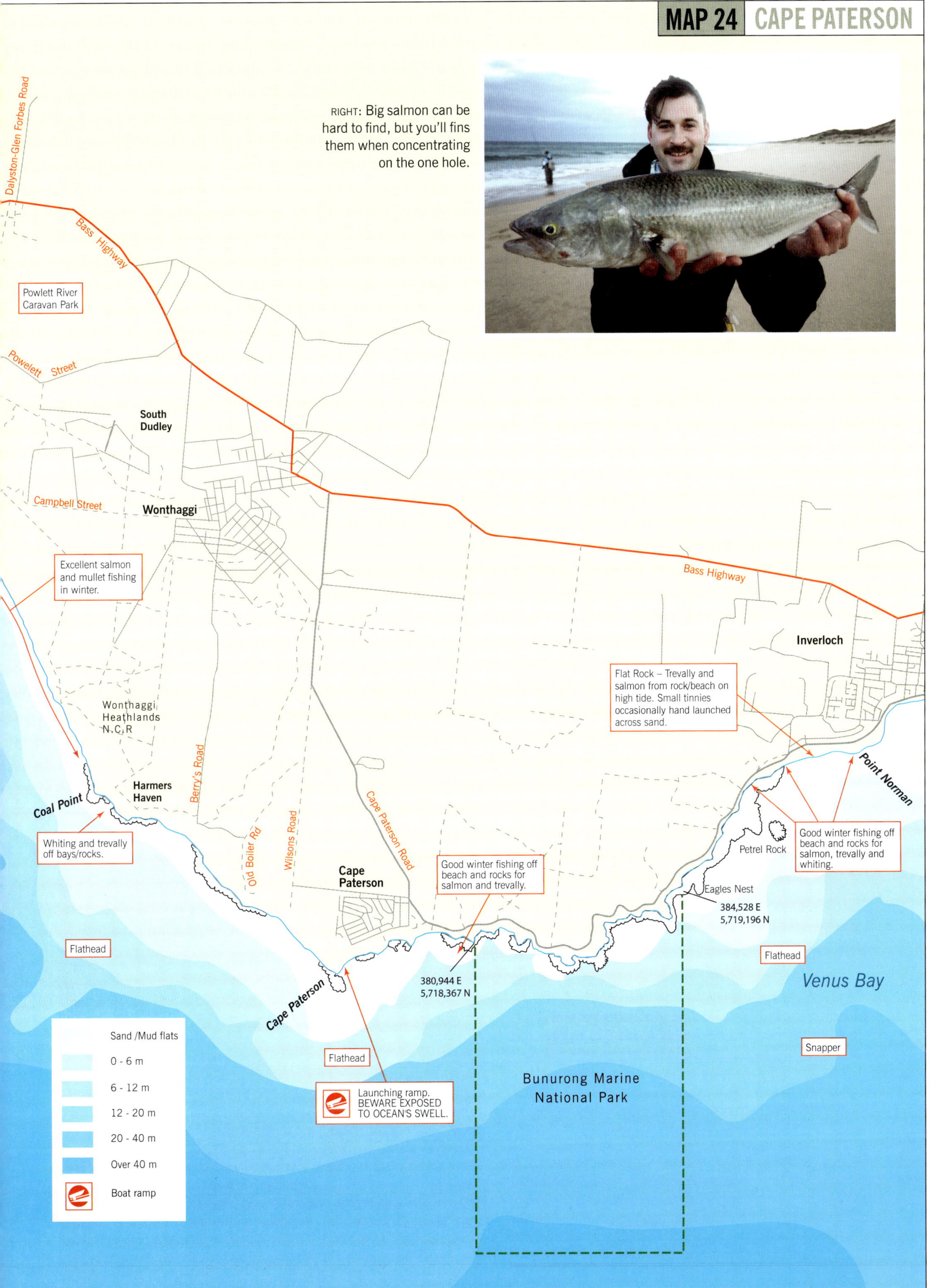

RIGHT: Big salmon can be hard to find, but you'll fins them when concentrating on the one hole.

sometimes shallow enough to wade across. The adjacent beach is exposed and uncomfortable during a southerly but produces small salmon and mullet.

The Powlett River estuary produces estuary perch and bream. The average size of both species is excellent, although they are not taken in large numbers. Bream become active within the Powlett from October and continue through until May at least. Most perch and bream are taken upstream from the road bridge above the mouth. The favoured access is from the car park beside the bridge, over the stile, and along the bank until you find a place to your liking. Fishing the edges of the weed beds and in amongst the snags will yield good catches. Most of the perch action is during warm balmy summer evenings when flicking surface poppers and walkers. There are some big perch in this system so be prepared. A small rowing boat or canoe is easily launched beside the bridge.

In the vicinity of the highway bridge, and further upstream, anglers have taken small brown trout to approximately 500 grams but some are bigger. After rain, scrub worms are best offered.

Kilcunda

One of Victoria's best known surf fishing beaches, Kilcunda is less than 2km past the turn-off to the Powlett River mouth travelling toward Melbourne.

Kilcunda has a well-deserved reputation for producing consistent catches of Australian salmon and yellow-eye mullet throughout the year. One of the very best spots to fish is straight down from the car park after crossing the old disused railway line, and to the left from where the track leads out onto the beach.

There is another beach to the left or east of Bourne Creek as you drive into Kilcunda. It is well worth trying, provided the kelp is not too bad. Open to strong southerly, south westerly and westerly winds, excess kelp is ripped from the sea floor and discarded onto the beach. This makes it difficult to fish the area a day or two a heavy blow. The rocks in front of the headland to the right of the creek also provide another option at low tide should the sea be calm enough. Silver trevally, flathead, wrasse, salmon, sweep and pinkie snapper are common catches for the persistent angler.

When fishing from either the rocks of the sand, a paternoster rig suits best. This should be constructed from at least 15lb leader with two droppers containing either a size 2/0 Mustad octopus hook or Demon Circle and a size 6 long shank hook on the bottom dropper.

For best results along any surf beach—but in particular Kilcunda as it is quite shallow and doesn't have deep gutters—use plenty of berley to bring the salmon and mullet to your area.

Kilcunda Rocks

The main target species off the Kilcunda Rocks are sweep and wrasse, although some very nice trevally get caught at times, especially by anglers who use a bit of berley. Using berley from the rocks should be undertake using an onion bag will with pellets. This should be well secured so not to break off and pollute the ocean. Larger baits cast out further can find big whiting, snapper that range from pinkies to big reds, and some large sharks, especially threshers, which seem to love this stretch of coastline.

To target threshers and other sharks it is best to float bait out with a balloon when the wind is from the north or east. Experienced anglers also do this with smaller baits to get them out further, then break off the balloon allowing the bait to sink into deeper water. This method has resulted in landing some big snapper and gummy sharks.

South Head

The rock platform in front of the hotel is known as South Head. It is a low, flat table of basalt that is safe to fish provided the tide is out and the seas are calm. Whiting, small snapper and the usual varieties of rock fish are taken from here. A paternoster rig is most effective from this location. Snook may also be taken on size 35g and 50g metal lures, particularly early in the morning.

Coalmine Ledge

Other headlands fished by land based anglers include Black Head and Coalmine Ledge, which are accessible through the settlement of Anderson by taking Mabilia Street on your left on the way up the hill to the large roundabout and turn-off to Phillip Island.

The descent from where you can park off Gilbert Street, is fairly steep and at times slippery. But, if made with care, for experienced rock anglers used to such locations, it's a comparatively safe walk.

The main ledge is to the left and gives access to deep water. This is where shark fishing enthusiasts try their luck. Getting a balloon out under the steep cliff is difficult, even with an offshore wind.

The rock ledge immediately below and inside the small bay produces some excellent snapper on evening but very large leatherjackets biting through your line can be a nuisance here.

The ledge to the right hand side of the bay looks promising and reasonably safe, but experienced anglers consider it treacherous. It is recommended that you watch this ledge very carefully before fishing from it.

The Punchbowl

The ledge known as The Punchbowl is reached from the bottom of Punchbowl Road after taking the road to San Remo. The climb down is arduous and includes a razorback, so care and a reasonable level of fitness are required.

One of the better known ledges in the area but not necessarily for the right reasons: this ledge can be quite dangerous and more than a few anglers have lost their lives here after being swept in.

It is unfortunate that the reason the ledge is so good for fishing—deep water at your feet—is also what makes it dangerous, with swells jacking up out of nowhere and a sheer rock wall behind leaving nowhere to run. In the right conditions, however, it is still a great spot to fish, with good numbers of salmon, wrasse, sweep, and trevally. For those who fish larger baits and cast out into deeper water, the rewards come in the form of snapper, big salmon the occasional kingfish and the chance of a thresher shark.

TACKLE & GENERAL INFORMATION

Always be careful when fishing on the rocks and wear the appropriate clothing and footwear. Wearing an inflatable life vest is also a good idea.

Cargill Sports
Graham Street
Wonthaggi Vic 3995
Phone: (03) 5672 1194

Venus Bay Outdoor Store
135 Jupiter Boulevarde
Venus Bay Vic 3956
Phone: (03) 5663 7222

Spinners
144 Graham Street
Wonthaggi Vic 3995
Phone: (03) 5672 3527

Winch House
C/- Post Office
Port Albert Vic 3971
Phone: (03) 5183 2022

Alberton Marine
39 Johnson Street
Alberton Vic 3971
Phone: (03) 5183 2344

Alpine Country
6 Saskia Way
Morwell Vic 3840
Phone: (03) 5237 6434

Active Outdoor Sports
38 Palmerston Street
Warragul Vic 3820
Phone: (03) 5623 1944

Walkerville Kiosk
Bayside Drive
Walkerville North Vic 3959
Phone: (03) 5663 2321

Port Albert General Store
C/- Port Albert Post Office
Port Albert Vic
Phone: (03) 5183 2359

Alberton Roadhouse
South Gippsland Highway
Alberton Vic
Phone: (03) 5183 2450

Yarram Bargain Centre
225 Commercial Riad
Yarram Vic 3971
Phone: (03) 5182 6266

Allways Angling
Shop 13/68 Hotham Street Arcade
Traralgon Vic 3844
Phone: (03) 5174 8544

CHAPTER 7

WESTERN PORT

Western Port is a vast maze of shallow mudflats, rock bars, and channels that range from small drains right up to deep, fast flowing channels navigable by ships. This complexity can be quite daunting for anyone new to the area, however with time and patience Western Port has some excellent fishing on offer. Each year it produces many snapper over 10 kg, gummy sharks over 20 kg along with plenty of smaller ones, not to mention great whiting that are abundant through summer. Additionally, each autumn sees the annual run of elephant fish which come in to spawn, allowing anglers to target a unique fish that offers good sport. Calamari are in abundance throughout the year and the recent commercial netting ban has seen the return of rock flathead throughout the port.

At the entrance to Western Port lies Phillip Island. The island creates two entrances for the water to pass through. The great majority of the water flows through the western entrance which is much wider than the eastern entrance, however all species of fish travel through both.

Aside from the main target species of snapper, whiting, elephant fish and gummy sharks, Western Port also has some excellent fishing for species such as mulloway and kingfish for those willing to try different methods and locations. Both of fish are quite common at the right times. Additionally there are a number of species of shark present—all up an indication of a healthy fishery.

Offshore from Western Port anglers find some great fishing for various species of shark with makos, blues, bronze whalers and threshers being the most common. There are also big flathead and schools of pinkie snapper.

Each season Western Port becomes more popular, and for good reason. It not only offers anglers the opportunity to catch several great species in a day, it also has many options for sheltering from the weather, thanks to the protection of Phillip and French Islands.

FISHING WESTERN PORT

Western Port is a maze of mudflats and channels that can make navigating the waterway difficult for the newcomer; however by taking it easy and spending time on the waterway it becomes fairly easy to navigate.

For those starting out on Western Port it is advised to launch from some of the better ramps that have plenty of water at all stages of the tide, such as Hastings, Corinella, or Stony Point.

Head out on a low tide or close to it—this will mean many of the mud banks are exposed so you can actually see the shallow areas. It also means that if you do run aground there is a much shorter wait until the water comes back in and you can float off. Many people get stuck as they race around the port without really knowing where they are going—the risk here is running aground at speed will get the boat well and truly stuck. So if you are new to the area take it slow, and that way if you do run aground you should be able get off fairly easily.

Success in fishing Western Port doesn't usually happen overnight. Firstly you must develop an understanding of the tides and how they work. Tides are determined by the moon and its phase in the sky, which creates a magnetic pull on the earth, and this in turn dictates water movement. Understanding the difference between a spring and a neap tide and how these will affect the fishing and water movement through the port is a good start.

Spring tides occur during the new moon and first quarter 'waxing moon', and then again at the full moon till and last quarter 'waning moon'. During these times there are big high tides and low, low tides—meaning there is minimal water left when the tide is out, and also meaning there is substantial water flow as it enters and leaves the port. Fishing in these tides can be difficult due to the current however the results can be impressive as the fish actively feed in the fast flowing water.

Neap tides occur between the spring tides and are basically tides that do not have big high and low water differences, creating less flow. Neap tides give anglers the chance to fish for longer periods in some of the deeper channels that flow too fast on the spring tides.

In the upper half of Western Port, say from Stony Point and Tortoise Head in the west and from Corinella in the east, fishing trips should be planned to coincide with the last kick of the ebb tide and the beginning of the flood (incoming) tide. This will give the maximum fishing time with minimum tidal problems. Add to this the obvious fact that all fish must be confined to the channels when the sand and mud flats are exposed and this reasoning becomes doubly sound.

To complicate the tidal issue, the change of direction in the current flow does not always occur at the extreme top or extreme bottom of the tide, but may be delayed for some hours. This is because it takes a long time for the water to travel to and from the furthest extremities of the bay and slack water cannot occur until the water level in the upper reaches is at the same height as the incoming or outgoing water from the source. An example would be that an angler fishing near Crawfish Rock at the bottom of the tide would not experience slack water for some hours because of the amount of water still to drain from the furthest extremities of the system.

TAKING MARKS

Anglers fishing Western Port are fortunate in that there are numerous visible natural and artificial features that can be aligned to enable the angler to return to a productive fishing spot. We call these co-ordinates, and two sets are required. First look for the most prominent and permanent visible feature and align it with another object either beyond it or in the foreground. If such an alignment is not possible then you may have to take a gun sight alignment, placing an object between two or more other objects.

Having established such a mark, look to 90 and 270 degrees to see how close to those angles you can get another alignment on the same basis as the first. Remember, the closer your co-ordinates are to being at right angles from each other, the more accurately you will be able to relocate the spot from which you did so well.

While landmarks are a great way of locating fishing spots, not always is a particular tree or house going to always be in the same location over time. Today, GPS electronics packages can assure that you always fish exactly on the same mark once you have its position. Even then, you might opt for a dedicated GPS/Mapping unit which can give you a Melway's view of the ocean floor. Mapping systems will actually show you the channels and obstacles, as well as being able to pinpoint any marks you find so that you can go back to exactly the same location.

ANCHORING

In all locations correct anchoring can mean the difference between fish and no fish. Western Port is no different; however by using a few basic methods anchoring can be very effective and simple.

It does pay to have a good quality anchor that is capable of holding in anything from soft mud to rubble and a bit of reef, combined with a good length of chain, a boat length is recommended. Many people have trouble getting the anchor to hold bottom and believe the anchor is too small. While in some cases this is the case, mostly the length of chain is too short. By making the chain as long as the boat once the anchor has dug in, the majority of the boat's weight is taken by the chain, which in turn prevents the anchor from being constantly dragged through mud.

One bonus with Western Port is the tide often holds the boat steady and prevents it from swinging. However if the wind and tide are opposite, or the wind is from the side then it can cause the boat to swing or yaw. This causes the lines to move and drag, often creating snags and uncomfortable fishing. One way to stop this is through the use of a bridle. A bridle is a length of rope that is slightly longer than the boat. One end has a clip of some sort while the other end is tied off on the rear bollard. Once the anchor is locked in then take the end of the bridle rope to the front of the boat, tie a loop into the anchor line and attach the clip to the loop. Then it's a simple matter of letting out a little more anchor rope until the rear of the boat sits in the right direction—this will also stop any yawing of the boat.

Another option that works well, especially if you are anchored in a wind-against-tide situation, is to place a sea anchor or bucket off the rear of the boat. This creates drag in the tide, helping the boat to hold in position.

Other options include the use of two anchors, one at the bow and one at the stern. This can be a little tricky but is very effective in areas where there isn't a lot of tide flow.

Aside from all of this it is important to make sure you know where you will sit depending on the tide and wind. They will often move you 10 to 15 m sideways or away from where you thought you would sit. Always get ahead of the area you plan to fish so that you have the boat positioned above or slightly ahead of the mark, enabling you to fish back toward the area. If the boat isn't in the correct position, take the time to re-anchor until you get it right—it can mean the difference between fish and no fish.

WHITING

Probably one of the finest table fish available, whiting are a very popular species in Western Port and for good reason: they can be caught in good numbers, put up a great fight and at the end of the day you have a feed fit for a king.

King George whiting are a timid bottom feeding fish with a small mouth that is designed for extracting worms and small crustaceans form the bottom.

They can be caught in many locations around the port, from the deep fast flowing channels, which is where the big 'channel whiting' live, to the shallow weed-lined banks and channels which hold large numbers of school fish.

Due to whiting having no real teeth preferred baits tend to be pipi, mussel, tenderised calamari strips and sand worm while live Bass yabbies' are dynamite. Anglers chasing larger whiting in the deep water or closer to the ocean do extremely well with baits such as small fillets of pilchard.

While there are many great locations to chase the whiting some of the more noted ones are the Middle Spit, the banks around Warneet, Tortoise Head, Quail Bank, Tankerton, Stony Point, Balnarring, Flinders and Coronet Bay.

If huge whiting are your target then it's hard to go past McHaffeys Reef and Cat Bay. These areas receive clean ocean water that the big fish seem to love, and they fish well all year round with some of the winter fish being true kidney slappers.

Rigs for whiting are usually paternoster rigs or similar variations. Nowadays small ezi rigs or plastic sliders are also

BOAT RAMPS

LOCATION	BOAT SIZE	PARKING	BUILD
Stony Point	7 m	Excellent	Concrete
Hastings	7 m	Excellent	Concrete
Warneet	6 m	Very good	Concrete
Blind Bight	4.5 m	Poor	Asphalt
Tooradin	6 m	Very Good	Concrete
Lang Lang	5 m	Very Poor	Concrete
Granville	3 m	Very Poor	Concrete
Bass River	4.5 m	Very Poor	Crushed Rock
Coronet Bay	4.5	Average	Concrete Brick
Corinella	4.5 m	Very good	Concrete
Newhaven	7 m	Excellent	Concrete
Ryhll	7 m	Excellent	Concrete
Cowes	5 m	Good	Concrete Sand

popular as you can easily change sinkers to suit the tide. Whichever rig anglers choose most make sure they have a small red bead or piece of tubing above the hook to attract attention.

When targeting whiting it pays to be mobile. Many of the better anglers will make lots of moves until they find a good concentration of fish. This may mean fishing a location for 15 minutes or so, then if no bites occur or only a few fish are found then a move is made. The move usually only needs to be a short one, perhaps into slightly shallower or deeper water. This is repeated until a patch of fish is located.

To get the best catches of whiting berley is essential. Most anglers will use a berley cage filled with pellets, and crushed pipi and mussel shell. The cage is attached to a rope, weighted, and lowered to the bottom. This will help to not only attract whiting but hold the school near the boat. More recently, just a bag of pilchards mashed up into a berley cage has proven to be one of the better berley's to use. When placed on the seafloor, the fishy smell emits with the current immediately. It is imperative that the correct berley cage be used to not to fill the fish with large chunks of berley rather very small particles which will bring them in from vast distances.

Hooks for whiting are usually long-shank patterns with a size 6 being most common, although on bigger fish a 4 can be better. Another option and a great hook is the circle or shiner pattern, they work best by allowing the fish to hook itself and are amazingly effective. Using circle hooks requires anglers to reframe from striking to set the hook. If you strike, you will pull the hook out of the mouth as it would not have set correctly. The design of the circle hook is to allow the fish to swallow the bait, turn to swim off and the hook will set automatically. Striking will have you miss the fish 100% of the time.

Leader material in which to tie the rig from should be 15 lb fluorocarbon. Whiting are quite a shy species and with it's almost invisible properties and high abrasive resistance, fluorocarbon in a 15 lb strength can combat being wound through weed, over reef and considering you'll also come into contact with salmon, trevally, mullet, pinkie snapper and the odd gummy shark, you'll still be able to land them rather than when using lighter leaders.

SNAPPER

Without doubt snapper are the most highly prized species in Victoria, and Western Port is a great place to start looking for those who dream of catching a truly massive fish over 20 pounds.

Snapper are caught in Western Port all year round; however the main run of fish enters in spring (September), with some of the bigger snapper coming in at the start of the run. Early season snapper tend to be caught in either one of two locations, Long Reef off Lysaghts or around the Spit Point area north from Corinella. You can always be assured that the snapper are near when fishing reports appear on social media of big barracouta being caught off Lysaghts and Long Reef. By November there is usually a good spread of fish in a variety of sizes moving through the port.

Some key areas are along the western channel, and early season anglers will often fish the channel edge from areas such as buoys 1 to 12, then move up to locations such as Stony Point and Hastings. One of the most popular spots is an area called Lysaghts, where there is a lot of scattered reef that holds plenty of snapper. Lysaghts is the southernmost section of Long Reef which then runs in an arch direction north to north east incorporating Crawfish and Eagle Rock. Other areas worth fishing include Crawfish and Eagle Rock, Bagge and Yaringa harbour, and basically anywhere you can find some reef or rubble on the sounder.

The eastern side of the port also offers exceptional fishing with areas such as Rhyll, and out further to a famous ground called the Corals. This is a fairly shallow rubble ground that produces huge numbers of snapper each season, along with gummy sharks and more than the occasional big mulloway. Other areas to look at are Elizabeth Island and up towards Corinella with the deeper water near Pelican Island and the aptly named Snapper Rock producing some great fishing.

Snapper usually feed best when the water is flowing and can be found in anything from shallow banks to the deep fast-flowing channels, especially if any of these locations hold patches of reef or broken rubble where the snapper love to feed and hide.

A good main line for snapper is 20 to 30lb (mono) with many anglers nowadays choosing to use braid in 20 to 50 pound. Braid is very thin for its diameter and has no stretch, allowing the use of smaller sinkers and providing better bite detection. Braid is also an advantage due to its high breaking strain based on its diameter. Due to the large sting rays and banjo sharks amongst other oversized fishes, braid can allow you to reel them in to remove your hook rather than busting of on mono causing you to re-rig each time. As the saying goes "Those with baits in the water longer, will catch more fish" and spending the time re-rigging reduces your chances at success especially if there is a hot bite.

Rigs for snapper can and do vary. The paternoster rig remains popular, however many choose to use an ezi rig or plastic slider, which moves freely on the main line and allows sinkers to be easily changed depending on the current. It also allows the angler the option to let the snapper run with the bait, or you can have the reel in gear and let the snapper hook itself. The ezi rig runs to a swivel and a word of advice: use good quality swivels such as the crane or barrel type, as they spin under pressure unlike lesser quality ones. Another very important piece of advice to remember is to do with the Ezy Rig slider itself. Ezy rigs come standard with a metal clip to attached the sinker too. Remove this and replace it with a 30cm length of 8 or 10lb fishing line. This way, if your sinker becomes snagged in the reef, you'll bust off the sinker and not the entire rig.

The swivel then joins to about 1.5m of good quality 40 to 60 lb leader, matched to a snelled two hook rig. Hooks such as suicide and circle patterns are popular, in sizes ranging from 2/0 up to 8/0 depending on the size of the baits being used. Most anglers find 5/0 suicides a good hook for the majority of the snapper.

A recommended rig is 1.5 m of 40 lb leader running to a pair of snelled hooks, with the top hook a 5/0 circle and the bottom hook a 5/0 suicide. Smaller snapper tap at the bait and get caught on the bottom hook, while the big fish hit it hard and fast and normally have the top circle hook lodged firmly in their jaw hinge.

The bonus to the two hook rig as described is it allows you to rig the bait so it is straight and the tow point comes from the top hook—bait that bunches up or bends will spin in the current causing line twist, tangles and no fish. Single hooks can be used and a circle is recommended. This should be in a 5/0 or 6/0 size with a small bait just pinned on. This allows the fish to completely swallow the bait rather than attempting to tear it from a double hook set.

Snapper are often referred to as scavengers, and while this may be partly true they do show distinct preferences for certain baits, especially if they are fresh. Successful anglers will usually head out with a range of different baits, with some of the more effective ones being tuna fillet, pilchard, sauri, squid (frozen is okay but especially fresh), garfish and salmon fillet. All of these baits can be used either whole or cut into strips or fillets, either way just make sure that in the current you keep the baits thin and streamlined—this makes presentation more natural and also makes the baits easier for the fish to eat.

Snook

A far more common species in Western Port than most realise, snook can be found in any of the areas that have relatively shallow clean water near reefs or weed beds, such as the banks close to Hastings, Stony Point and along the Middle Spit. However if you are after snook in big numbers then it is often best to head towards areas such as McHaffeys Reef, Red Rocks, Cat Bay and down towards the Knobbies, then all along the reefy shoreline on the south side of Phillip Island

While not the best fighters in the world snook are good fun to catch especially on lighter line, and often decent numbers can be taken as they do tend to school loosely.

The best way to target snook is to troll with small diving minnow pattern lures such as Rapala Magnums, although snook just love the action of a lure called a Tilsan Barra which runs about 3 m deep.

Another very effective way is to troll with fresh baits like squid strips, small garfish or pilchards. Garfish rigged on ganged hooks are probably the best, although make sure the bait is rigged straight or it will spin.

When trolling lures or baits for Snook, it is imperative that you attach a small length (30cm) of wire between the mainline and the lure or bait. Snook have quite an array of sharp teeth as do short finned pike and barracouta which are also caught while trolling for snook. Snook are often mistaken as Pike and vice versa though both look extremely different from one another. Snook are more rounded in shape with a brown yellow tinge over their back and yellow fins. Pike on the other hand are more short and much darker brown with a red tinge.

Troll for snook at a fairly slow to medium pace and once one or two are caught in quick succession, keep working the area as there should be more. A bonus of trolling for snook is that they often live in the same location as species such as salmon and kingfish, both of which also love the same style of lures and baits.

Eating-wise snook are fairly poor if they have been frozen, although fresh they make a good meal when filleted and de-boned.

Snook make great bait in Western Port when used fresh for a variety of species such as snapper and gummy sharks.

Salmon

Salmon are a Victoria's most popular pelagic sportfish being accessible to most anglers. Their energetic fight and acrobatic display's is what makes them an attractive light tackle species. Salmon are well known for bringing baitfish to the surface and "bust up" causing the water's surface to resemble a spa bath.

Through the cooler months many anglers fish the surf beaches for salmon. For best results in the surf successful anglers use berley to attract the salmon. A paternoster rig with two droppers is a good surf option, with one hook baited with pilchard or blue bait, and the other with pipi or the more popular surf popper.

While surf fishers do catch good numbers, for the most part the bigger fish tend to move in large schools and hold towards the eastern and western entrances. Here they can be seen turning the water to foam while chasing baitfish. One option is to troll a range of lures such as small skirts, metal slices and diving minnows around the school—don't drive through the fish as this will send them deep. However, the best option is to get up wind or up tide of the salmon, cut the motor and let them come to you, then cast lures. This is far more fun and a lot more effective. Metal slug lures are perfect in this instance.

In Western Port there are good numbers of smaller salmon to

be found in most areas, especially along the shallower banks where whiting are caught. Use a fine berley and baits such as pipi and pilchard fillet. These smaller salmon make great bait when used fresh for species such as snapper, sharks and mulloway, but be sure to adhere to the bag limits and size limits applying to salmon: see the latest Recreational Fishing Guide for details.

YELLOWTAIL KINGFISH

Since the removal of the kingfish traps up in NSW several years ago we are starting to see good numbers of kingfish returning to Victorian waters. Both entrances to Western Port are great spots to look for kingfish, where strong tides sweep past rocky headlands and islands that the kingfish like to live around.

The ideal times to target kingfish is in summer when the water is at its warmest. This is when they are most active, and while they can be found in cooler water it can be very hard to get them to eat a bait or lure.

When targeting kingfish, trolling around the rocky headlands and islands with lures such as large diving minnows or small skirts can be effective. Another good tactic is trolling larger lures around feeding salmon schools. The kingfish love to hold with the salmon but they will sit deeper under the school and prefer the bigger lures. Slowly trolling live baits such as small salmon, yakka's, squid and garfish around the school is a sure-fire way to see if there are any kingfish around. Offshore around Seal Rocks and towards Cape Shank are two popular locations t troll live baits for kingfish. In recent years, caught kingfish have fetched 15 kilos. Trolling live baits requires special rigging techniques with bridling the most effective. A special "kingfish" sinker will be required to allow the live bait to swim freely while being trolled while the weight of the sinker will hold it down under the water while in a forward motion. Without the kingfish sinker, the live bait will be trolled high on the surface of the water and most likely perish due to skipping on the water surface and being exposed to the outside air and surface wave action.

Other great methods include anchoring over chosen patches of reef or close to islands, then berleying while fishing live and dead baits such as squid and garfish (either suspended under floats and near the bottom). Casting soft plastic lures and poppers while you wait is also a great way to attract the kings. Teasing kingfish is another effective method. Dredge style teaser bars can be deployed to raise the schools to the surface. Anglers can then cast 145mm soft plastics to them with great success.

While most the kingfish tend to hold around the entrances to Western Port in locations such as Woolami Headland, Pyramid Rock, Seal Rocks and the Knobbies, at times they will move up in the system. Sometimes they can be found holding on some of the channel marker buoys and as far up as Crawfish Rock which is a well-known location for kings. Some of the more effective techniques include casting lures such as poppers, metal slugs and soft plastics at a marker buoy or around a rocky outcrop for 5 to 10 minutes before moving on to the next. This can produce some white knuckle fishing as you try to stop the kingfish before they bust you up on the chain or reef below.

FLATHEAD

Just like Port Phillip most of the flathead to be found in Western Port are of a small size. In saying that, with the removal of the netters in the Port some years ago, larger flathead are becoming a more regular catch. Anglers who like to fish the shallower banks, especially with lures, often encounter the odd nice flathead. Try to find banks that have a decent-angled drop from shallow to deeper water. This way you can work the lure from the shallow water over the ledge to the deeper water, where the flathead will lie in wait for food. The best time to target flatties is on the run out tide, when the baitfish are pushed off the banks into deeper water. One popular location is along the edge of Middle Sand in the Eastern Entrance near Sam Remo as well as at the Corals and in Coronet Bay. They are usually caught as a by-catch when fishing for whiting. Rock flathead do like reefy/rocky locations. Flathead are a very common catch for bait fisho's, especially when berley is being used. The smell or attractant brings them in and those anglers that regularly target whiting tend to also catch a good feed of flathead too. Flathead like soft sand and mud so where there are whiting to be found, there will be flathead. Flathead can be caught on the basic of rigs but a paternoster rig is best offered with size 1/0 long shank hooks attached. Sinker weight will vary according to the strength of the tide.

GUMMY SHARK

Western Port is a great location to find gummies. With its maze of tidal flats and deep channels it is the ideal feeding area for smaller gummies to live and grow, and also a perfect place for the big gummies to breed.

Gummy sharks are one of the favoured species in Western Port and for good reason: they put up a strong fight and a feed of fresh flake is pretty hard to beat.

When targeting gummies, anglers have two real options location-wise. First, there are the deeper main channels such as the whole western channel from buoy 1 right up to around Warneet. In the deeper water the tide flows hard; requiring large lead to hold bottom. Here the trick is to find the edge of the channel where the bottom just starts to level out a bit after dropping away from the bank, then try to locate some bottom structure in the form of reef or a ledge. Just make sure you are outside the shipping channel as it is illegal to anchor in it.

In the deeper spots gummies of any size are possible; however these areas tend to produce bigger fish with 20 kg specimens not uncommon. Many anglers now choose to release these big fish as they are all females that come in to breed and repopulate the fishery. They are also old fish that don't taste anywhere near as good as the smaller ones. If you are looking to take one home for the table, the sweetest flesh comes from fish in the 4 to 8 kg bracket.

The other area to look for gummies is on the shallower tidal flats found up toward the top end of Western Port. Mazes of deeper channels run through large mudflats here that are often dry on low tide. In these spots the trick is to fish in the channels on a run out tide—as the water gets lower it pushes the fish off the flats into the deeper water where you are fishing. Although your baits will attract them, berley is essential if you want to catch numbers of fish. You will attract stingrays as well but this is part and parcel of fishing on the bottom. In the deeper areas and due to the sinker weight required to hold bottom, your rods and reels need to be able to cope with not just the sinker weight and water pressure but also the size of the fish that can be hooked and fought. In fast tidal locations, a 7ft 8-12kg rod will be adequate with either a 6000 or 8000 size spin reel or small overhead reel capable of holding 300m of 30-50lb braid.

In the shallower channels it is uncommon to find the very large gummy sharks; however fish ranging from 3 to 8 kg are usually found in good numbers, especially during the warmer months. In this case, lighter tackle can be used with rods in the 6-8kg bracket matched to a 4000-5000 spooled with 30lb braid or monofilament.

Best methods to target gummies include the use of a plastic slider called an ezi-rig or similar, allowing you to easily attach and remove sinkers. This slides on the line to a swivel, attached to a metre or so of 60 lb leader with one or two hooks. Suicide hooks in a 5/0-6/0 size are ideal when snelling two hooks together otherwise should a single hook be chosen, a 6/0 circle is best offered. Many anglers choose to use a wire trace although it isn't really necessary as gummy sharks have no teeth and you will get more bites without the wire. If you do get bitten off it's not gummies but more likely school sharks. School shark won't take wire leaders as they have highly sensitive sense organs. The most effective way to catch them is by using 80 or 100lb leader with a size 8/0 circle hook.

A variety of baits work with some more effective than others. Pilchards, tuna, salmon and trevally fillet are very common while fresh calamari and cured eel and the top two.

MULLOWAY

Mulloway are a truly mysterious fish that have become a more common catch over recent years. Some say there are more around than there used to be, which is probably true. It may also be something to do with the fact that anglers are learning more about the areas mulloway like to live within the port, and are taking the time to use the right baits and fish at night, when they are most active.

If you want to catch one of these awesome silver fish, then first of all it is important to become efficient at catching bait. This means catching mullet, small salmon or squid, all of which are favoured by mulloway when used fresh or live.

Once this is achieved then fishing around tide changes in the new to full moon period seems to produce the best results. However mulloway can be taken at any time of the day or night and at any stage of the moon phase. What is really important is to be patient as it usually takes many hours to catch just one. Over time, patterns will emerge as to when your chosen spot fishes best.

Mulloway grow very large with fish of 50lb being caught every year by lucky anglers, however for the most part fish of 10 to 25lb are more common. The smaller ones are often referred to as 'soapys' as their flesh is often soft and mushy, with fish under 6lb not highly rated as table fare. Fish ranging from 10 to 30lb are a different story and make great eating.

Rigs for mulloway are the same as those described for snapper and gummy sharks, but with extra emphasis on the bait being fresh or live. Look for locations where there are drop-offs and holes for the fish to ambush prey, and work these areas. Locations that have a rubble bottom or reef nearby seem to be prime habitat.

One of the bonuses with mulloway is that some of the better fish are caught each year by land based anglers as the mulloway will hold around piers and wharves where there are good numbers of bait fish. Tenby Point and Settlement Point at Corinella are known land based locations.

The bite from a mulloway is usually unmistakable, being amazingly fast and powerful. If fishing in gear the rod will buckle and the drag on the reel will howl. In that instant the fish is either hooked or gets away. There are some anglers who prefer to let mulloway run with the bait, but many have success fishing with the reel in gear.

If fishing out of gear and allowing the fish to run with the bait before hooking it, allow the fish to run then calmly put the reel in gear while holding the rod steady. If all goes well the rod will load and you will feel the powerful run and headshakes from what many anglers class as one of the ultimate species. Knowing how powerful they are, anglers should rig up with heavy tackle. The same setup used for gummy sharks is suitable for mulloway.

ELEPHANT FISH

Elephant fish are a very strange looking species, which come into Western Port to spawn each year. They're a member of the spook fish family, which includes the Pinocchio fish and other deep water species.

What makes the elephant fish so unique is that it is more closely related to a shark and is often called an 'elephant shark'. It has a cartilage backbone and no ribs, a tail like a rat, and uses its large wing-like pectoral fins to glide along the bottom while its trunk-like nose glides along the sea floor helping it to find food.

Each autumn huge schools of elephant fish swim out of extremely deep water into the shallows of Western Port to lay their single egg in the port's soft mud bottom. At this time they offer anglers the opportunity to have some great fishing for a species that can only be found in one other area in the world, South Africa.

When targeting elephant fish, look for areas with a soft mud bottom. The most popular locations include Bouchier and Boultins channels in the top end of the Port along with a location known as The Elephant Triangle. This can be found by taking a ruler to a Western Port map and drawing a line from Corinella to Rhyll, from Rhyll to San Remo and then back to Rhyll. The well known as "the corals" is also one of the biggest producers of Elephant's from the area. Gear can be anything from the standard Western Port tackle of 10 to 15 kg monofilament or 20 to 30 lb braided line on a suitable reel and 8 to 15 kg rod, through to lighter tackle such as spin and whiting rods; on the latter elephants put up a great fight. Rigs are either paternoster style or the more common plastic slider with a leader of about 40 lb to either a single or double 3/0 sized hooks—usually a suicide pattern, 3/0 circle hooks are also extremely popular with light tackle users as the hook will set itself.

While elephants have no teeth being crustacean and shellfish feeders, the heavier 40 lb leader is handy as they tend to roll on the line and the spike on the top of their head is quite sharp and serrated, easily cutting through light line.

If you have always wanted to catch a decent sized fish without too much effort then you could do a lot worse than heading out on Western Port over autumn to chase this unique species.

Landbased anglers can easily catch elephants too. The most productive locations are Stockyard Point, Lang Lang, Grantville Jetty, Tenby Point, Corinella Jetty and Settlement Point.

OTHER REFERENCES

If you are new to Western Port, a sound investment is the Australian Fishing Network's Fishing Map No 6 'Western Port', available from fishing tackle outlets. Another must-have item is a book called *Fishing Western Port*, which covers the whole of Western Port in depth, including species and locations, best fishing times and even GPS marks. Land Based anglers are not left out either, AFN's Land Based Fishing Guide to Western Port, Phillip Island and surrounds will provide land based anglers with plenty of tried and proven new locations from which to catch a fish.

After crossing the bridge from San Remo to Newhaven on Phillip Island, the angler can fish from numerous spots. However, those facing the ocean should be avoided by all but the most experienced anglers.

PHILLIP ISLAND

SAN REMO

The last stop before crossing the bridge that joins Phillip Island to the mainland, the small township of San Remo is a quiet little location that is home to a solid wharf and several trawlers that fish out in Bass Strait, mainly targeting gummy sharks and silver whiting.

San Remo is also the last stop before heading out the eastern entrance to Bass Strait, and while much smaller and shallower than the western entrance the water flows very fast through the channel past the wharf and under the bridge, rushing powerfully through the pylons with each tide change.

The channel itself produces some good fishing for those who work around the tides and fish in the periods when it runs slower. Along the edges, whiting, garfish and salmon make up the bulk of the catches.

From the wharf anglers catch trevally, calamari and a few whiting together with the odd nice gummy shark, although catching any species is possible as they have to swim past the wharf to get into Western Port. Fishing the tide changes is imperative otherwise your baits won't reach the bottom. This means fishing about an hour each side of either the high or low tide. During the slack tide, anglers are able to fish from the sand and can catch yellow-eye mullet. Small hooks are required with pilchard the top bait.

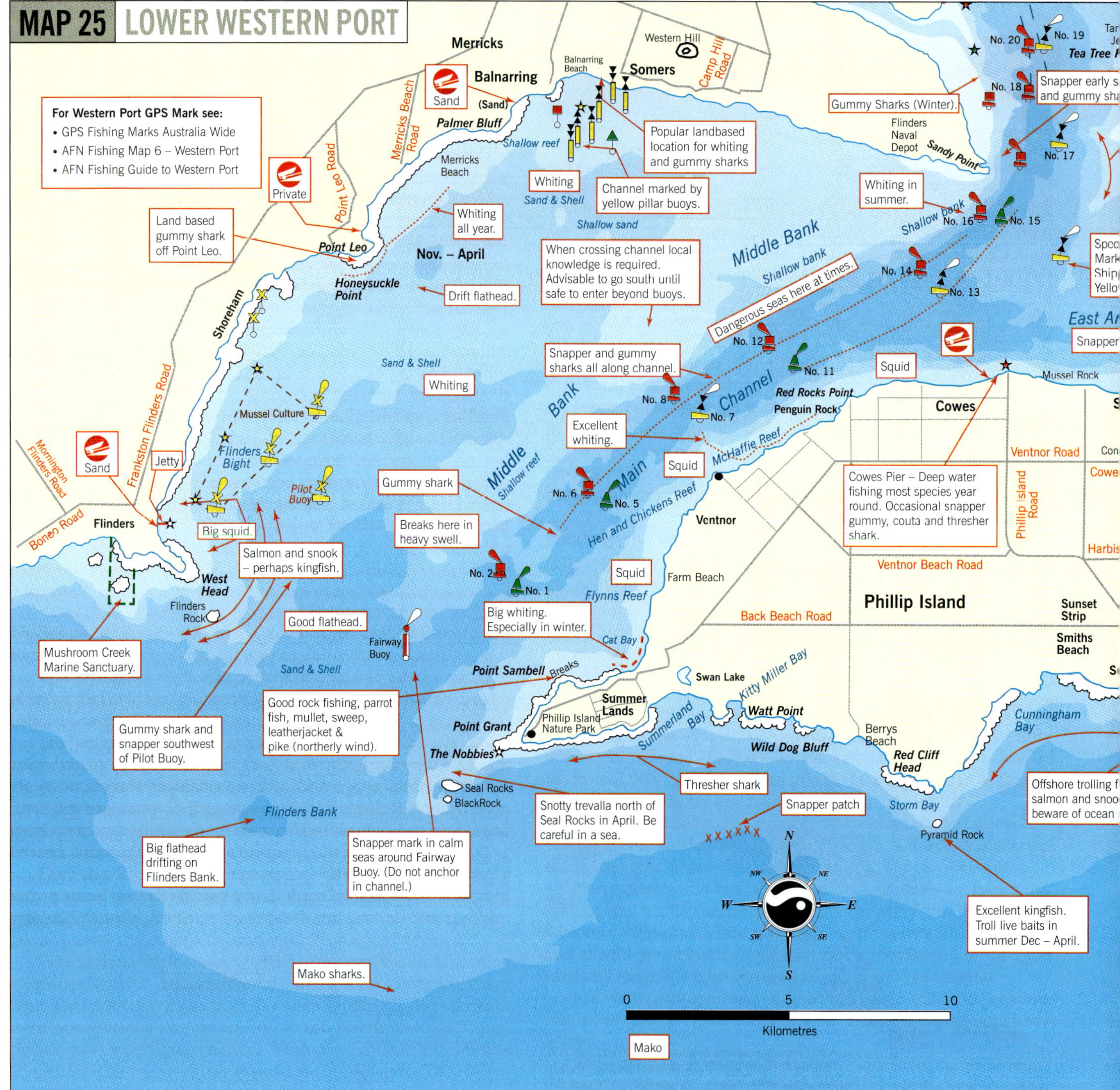

San Remo Back Beach

At low tide, there are several rock ledges within walking distance of the parking area at the bottom of Back Beach Road, which provide the land based angler with the opportunity to catch squid, whiting and a variety of other fish, including salmon, particularly when using lures. Flathead are also a common catch, especially on low tide along the edge of the channels. Be careful though, the water can come in quick and you could get stranded on one of the many sand bars. On the lead up to a full moon, this location is quite popular for angler searching out flounder. The most productive way to catch them is with the use of a spear but check the rules and regulations before doing so.

Newhaven

A decent boat ramp can be found at Newhaven even though it is rather exposed in a northerly wind and the fast flowing tide can also be a nuisance when endeavouring to launch and retrieve a boat. However, it does offer access to many nearby fishing locations and is also the closest point to launch for anglers who are heading out into Bass Strait, hence it is popular with shark fishermen and also to those who want to fish offshore. When seldom quiet in the Newhaven channel, whiting can be caught along the edges on the high tides.

The Newhaven jetty can produce good fishing for those who are prepared to put in a bit of time and fish around the tide changes when the water isn't flowing as fast. The simplest method used to attract fish is with the use of berley. You don't have to go to any extreme but a small berley put with some fish oil and pellets will do the job. A paternoster rig tied from 15lb trace with 2 size 6 long shank hooks will suffice. Sinker weight will vary according to the strength of the current.

Species caught from the pier include whiting, flathead, snapper, garfish and mullet along with the occasional gummy shark. For the smaller species, small pieces of pilchards work well while for snapper and gummy sharks, oilier baits such as tuna, calamari, trevally or salmon fillet are ideal.

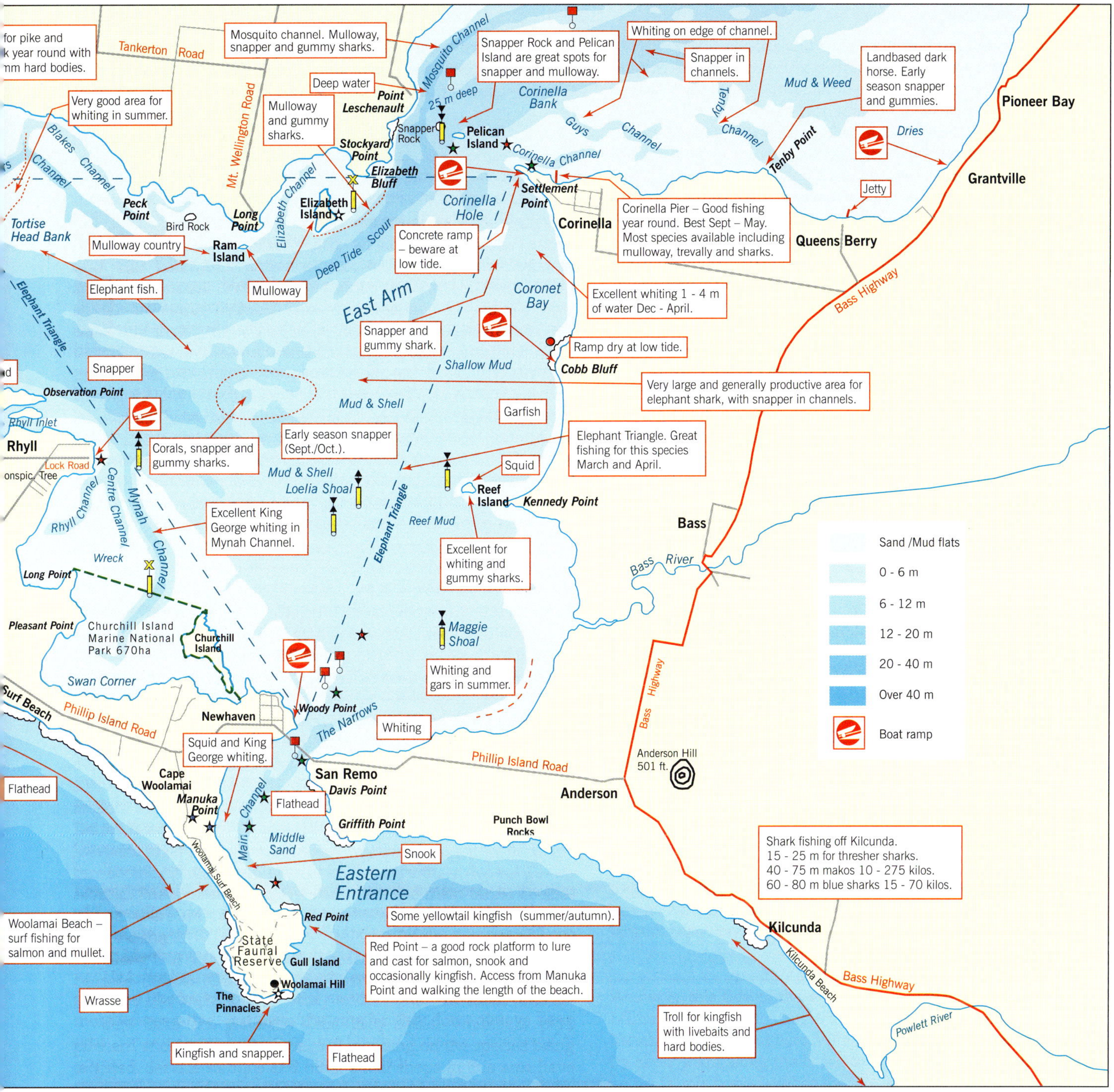

Mosquito channel. Mulloway, snapper and gummy sharks.
Snapper Rock and Pelican Island are great spots for snapper and mulloway.
Whiting on edge of channel.
Snapper in channels.
Landbased dark horse. Early season snapper and gummies.
Very good area for whiting in summer.
Deep water
Mulloway and gummy sharks.
Mulloway country
Elephant fish.
Mulloway
Concrete ramp – beware at low tide.
Corinella Pier – Good fishing year round. Best Sept – May. Most species available including mulloway, trevally and sharks.
Jetty
Excellent whiting 1 - 4 m of water Dec - April.
Snapper and gummy shark.
Ramp dry at low tide.
Snapper
Very large and generally productive area for elephant shark, with snapper in channels.
Garfish
Corals, snapper and gummy sharks.
Early season snapper (Sept./Oct.).
Elephant Triangle. Great fishing for this species March and April.
Squid
Excellent King George whiting in Mynah Channel.
Excellent for whiting and gummy sharks.
Whiting and gars in summer.
Whiting
Squid and King George whiting.
Flathead
Snook
Shark fishing off Kilcunda. 15 - 25 m for thresher sharks. 40 - 75 m makos 10 - 275 kilos. 60 - 80 m blue sharks 15 - 70 kilos.
Some yellowtail kingfish (summer/autumn).
Woolamai Beach – surf fishing for salmon and mullet.
Red Point – a good rock platform to lure and cast for salmon, snook and occasionally kingfish. Access from Manuka Point and walking the length of the beach.
Wrasse
Troll for kingfish with livebaits and hard bodies.
Kingfish and snapper.

Sand /Mud flats
0 - 6 m
6 - 12 m
12 - 20 m
20 - 40 m
Over 40 m
Boat ramp

Red Rock

Red Rock, also known as Red Point, is located right at the southernmost point of the Eastern Entrance. To access it, you can park at Cleeland Bight located at the end of Cottosloe ave, and then you will have to walk along the water's edge towards the mouth of the entrance. A faster route is along a passage through the Cape Woolamai Fauna Reserve from Woolamai Beach Road.

Dropping almost straight into deep water with a sandy bottom, the rocky outcrops collectively known as Red Rock are the safest and most productive rocks to fish from on the whole of Phillip Island. This area produces salmon, barracouta, pike, snook, calamari, King-George whiting, Sand whiting, flathead, gummy shark, various wrasse species, snapper and the very occasional kingfish.

While the platforms are safe, the walk out on Woolamai Peninsula is hazardous, particularly should you make it in pre-dawn darkness though the mutton bird burrows and take note, during the summer months, red belly black snakes can be a problem along the hot dry paths. The tide can run hard here at times so it pays to have a variety of varied sinker weights at your disposal. for numbers of fish, place some berley such as fish based pellets into an onion bag and suspend it on a rope over the edge of the rocks. As the water splashes onto it, the berley will disperse and thus, attract fish. Casting baits out into the trail is where you'll see most of the action. When targeting gummy sharks and snapper here a running sinker works best while a paternoster rig will suit all other possible species.

Manuka Point

Between Red Rock and Newhaven, the beach below the sand escarpments at Manuka Point provides opportunities for land based anglers to fish for squid and whiting with surf casting tackle. However, this area is covered when the tide comes in so you may have to retreat to higher ground if you stay too long. When fishing for whiting use a paternoster rig as you will increase your casting distance. This will allow you to access the deeper water where they are abundant in season. Calamari are taken on a high tide with night time most productive. When fishing for calamari, use a float setup with baited jig suspended around 50 cm under the float. There is a lot of red weed throughout this area and it is very easy to become snagged. A silver whiting is best offered as bait for calamari.

Rhyll

This is a great starting point that puts you in close proximity to some of the best locations in Western Port. Beginning at the pier, anglers can chase mullet and whiting with light rods and baits such as pipis, while a larger bait can find gummy sharks and elephant fish in autumn. The Rhyll Channel is a well-known location to fish for whiting, especially at its northerly most point. Berley is a must, especially during the begging in of a run out tide. A Paternoster rig will suffice with pipi and mussel baits the best bait choice. There are some sizeable flathead about. Pilchards fished on running sinker rigs seem to work well.

The ramp and nearby waters get quite busy so for land based anglers the best fishing is usually at night and early in the morning.

Observation Point

Though not too far from Rhyll, Observation Point offers anglers good access to deep water where snapper are the prime suspect throughout their annual migration. Averaging 13 meters deep, this area has steady tidal movement requiring anglers to use a substantial amount of lead to hold bottom. A running sinker rig works very well with size 5/0 hooks suitable. A cube berley trail will bring fish to the immediate area along with gummy sharks, schools and elephants in season. Oily baits such as salmon, trevally, mullet and eel are the key in this area as it is very tidal and the water clarity low.

SilverLeaves

A little around the corner from Observations Point towards Cowes is a relatively small sand beach known as SilverLeaves. Well known for land based flathead during a rising tide, from a boat, anglers can target snapper along the edge of the drop off in season. Throughout the season, various sized snapper are caught but each January at least one 20 lb red is reported. Fishing along here requires patients as it is more of a thoroughfare than a holding location. Fishing the flood tide is paramount. A running sinker rig tied from 60 lb trace with a 5/0 hooks will suffice. From the shore is a series of sand divots made from the force of the tide. It is a land based access only location and fishes best late in the evening on a high tide for flathead. Anglers flicking soft plastics do quite well. Fishing the dead low tide will have you casting into 7 meters of water where flathead can still be caught. At this time of the tide, you're best to fish using a surf rod outfit with a paternoster rig and blue or white bait offered. Some flathead can be in excess of 60 cm during the summer months.

Cowes

Also known as Erehwan Point to the right of the Cowes jetty, anglers access to reasonably deep water. Snapper have been caught here but the tidal current can make fishing difficult should there be much weed about. It is best to time your visit here with the change of tide. Whiting are also common for those fishing with surf type tackle.

Cowes Jetty

Cowes Jetty is one of those locations that can produce anything at any time for anglers who are prepared to put in the effort.

For the most part anglers who fish the jetty do so for species such as silver trevally, barracouta, pike, snook, flathead, mullet, small salmon, calamari and whiting. However for those who fish late evening and through the night with larger baits and heavier tackle, the rewards can be great. Each season good numbers of snapper are taken, some of which are over 10 kg, along with gummy sharks of all sizes. Effectively fishing for larger species can be difficult having too cast out such large and heavy baits. A new specially designed land based rig call the ICON Surf Casting rig is ideal in this situation. Together with an attached float, the rig can enable a further cast with large baits and sinker. Fitted with 5/0-6/0 circle hooks, it is perfect in all land based situations.

Aside from this many anglers like to put out large shark baits to target some of the big sharks which cruise in the deep water that runs close by. Most of the sharks hooked are seven gills and some huge bronze whalers, which prove hard to stop in the strong current.

During the night, anglers fishing with baited jigs under floats tend to catch some very impressive calamari under the jetty lights. Approaching the slack tides is the prime time for this.

Boat Ramp

There is a reasonable launching ramp at the bottom of Anderson Road, giving boats to five metres access to deep water within a few hundred metres of the ramp. Care must be taken when launching here as rolling swells can make launching and retrieving difficult and unsafe at times. It is advisable that you do not launch during a Northerly wind over 10 knots.

Penguin Rock

There is marginal land based access between Penguin Rock (to the left of where Red Rocks Road meets the sea) and at various places south-west to Grossard Point (at the end of Grossard Point Road). However, while some dedicated anglers have taken fish from this part of Phillip Island, most will find the degree of difficulty a little too much.

A weedy area, whiting and wrasse are the most common species caught. A paternoster rig works well with small hooks such as a Mustad 92647S.

Ventnor Beach

This spot may just look like any other small beach but it does produce some great fishing for a variety of species, with the most common being gummy sharks and the odd decent snapper. A good cast is needed to get into deeper water, however at night time the gummies in particular will move up into the shallows on a high tide.

The area can also produce some very big squid for anglers who fish with fresh fish baits suspended under a float. Whiting are also worth targeting although it is weedy; a paternoster rig is highly recommended.

McHaffie Reef

Land Based anglers have quite good access along the board walk at the end of Grossard Point Road at Ventnor. Fishing from the rocks is a popular affair during the summer months for whiting, pike, snook and calamari. Each species has its own specific technique with calamari being more abundant at night. a baited jig suspended under a float is the best method used. Pike and snook can be caught spinning with metal slug lures whiting whiting will take a pipi on a paternoster rig. Fish high tide for best results.

Hen and Chickens Reef

Further along the Phillip Island coastline, Hen and Chickens Reef is a popular location fished only by boat anglers. Land Based access is a non-event due to its proximity to Access points.

Predominantly calamari are the main target by those flicking size 3.0 artificial jigs about. If bait fishing, the area is plaqued by wrasse.

Flynns Reef

Known for delivering killer waves if you're a surfer and opposite the Penguin Parade on Phillip Island, Flynns Reef adjoins Cat Bay to the east. Flynns Reef has sand patches in which whiting and salmon can be caught but around its reef and weed lines bottom, calamari and wrasse can be caught. Setting anchor just out from the reef and setting a berley trail is an effective method. While fishing with a paternoster rig for whiting, salmon and wrasse, also suspend a baited jig in the trail for a calamari.

CAT BAY

It's a fair walk to get here, however the results can be worth it for anglers who want to chase some huge whiting from the shore. Try the area near the old pier and cast into the areas of broken bottom.

Aside from whiting there are some big flathead and trevally to be found, and a larger bait is always a chance to take a gummy shark or snapper. Seven gill sharks are also a common capture and more often released. Fishing in Cat Bay is tricky as it is exposed to ocean swells and North, North West and westerly winds. This makes fishing very difficult and it is best fished in an easterly or southerly when swells are low.

When fishing from the boat, calamari, whiting and gummy sharks are the man targets. For whiting, use a paternoster rig and move in close to 8m of water directly out from the old jetty ruins. Berley is essential and you will attract various species of wrasse too. Calamari can be caught by drifting over the weed patches. Use large size 3.0 and 315 jigs in this area. Some calamari have been known to have weighted over 3kgs. These larger calamari tend to be caught in September and October.

Gummy sharks are caught further out in 10-12m pf water. One particular productive location is around Buoy 5 on the edge of the channel. Fish the last of the ebb tide for best results during the lead up to the full moon.

THE NOBBIES

At the end of Ventnor Road, The Nobbies is a popular location for tourists. There is land based access to deep water from the rocks and good size snook can be taken on lures here. However, the weather and tide govern access to The Nobbies, which is a spot not recommended for any but the most experienced rock anglers. Various species of wrasse and sweep are in abundance which often deters anglers from fishing this location. Throughout February to April, Snotty Trevella also known as Warehou can be caught by those fishing from a boat. A float setup with bread used for bait makes the perfect bait. Snook can be caught by trolling lures and Kingfish are a common catch for those trolling live baits.

KITTY MILLER BAY

This sheltered little bay at the bottom of Kitty Miller Road has produced some large whiting to anglers who don't mind losing most of their sinkers on snags. To eliminate this, use spoon sinkers on paternoster rigs. Berley pellets placed into an onion bag and hung from the rocks on the western wise works well. Garfish can also be taken in calm weather using a float setup.

PYRAMID ROCK

At the end of Pyramid Rock Road, the east side of the rocky promontory extending out to Pyramid Rock does offer scope to lure casting enthusiasts seeking large snook in calm seas. However, it's a big climb down with fishing tackle, the bottom is snaggy and you have to be fairly dedicated to fish here. Extreme care must be taken as rock fishing can be very dangerous. Anglers in boats can also fish around Pyramid Rock in calm seas. Flathead, wrasse, pinkie snapper, salmon and kingfish are all common captures. Those wanting to catch kingfish tend to troll squid strips and live baits around the reefs.

WOOLAMAI BEACH

At the end of Woolamai Beach Road, Woolamai Beach is badly exposed to weather from the south-west. However it is popular with surf anglers who catch quite a lot of respectable salmon here. Most of the better catches of salmon come in the winter months, while during summer and autumn anglers catch decent gummy sharks from the beach at night around the full moon.

There are also reports each season of kingfish being taken from Woolamai, especially in some of the deeper gutters towards the eastern end of the beach.

In particular, Anzacs beach is the first car park located along Cape Woolamai road. A gutter lies to the right of the beach and it's quite deep. The bottom is rocky which attracts and holds silver trevally and salmon throughout the year. The odd pinkie snapper has also been taken here. Berley is very effective here and can attract schools of fish fairly quickly due to the strong currents. A paternoster rig works well when tied from 20lb fluorocarbon leader. Two size 1/0 bait holder hooks work well for all species

OFFSHORE

The offshore waters of Bass Strait out the front of Western Port and Phillip Island are very popular with anglers, and for good reason. During the summer months warm water flows down from the eastern seaboard bringing with it several shark species such as blues, bronze whalers, threshers and probably the most prized of all, mako sharks. While most of the makos encountered are usually between 20 to 50 kg there are some monsters amongst them.

Areas such as 25 m of water off Powlett River, 50 to 70 m of water out from Woolamai, and locations such as the Flinders Bank are all noted shark spots.

Shark fishing techniques aren't too complex; actually shark fishing is one of the easiest fishing techniques to understand. Once you have your chosen rods and reels at the ready, simply head out to a location you have picked based on the direction of the wind and tide and begin a berley trail. Ideally, a light southerly, westerly or easterly wind is recommended as it will push you back or to the left or right of the western entrance should you head out trough there.

You will require a substantial amount of berley to get you through your drift so take along a mixture of pilchards and shark berley blocks. You will also require a few different baits as the large schools of arrow squid will devour a whole striped tuna in minutes. In a perfect world, 6 baits such as whole slimey mackerel, whole tuna and whole mullet are good options. These should be suspended under balloons at different depths in the berley trail as your drifting. Remember, it pays to check your baits every hour or so as the arrow squid could have devoured them. One think to note is that when attempting to land a mako, care must be taken as they are quite dangerous. Ensure you have a full set of gaff's on board for when the time comes.

While drifting for sharks it is also worth having a line on the bottom as there are some great flathead to be found, along with large barracouta, gummy sharks and the occasional snapper. Just out from the Western Entrance, The Flinders Bank is a popular location for flathead on the run out tide. Silver whiting are also caught offshore mainly during the warmer months. These can be caught on the bottom with paternoster rigs and size 10 long shank hooks as silvers have extremely small mouths.

A large squid jig will also find any of the very aggressive arrow squid, which live in the big numbers in these waters. Along the headlands, trolling minnow type lures is effective for snook, pike and the odd salmon.

Huge schools of striped tuna are common from February through to April and although the species was almost decimated around 20 years ago, they are back in full swing. Anglers wishing to catch a Melbourne tuna can do so by trolling small 2 and 3 inch white occy skirts around the busting schools. Casting metal slugs is possible although the schools often move too fast to allow this to occur.

In close to the Phillip Island coastline is popular with anglers seeking big whiting. Great care must be taken when anchoring in ocean swells but if the conditions are ok to do so, some very big fish can be caught. Garfish are also popular in these areas and are usually of good size.

MAP 26 UPPER WESTERN PORT

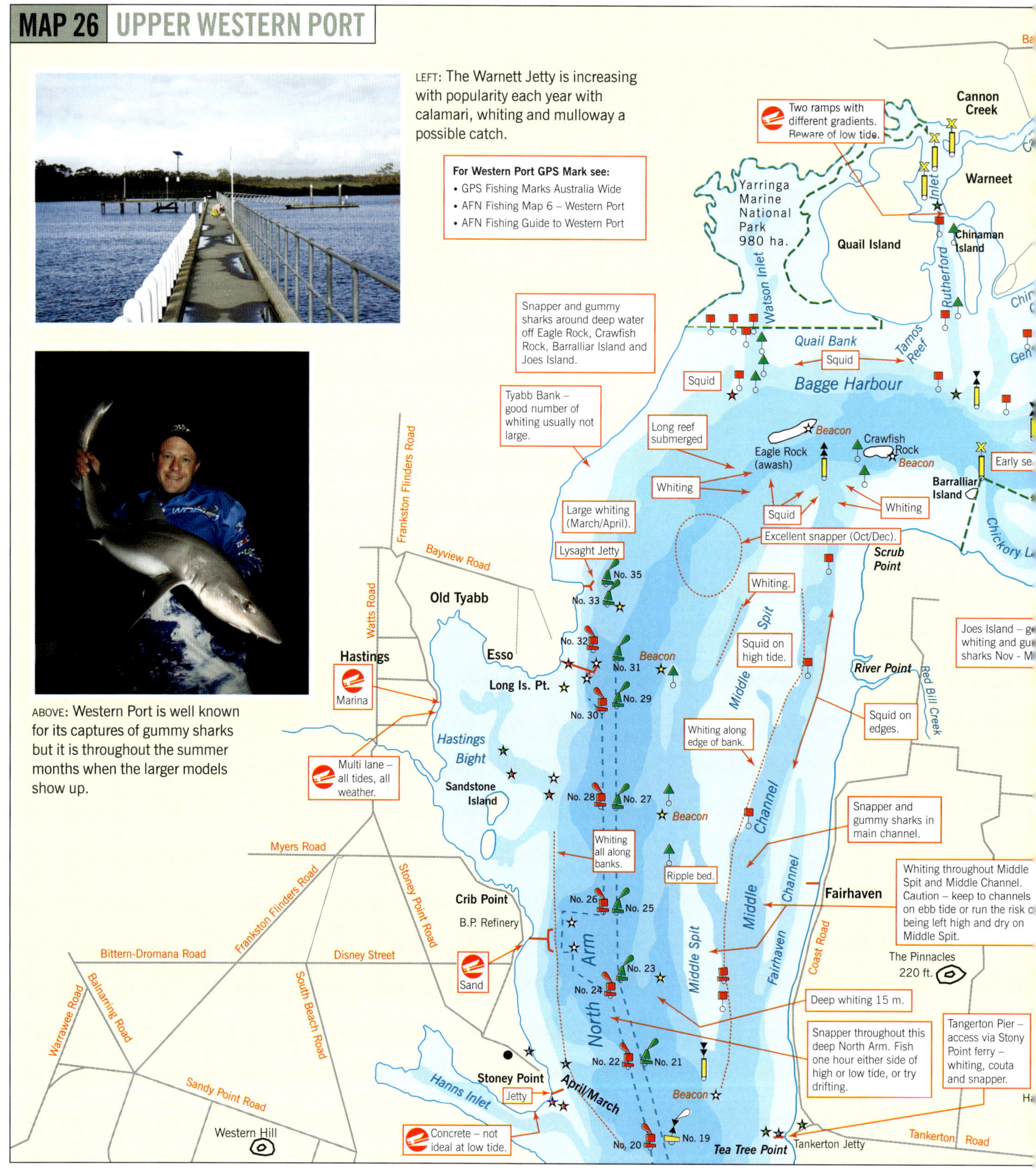

LEFT: The Warnett Jetty is increasing with popularity each year with calamari, whiting and mulloway a possible catch.

ABOVE: Western Port is well known for its captures of gummy sharks but it is throughout the summer months when the larger models show up.

WESTERN PORT

Dickies Bay

Tucked away under the cliffs of San Remo, Dickies Bay is as synonymous with whiting and garfish as Snapper are to Port Phillip Bay. Despite seasonal runs of fish, whiting and garfish can be caught at Dickies bay throughout the year.

Fishing the high tide is most productive and berley is a must to bring the fish on. Whiting are very fond of mussel and pipi baits while garfish prefer silver fish on a float setup. This locations is best fished in 3 meter of water but as the tide abates, you will have to up anchor and move out into deeper water towards the low.

Bass River

The Bass River is a great location to fish for both Land Based and boat anglers. Land based anglers can access the river at the end of Bass Landing Road. From this point, anglers can walk along the

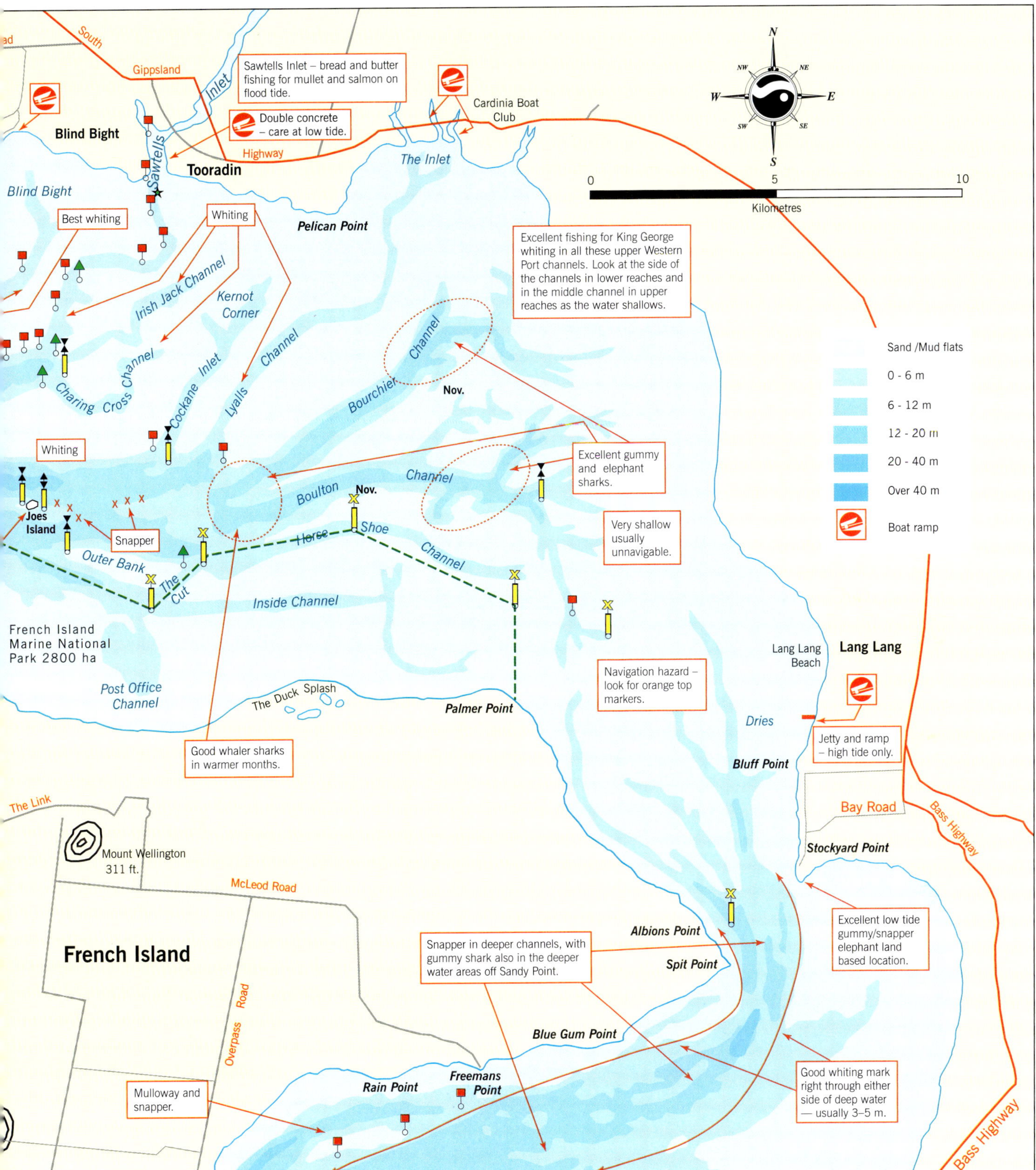

river flicking soft plastics or soaking baits for bream, salmon and trevally. There is an unmaintained boat ramp where anglers can launch tinnies up to 4.5 m. Kayak anglers can also take advantage of this launching facility but tidal strength can be an issue at times.

Around the Mouth, anglers can catch whiting and calamari. Larger vessels should launch at Newhaven and drive over fishing around the mouth on a high tide.

Reef Island

Situated between Bass River and Coronet Bay is a large rocky outcrop called Reef Island. Land Based anglers can venture out onto Reef Island during low tide but are limited to around an hours fishing time before the tide floods over the exposed walkway stranding them.

Fishing from the shore at the end of Soldiers Rd is popular for land based anglers targeting whiting, flathead and silver trevally. A paternoster rig is best offered with blue bait, white bait and pipi's working well.

Corinella

The township of Corinella is clearly signposted off the Bass Highway. It has an excellent boat ramp and a jetty extending out to the channel where anglers can fish with the hope of catching mullet, silver trevally, small salmon, whiting and a variety of other fish.

This also offers great land based opportunities for the chance of catching a big fish such as a mulloway or gummy shark. Fresh baits are the key with the prime time being three days leading up and down from the full moon. Snapper and elephant fish can also be caught from the pier by those in tune with the tides and times of the month when the fish will be at their most active. The best fishing is usually found on the last few hours of the run out tide, especially at night when there is less boat traffic around. For elephant's, gummies and mulloway, a paternoster rig suits well when rigged from 60lb trace. Circle hooks ranging in size from 3/0 to 6/0 will suffice. Using berley is an effective way of attracting fish to the pier. Simple methods include using an onion bag with pellets and tuna oil mixed together to hang on the water's surface.

Corinella has a very good boat ramp along during strong northerly and north easterly winds, launching and retrieving can be challenging. Fishing in close can see flathead, silver trevally, gummy shark, whiting and elephant's caught. A running sinker rig works best for all species.

Tenby Point

Well known by the Land based fraternity, Tenby Point is quite a unique location. The most productive area to fish is next to the old jetty ruins casting in an easterly direction. Best fished on a high tide, mulloway, gummy shark, salmon and silver trevally are the most common species caught. The bottom is quite rocky and snags are unavoidable at times. Fresh baits are the key with calamari being the most consistent. Fishing a few days either side of a full moon is profitable.

Grantville

There is a small boat ramp at Grantville suitable for small craft from half flood to half ebb. There is no low tide access here. The small jetty at Queensferry, south of Grantville, is also a high tide proposition only. This jetty can only accommodate one or two anglers at a time and is a very popular during elephant shark season. Kayak anglers can launch from here to access the wide gummy shark grounds. It is around a 200m paddle/peddle to the drop off into 3 meters of water. Here, anglers can expect to catch elephants in season, mullet and gummy shark year round.

Stockyard Point

Undoubtedly, Stockyard Point is the most well-known land based fishing location in Western Port. Being so, it is also requires the longest walk to get to. This location is a low tide only fishery and can produce snapper, elephants, gummy sharks, school sharks, bronze whalers, seven gill sharks, tailor, silver trevally and yellow eye mullet.

Fishing the low tide gives access into the deeper water which is within casting range. Ideally, fish two hours either side of the low tide for best results. A paternoster rig will pay dividends here.

Lang Lang

The jetty at Lang Lang has now been dismantled; however, fishing from the shore on a high tide will still produce elephant sharks, gummy shark, mullet, silver trevally and salmon.

Similar to that of Grantville, Lang Lang has become a very popular launching location in recent years for kayak anglers. Once again, launching is paramount on the high tide and the paddle to deep water is around 300m. On the high tide, anglers would be fishing in around 3 meters of water and perched on the edge of the bank where they do very well when fishing with banana prawns for bait. Calamari also works well.

Tooradin

Tooradin is situated on Sawtells Inlet on the South Gippsland Highway. There are numerous places where one can fish either from the bank of the inlet, or from the jetty. Mullet are the dominant species followed by silver trevally. Bream and estuary perch have also been taken from time to time but do not seem to be a regular capture. Small hooks are recommended with pipi and pilchard fillet being popular baits. In recent years, kayak anglers have taken advantage of the launching facilities giving easy access to the mangrove lined channels on a high tide. Estuary perch are the main target with soft plastics and small diving hard body lures best offered.

Tooradin Channel

This channel sits at the outlet of Sawtells Inlet and is reached via boat. Launching is at the excellent boat ramp at Tooradin as it has had a recent upgrade. Make sure you know where the channels run as many anglers have been left high and dry on the soft mud and sand in front of Sawtells Inlet.

Best known for its fantastic whiting fishing, the Tooradin Channel also produces good flathead and elephant fish in season.

When fishing the channel for whiting it is always worth putting out a larger bait on heavier tackle, as good sized gummy sharks and the occasional big snapper will often feed on the shallow banks in here, especially on cloudy or rough days.

Blind Bight

Off the Warneet Road, after taking the Baxter Tooradin Road from the Highway, Blind Bight has a small jetty and boat ramp that gives access to the channel known as 'Gentle Annie'. The jetty produces good fishing for mullet and small silver trevally. Occasionally it can produce a snapper or gummy shark for a lucky angler, and more than an occasional mulloway has been seen or caught as they harass mullet in the channel from half flood to half ebb tide. There is little or no water here with the tide out.

Gentle Annie Channel

Of all the channels in the top end of the Port, Gentle Annie is the most renowned of its abundance of whiting. Though a small channel in retrospect of the others throughout the Port, Gentle Annie always produces quality fish. The best fishing is two hours either side of the high tide change with pipi and mussel baits working well. It is mostly 4 meters deep in the middle with the fish being found on the edges of the bank.

Blind Bight

Off the Warneet Road, after taking the Baxter Tooradin Road from the Highway, Blind Bight has a small jetty and boat ramp that gives access to the channel known as 'Gentle Annie'. The jetty produces good fishing for mullet and small silver trevally. Occasionally it can produce a snapper or gummy shark for a lucky angler, and more than an occasional mulloway has been seen or caught as they harass mullet in the channel from half flood to half ebb tide. There is little or no water here with the tide out making launching impossible.

Warneet

Situated on Rutherford Inlet, the Warneet boat ramp gives access to good fishing in the inlet and in Bagge Harbour in northern Western Port.

There are two main jetties in Rutherford Inlet that land based anglers can catch quality fish from. Firstly is the one located further up the inlet. This is a small jetty that is completely dry on low tide. On high tide anglers fishing with pipi or blue bait catch small salmon, silver trevally and yellow eye mullet. Live baiting with mullet can see the odd estuary perch be caught. Anglers fishing the high tide from their kayaks also catch a few perch when casting shallow diving lures into the mangroves.

The main pier at the boat ramp provides anglers with access into deeper water. The best fishing is from the end of the pier during the run out tide. All the fish up in the system, flush out with the force of the current and swim within casting range of the pier. Yellow eye mullet, King George whiting, silver trevally, salmon and calamari are the most common species caught. Mulloway are also an option for those fishing with live baits. The odd Elephant fish has also been taken during their season.

Warneet is also a very popular location for whiting anglers to gather fresh bait from before heading out into the Port. Bass Yabbies can be pumped on the mud flat at half tide before heading out.

Quail Bank

Located between Rutherford Inlet and Watson Inlet, the Quail Bank is a relatively shallow sand and seaweed covered flat. During a high tide, fishing for calamari, whiting and flathead is popular amongst anglers. Calamari can be taken on baited jigs along with various artificial jigs. Whiting respond well to berley with pipi and mussel baits working best.

Watson Inlet

Watson Inlet provides anglers with access from the Yaringa Boat Harbour into Western Port. Although it is mainly used as a thoroughfare, the fishing in the entrance is extremely good for whiting. These can be productively targeted all along the edges of the banks between the channel markers.

There is a Marine Park located just above the entrance into the Yaringa Harbour. Yaringa Marine National Park prohibits the removal of any fishes, shells or crustaceans —contact Parks Victoria for details.

Tyabb Bank

The Tyabb Bank can be found from Watson Inlet to the Lysaghts shipping jetty. The bank ranges from 2 to 5 m deep which is a popular area for whiting but also supports a good population of calamari.

This bank fishes best on a high tide and can become very weedy after strong south easterly and easterly winds. Setting a berley trail and fishing baited squid jigs into the trail is a very effective method for big calamari.

Middle Spit

The most popular area for whiting fishing is the Middle Spit. The Middle Spit runs from Bagge Harbour to Stony Point. This length of shallow sandy bank is a known location to catch whiting, garfish, salmon and silver trevally. It is fully exposed on a low tide and care must be taken when boating around the area. Whiting can be found everywhere but best depths are 2 to 4 meters. Whiting respond well to pipi, mussel and squid strips. Berley is essential. Yellow eye mullet, Australian salmon, silver trevally and flathead are also common catches.

Anglers fishing for whiting can also pump live bass yabbies from the mud flats but be aware, this should only be done on a half tide otherwise, when you jump in, the mud will be soft, and you will sink up to your knees. Live bass yabbies are the number one bait for whiting.

Calamari are also a viable option for those wanting a good feed. There are scattered weed beds at the northern most tip of the Spit where anglers can use the current to their advantage and drift the edge of the bank casting and retrieving artificial jigs.

Sunken Island

Unbeknown to many, a small shallow sand bar known as Sunken Island sits some 2 km east of Long Island Point in the north arm. Sunken Island begins at channel marker no. 5 and heads in a southerly direction. A very popular location for garfish up to 50 cm in season, whiting, salmon and silver trevally. For best results, set anchor on the island's edge and fish the last hours of an ebb tide.

Hastings

There is an excellent marina and multi-lane boat ramp at Hastings with all facilities for anglers. Landbased access is strictly limited.

Fishing close to the ramp and its surroundings such as the pier is a great spot to find schools of hungry mullet, while a larger bait is usually eaten by stingrays. Occasionally anglers catch mulloway from the pier. Whiting and yellow-eye mullet are a viable option from both the pier and the concrete steps at the boat ramp but tend to be on the smaller size. Berley is essential with small long shank hooks a recommended.

Launching from Hastings gives access into the North Arm where anglers can head to the top of the Port, Tyabb and Quail Banks and the Middle Spit.

Fishing for snapper, whiting and gummy sharks is extremely productive in the North Arm.

Sandstone Channel

Exiting the Hastings Channel, Sandstone Island to the south has a small channel running west from the north arm. Entering this should be done with great care even with a GPS MAP system. The channel produces good whiting and calamari on the edges of the banks.

Stony Point

The large Port Authority jetty at Stony Point is at the bottom of Stony Point Road and gives access to deep water. Fishing at the change of tide is recommended here because the current runs strongly.

Possibly one of the better piers in Western Port, Stony Point enables anglers to catch just about any species of fish that comes into Western Port.

Each year there are snapper of all sizes caught from the pier, along with gummy sharks, mullet, trevally, whiting, squid, garfish, barracouta and, in season, elephant fish and the occasional mulloway. The best thing about this spot is that the species available can change from day to day, and every cast sees you in with a chance of a big fish. It does pay to fish with heavy tackle such as a surf rod with the reel spooled with 30-50lb braid. Fishing during the night throughout the year is particularly productive for calamari. A baited jig is the best approach but artificial jigs work well also. Try flicking white coloured metal slugs under the lights at night for snook and barracouta.

Anglers can use berley in a bucket and fish from the third light post along the pier during the first and last two hours of the ebb tide. Silver trevally, salmon, yellow-eye mullet and whiting are a common catch. A paternoster rig works best.

The Stony Point boat ramp is concrete and can accommodate three boats launched at any one time. This ramp also offers low tide access and all facilities are nearby.

Balnarring Beach

Balnarring Beach is at the bottom of Balnarring Beach Road, which runs off the Frankston Flinders Road at the Balnarring Traffic Island. To the east, the foreshore reserve between the entrance of Merricks Creek and Somers Yacht Club gives anglers pedestrian access to both the shallow tidal estuary of the creek and the beach.

The curved beach in front of the foreshore reserve, between the entrance of Merricks Creek and Balnarring Beach Road, shelves into approximately 2 m of water within casting distance and has produced whiting, gummy shark and snapper. This beach fishes best from sunset until an hour or so after dark, with a high tide recommended.

The rocky bank between the Western Port and Somers Yacht Clubs becomes sufficiently exposed on the lowest of tides to give shore-based anglers access to the channel running east from the yacht club anchorage. Both whiting and snapper have been caught here along with gummy sharks. Gummy sharks are a more viable catch on the lead up to the full moons.

Similarly, the headland several hundred metres south-west from the Western Port Yacht Club gives anglers access to productive water on these same low tides that occur in the evening during late spring and in the morning during late autumn. Be careful when fishing the rocks as the tide can come in fast leaving you stranded having to wade back to shore.

Merricks Creek

Merricks Creek has produced bream, but small mullet are the usual catch made by anglers fishing from the foreshore reserve. Best results are to be had with the tide rising toward full.

Point Leo

Point Leo is off the Frankston-Flinders Road and is popular with beach anglers seeking gummy sharks at night. The most productive time to fish here is at the top of the tide when it occurs shortly after dark. Large Sevengill sharks are also quite a common catch, especially when fishing the high tides and night. Oily baits such as salmon, trevally, and calamari are a hot favourite. Salmon are a viable catch in the winter along with some very sizeable flathead.

Flinders

The coastline surrounding Flinders offers marginal access for land based fishing and a very ordinary sand boat ramp that requires caution so as not to get the car bogged in the soft sand. While the ramp is not great, it does enable anglers to launch smaller boats and kayaks into some prime fishing water where the main targets are squid and large whiting.

The area is probably best known for the numbers of good squid that are caught from the Flinders Jetty, especially each spring when it offers anglers the opportunity to fish for some of the truly huge calamari that move into the area to spawn. Most successful anglers use whole fish on a squid prong, which is suspended under a float, although casting with artificial jigs also produces plenty of calamari. Those fishing from boats or a kayak should move out into 10 meters of water and drift while casting jigs about. Once a calamari is hooked, mark it in your GPS and drive back to re-drift over the same spot. Often, calamari will school in numbers of be found tight in the same area.

With lots of broken reef and weed the area surrounding Flinders is also great for big whiting that move through, especially on a rising tide at dawn and dusk. During these periods whiting move into the shallows to feed, enabling land based angler's good opportunities to catch them. Best baits include mussel and pipi, although a tenderised piece of fresh squid is likely to produce a really big whiting. Grass whiting are also popular along with garfish and leather jackets. Pike and snook can be caught by those spinning with metal slugs on a high tide. Night time is preferred.

When targeting whiting from a boat or kayak, move east towards the mussel farm and fish amongst the sand patches. There are a lot of big whiting in their area.

Snook are also abundant around the mussel farm and are often taken by those flicking soft plastics about. Some big six spine leather jackets are a common bi catch.

A Flinders squid

Flinders Head

Taking the road to the Royal Australian Navy depot on West Head, turn right through the golf course just before the gates, to the parking area from where you can walk down to the beach.

The sheltered area on the left side is an excellent whiting spot at the bottom of the tide, particularly when this occurs on evening.

The extensive rock platforms provide ample scope for bait and lure anglers at low tide, but the bottom is snaggy and has accumulated a good deal of fishing tackle over the years! The deep channel between the outer rocks and the main ledge is the most obvious fishing spot but the reefy drop-off requires a long rod to avoid getting your line caught on the retrieve. Wrasse, pike, snook, salmon, silver trevally and whiting are all commonly caught. This location also produces some big calamari. A baited jig approach is the most effective technique to use.

Boat fishing around Flinders Head is also very effective for flathead, gummy shark and pinkie snapper. Salmon can also be caught when seen busting the surface.

Located on the southern side of Flinders Head is the Mushroom Reef Marine Sanctuary. Fishing is prohibited in this area —contact Parks Victoria for details.

The Blow Hole

Taking the road to Cape Schanck, you will come to the track leading to the Blow Hole after about two and a half kilometres. The most obvious feature is the pinnacle to the left below the cliff at the bottom of the track.

Although the Blow Hole is fished regularly by anglers for sweep, the rocks are dangerous and should be avoided by all but the most experienced rock anglers. There are better ledges dropping into very deep water between the Blow Hole and Cape Schanck but access needs to be negotiated through private property. Other species that can be caught are pike, snook, leather jacket, wrasse, silver trevally and the odd salmon.

Cape Schanck

The turn off to Cape Schanck is clearly marked approximately 13km west of Flinders on Boneo Road, or access is from the Rosebud-Flinders Road should you be coming from Melbourne.

There is only one place to fish at Cape Schanck and that is on the rock ledge right out on the east side of the point looking across Bushranger Bay. Lure casting here often produces large snook, and bait fishing the bottom will almost guarantee anglers a large parrot fish or two. The odd pinkie snapper has been taken but it is a rare capture. It is quite a walk from the car park along the fairly steep track around the sloping mounds of the headland, but the rock platform is reasonably safe provided you make an intelligent assessment of the conditions.

The deepest spot on the ledge is as far out as you can go. It's a great pity you can't get on to the outer part of the headland (Pulpit Rock) where it drops down into very deep water—spear fishers have taken some large kingfish here at times.

Boat anglers can access this area by launching from Stony Point but it is about a 40km run. Fishing around here can lead to some great catches of salmon, silver trevally and gummy sharks. Inside Bushrangers Bay is productive for whiting but don't get in too close as it is a surf beach and swells can be overpowering at times. Fishing over the sand is where the whiting and silver trevally can be found. Out deeper in 15 meters of water, the bottom is thick reef with huge kelp forest, Pike and Snook are common catches for those trolling small diving hard body lures. Mako sharks can be caught out here in 40 m of water. Kingfish are also an option for those willing to put in the time to find them. Trolling live baits is the preferred method used.

Providing the weather is in your favour, setting anchor in 20 meters off the Schanck is productive for gummy sharks, seven gill shark, school shark, bronze whaler's and thresher sharks. Try to avoid from using wire leader, rather a big circle hook with 80lb trace will see more quality fish hooked. Live baiting is also a very effective technique for sharks here.

WESTERN PORT TO PORT PHILLIP BAY

Gunnamatta

Approximately 3km west of Cape Schanck on Truemans Road, Gunnamatta Beach has gained a deserved reputation for producing salmon for surf anglers throughout the year. Anglers setting berley trails catch the majority of fish throughout the season. In recent years, spinning with metal lures has become extremely popular and effective. Small metals ranging 25-50g fitted with a single hook work best. For this type of sport fishing, a specific 9ft casting rod will be required. Many brands are available but ensure the one you choose is rated to casting a 60g lure. When flicking lures along the surf beaches, simply walk from gutter to gutter casting in each. It is best to put in around 30-40 casts before moving to the next if no luck. Casting metal lures throughout the summer months is extremely productive on first light. During the full moon period this beach also produces good gummy sharks for those anglers who fish during the night. Silver trevally and yellow eye mullet are also caught when anglers use smaller sized hooks.

There are public toilets and a car park at Gunnamatta but little else. Access from the east or from the direction of Cape Schanck is from Boneo Road (Rosebud Flinders Road), then along Limestone Road to Truemans Road.

Rye Back Beach

Similar to Gunnamatta, Rye back beach has its devoted adherents who take excellent bags of salmon throughout the year. Access is from Rye by Dundas Street or by the unmade road from Gunnamatta. Beware of rocky outcrops that jut out from the shore. Many quality fish have been lost here.

St Andrews Back Beach

From Point Dundas Street, turn right into Bass Meadows Boulevard. Here you will find a good car park with access to the beach. St Andrews is popular with anglers seeking salmon although it is a very popular beach to target gummy shark at night. The lead up to the full moon is prime time. A high tide is recommended. Silver trevally and yellow eye mullet are common catches when fishing for salmon. St Andrews beach is the most reliable gummy shark beach along this stretch. Though Gunnamatta is more publicised, St Andrews gets little attention and is kept quiet. You will have to get there early to get a good gutter before the locals do.

Diamond Bay Back Beach

Diamond Bay Back Beach is quite small and can only accommodate a few anglers. It is not very popular but yields some great fishing at times. During a high tide, silver trevally and salmon enter the bay. The rocks can be fished to gain access into deeper water but they can be very slippery and care must be taken. Sweep, leatherjackets and salmon are popular catches. An onion bag containing pellets infused with tuna oil can be hung over the edge of the rocks on a long rope. Fishing unweighted pieces of pilchard or squid is an effective technique. Weighted rigs such as a paternoster can and will become snagged on the bottom as it is very rocky. Take extra sinkers if you're going to fish this way.

Diamond Bay can be found at the end of Diamond Bay Road.

Sorrento Back Beach

During the summer months, Sorrento Back Beach is extremely popular with swimmers but during the winter it becomes an angler's domain. Each side of the beach is bound by rocky headlands with plenty of fishing opportunities. Directly out, it can be up to 5 meters deep with sweep, salmon, silver trevally and wrasse all common captures. During the summer months it is very busy with surfers and swimmers. Fishing the evening or on first light will be your best options. Ensure berley is used to bring the fish to within casting distance.

Portsea Back Beach

The Portsea Back Beach has a series of deep gutters along its length. Once located, these gutters hold good numbers of salmon and mullet during winter. Berley is essential for success. Those fishing into the night have the chance of hooking a good gummy shark. Portsea has adequate car parking and a well maintained boardwalk to the beach.

Tackle & General Information

Tackleworld Cranbourne
270 South Gippsland Highway
Cranbourne Vic 3977
Phone: (03) 5996 6500

Phillip Island Motors & Fishing Centre
157 Thompson Avenue
Cowes Vic 3922
Phone: (03) 5952 2567

P & J Marine Service Centre
Factory 1
101 Tooradin Station Road
Tooradin Vic 3980
Phone: (03) 5998 3107

Popeye's Marine Centre
Lot 2 Factory 5
Grantville Drive
Grantville Vic 3305
Phone: (03) 5678 8765

Fish Tales Bait & Tackle
14 Station Street
Pakenham Vic 3180
Phone: (03) 5941 3310

Jim's Bait & Tackle
151 Marine Parade
San Remo Vic 3925
Phone: (03) 5678 5462

BP Service Station Cowes
160-162 Thompson Avenue
Cowes Vic 3922
Phone: (03) 5952 2024

Byrneside Store
5385 Midland Highway
Byrneside Vic 3617
Phone: (03) 5854 8219

Seaside Marine
1885 Point Nepean Road
Tootgarook Vic 3941
Phone: (03) 9589 1011

Marine Motors, Sealand Marine & Elect
Westernport Marina
PO Box 35
Hastings Vic 3915
Phone: (03) 5979 1211

Hastings Bait & Tackle
112 Marine Parade
Hastings Vic 3915
Phone: (03) 5979 4332

Warneet Bait and Tackle
Warneet Boat Ramp
Rutherford Pde
Warneet Vic 3980
Phone: (03) 5998 7163

CHAPTER 8

PORT PHILLIP BAY

Covering some 2000 square km, Port Phillip Bay is a huge expanse of water that is completely different from its neighbour Western Port, such a very short distance away. While Western Port has strong tidal flow throughout, Port Phillip has minimal flow, except near its entrance.

Port Phillip Bay is fed by ten tidal creeks and estuaries, the main one being the Yarra River, which is found at the top of the bay.

The bay's entrance is appropriately known as The Rip—it's less than 2 miles wide. The entire tidal flow for the expanse of the bay must enter and exit through here—and it does so at an amazing rate.

With such volumes of water coming through the entrance it creates large pressure waves that make The Rip one of the most dangerous pieces of water in the world. There are deceptive exceptions when The Rip is dead flat and easy to pass through, but on a strong run out tide and a big southerly swell or wind it becomes extremely treacherous, and it has claimed many water craft over the years including big ships. But as well as being so dangerous, the strong tides and turbulent water of The Rip are also the 'lifeline' that feeds the bay with clean ocean water and large numbers of fish.

While The Rip may be off-putting for newcomers, with proper care and preparation, fishing it on a slack tide or when the wind and tide are going the same way can offer some fantastic fishing—especially for salmon and large kingfish. The Rip also enables anglers to get out into Bass Strait where they can find good numbers of snapper and gummy shark, and also gamefish such as mako and thresher sharks.

Without doubt Port Phillip Bay is best known for the snapper that move into it each spring to feed and spawn. They come through The Rip in huge numbers before spilling out into various parts of the bay. While snapper are the prize fish on offer, there are plenty of other great species to be caught such as whiting, salmon, flathead, trevally, kingfish, squid and garfish.

The Australian Fishing Network's Fishing Map 1 Port Phillip Bay covers all boat fishing marks in detail and is a highly recommended source of information.

Nepean Bay

This is a sheltered bay on the inside of Point Nepean, much of which is now inside Port Phillip Heads Marine National Park where fishing is prohibited—contact Parks Victoria for details of the park boundaries. Nepean Bay was a noted spot for huge whiting but many of the best areas are now in the park and can no longer be fished. However, there are still some good locations in the deeper water that lies just along the outside edge of the park. Salmon are targeted by means of trolling and deep diving lures work exceptionally well. When the salmon are busting on the surface, soft plastics and metal slugs can be cast into them.

From September until November large spawning calamari can be found in this area. Although calamari can be caught throughout the year, the spawners can be in excess of three kilograms. Artificial jigs and baited prongs are the most effective techniques used.

This location can also produce some memorable whiting fishing. Fishing two hours either side of a tide change is very productive with some very large fish caught. A paternoster rig works best.

About 600 m out from the end of the stone wall in front of the power lines is a good spot to catch yellowtail kingfish. Most boats anchor up and let their baits or lures work in the tide behind the boat. The ebb tide is considered best.

If you anchor out much further than this, you are likely to be booked by the Port Authority for anchoring in the rather liberally defined shipping lanes. If you go no further out than 12 m of water, you should be safe.

When the kingfish are feeding on the surface on squid or garfish, as they frequently can be seen doing in this area, it is possible to cast lures to them with the expectation of getting a strike—Cotton Cordell poppers are effective but anything in the 100 to 120 mm length range will work

BOAT RAMPS

LOCATION	BOAT SIZE	PARKING	BUILD
Queenscliff	7 m	Excellent	Concrete
Swan Bay	4 m	Average	Concrete
St Leonards	6 m	Good	Concrete
Indented Head	6 m	Excellent	Concrete
Point Richards	4 m	Good	Concrete
Portarlington, Fairfax Street	5 m	Good	Concrete
Portarlington, Boat Avenue	5 m	Good	Concrete
Portarlington, Point Richards Road	5 m	Good	Concrete
Clifton Springs	4 m	Poor	Concrete
Limeburners Point	7 m	Good	Concrete
St Helens	6 m	Average	Concrete
Geelong Grammar School	5 m	Poor	Concrete
Avalon Beach	4 m	Poor	Concrete
Kirk Point	6 m	Poor	Concrete
Werribee River	7 m	Excellent	Concrete
Altona	7 m	Excellent	Concrete
Williamstown — Newport	5.5 m	Excellent	Concrete
The Warmies	7 m	Excellent	Concrete
St Kilda Marina	8 m	Excellent	Concrete
Brighton	5 m	Excellent	Concrete
Black Rock	5 m	Good	Concrete
Mordialloc, Beach Road	5 m	Average	Concrete
Mordialloc, Governor Road	6 m	Very good	Concrete
Patterson River	8 m	Excellent	Concrete
Kananook Creek	6 m	Excellent	Concrete
Olivers Hill	5 m	Very good	Concrete
Mornington, Schnapper Point	7 m	Good	Concrete
Mornington	5 m	Average	Concrete
Fishermans Beach	4 m	Average	Concrete
Martha Cove	8 m	Excellent	Concrete
Safety Beach	5 m	Average	Concrete
Anthony's Nose	5 m	Average	Concrete
Tootgarook	4 m	Average	Concrete
Rye, Leonard Street	4 m	Average	Concrete
Rye Pier	5.5 m	Very good	Concrete

Ticonderoga Bay

The ruins of the old Portsea cattle jetty are on the rounded, sandy headland that divides Nepean Bay from Ticonderoga Bay.

Good numbers of arrow squid can be taken from this area using squid jigs or baited jigs and for the best results try fishing there before dawn or just after dark. This is also a favoured spot for anglers who chase yellowtail kingfish, both for catching bait and fishing nearby. A good indicator of the presence of kingfish is the abundance of arrow squid on offer—if there are plenty then it's a fair bet the kingfish will be nearby. The prime months for kingfish are from Mid-January throughout mid-April. Live baiting is the preferred method used for kings. Live baits should be rigged carefully and placed on either an extended paternoster rig or a kingfish sinker rig and trolled around the area.

The wreck of the Eliza Ramsden is about halfway between Portsea and Queenscliff along the line-up of the outermost point of the Point Lonsdale headland with the back slope of the Barwon Heads Bluff. You can't anchor here, but a lot of yellowtail kingfish have been caught on the troll just as the tide eases off—particularly the ebb tide. Lead lines baited with fresh squid are favoured for catching kingfish here. You will see the other boats trolling around in circles if the kingfish are on the bite. It's also always worth having a heavy spin or overhead setup ready with a large popper as often the kingfish will push bait to the surface turning the water to foam as they feed. This can happen at any time but usually early morning or late in the afternoon is best. Don't underestimate a soft plastic either, if the fish are on the surface, unleash a softie and hold on.

Portsea to Sorrento

Good fishing can be found all along this part of the coastline, and conveniently, most of the best fishing can be found within 500 m of the shoreline so it is accessible to smaller boats. For land based anglers there is some great fishing on offer at Portsea Pier.

From the pier—calamari, whiting and salmon are a viable option throughout the year but it is the winter calamari fishery that is impressive. During the warmer months, snapper can be caught from the end of the pier. Garfish are also in abundance year round. Garfish will be in greater numbers during the flood tide on dawn. Berley is essential with a float setup required. The best location to catch them is from the first landing on the eastern side of the pier.

When fishing for calamari, set a baited jig or two under floats then cast size 3.0 artificial jigs about the weed beds.

In the boat, anglers should work over the broken reef and weed that abounds here; drifting is the preferred method used to catch calamari. Some of the most productive area is just out from Pt Franklin in 5 m of water. While numbers of fish may be better during the summer months, it is the winter that seems to produce the big whiting and some huge squid for patient anglers, especially late winter. For best results fish the tide changes, when the water isn't flowing as hard. The sand holes out from Point Franklin are very productive for whiting. The ebb tide fishes best for them.

Sorrento

At the ferry pier, anglers catch good numbers of whiting and squid on a regular basis, while occasionally schools of salmon or trevally come past the pier, giving anglers some great sport on the light gear being used for whiting.

For the angler who wants to catch big fish, it's worth noting that over the past few years there have been good reports of kingfish coming from this area, so it would certainly be worth trying a live squid or garfish under a float. You will have to be on your game due to the boat traffic but it is worth the effort. Calamari can also be caught from the pier although the current does rip through the area so running your jigs above a sinker helps. Boat anglers can drift the edge of the Sorrento channel for calamari. Look for the weed beds and work these with artificial jigs. Drifting in the channel is also productive for flathead when using paternoster rigs.

Sorrento Boat Ramp Rocks

At the Sorrento Boat Ramp, a man made rock wall juts out. Anglers fishing from there can catch calamari, salmon, silver trevally and garfish. Anglers must be careful of boat traffic at all times.

Kayak anglers can launch from the beach and paddle out to the moorings. Calamari and garfish are the main targets and are plentiful.

Blairgowrie

Through the summer months, anglers who wade the shallows and cast lures towards some of the deeper drop-offs catch some great flathead, and while you may not get lots the reward is certainly there in the size of the fish. Other options include good whiting in the general area—just look for broken weed and reef. Squid like the same terrain.

In a strong westerly blow, salmon push right into the shoreline. Anglers armed with metal slugs generally pull some quality fish up the sand when casting off the beach on the southern side where the water depths drops to around 3 meters.

From the marina jetty, fishing is only allowed on the northern side. Garfish, salmon, and calamari are most commonly caught. Berley is essential for garfish and they are usually in quite good numbers.

The edge of the shipping channel also offers some fantastic fishing for snapper early in the season as they move into the bay to spawn. As the tide flows quite fast here it is best fished with a Western Port style rig—see Western Port chapter.

While the snapper are fantastic, over the past few years anglers have come to realise the excellent autumn and winter gummy shark fishing on offer in the same area. Many of these fish are over 20 kg and provide great sport, and in between the monsters are numbers of smaller 4 to 10 kg specimens. The latter are best taken for food, while releasing the large ones to breed.

Once again, if fishing in the vicinity of the shipping channel make sure you anchor outside the actual shipping lane, or you will be quickly fined by the Port Authority. Try to reframe from using berley in this case as you will also attract sting rays and other unwanted fish species. Stick to using good fresh baits such as calamari, salmon fillet and trevally fillet.

Rye

Capel Sound is a large basin at the end of the Sorrento Channel and the nearby south channel and is a known snapper spot especially in October and then in April, although big fish are often taken here year round.

While the edge of the south channel produces good gummies and snapper as per Blairgowrie, it does also produce good whiting fishing in the nearby shallow waters, and often there are also great numbers of squid and big garfish to be found in the same areas. Drifting through Capel Sound can lead to some great catches of flathead, some of which are of exceptional size. A paternoster rig running along the bottom is highly effective.

If you're into snorkelling and or diving, scallops can be gathered from the sea bed in3 to 4m of water seems to be favoured and worth the effort for a tasty treat.

Where the Rye channel meets the main sipping channel, fishing the edge of the bank for gummy sharks is productive throughout the year. Snapper are also a possible catch during spring.

Rosebud

Lots of shallow water with good patches of broken bottom abounds off Rosebud. In these locations, which are usually in less than 7 m of water, there are some great whiting to be caught in summer months.

This area is also good for flounder spearing as the fish move into the shallow water under the cover of darkness. The pier sits in mainly shallow water but does drop-off towards the latter stages. Squid, garfish and flathead can be caught here and somewhat surprisingly, bronze whalers from the end of the pier.

LEFT: A Port Phillip Bay snapper.

Below: Port Phillip snapper.

DROMANA TO SAFETY BEACH

Flathead to 2 kg can be found close inshore here, with extensive snapper and whiting grounds. It's also an excellent area for flounder spearing as it is sheltered from prevailing southerly winds. The piers at both Dromana and Safety Beach are popular for garfish.

During the warm balmy summer evenings, fishing from the beach adjacent to the Safety Beach boat ramp is productive for whiting. A paternoster rig with pipi baits works best. At certain times of the year, bream have also been caught from the pier while on route to Martha Cove (Fishing in Martha Cove is prohibited).

MOUNT MARTHA TO MORNINGTON

This whole stretch of coastline enables anglers to get to deep water quite close to shore, and along with this the rocky foreshore provides great food and cover for a range of species from squid and whiting to large snapper. There is plenty of weed growth on the rock which provides calamari with plenty of areas to hide. Anglers wishing to catch them can do so by casting artificial jigs into these areas. Whiting are also in abundance especially around the Mount Martha mussel farm and the beginning of the Mount Martha cliffs. During snapper season some great fishing can be had by anchoring close to shore in anything from 5 to 10 m of water, especially in areas of broken reef, and the best time for this is definitely during or just after a strong blow from the west. Snook are in quite good numbers and are caught when trolling small diving minnows along the edge of the rocks. This area is also popular for salmon which often round up bait and bust the surface.

The newly opened Martha Cove Marina enables anglers to launch safely in close proximity to the great fishing on offer. (Before the marina opened the only launching facility was a ramp on Safety Beach that was very exposed to weather from the north and west.)

MOUNT MARTHA ROCKS

Possibly one of the best land based spots on this side of Port Phillip Bay, the rocks at Mount Martha drop into deep water directly at your feet, while a good cast will see baits landing in 7 to 9 m of water. While quite exposed to any wind from the south-west, west, and anything from the north, it is these rough conditions that bring snapper close to shore for land based anglers to target. Other species on offer include squid, garfish, flathead, salmon and over the past few summers there have been good reports of kingfish from this area. Access to the best area is below Hearn Road. Here you'll catch whiting, garfish and snapper. Garfish can be caught using a float setup, whiting a paternoster rig and snapper a running sinker rig.

Large snapper are also caught when strong westerlies and south westerly winds are blowing. Fish to 9 kilos are caught by those dedicated enough to put in the time and effort.

BALCOMBE CREEK

North of Bay Road Mount Martha, Balcombe Creek is popular with family groups fishing for mullet. While the creek is usually closed to the sea it does hold a good population of big bream although the weedy bottom makes bait fishing in the deeper holes difficult. It is however perfect for anglers who like to use lures for bream and some great fish are often taken with this method. Bait fishing is also effective with peeled prawns under a float working very well. Try fishing under the road bridge near the pylons or up the system behind the footy oval.

NUNNS WALK

At the bottom of the cliff below Strachans Road in Mornington, Nunns Walk is well worth fishing for snapper during the warmer months of the year. The water is deep, but a submerged ledge in front of the platform can cost anglers a lot in tackle losses.

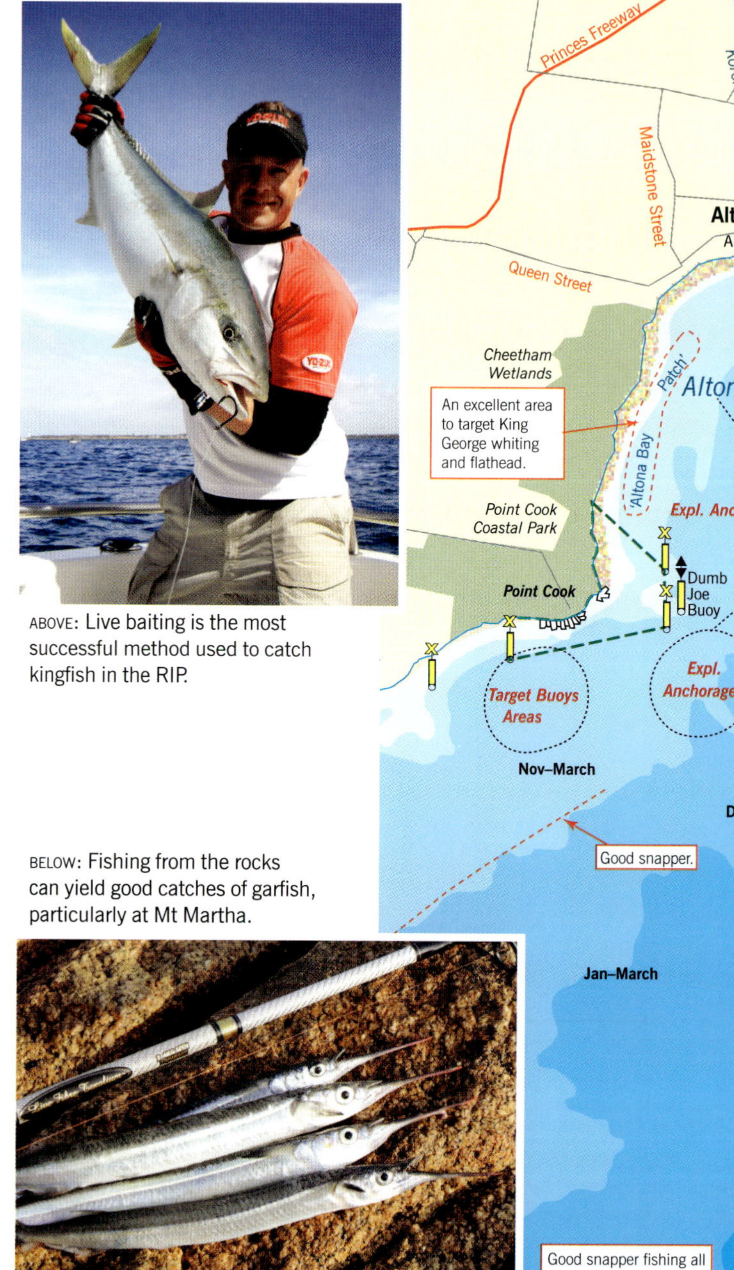

ABOVE: Live baiting is the most successful method used to catch kingfish in the RIP.

BELOW: Fishing from the rocks can yield good catches of garfish, particularly at Mt Martha.

ABOVE: Port Phillip Bay snapper.

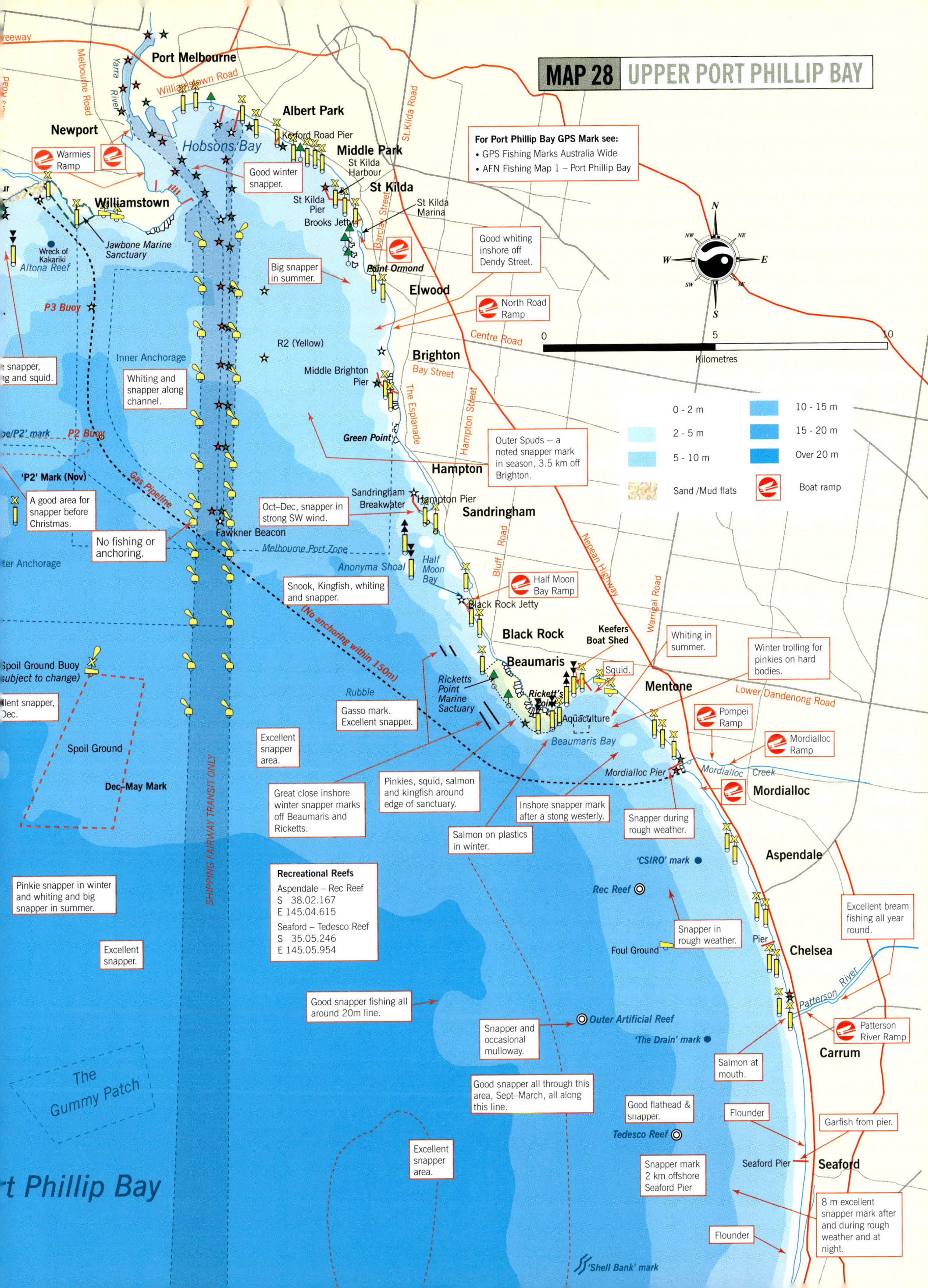

MAP 28 UPPER PORT PHILLIP BAY
For Port Phillip Bay GPS Mark see:
• GPS Fishing Marks Australia Wide
• AFN Fishing Map 1 – Port Phillip Bay
Port Melbourne
Williamstown Road
Melbourne Road
Yarra River
Newport
Albert Park
Kerford Road Pier
Middle Park
Hobsons Bay
Warmies Ramp
Good winter snapper.
St Kilda Harbour
St Kilda
St Kilda Pier
St Kilda Marina
Brooks Jetty
Williamstown
Jawbone Marine Sanctuary
Wreck of Kakariki
Altona Reef
Barclay Street
St Kilda Road
Point Ormond
Good whiting inshore off Dendy Street.
Big snapper in summer.
Elwood
North Road Ramp
P3 Buoy
Centre Road
R2 (Yellow)
Brighton
Bay Street
Middle Brighton Pier
Inner Anchorage
Whiting and snapper along channel.
The Esplanade
Hampton Street
Green Point
P2 Buoy
'P2' Mark (Nov)
Outer Spuds -- a noted snapper mark in season, 3.5 km off Brighton.
Hampton
A good area for snapper before Christmas.
Gas Pipeline
Sandringham Breakwater
Hampton Pier
Oct–Dec, snapper in strong SW wind.
Sandringham
Fawkner Beacon
No fishing or anchoring.
Melbourne Port Zone
Anonyma Shoal
Half Moon Bay
Bluff Road
Nepean Highway
Half Moon Bay Ramp
Snook, Kingfish, whiting and snapper.
Black Rock Jetty
(No anchoring within 150m)
Black Rock
Keefers Boat Shed
Warrigal Road
Whiting in summer.
Winter trolling for pinkies on hard bodies.
Spoil Ground Buoy (subject to change)
Beaumaris
Squid.
Ricketts Point Marine Sactuary
Rickett's Point
Mentone
Lower Dandenong Road
Rubble
Gasso mark. Excellent snapper.
Aquaculture
Pompei Ramp
Spoil Ground
Excellent snapper area.
Beaumaris Bay
Mordialloc Ramp
Dec-May Mark
Mordialloc Pier
Mordialloc Creek
Great close inshore winter snapper marks off Beaumaris and Ricketts.
Pinkies, squid, salmon and kingfish around edge of sanctuary.
Inshore snapper mark after a stong westerly.
Snapper during rough weather.
Mordialloc
Salmon on plastics in winter.
SHIPPING FAIRWAY TRANSIT ONLY
Recreational Reefs
Aspendale – Rec Reef
S 38.02.167
E 145.04.615
Seaford – Tedesco Reef
S 35.05.246
E 145.05.954
'CSIRO' mark
Aspendale
Pinkie snapper in winter and whiting and big snapper in summer.
Rec Reef
Excellent bream fishing all year round.
Snapper in rough weather.
Pier
Chelsea
Foul Ground
Excellent snapper.
Patterson River
Good snapper fishing all around 20m line.
Outer Artificial Reef
Snapper and occasional mulloway.
Patterson River Ramp
'The Drain' mark
Carrum
Salmon at mouth.
The Gummy Patch
Good snapper all through this area, Sept–March, all along this line.
Good flathead & snapper.
Flounder
Garfish from pier.
Tedesco Reef
Excellent snapper area.
Seaford Pier
Seaford
Port Phillip Bay
Snapper mark 2 km offshore Seaford Pier
8 m excellent snapper mark after and during rough weather and at night.
Flounder
'Shell Bank' mark
0
5
10
Kilometres
0 - 2 m
2 - 5 m
5 - 10 m
10 - 15 m
15 - 20 m
Over 20 m
Sand /Mud flats
Boat ramp

It is also a great spot for squid and thinking anglers are quick to catch a few of these and use them for fresh snapper bait.

Fishermans Beach

Though there is a boat ramp at Fishermans Beach, it is best to only launch boats 4 m and under. Kayak fishing is very productive out from here. There is a Keep West Cardinal marker just out from the boat ramp signalling shallow reef, this are worth casting artificial jigs at as is always produces calamari. Either side of Fishermans Beach there is plenty of weedy areas to fish for calamari. Whiting are also taken in the sand holes with berley a must.

Land Based anglers can fish off the rocks to the east for calamari usually in abundance throughout the year, but often small in size.

Mornington Pier

Mornington Pier is one of the most popular piers within Port Phillip Bay. On any given day you can see anglers chasing garfish, salmon, pike, barracouta, flathead, whiting, and snapper.

In rough weather when the wind is from the north-east and hard enough to drench you with spray, snapper come on the bite to reward the stoic angler. One of the great things about this location is that it has something for everyone. There are squid that can be caught all year round, garfish and whiting, while a larger bait can catch anything from flathead to big snapper and even kingfish, which have become common over the summer months as they patrol the pier terrorising baitfish. Those fishing for snapper do so from the rock wall at the beginning of the pier.

The jetty to the right of the pier is a great location to catch whiting and squid in the summer months. Night time fishing is preferred as there is less boat traffic around to spook them. Storm damage saw the pier close for a period of time. It is now open and fishing as good as it ever was yet is only half the original length.

Whiting fishing is also very popular from the pier, particularly for calamari and whiting. Whiting can be caught from off the rock wall with a paternoster rig and size 6 long shank hooks, fresh calamari strips are the top bait.

Canadian Bay to Olivers Hill

This stretch of coast contains mostly a sandy bottom with broken reef and weed beds that are scattered throughout the area. This attracts numbers of calamari during winter. Around 3-5m in depth for the most part, boat and kayak anglers can access it simply. Due to the size of the calamari being somewhat smaller in size compared to the ones caught ant Sorrento and Portsea, smaller jigs in the 2.0 and 2.5 sizes are best offered.

Salmon and garfish are also frequently caught throughout the year. Salmon can be found by locating the birds which can be seen when dive bombing the water's surface. When this occurs, anglers are best to sneak in quietly and bombard the mayhem with soft plastics and metal slugs. Garfish are abundant throughout the area but do require berley to be lured into one specific location. Once concentrated into a berley trail, a float setup with silverfish offered as bait works well.

Frankston Pier

Like the Mornington Pier, this pier produces good catches of garfish from time to time. As with many of the piers the best fishing is found in rough weather for the keen angler who is willing to brave the wet and cold.

Fishing from the pier in strong south and south-westerly winds often produces big salmon action as they move into the shallow water to feed. In these conditions they can be taken on lures and bait—the best spot for them appears to be about half way along the pier. A good berley trail is sure to bring them into casting range. Often an unweighted pilchard fillet sinking with the berley is effective.

Fishing at the end of the pier in rough weather at night during October and November sometimes results in big snapper getting caught. Flathead are also a viable catch for the patient angler.

Frankston Wide

Out from Frankston, snapper fishing is very popular amongst anglers from September until January. The Wreck of Perseverance is a popular mark just out from the pier. Snapper hold up around the wreck and bite well in a westerly blow. A hooked fish will try to run back to the reef so be ready or you'll become busted off.

The best method is to anchor within casting range of the wreck and use berley to encourage the fish to move off the reef and into your trail.

Further out off Frankston, a location known as the Hospital is particularly popular through summer. Getting its name because of the visual hospital roof that can be seen while on the bay. This location can vary between anglers but is mainly in 17 m of water.

GPS co-ordinates are a good guide of where to find snapper, but it pays to watch your fish finder and locate your own patch of fish.

Kananook Creek

Running into Port Phillip Bay at Frankston, Kananook Creek is accessible from Gould Street after leaving the Nepean Highway and crossing the Mile Bridge. The creek offers mullet, bream and occasionally something surprising like a red mullet or flathead. Though bream are the main target, fish for them using unweighted prawn segments or small piece of sand worm fished under a float. There is an excellent multi-lane boat ramp within the creek—although the creek entrance is often shallow as a sandbar always builds up, so care needs to be taken entering the bay, especially if it is rough.

Seaford to Carrum

Definitely one of the better known big snapper areas in this part of the bay, the water ranges from 8 to 11 m around Seaford Pier and is known as Mile Bridge. The bottom here is scattered with mussel and scallop beds, along with reef and is a favoured snapper haunt, especially after a few days of strong winds from the south or west.

Aside from this area there are great snapper grounds to be found all the way through Carrum, Chelsea, Edithvale and Aspendale, with plenty of good snapper ground to be found in water that ranges anywhere from 8 to 20 m in depth.

Through these areas the majority of bottom is made up of mud interspersed with mussels and scallops, along with natural and manmade reefs. Snapper respond well to a cube trail of berley.

Fishing from the Seaford Pier is particularly good for flathead and garfish. Floundering is also popular during calm nights in summer.

Patterson River

Home of one of the busiest and best boat ramps on the bay, Patterson River also produces some great fishing for bream using bait and especially lures. Inside the system bream can be found hiding under the numerous moored boats, jetties and along the rock walls. Casting at the road bridge pylons is also effective. There is also a healthy population of estuary perch that tend to be caught after heavy rain under the train bridge on lures. Mullet are found throughout the whole system, along with decent numbers of mulloway during spring and summer. Each season several mulloway are taken by accident on baits and light line while fishing for bream, giving the lucky angler the thrill of a lifetime. Fishing for them usually occurs around the lead up to a full moon. Walking the bank edges casting and retrieving 100 mm diving hard body lures is very successful. At certain times of the year, calamari can be caught under the train bridge. A small reef on the south side bank is where they congregate.

Other species are occasionally caught such as big pinky snapper, and at times schools of salmon will invade the mouth area. During the winter months when the rock groynes are batted with strong winds, casting metal slugs for salmon is very productive. Cast in a northerly direction with a 15 g–25 g lure for best results.

Chelsea

Just out to the left of the Patterson River, Chelsea supports a good population of snapper in the warmer months. One of the most popular locations to fish is in 13 m of water where the bottom has an extensive covering of cunje. This is what holds snapper in the area. The most productive fishing is first light. Popular baits for snapper include pilchards and silver whiting. This area gets a lot of attention when the wind is blowing from the north. During these times, it is quite sheltered and some big fish are caught. However, by November, this location gets infiltrated by smaller pinkies often referred to as "piranhas" for good reason. Providing you can continually check and replenish your baits while keeping a good berley trail going, a big fish will be taken.

Mordialloc

A great place to fish in safe surroundings, the creek offers good fishing for mullet—just look for the local anglers and watch how they fish, if you do the same you too will catch them.

There are good numbers of bream in the creek and some of them can be huge. However they aren't easy to catch as they hide in amongst the moored boats and only seem to eat tiny crustaceans off the hulls.

Out on the pier there can be good squid over the broken bottom on the north side. This bottom also holds good whiting through the summer months, especially late in the evening. Aside from the squid and whiting being the main targeted species from the pier, mullet and garfish are also a viable option. Both can be caught in good numbers with the use of a float and berley—again, watch how and where the locals fish.

On the end of the pier a larger bait will see anglers in with a chance of catching a decent salmon or flathead, while fishing here at night or in rough weather sees good numbers of pinky snapper through winter and some big snapper on offer during spring and autumn. Big silver trevally are also a common catch. Pipi baits fished on paternoster rigs is an effective method.

Beaumaris Bay

A very productive fishing area, the pier itself which lies in front of the Beaumaris Motor Yacht Squadron is a noted squid spot, while a bait cast out from the pier can catch anything from small to large snapper, whiting and flathead. Snapper are the main target species especially in the right weather. Dawn and dusk are popular times to catch them with fresh baits best offered.

Boat fishing around the mussel farms can produce good whiting, while during rough south-westerly weather; the back of the mussel farms can produce big snapper in October and November, and pinkies in winter.

For the area as a whole, trolling or casting with lures through the summer months can see great action on salmon and the occasional kingfish, while the cooler months produce good numbers of smaller pinky snapper, barracouta and snook that love to eat lures and baits. Kayak fishing is becoming very popular in this area due to its proximity to car parking. Salmon fishing is particularly the prime species for anglers flicking lures.

Beaumaris

Decent land based options in Beaumaris Bay are now limited to the pier at the yacht club and the scout hall pier. Although the bottom here is very shallow and rough resulting in lots of lost tackle, casting into the sand holes nearby does produce good whiting.

Big snapper to 5 kilos are regularly targeted and caught during spring. The prime time is a strong south westerly wind from the yacht club pier. Fishing from the Scout Hall Jetty is where you'll catch a lot of calamari and red mullet on soft plastics.

Unfortunately the best locations such as Table Rock are now in a marine park that stretches from the scout hall pier to just near Fourth Street down towards Black Rock. The marine park is clearly marked with yellow buoys and signs.

Rickets Point

Fishing outside of the marine park in this area by boat offers some great fishing for a range of species. The most commonly targeted fish are the smaller pinky snapper, which are found in huge numbers through the cooler months as they live and feed on the extensive reef in the area. The reef from Rickets Point to past Black Rock is also great for catching red mullet. These are a small red fish with loose scales that are great eating, and they're becoming far more common captures for anglers who fish with soft plastic lures.

During spring and summer there are some big snapper to be taken here at night in the shallow water, especially if it is rough, while there are great snapper grounds out in deeper water off Ricketts Point such as the famous 'Gasso' mark.

Other common but seasonal species to be found along here include whiting, salmon, flathead, squid, snook and increasing numbers of kingfish. Probably the most surprising thing about all these species is that they can all be readily caught on lures, especially soft plastics. Live baiting also works well with garfish a prime bait. Ideally, targeting garfish with a berley trail then live baiting one under a float does the trick.

Trolling lures for snapper has become a popular affair and is very productive. Lures such as Tilsan Barra's, Yo-Zuri Crystal Minnows and Duel Hardcore Minnows are proving to yield the goods. While a lot of pinkie snapper are caught, fish to 4 kg are a common catch on first light in season. Other species caught while trolling include salmon, pike, silver trevally and barracouta.

Quiet Corner

Making sure you are outside of the marine park the reef before fishing here. It's a known area for pinky snapper and good whiting on first and last light as the fish move into the shallows to feed.

Half Moon Bay

This bay has a small but decent ramp suited to smaller boats. Care is needed as it is quite exposed in winds from the north and west.

The grounds off here take anglers to similar water and the same sorts of species that are found up at Ricketts Point, as there is an extensive reef system that is all along this part of the coast line.

Fishing from the pier itself or the carpark at Half Moon Bay produces squid, whiting and pinky snapper on evening, while in rough weather in October and November some big snapper can also be taken by land based anglers.

Heading north towards Sandringham Harbour there are excellent whiting and pinky grounds on a shallow reef called Yorkies, it lies in about 4 to 7 m of water and is a favoured location for many local anglers.

Wide of here you will see a pair of cardinal markers indicating another reef called the Anonyma Shoal. This is a favoured location for anglers who troll for snook, although it does also produce great pinky fishing during winter, while the summer months can find big whiting along the edge of the reef. While berleying for the whiting you will normally also find good numbers of garfish and this also helps to attract the rat kingfish that often inhabit the area.

Surprisingly the reef doesn't seem to produce big snapper in season, which seems strange as it is such great reef, rising out of close to 10 m of water nearby.

Sandringham Harbour

The pier and other structures at Sandringham Harbour provide excellent fishing platforms.

Fishing along the break wall and berleying the inside where the boats are moored produces good mullet and bream, while fishing the outside in weather rough enough to send waves and spray over the wall produces some very big snapper for the dedicated angler.

Fishing at the end of the rock wall at first and last light produces good numbers of garfish and pinky snapper. If you leave your bait on the bottom long enough, flathead can also be caught and their size is quite impressive.

GREEN POINT

While known as Green Point this area also includes the rock groynes near Sandringham through to Brighton Break wall, all of which can produce great land based fishing for a range of species including garfish, squid and snapper.

Boat anglers also do extremely well fishing out of the rock groynes in an area called the Gully, which is well known for big snapper in rough weather and at night. The area also does produce good whiting and plenty of garfish all along the broken ground.

MIDDLE BRIGHTON PIER

This pier is popular with anglers and has produced some good snapper catches over the years, particularly during late spring. Garfish are also an option and are taken on a float setup. Silverfish is best offered. If you're after calamari, the best place to try is just beyond the sea baths on the left hand side of the pier. Use a small quill style float and number 12 Mustad 4540 ½ hook.

BRIGHTON TO ST KILDA

Good fishing for snapper and whiting. In 8 to 15 m of water there are extensive cunjevoi beds where snapper is found over summer. It is also a noted stretch of coastline for garfish and good catches of whiting.

Drifting in the deeper water will produce flathead though you will have to sift through the smaller models to get a good feed.

ELWOOD DRAIN

A great area to chase snapper at night, the waters not far offshore from here have extensive cunjevoi and mussel beds that the snapper move onto under the cover of darkness. Fishing here in as little as 4 m of water late at night can produce memorable fishing as the snapper are often big and hit very hard and fast. The rough bottom is the only downside as it is hard on tackle and occasionally aids fish to escape if the line is cut. Fishing in shallow water requires anglers to be silent. After anchoring and setting the berley trail, refrain from making any noise at all or you might spook any fish in the area.

ST KILDA

St Kilda Pier is not renowned for its fishing, however the break wall is home to a dedicate bunch of anglers who fish for snapper during late spring and early summer.

But the pier can have its moments, especially if large schools of trevally or garfish move into the area. Numbers of big kingfish have been found cruising along its length over the past few summers. Kingfish respond well to live baits but lure fishing is also effective.

There are plenty of good sized flathead regularly caught from the pier but you do have to sift throughout the smaller ones. A running sinker rig with blue bait or white bait offered works well.

It usually pays to get the latest on this pier from a local tackle store before heading down.

KERFORD ROAD JETTY

This jetty is very popular with anglers who catch a wide variety of fish including garfish, flathead, salmon, barracouta and occasionally snapper. When the fish are biting the jetty will be crowded. Get there early to gain a spot.

LAGOON PIER

Similar fishing and the same species are to be found as at Kerford Road Pier, however Lagoon Pier does produce some very big snapper and exceptional mulloway for anglers who are prepared to put in the hours fishing at night with live or fresh baits.

STATION PIER

Access to Station Pier depends upon what ships are using the facility at the time. Fishing vertically next to the pylons produces the best results on silver trevally, mullet and a variety of other fish. Lines cast out from the pier can turn up snapper, flathead, or stingrays.

Another popular option these days is to cast small soft plastics along or back under the pier to catch some of the big bream and trevally that live in the shadows. Unweighted prawns also work well when allowed to slowly sink beneath the pylons. Although an effective fishing method, many fish are lost.

HOBSONS BAY

Again an excellent area in the cooler months when boat traffic is minimal. Many species including bream, snapper, barracouta and Australian salmon are taken on bait from an anchored boat in depths from 4 to 10 metres. Access to the bay is from the Warmies boat ramp. Good prospects for big snapper in August and September at night.

THE YARRA ESTUARY

The estuary of the Yarra River produces excellent fishing for bream and mullet for anglers using light lines and soft baits such as sandworm. Lure fishing is making a big impact here, but regulations are in place which restrict access to certain areas and it is suggested you check with Parks Victoria before fishing.

For the angler who dreams of catching a mulloway, you could do worse that putting time in around the Yarra River. The hours may be long, however the rewards are there for the angler who takes the time to catch and use small live mullet for bait. There is in fact a very good population of mulloway in the Yarra, many of which are over 20 kg in weight. Mulloway are also caught by lure anglers. Small soft plastics and or metal vibes work exceptionally well when worked around the bridge pylons.

Anglers fishing from Kayaks are a regular sight in the Yarra these days. You will notice many of them working around the wharves where the bream hide under. Casting small diving minnows, vibes and soft plastics works well.

THE WARMIES (THE HOTTIES)

This popular fishing destination is the outlet canal for warm water from the Newport Power Station. Access is from Douglas Parade or North Road in Newport. The variety of fish caught in the warm water canal is staggering. The list includes mullet, tailor, salmon, garfish, bream, mulloway, snapper, flathead and barracouta. Because of this fact, it is rare to find yourself the only angler fishing.

While there are always good fish to be caught here, the best fishing is when the warm water is pumping from the power station. Casting metal slugs works well for tailor and a little piece of wire above the lure will prevent being bitten off. Having caught a tailor or salmon, rig it up as a live bait and cast it out for a mulloway.

WARMIES BOAT RAMP

A recent addition to the Warmies has been the excellent two lane boat ramp. This boat ramp has all facilities including a fish cleaning table, boat wash area, enormous car and trailer parking area and billboards with current fishing regulations.

BREAKWATER PIER

The Williamstown Pier is popular with anglers because you can drive onto the breakwater section and fish from the comfort of your car.

Snapper are the main quarry sought and rough weather produces the best results, making car-based fishing more sensible.

KOROROIT CREEK

Although the Kororoit Creek looks an unlikely venue to find good fishing, there are good populations of mullet to be caught here and the occasional bream. Snapper have even been caught in Kororoit Creek, but this is by no means a regular occurrence. The best success comes to those using berley. Mullet respond well to a variety of baits but pips are by far the top favourite.

ALTONA BAY

This is a top location during October and November as large schools of big snapper often move into shallow water at night for weeks on end, and it can also produce the odd beauty in winter. However, for the most part the area produces good whiting in the shallow water as well as good pinky fishing. In being successful, anglers are best to set anchor and establish a berley trail. Pinky snapper will quickly move into the area and will take any baits on offer. Keep baits small, often just a half pilchard threaded onto a 3/0 or 4/0 size hook.

Altona Pier

Not regarded as a productive fishing platform, Altona Pier does produce whiting in the summer and the very occasional snapper. Small flathead are the most common capture when fishing bait on the bottom. Some big flathead reside in the area and are generally caught by anglers wading the shallows on the right of the pier. There are some very deep gutters throughout here where the flathead lie in wait of a meal. Soft plastics work exceptionally well. Garfish can be caught on small baits suspended under floats.

Altona Boat Ramp

There is an excellent boat ramp at Altona with all facilities giving access to many productive areas in Port Phillip Bay. Having exited the boat ramp, casting artificial jigs at the weed beds that run near them is popular for calamari.

Point Cook Jetty

The jetty at Campbell's Cove, Point Cook is now open to the public and may be reached from Laverton via Point Cook Road, or from Werribee South via Aviation Road. Fishing from the Point Cook Jetty is popular so it is advisable to be early on weekends to gain a spot. Flathead, whiting and snapper may be taken by anglers casting out from the pier while those fishing down by the pylons will take leatherjackets, silver trevally and mullet.

Point Cook

Point Cook is one of the most popular and well-known locations for whiting. Fishing in 2 to 5 m of water is the prime area with berley essential. At times some good flathead are also caught.

Campbells Cove

Notable for whiting in less than 5m, and also flounder and flathead in the shallows at night. There are some excellent snapper marks in 10 to 20 m of water.

Werribee River

Access to the east side of the river is from Duncans Road to Werribee South, then north along Diggers Road. Upstream access to the Willows and the Barnacle Hole is from K Road. Access to the west side of the river is through the Board of Works farm for which you need a permit.

The Werribee River is renowned for its bream fishing, but surprisingly it can turn on some excellent whiting and mullet. At the entrance of the river, anglers can cast lures for bream alongside the boat hulls. Further up the system, work the weeded edges, rock walls and below the cliffs. The occasional mulloway have been caught in the river and although elusive are still worth targeting in the warmer months.

Werribee Offshore

Access out from the Werribee River is safe and should be made by adhering to the navigation lights. Most of the fishing is well out in 8 m of water. There are also some good snapper marks to the south in 4 m of water, which are best fished at night. A well-established cube berley trail will bring snapper to your area.

Flathead and whiting can be found from the shallows out to about 5 m depth. Drifting is the preferred method for flathead although when fishing for whiting at anchor, the odd flathead will take any bait offered.

Wedge Spit

A noted area in less than 5 m of water. Safest access is from the Werribee River. Whiting are mostly caught around here.

Kirk Point

There is a small boat ramp at Kirk Point and caution must be taken as it is very exposed to the wind and sea. To the north-east is Long Reef, a noted area for small snapper and squid. There are extensive whiting grounds, extending down to Point Wilson. Berley is a must.

Arthur the Great

This is a good area for a wide variety of fish including whiting, flathead and snapper. Whiting and flathead are often caught together in the sand holes. Using berley with enhance success.

Point Wilson

Some of the best fishing is near the pier, but boats must keep 200 m away. There are good snapper and whiting grounds all around the pier. Once again, use berley and success will be imminent.

Outer Harbour

There are very good snapper marks along both the Point Richards and Wilson Spit Channel. There are whiting to be caught on the north and south banks of the Outer Harbour. Setting anchor and a light train of mashed pilchards as berley works well.

Corio Bay

Most fishing in Corio Bay is done by boat, but there are jetties and some other land based spots where anglers may fish as well. The bottom of both the inner and outer harbours is substantially muddy with few features. Nevertheless, both areas sometimes produce good fishing for flathead and snapper. Whiting and garfish are regularly caught in the shallower seagrass areas close to shore.

Anglers in boats frequently fish in close proximity to various structures like channel beacons and wharves, which attract species like warehou (snotty trevalla), silver trevally and good size mullet. Snapper are sometimes taken in these areas as well.

Avalon Ramp

Avalon boat ramp is located near the fisherman's huts on Avalon Beach. There are toilets nearby but parking space is limited. The ramp gives access to good whiting grounds in the old north channel, which is marked by poles in the water almost straight out from the ramp.

Heading to the east, past Point Lillias, productive water for snapper is encountered shortly after rounding Bird Rock and altering course to the north-west so that Point Lillias is on your left hand side. On a cautionary note, there is no passage between Bird Rock and Point Lillias as a number of boating enthusiasts have found to their cost!

Point Lillias

Turning from the Princes Highway into Avalon Beach Road you will pass through a roundabout, and shortly after that, there is a left hand turn through a gate in the salt works fence leading to the tiny settlement of Avalon.

Park your car at the end of the fishing shacks and walk to the rocks from where you can cast into approximately 4 m of water. Flathead, snapper and gummy shark have all been taken here. The walk in takes from 15 to 20 minutes so pack light. The rocks can be slippery so be careful. When fishing from the shore, a paternoster rig containing two droppers works extremely well. Fish a half pilchard on a 4/0 suicide hook from the top dropper and a size 6 Mustad Demon Light Circle hook from the bottom dropper with a slither of calamari. This way you can target whiting and snapper at the same time.

Limeburners Bay

Known locally as the 'Grammar School Lagoon', Limeburners Bay is the Hovells Creek estuary, a tidal lagoon running to sea through a narrow entrance between the Point Abeona sand spit and the beach in front of the Geelong Grammar School. You may reach

Limeburners Bay by turning off the Princes Highway on School Road.

Once you could drive past the Grammar School to the beach. Access is now blocked so you have to detour right at the roundabout to reach the beach and small boat ramp via Foreshore Road.

The beach used to be popular with anglers who enjoyed fishing from their cars, but access has been blocked by a large log placed across the beach by the Geelong City Council.

Small salmon, whiting, bream, flathead and gummy shark are caught along here, along with the very occasional snapper. The first two hours of the incoming tide are most productive. The tide begins coming in here about two hours after low water at Port Phillip Heads. A cube berley trail works extremely well for snapper in this area.

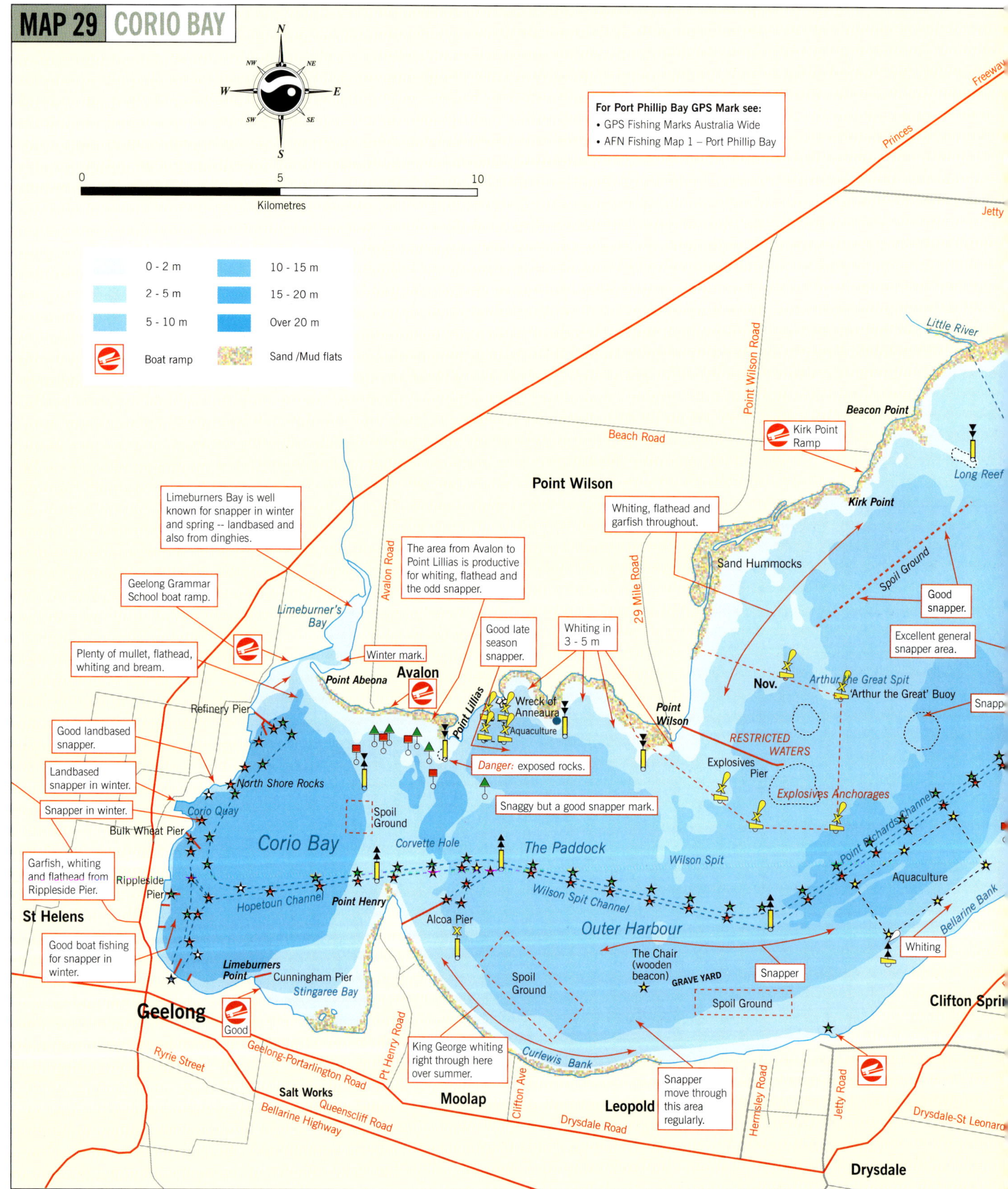

The small boat ramp on Foreshore Road, just before Biddlecombe Avenue, is suitable for small boats only. Though parking is limited, it is usually adequate.

POINT ABEONA

Until recently you could walk out to the end of the Point Abeona sand spit from the bottom of Avalon Beach Road. Unfortunately, the sand spit has now regressed to the point where only the tip emerges at the bottom of the tide, and then sometimes for only a couple of hours.

Should you have a small boat to cross the channel from the Grammar School side, it is worth fishing from the spit, even just for a couple of hours. This is because the first two hours of the rising tide is probably the best time to fish here regardless of what time of the day or night it occurs. Species to be caught here include small salmon, mullet, flathead, bream and the very occasional snapper.

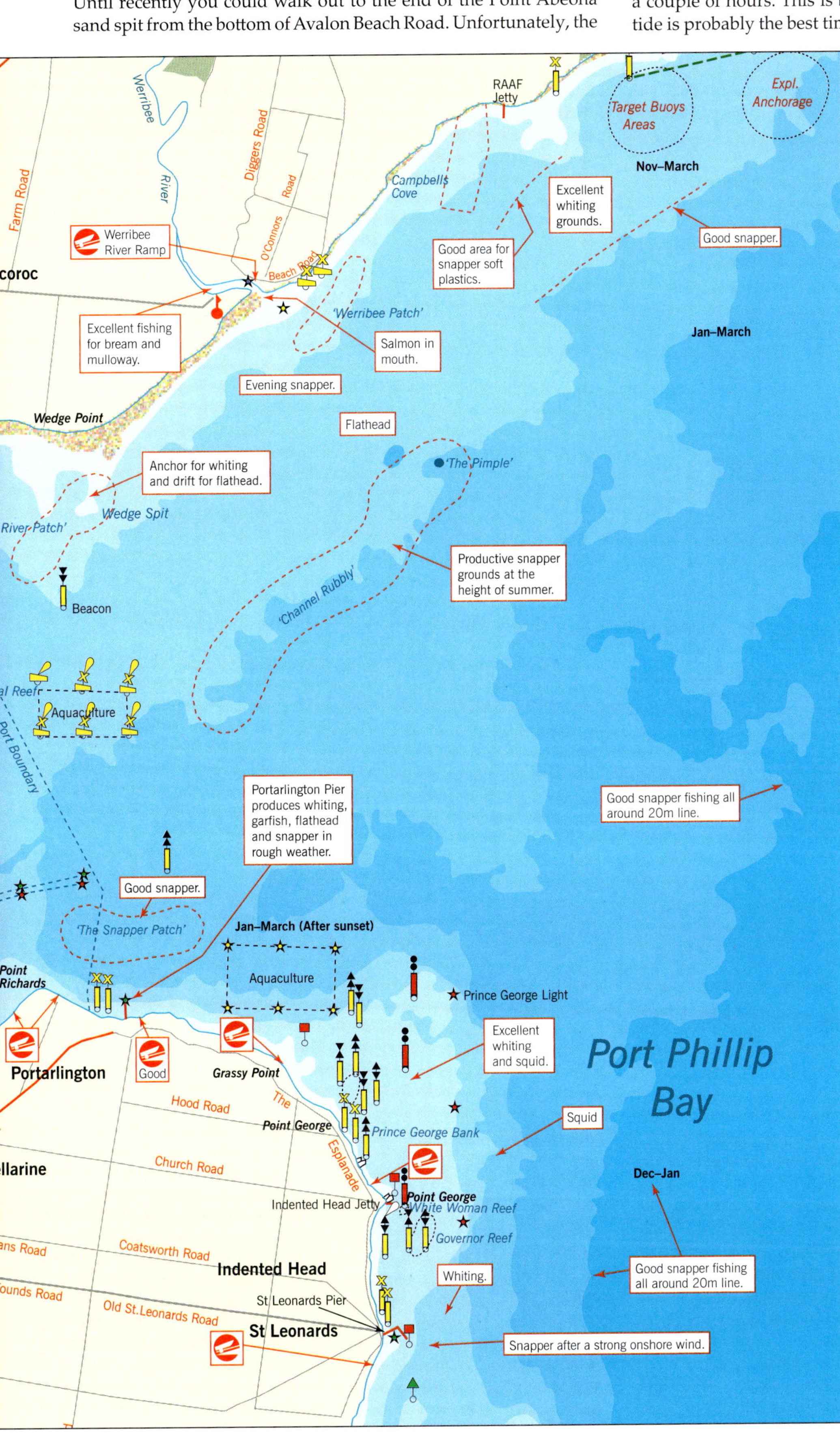

HOVELLS CREEK

Hovells Creek sometimes produces good size bream. Access is from the Princes Highway, Corio. Take the North Shore exit from the Princes Highway into Shell Parade then Cummins Road to the high ground overlooking the creek. While a variety of baits will work, prawns are best offered.

NORTH SHORE ROCKS

The North Shore Rocks are in the Geelong suburb of North Shore and extend from the Phosphate Company weighbridge to Moorpanyal Park. These rocks give the land based angler access to about 7 m of water with a decent cast.

The platform below the weighbridge is fishable on all tides, but you can only fish from the other rocks—those around to the right—when the tide is out. Once you could drive your car down the track below the Phosphate weighbridge. In fact you may still be able to sometimes, but the track has deteriorated.

Grass whiting (stranger) may be caught from the rocks using sandworms and pipi's for bait while large King George whiting often give the angler a pleasant surprise. A running sinker rig or paternoster rig with either size 6 long shank hook or a size 6 circle hook works well. Casting out with large baits like pilchards will occasionally tempt a snapper, but small flathead are a nuisance. Lure casting enthusiasts sometimes take large snook here at dawn and dusk in spring. Good size bream, and the occasional large luderick have also been caught here by anglers who know their trade.

ST HELENS

This two lane boat launching facility at the bottom of Swinburne Street in North Geelong has adequate parking, boat washing facilities and toilets. There is a KFC on the corner of Swinburne Street and the Highway.

St Helens ramp is arguably the most popular ramp on the Corio Bay inner harbour, providing sheltered access to reasonably good fishing for flathead and whiting within a few hundred metres.

St Helens is also a popular spot for land based anglers who fish from the reclaimed land and adjacent jetties for a variety of fish including snapper and flathead. Sandworms fished close in may produce a bream or two but leatherjackets and small whiting are more common.

Rippleside Jetty

Rippleside Jetty is reached by turning off the Princes Highway at Bell Parade, Drumcondra, then into Rippleside Park to the left from where it is a short walk to the jetty.

Good catches of King George whiting and garfish are made here on light tackle at times, while a large bait cast right out will occasionally tempt a nice flathead or snapper.

When targeting garfish they respond particularly well to a light berley trail. A float setup with silverfish used for bait yields a good result.

Griffins Gully Jetty

This popular jetty is reached from The Esplanade at the beginning of Western Beach. It produces small flathead, whiting and garfish. Here you can drive your car down the track from the Esplanade and park beside the jetty.

Cunningham Pier

Located at the junction of Western and Eastern Beach Roads, Cunningham Pier has long been a Mecca for young anglers and those of more senior years. Mullet are the main fish caught from the pier, but leatherjacket, silver trevally, warehou, slimy mackerel and barracouta are all taken here at times, usually right down beside the pylons of the pier.

Unfortunately access to Cunningham Pier has been restricted by the owners of Smorgy's Restaurant who are also the new owners of Cunningham Pier. Check the signs at the pier for times of access.

The rock wall between the Cunningham Pier and the Western Beach Boat Club is also a popular area with anglers who are able to cast well out for flathead, whiting and the occasional snapper.

Fisherman's Jetty

The jetty and rock groyne complex at the bottom of Yarra Street is not fished heavily, but leatherjacket, mullet, silver trevally, mackerel and salmon have all been taken here in good numbers.

Stony Pier

Adjacent to the Geelong Yacht Club, Stony Pier and the adjacent rock groyne produce silver trevally, leatherjacket, flathead and zebra fish. Other species like garfish and mullet may sometimes be caught here as well.

Limeburners Point Boat Ramp

The boat launching facility at the end of Hearne Parade at Limeburners Point gives boats to 6 m access to Corio Bay. Landbased anglers sometimes fish from the sheltering breakwater.

Whiting and small snapper are sometimes caught from the breakwater, but small flathead is the most common catch. Larger snapper are occasionally taken here at dawn or dusk, and following very rough weather, particularly from the north or north-east.

Bellarine Peninsula

Geelong is the gateway to the Bellarine Peninsula and Port Phillip Heads. While boat fishing is good, there are very few spots from which you can fish Corio Bay land based along the section of the peninsula that skirts the outer harbour, with any expectation of success.

Clifton Springs

The Clifton Springs boat launching facility at the end of Jetty Road is protected by a sheltering breakwater. It has a mooring jetty, toilets and boat wash facilities. The ramp itself is adequate for boats to 6 m, but the passage to the sea is shallow making it virtually unusable at low tide.

Anglers fish from the breakwater, but the water is shallow and very weedy. Casting for calamari is the most productive with artificial jigs.

Point Richards

There is a boat launching facility at the end of Point Richards Road, and another at Portarlington nearby, giving anglers access to whiting and snapper grounds within two kilometres. Both facilities are badly exposed in rough weather.

The north side of the shipping channel, between beacons 3 and 5, is a well-known snapper mark and boats congregate here from September onwards. Whiting enthusiasts need not go half that far to find productive ground.

Portarlington

This jetty is a little difficult to fish from because the decking does not extend right to the edge all the way around. However, whiting are sometimes caught here, along with small flathead. Snapper have been taken here at dawn and dusk or through the night by anglers casting well out, but only very occasionally.

There is a concrete boat ramp at the bottom of Boat Avenue in the caravan park and another at the bottom of Fairfax Street at Steeles Rocks. Both ramps are difficult at low tide, particularly the one at Steeles Rocks that is suitable for small boats only.

Steeles Rocks

Adjacent to the small boat ramp at the bottom of Fairfax Street, Steeles Rocks provide a marginal platform for anglers seeking squid and whiting. Being able to cast well out with light tackle is an advantage when seeking whiting here.

Yabbies may be pumped from the muddy sand between the Portarlington Pier and Steeles Rocks provided the tide goes out far enough to expose their holes.

Grassy Point

Grassy Point is one of the best known whiting producing areas on the Bellarine Peninsula although it does get a hiding from commercial fish harvesting operations. The boat ramp at Grassy Point offers marginal access for small to medium boats although it is difficult at low tide.

Whiting are usually plentiful at the edge of the mussel leases where they can't be netted, and squid are usually small but prolific over the grass beds throughout. Get in close and set a berley trail to coax the fish to your location. A paternoster rig will work best here. Best baits include pipi and mussel.

Indented Head

There is an adequate boat launching facility at Indented Head, but nowhere for land based anglers to fish with any expectation of success. The St Leonards pier nearby is a better proposition.

The Governor Reefs, clearly marked with isolated danger marks and cardinal marks, and all within a kilometre or so of the Indented Head ramp, are good whiting and squid grounds, principally because they are difficult for commercial fishermen to net and consequently retain good populations of fish.

This area is also the best location to catch whiting throughout the winter months. Continues to work the sand holes for best results. Calamari are in abundance over the weed year round. Size 3.0 jigs are best offered.

St Leonards Pier

The pier at St Leonards has gained a deserved reputation for producing both snapper (to those who are prepared to put in the time) and squid. Sadly, the wooden decking over the rock breakwater has now been removed and the breakwater itself is an unsafe fishing platform.

ST LEONARDS

The St Leonards boat ramp at the end of Leviens Road is badly exposed to an onshore breeze or swell, and rocks in the water are a potential hazard. However, under favourable conditions, craft to 5m can be launched and retrieved safely

SWAN BAY ENTRANCE

Keeping in mind that the Queenscliff boat harbour is the south entrance to Swan Bay, the recognised entrance for navigation purposes is between Duck Island and Point Edwards, some 3 or 4 km to the north-west of Coles Beacon.

The channel forks in two and the lesser channel runs close in to the north end of Duck Island from where you can fish from the shore, particularly at the very bottom of the tide when eel grass is not such a problem. Here you are likely to catch good size gummy sharks. Other species like snapper and mulloway have been caught here too, but not very often.

Up on the shallow banks, just inside the entrance, big flathead bask in the shallows on warm days, particularly in December, January and February.

The preferred technique of catching these is to anchor up in the shallows, in less than a metre of water, then drift a whitebait down the tide about half a metre under a float. If a flathead is on your drift, you will pick him up. If you don't have any success after a couple of tries, up-anchor and move somewhere else, but not into deep water. On the banks of the entrance, calamari are a worthy target. The weed beds in this area are quite extensive, supporting a good calamari population throughout the year. From September until November, big spawning calamari can be found.

SWAN BAY

The vast majority of Swan Bay is part of the Port Phillip Heads Marine National Park and fishing is prohibited. Anglers should visit the Parks Victoria website for details of the very limited area still open to fishing. Tailor are sometimes caught in the vicinity of, and from the jetty at the bottom of Swan Bay Road, particularly in the evening. Anglers fishing from the Swan Bay jetty at night sometimes catch good size gummy sharks, and the occasional good size flathead on baits of fish fillet.

THE KELP PATCH

The kelp patch is a kilometre offshore from Clarkes Beacon, which is on the shore about halfway between Queenscliff and Point Lonsdale. It is easy to find because the long tendrils of kelp reach the surface of the water. Be aware of the marine park prohibited fishing area immediately south of Clarkes Beacon.

Trolling in this area produces a variety of predatory fish including salmon and snook, and the occasional yellowtail kingfish.

Just inside the kelp patch, excellent catches of big whiting are sometimes taken and garfish will respond to berleying. Squid are also taken here in good numbers.

BELL REEF

This rock platform underneath the white lighthouse on Shortland Bluff is exposed at low tide. It is a favourite spot for catching squid, but does produce other species as well, particularly small flathead from the north end. Anglers casting out from the north end adjacent to the beacon have also taken snapper.

A baited squid jig-fished on rod and reel is the favoured technique of catching squid from this ledge because hand lining is difficult.

In October and November, good catches of silver trevally have been taken here during the day, and from September through until mid-November, you likely to catch a good size snapper on evening by using freshly caught squid for bait.

Yellowtail kingfish have often been hooked from this ledge, usually on freshly caught squid baits of generous proportions. Most of these get away, others have been broken off on purpose in the mistaken belief the protagonist was a stingray.

Early in the 1970s this platform was a favourite among lure casting enthusiasts; target species included yellowtail kingfish, but more often the catch comprised salmon and barracouta, particularly on summer evenings.

Remember that in summer, the low tides occurring from say late afternoon to dusk are most suitable here because they fall lower than the morning low tides that sometimes barely expose the platform at all.

LAKERS CUTTING

This water adjoins the Swan Bay section of the Port Phillip Heads Marine National Park and anglers should acquaint themselves with the park boundaries, inside which fishing is prohibited. The shell grit cutting on Fellows Road, and Burnt Point, produces good size bream in late winter and spring. They come right up into the pen above the road at times, but usually you have to do a bit of prospecting until you find them.

There is pedestrian access to Burnt Point from the end of McDonald Road, off Fellows Road, but parking space is limited and gumboots are required for the walk through the swampy ground to the shoreline.

QUEENSCLIFF PIER

Small flathead, garfish, leatherjacket and squid are the main species caught from the Queenscliff pier. Garfish are sought when the current is running out so that the float is drawn away from the pier in the berley trail.

Leatherjacket are regularly caught down around the pylons of the pier by anglers using fresh squid or pipis. Long-shanked hooks are advised as these fish that can bite through your line.

Squid are taken from the pier in good quantities at times, but the best catches are taken at night about halfway along the pier. Look at the pier's timber planks and you'll see they are stained black with calamari ink. Where the ink is, is where you should be casting out jigs from. Lure casting from the pier at daybreak will sometimes pick up a good salmon or two, but after sunrise your chances will have faded.

Fishing on the bottom will produce a variety of fish, but small flathead predominate. Large baits fished on the bottom will attract stingrays. Big sharks can also be caught from the pier by those in the know. Specialised techniques are required by those embarking on such a mission.

QUEENSCLIFF BOAT HARBOUR AND RAMP

The boat ramp and harbour are both inside the narrow southern entrance to Swan Bay, which is a shallow tidal lagoon some five nautical miles in length by two miles across. Once again, anglers should acquaint themselves with the boundary of the Swan Bay part of the Port Phillip Heads Marine National Park, where fishing is prohibited.

Swan Bay is navigable for only a short distance from the Queenscliff ramp, but good catches of silver trevally can be made inside the harbour near the ramp, particularly on the incoming tide.

From a boat, the best place to fish is between the yacht club (on the north side opposite the slipway) and the bridge, but keep out of the channel and beware of large commercial fishing boats.

Landbased anglers can fish from the entrance wall near the ferry terminal and from the wharves and structures inside the harbour with the expectation of catching mullet and silver trevally. The wharf at the bottom of Bay and Beach streets, near the abalone shed, is a popular spot to fish on the incoming tide, provided there are no vessels tied up.

The boat ramp at the bottom of Hesse Street, Queenscliff, is the best on the Bellarine Peninsula. It gives access to several areas, including the turbulent waters of Port Phillip Heads where a variety of fish are sought including big yellowtail kingfish. Boats to 7 m can be launched comfortably from here, and the ramp is adequately sheltered in all conditions except a very strong northerly. The car park is adequate most of the time, but becomes crowded when public holidays coincide with good weather. You can overcome problems by arriving early in the morning.

When the weather is rough, you don't even have to leave the boat harbour to catch fish. As long as you keep out of the main access channel, you can fish in the harbour with an expectation of catching mullet, whiting, small salmon, good size silver trevally and even the occasional good sized tailor.

One of the best places to fish from a boat in the harbour is between the bridge and the yacht club corner. The best time of the year to fish here seems to be from mid-September through until mid-December.

The Grass Beds

Aligning the black water tower on Shortlands Bluff over the shed on the Queenscliff Pier will take you past some of the most productive whiting grounds as you head north-east in front of Swan Island along that alignment. This is the area referred to as The Grass Beds.

The White Lady

This is the name given to the prominent Coles channel marker off the northern tip of Swan Island. North and east of this marker, good catches of whiting are made, particularly during the ebb tide.

To the east of the marker, about another 400 m out, the bottom drops away into the blind fork of the West Channel. In the spring, good catches of snapper are taken right along this drop-off that is marked by three red floating buoys. The last of these three buoys is about 300 m out from the row of red or orange buoys that have been placed in front of Swan Island about 200 m from the shore. You are not allowed inside this row of markers.

Also, at the approach to the channel around the northern tip of Swan Island, there is a sign indicating that you cannot approach the army base on Swan Island. Additionally, during demolition exercises and range target practice, you will be required to keep clear of the area to the east and north-east of Swan Island. This area is patrolled prior to such exercises.

There are plenty of good weed beds around this area too which hold good numbers of calamari year round. Drifting the area is the preferred method to cover ground so to locate where the calamari are holding. The most effective technique is to cast size 2.5 or 3.0 artificial jigs about, working them just above the weed.

Whiting are also prolific in the area and hold in good numbers year round. In fact, this is the most popular location to fish for whiting throughout winter. Pipi and tenderised strips of calamari are top baits.

The Submarine

There is excellent fishing for whiting and trevally around the wreck of the old J-class submarine just off Swan Island but stay outside of the orange markers. Some 200 m north of the submarine, drifting for calamari is popular. Once you locate them, double back and continue to work the same area. the best fishing is two hours either side of the high tide change.

Point Lonsdale

Although surrounded by the Port Phillip Heads Marine National Park, fishing is permitted for a distance of 50 m either side of the Point Lonsdale pier. The pier does not produce the catches of fish one might expect, considering its location. However, it does fish moderately well on a rising tide for salmon. Best results are usually had early in the mornings when salmon will readily take a lure.

Big whiting are also caught from the pier, particularly during the evening after a hot day. Halfway up the pier is a good spot to catch these. Garfish are a worthy target and can be attracted in large schools. More often than not, these garfish are of exceptional size due to the proximity of the pier to the ocean.

Snapper are caught from the pier from early September till late October, both during the night and day. Sometimes there are some big fish among these.

Anglers equipped with game fishing tackle catch a variety of sharks from the pier including seven gill, gummy and bronze whalers. Most of this action occurs in February. Large balloons, or floats, provide the means of deploying their large baits (usually tuna), when the wind is offshore, but be aware of the park boundary.

THE HEADS

The entrance to Port Phillip Heads is known as 'The Rip' because of the speed the tide flows through here.

Unlike the rest of Port Phillip Bay, which tends to be a muddy, flat basin surrounded by shell and weed banks with some reef, the waters immediately inside Port Phillip Heads are mostly heavy reef interspersed with sandy patches and kelp beds. Inside the marker, between the beacon and Swan Island, extensive grass beds harbour a good population of pike to 3 kilograms. The favoured method of catching these is to troll with a leaded hand-line or snook line, baited either with a diving minnow type lure, or with a pilchard rigged on ganged hooks. (Remove the bottom jaw of the pilchard to prevent the bait spinning if you choose the latter).

Anyone fishing Port Phillip Heads for the first time should obtain a copy of the boating rules and regulations pertaining to the area from the Port of Melbourne Authority because Port Phillip Heads handles all shipping to every terminal inside Port Phillip and Corio Bay. Also, a large area on the western side of the entrance is inside the Port Phillip Heads Marine National Park, as is a smaller area on the eastern side. Fishing is prohibited here—contact Parks Victoria for details

Two ramps service the Port Phillip Heads area—one is at Sorrento on the Mornington Peninsula, the other is at Queenscliff on the Bellarine Peninsula.

The ramp at the bottom of Hesse Street, Queenscliff, is the better of the two being ample for almost any trailer-able craft. Parking facilities at Queenscliff are adequate on all but the busiest weekends and public holidays. All boating directions in this chapter are given from the Queenscliff Ramp.

On both sides of The Rip, anglers troll for salmon and sometimes snook. Salmon perform well on light tackle and are often spotted when they bust up balls of baitfish on the surface. The commotion attracts birds too which is an anglers visual queue that salmon are in the area. Approaching the school should be done with care so not to spook them before bombarding them soft plastics and small surface poppers. Out in the centre of The Rip, yellowtail kingfish are usually the quarry. At slack water, particularly early in the morning, you can jig squid out in The Rip.

When the tide slackens off, you can jig with knife style jigs in the deep trench out past the Nepean Bank with some expectation of hooking a yellowtail kingfish. Minimum lure weight required is 200g; minimum tackle required is 15 kilograms. Live baiting is the preferred method when targeting kingfish. Anglers catch yellow-tail scad and slimy mackerel off Blairgowrie and Sorrento before heading to the RIP in search of kings. Live baits, tend to be rigged on extended paternoster rigs then dropped to the bottom where they drift within reach of where the kingfish are schooled up.

Landmarks to give you your point of drop are the two lighthouses at Queenscliff; the black and the white in line to the north, and to the west, you should just be able to see daylight between the pylons of the Point Lonsdale Pier.

Big bluefin tuna are sometimes seen in The Rip, and occasionally an angler fishing for yellowtail kingfish hooks one. Almost all hook-ups on big bluefin occur at the end of the ebb tide. Sometimes small specimens are landed; to date no one has landed a big one.

Fishing during sunrise throughout winter will see very few other boats on Port Phillip Bay, meaning that the fishing can be more productive.

LANDBASED FISHING IN PORT PHILLIP BAY

The Tides

Some explanation of the tides at Port Phillip Heads is necessary because inexperienced mariners and anglers get it wrong too often, and this can introduce an element of danger.

High and low tide as given for Port Phillip Heads represents the tide height and not the direction of the current flow. For example, the published time of high tide might be 12 midday, but an observer standing on the Point Lonsdale pier would notice the tide was still coming in strongly with no sign of slowing down.

The situation is, that, although the tide is indeed at the highest point it is going to reach for some twelve hours at The Heads, the level inside the bay has not yet caught up and is still covering ground exposed by the previous low tide.

One hour into the ebb tide, the level outside The Heads may have dropped 20 cm, yet still be higher than the water inside the bay, so the current continues flowing into the bay. Not until approximately three hours into the ebb tide does the level outside The Heads fall sufficiently to equalise with the rising water inside the bay. Only then will slack water occur. The same thing happens on the flood tide. When fishing the RIP, especially for kingfish, it is vital an understanding of this situation is understood otherwise you will not be able to get baits or lures to the bottom or worse, get yourself into trouble should the conditions not be favourable.

Times to Fish

Contrary to popular belief, land based fishing in Port Phillip Bay can be quite exceptional, especially during spring and summer. With a bit of knowledge and persistence, all of the species on offer within the bay can be caught from land. Snapper, King George whiting, squid, flathead and garfish are all readily available from shore if you know when and where to fish. Piers and jetties aren't the be all and end all of land based fishing platforms in the bay and the beaches are worth a serious look. Anglers should target beaches that are in close proximity to broken ground such as weed beds and rock. Fish these areas during sunrise and sunset, or even better; after dark. Fish come in close to feed on these inshore reefs and due to the lack of fishing pressure most of these locations receive, they will readily take baits. During or after big onshore winds are often the most productive times to fish from the local beaches as the water becomes discoloured and food becomes dislodged from the bottom.

Snapper are most likely to move in close to shore during and immediately after an onshore blow. This is particularly true along a rocky shoreline where there is more than 3m of water within casting distance. As long as the water remains discoloured, snapper will feed within casting distance of the shore, even in daylight.

Good examples of this are at Mornington Pier, Mount Martha Rocks and St Leonard's Pier, all of which produce good catches of snapper after an onshore blow.

Dawn's first light is another excellent time to be fishing from a land based location because snapper frequently move in close to shore during the early hours of the morning to feed on grapsid crabs and remain in close until sun up.

Snapper are known to feed on evening, but it is usually only land based locations having an interface with deep water that produce many fish at this time. Usually it is not until quite late at night that snapper are caught from land based situations, particularly if the weather is relatively calm.

At Limeburner's Bay (Grammar School Lagoon) where many snapper were once caught from both the shore and the little jetty, the change of tide was an excellent time to catch a fish, particularly if that tide change occurred late at night or around daybreak. Mt Martha Rocks has been particularly productive for snapper, especially during a strong westerly or south westerly blow were fish will move in close to the rocky shoreline.

Good sized flathead can be targeted by those wading in the shallows, targeting drop-offs and sand bars with soft plastics. These fish will general be better in size than those found in deeper water and should be targeted during the warmer months.

Technique

Your proximity to productive water does not alter the advantage you have if you can cast, because wind and sea are often against the angler in the most productive snapper situations. Making good casts is not simply a matter of having the best tackle for the job, although careful choice of tackle for the particular place or places where you fish, is certainly a great advantage. If long casts are required, then you must use aerodynamically designed sinkers like the teardrop and bomb patterns, which have most of their weight forward and don't tumble like pyramid, bean, barrel and star sinkers. To take things further, specially designed rigs such as the ICON Long Cast rigs have the bait hooked onto the sinker when the cast is made. This enables a further cast as all the weight is confined to the end of the rig. Once the rig hits the water, the bait breaks free due to a float and sits elevated in the water column. Baiting up is critical also. Remember you have to make your bait travel further and at higher speeds than the boat angler does, therefore your bait has to be cut aerodynamically also.

Another advantage of the well cut bait is that it doesn't have the same tendency to spin as it is being retrieved through the water and this is a big advantage because spinning baits mean twisted leaders and tangles. When very long casts are required, shorten the leader to about 30 cm because a long leader will reduce the distance of your cast by many metres.

It is also recommend that you use a leader of approximately twice the breaking strain of your line to minimise damage to the leader by crabs, toadies and shell. No part of your line is more vulnerable to damage than the leader.

Running sinkers are preferred to fixed sinkers because they give the fish just that much longer to pick up the bait and race off with it before feeling any resistance. If casting distances are not extreme, than a No. 8 ball sinker can be allowed to run down the line to a swivel or ring stop above the hook and leader. However, if casting requirements are beyond about 40m, it can be advantageous to use a teardrop sinker rigged on a leader attached to a ring, which slides along the line.

When fishing from land, it is a great advantage to be able to sit your rod up at about 45 degrees so it holds the line up from inshore hazards, and, at the same time allows you to observe the rod tip without too much discomfort. Where possible, use a solidly made rod holder to prevent your rod from falling over, or in the case of a good bite, being pulled over into the water.

Leave your reel in gear with enough tension on the drag to put a working curve in the rod. This will hook the fish better than you can in all but the most unusual circumstances.

Another effective fishing method is to fish in close with berley at your location. Anglers who use this method from a pier or jetty are very successful especially if they are targeting salmon, garfish and whiting.

TACKLE & GENERAL INFORMATION

Tackle World Cranbourne
270 South Gippsland Highway
Cranbourne, VIC, 3977
Phone 03 5996 6500

BCF
878 Springvale Road
Keysborough Vic 3173
Phone (03) 9798 8883

Tackle World Geelong
105 Shannon Avenue
Manifold Heights Vic 3218
Phone: (03) 5222 3257

Southern Sportfishing
598 Balcombe Road
Black Rock Vic 3193
Phone: (03) 9589 5666

Spinners Bait & Tackle
251 Dorset Road
Boronia Vic 3020
Phone: (03) 9761 1343

Tackle World Laverton
37 – 39 Boundary Road
Laverton North Vic 3026
Phone (03) 9314 4900

Hooked on Bait & Tackle
159 Old Geelong Road
Hoppers Crossing Vic 3029
Phone (03) 9748 3811

Noel Clark's Tackle Bar
158 Deakin Street
Essendon Vic 3040
Phone: (03) 9379 4623

Dromana Camping & Fishing
3 Pier Street
Dromana Vic 3936
Phone: (03) 5981 4457

Pro Angler Bentleigh
PO Box 236
East Bentleigh Vic 3165
Phone: (03) 9576 5012

Pro Angler Geelong
22 Boundary Rd
East Geelong 3219
Phone (03) 5248 8338

Compleat Angler Geelong
205 Melbourne Rd
North Geelong 3215
Phone (03) 5272 3201

Northside Angler Pty Ltd
530 Mahoneys Road
Campbellfield Vic 3061
Phone: (03) 9357 2233

Regal Marine Forest Hills
514 Cantebury Road
Vermont Vic 3133
Phone: (03) 9874 4624

Masterfish
8/1488 Ferntree Gully Road
Knoxfield Vic 3180
Phone: (03) 9763 7922

Douglas Parade Bait and Tackle
365 Douglas Parade
Newport Vic 3015
Phone: (03) 9399 3066

Lilydale Lakes Fishing
3 Castella Street
Lilydale Vic 3140
Phone: (03) 9735 3987

Hook-up Bait & Tackle
Shop 4 / 718 Burwood Highway
Ferntree Gully Vic 3156
Phone: (03) 9758 4332

Prestige Fishing
4/145 Salmon Street
Hastings Vic 3915

Amazing Bait & Tackle
112 Marine Parade
Hastings Vic 3915
Phone (03) 5979 2899

Compleat Angler Melbourne
387 Flinders Lane
Melbourne Vic 3000
Phone: (03) 9620 3320

Compleat Angler Bentleigh
915 Nepean Highway
Bentleigh Vic 3204
Phone: (03) 9557 8011

Compleat Angler Dandenong
241–243 Princess Hwy
Dandenong Vic 3175
Phone: (03) 9794 9397

Compleat Angler - Ringwood
27 New St
Ringwood Vic 3134
Phone: (03) 9870 7792

Aussie Angler
30 Sherbourne Road
Greensborough Vic 3088
Phone: (03) 9423 1501

Armadale Angling
1125 High Street
Malvern Vic 3144
Phone: (03) 9822 3896

Compleat Angler Rosebud
11 Boneo Road
Rosebud Vic 3939
Phone: (03) 5981 1994

Capacity Sports
225 Bay Road
Sandringham Vic 3191
Phone: (03) 9598 9821

Gone Fishin Sales
29 Lathams Road
Carrum Downs Vic 3201
Phone: (03) 9770 8142

Melbourne Marine Centre
1/92–94 Hullam South Road
Hallam Vic 3803
Phone (03) 9111 7794

Fishing Fever
303 Boundary Road
Mordialloc Vic 3195
Phone (03) 9580 9899

CHAPTER 9

NEAR WESTERN COAST

Heading west from Port Phillip Bay, anglers are greeted with some of the best land based and inshore fishing on offer in Victoria. There's a range of species available to target in a variety of appealing locations.

Starting at Ocean Grove the shallow and featureless beach known as Collendina holds some amazing fishing for big snapper and often massive mulloway, and while it may be a bit of a wait between bites the results make it worthwhile.

Next in line is the famous Barwon River, best known for its huge mulloway, especially during the cold winter months, not to mention great bream and salmon fishing at times.

The water offshore from Barwon Heads is home to some good reef systems that hold snapper and gummy sharks, while trolling lures in close often produces salmon, snook and more than the occasional kingfish.

BOAT RAMPS

LOCATION	BOAT SIZE	PARKING	BUILD
Barwon River (Ocean Grove)	6 m	Excellent	Concrete
Barwon River Sheepwash	6 m	Good	Concrete
Torquay	5.5 m	Good	Concrete

For game fishers the offshore water also hold good numbers of mako, thresher and bronze whaler sharks.

Meanwhile the coastline between Collendina and Torquay has quality beach fishing on offer for species such as salmon, mullet and trevally, while the rocks produce wrasse, sweep, snapper and several other species.

PORT PHILLIP TO BARWON HEADS

COLLENDINA

Collendina is a shallow and an unattractive beach at first glance but has produced snapper and mulloway for prepared anglers. Low tide seems to be best, and the best places to fish are adjacent to the obvious exposed patches of reef at either end of the beach.

One good spot to start looking would be about halfway between the Collendina Hotel and Ocean Grove where there is deep water interfaced with exposed reef accessible at low tide. Long casts are required to reach the desired distance as to where snapper may be holding. A long cast land based is highly recommended at this location. These can be purchased at most good tackle stores.

In common with all of the other beaches close to Port Phillip Heads, the most common fish are small salmon and good size mullet. These can be caught on light tackle in the wash, particularly at low tide. A paternoster rig tied from 10 lb fluorocarbon leader with two droppers each containing a size #8 or #10 long shank works best. Both species will take a variety of baits but pipi is favoured over all. Access to this area is from Bonnyvale Road.

There are some other big fish that lurk about in this area and it is always worth putting out a larger bait of salmon or mullet fillet especially if fishing the beach of a night.

OCEAN GROVE BEACH

This is another shallow, featureless beach that produces good results throughout the year for snapper and mulloway. Although the fish have been caught at all the stages of all tides, and both during the day and at night, fishing the beach on the low tide is recommended when you will be able to wade out far enough so as to cast into productive water.

Low tides coinciding with evening in late spring and summer, and with daybreak in late autumn and winter, give the best fishing opportunities here. Target species are snapper and mulloway and a popular stretch of beach is from the car park all the way back to the sand spit at the river mouth.

Either a running sinker rig or paternoster rig will work well at this location. Live baiting salmon is effective for mulloway, especially on the lead up to a full moon. Strong currents can make fishing difficult from time to time so ensure you pack some heavy star sinkers to 7oz.

When fishing any of these beaches, it is a good idea to have a decent pair of waders and a sand spike to hold your rod. A folding chair is another good investment here, not just to sit on, but to put your gear on when the tide begins to rise.

BARWON RIVER ESTUARY

The Barwon estuary consists of a narrow entrance to the sea, with minimal siltation, a broad-water extending about 2.5 km upstream from the bridge, and a long winding section of another 4 or 5 km up to Lake Connewarre.

Lake Connewarre is shallow, but there is a channel of sorts along the west side of the lake roughly joining the estuary below with the river above. Nowhere would this channel exceed 3m in depth.

Above the lake, the stretch of river to the weir is relatively deep and can be navigated in a small boat or kayak. It is very narrow and reedy, but this deep stretch of river is popular with bream anglers, most of whom have negotiated access through private property from Matthews Road.

THE MOUTH

The rocky platform under Barwon Heads Bluff on the right side of the river mouth offers some fishing platforms at low tide, both facing the ocean and in the river itself. Here, bait anglers usually encounter various species of rock fish, but of these only the blue throat tusk fish is prized. Sometimes a low tide on dusk will produce a more interesting catch including small snapper, whiting and the occasional gummy shark.

Lure casting enthusiasts who don't mind losing a lure or two in the kelp sometimes encounter large snook or long fin pike. These two species have sharp teeth so you might opt for tying on some wire between the lure and leader to prevent bite offs. Spinning with metal slugs will also catch the attention of salmon and silver trevally. The ideal lure weights range from 15 g to 35 g for this area.

Access to the bluff is from Ewing Blyth Drive then Bluff Road.

FISHERMAN'S JETTY

The Fisherman's Jetty, around which several commercial fishing vessels are moored, is a popular spot for anglers during the day, but

due to the extreme narrowness of the river at this point, the tides run very fast. For this reason, time your trip to coincide with the low tide change that occurs some two hours later than low water at Port Phillip Heads.

On the Fisherman's Jetty, the first couple of hours of the incoming tide will usually produce mullet and small salmon. As the tide picks up speed and the water clears, big silver trevally become a distinct possibility. The best baits for these include fresh whitebait, clams, prawns, mussels and rabbit. If you secure an onion bag full of mashed pilchards to the side of the jetty and let float on the water's surface, you'll attract fish in no time.

The steep beach downstream from the Fisherman's Jetty is also a productive spot to fish on the low tide change, with a variety of species to be caught, including mulloway when they are about.

Access to the Fisherman's Jetty is past the roundabout on Flinders Parade and then past the ranger's building in the Foreshore Caravan Park, just downstream from the bridge.

The Spit

There is a sand spit opposite the Fisherman's Jetty and a little bay back upstream toward the bridge. This is a popular spot for anglers fishing the rising tide because there is little current in the bay until the tide has covered the sand spit. There is good access to this spot from the car park on the Ocean Grove side of the bridge. It can be a great spot to berley up small mullet and salmon that can be then used as live baits to hopefully tempt a mulloway. A lot of stingrays come into this bay and they can be a nuisance on almost any tackle. There are moorings not far out in the river here, and most of the bigger rays that get hooked manage to wrap the angler's line around one of these, or sometimes a bridge pylon.

Overall this spot is not wholly negative; it is probably one of the most comfortable spots for the angler to fish the incoming current, and a wide variety of fish, including mulloway, have been caught here.

The Bridge

The bridge is a popular spot for anglers fishing for small mullet and salmon during the first two or three hours of the rising tide. Most fish seem to be caught on the Ocean Grove side of the Bridge; one favourite spot is beside the third light pole from the Ocean Grove side of the river.

The bridge draws quite a different crowd after dark, particularly in the autumn and winter when mulloway can sometimes be seen cruising up and down in the lights of the bridge as the water clears at the change of tide.

Mulloway spotting has become a regular activity with several local anglers who spend hours on the bridge at night looking for a big ghostly shapes in the mercury vapour lamps of the bridge. Catching them is a different story though, for although a few are caught in the course of a season they show extreme caution when presented with bait. Most baits, even live baits, are ignored altogether.

Experience has shown that mulloway are much more likely to take bait from the bridge when the water is cloudy and they can't be spotted. Under these conditions, several have been caught on lures jigged under the lights of the bridge. A red rubber octopus pattern has been responsible for several captures from the bridge under these conditions however, some have been taken on bibbed lures as well.

Watching mulloway ignore baits presented to them from the bridge makes you wonder just how often baits intended for mulloway are ignored in other parts of the river as well when the quarry is not visible.

Big mulloway seem to be most plentiful in the Barwon from March until the end of June or July and then perhaps again in November. School mulloway appear in November and December.

Ozone Jetty

This little jetty at the bottom of Ozone Road is popular with anglers and produces mullet and salmon during the first two hours of the incoming tide. Mulloway seekers fish from the Ozone Jetty with some success, the best time to get a run being from the last hour of the outgoing current until the slack water and first two hours of the incoming current. Mulloway can be quite decisive about what they choose to eat and with mullet and salmon capable of being caught here, presenting them live is the best chance at success. If you do choose to live bait for mulloway, send them out under a small bobby cork float or balloon. Mulloway fishing is best leading up to the full moon throughout the summer months.

The Mulloway Hole

At the bottom of Talbot Avenue, and between the Ozone Jetty and the creek draining the mud flats in front of the river front houses, is a popular mulloway spot. It tends to get crowded when there are a lot of fish about, and because of this, fish are lost around anchor ropes quite regularly. Live baiting salmon and mullet is the preferred and most successful fishing method.

The Broadwater

This shallow section of river between the Ocean Grove boat ramp and the bridge regularly claims the propellers of boats traveling between the ramps and the sea. The only remedy for this is to build another boat ramp downstream from the bridge.

There are a lot of small mullet and salmon in the Broadwater when they don't seem to be in the deeper stretches of the river, and boats can often be seen anchored up along here with anglers catching live bait for mulloway.

Ocean Grove Boat Ramp

The Ocean Grove boat ramp is adjacent to the car park at the bottom of Guthridge Street in Ocean Grove; toilet block and boat washing facilities are adjacent. Don't use the ramp that is in a state of collapse at the very bottom of Guthridge Street, use the one at the other end of the car park adjacent to the pontoon.

Navigation to the river mouth and back to the ramp is difficult because the water is shallow and it is rocky in many spots, particularly at low tide.

Anglers fish from the shore beside the boat ramps and good catches of mullet and small salmon are common. Silver trevally can also be caught here at times, particularly when the tide is rising.

The exposed mud flats, both upstream and down from the Ocean Grove boat ramp, are a good source of Bass yabbies for anglers equipped with pump and bucket.

The Tributary

Several creeks drain the swamp and enter the Barwon. The most substantial of these enters the river opposite the Sheepwash boat ramp, about 1 km upstream from the Ocean Grove boat ramp.

Although anglers overlook this smaller water, it is relatively deep and contains bream, luderick and some estuary perch. Bank access to this stream is limited to a swamp trail right at the bottom of Thacker Street.

The Sheepwash

Access to the Sheepwash is down Sheepwash Road, which runs off the Barwon Heads Road to the left just after you enter Barwon Heads coming from Geelong. To get to the Sheepwash boat ramp, turn right at the bottom of Sheepwash Road along the river and past the caravan park. The boat ramp is situated on the river in the fourth clearing on the left-hand side of the road.

There is enough parking for about ten cars and trailers, but no other facilities. The section of river known as 'The Sheepwash' extends upstream from the boat ramp to the third fence running to the water's edge.

The Sheepwash fishes well for bream and luderick, particularly from April to August when the weather is cold. The best time to catch these fish is during the last hour of light, particularly if the tide is running in toward full. Sand worms and locally pumped bass yabbies will take both species, and abalone gut is excellent if you are just seeking luderick.

Casting out into the middle of the river from the bank is not a good idea when the tide is running because your line just gets swept back into the bank. Putting a heavier sinker on to prevent this only makes matters worse because more weed gathers along the line before the sinker pulls.

The Thunderbolt

Upstream from the Sheepwash, between the last fence and the lake, the winding section of river is known as 'The Thunderbolt' because of the speed it can run at. There is dry weather access to the Thunderbolt from the elbow in Lake Road. Lake Road runs off the Barwon Heads Road between Connewarre and Marshmallow Road, makes a right angle bend, then runs back to the Barwon Heads Road by the Barwon Heads airfield. Never use this access if there is any suspicion of wet weather, because it winds down through the lowlands swamp to the river and often the surface is merely a crust over soft mud.

Most anglers who fish the Thunderbolt do so from boats launched at the Sheepwash. However, the majority of anglers launch boats into the river with the intention of fishing outside. There are some deep holes in the Thunderbolt area, particularly on the east side of the river and these are the places to look when there is a mild fresh running.

Lake Connewarre

Upstream from the Thunderbolt is Lake Connewarre, which covers about 1000 hectares. It is a game reserve with many water birds nesting there, ibis in particular. Motors above five horsepower are not permitted in the lake for this reason.

There are a lot of fish in Connewarre that never seem to get caught, including big sea mullet. Apart from these there are yellow-eye mullet, bream and eels. The lake is also popular with shooters in the duck season and some shooters have reported sighting very large fish in the lake. These would undoubtedly have been mulloway.

Landbased anglers do have access from the point at the bottom of Stacey's Road where there is about a metre and a half of water.

These days with the popularity of lure fishing, especially soft plastics, anglers in small craft such as canoes or kayaks are catching some great bream by fishing the lake, working weed and reed beds snags and any other likely looking areas.

The Second Break

The Second Break is the name of the weir across the river approximately a kilometre above the lake. Bream anglers who have negotiated access through private property to this section of the

MAP 31 BARWON HEADS AND OFFSHORE

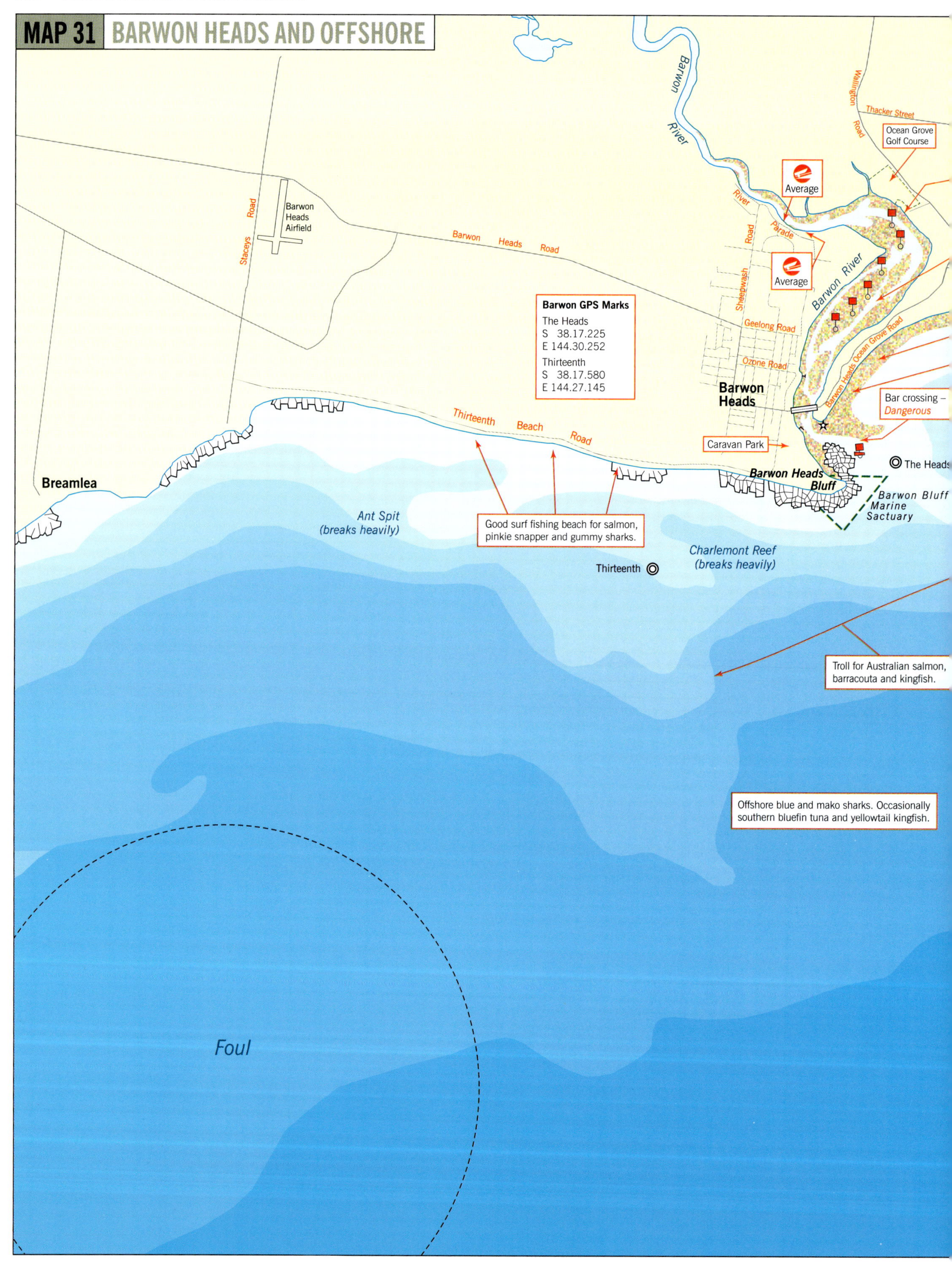

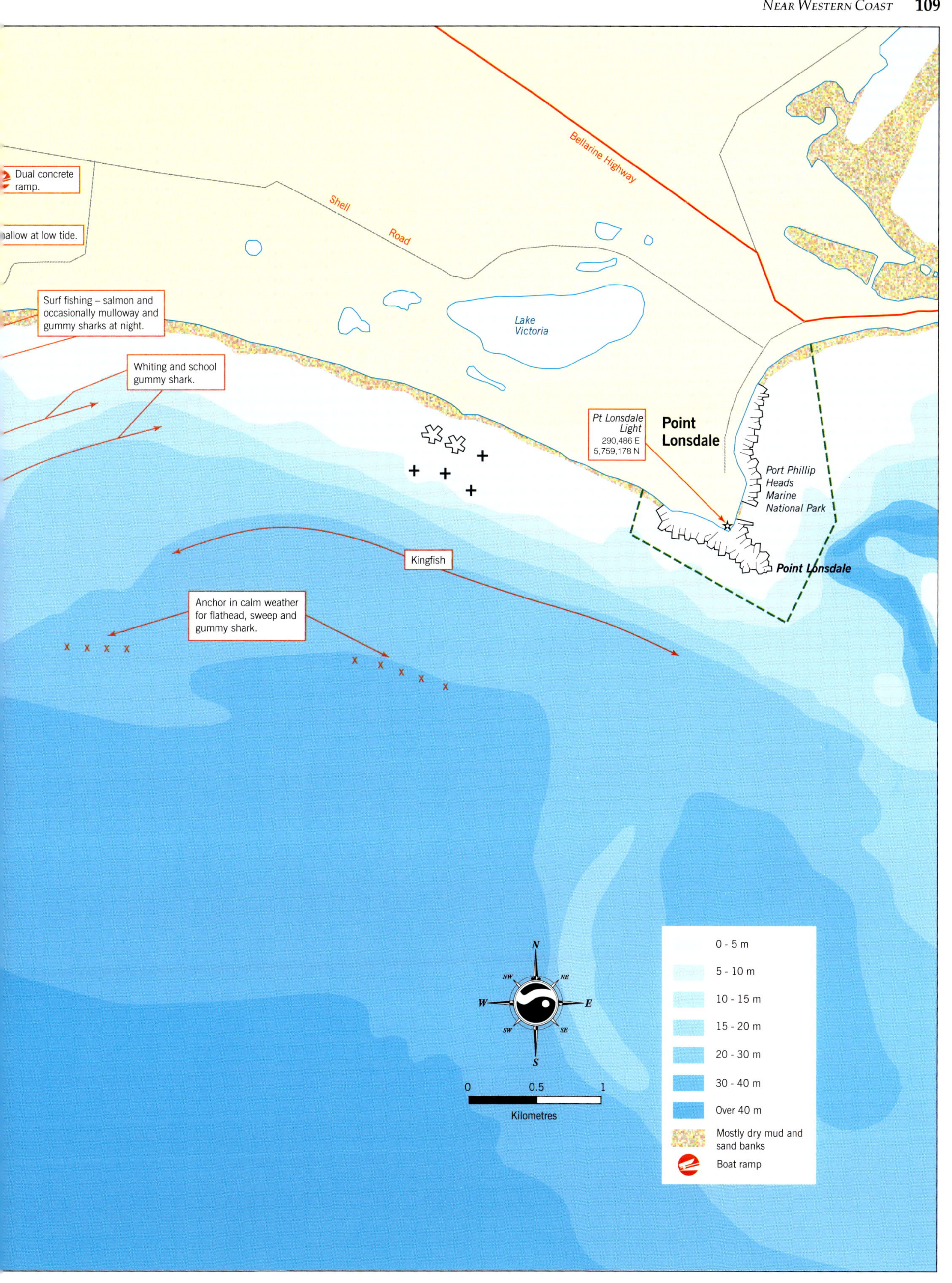

Dual concrete ramp.
allow at low tide.
Surf fishing – salmon and occasionally mulloway and gummy sharks at night.
Whiting and school gummy shark.
Bellarine Highway
Shell Road
Lake Victoria
Pt Lonsdale Light
290,486 E
5,759,178 N
Point Lonsdale
Port Phillip Heads Marine National Park
Point Lonsdale
Kingfish
Anchor in calm weather for flathead, sweep and gummy shark.
N
NE
E
SE
S
SW
W
NW
0
0.5
1
Kilometres
0 - 5 m
5 - 10 m
10 - 15 m
15 - 20 m
20 - 30 m
30 - 40 m
Over 40 m
Mostly dry mud and sand banks
Boat ramp

river, refer to the whole stretch between the weir and the lake as 'The Second Break'.

There is another access to the Second Break from the west arm of the lake. At the bottom of Stacey's Road there is a makeshift cutting in the bank where dinghies and canoes can be launched. From here, one can proceed north up the west arm to the opening of the river.

The entrance to the river is the second opening in the reeds on the right of the east side of the arm. It is shallow at the entrance and you might have to get out of your craft to push it over the bar, but, once inside, there is deep water—up to 3m in places.

The most sought after species here is bream, which can be taken up to a good size on a variety of baits including bass yabbies, squirters and crab. However, there are several freshwater species as well including trout, carp and redfin that come over the weir and can't get back up again.

In the past there have been a number of big brown trout caught below the weir by anglers patient enough to keep coming back until they manage to tempt one. Successful bait for these big fish is shrimp netted from the river.

In summary, the Barwon estuary is not the easiest Victorian estuary to fish, and big catches of worthwhile fish are the exception rather than the rule. The fast tides and the constant colour changes in the water drive many anglers away to fish less hostile waters.

However, the Barwon does have rewards for dedicated or specialist anglers who are prepared to spend enough time getting to know this water. Without a doubt, big mulloway are the prize fish of the Barwon, and some anglers take their share of these every year while others after years of trying, have yet to catch their first.

BARWON HEADS OFFSHORE

Anglers fish offshore from Barwon Heads regularly and take good catches of a fairly wide variety of fish. However, the passage to the sea from the boat ramps upstream is shallow and some knowledge of the river is required before attempting this passage. There is no bar to cross at the Barwon, the entrance is fairly shallow and low tide crossings should be avoided. Many anglers who fish the offshore waters here do so by launching in Port Phillip Bay then heading through the Rip.

Extensive reef systems offer anglers the opportunity for great fishing for highly prized species such as snapper and gummy sharks, both of which can be taken by either drifting or by finding likely looking patches of reef or drop-offs, then anchoring up to fish with baits held on or near the bottom. Using berley followed up with lightly weighted baits, anglers can also enjoy great snapper fishing as they move up off the bottom to feed mid water.

Some of the reefs out from Barwon Heads that lie in 20 to 30 m of water also produce great fishing for kingfish during summer, and while most of the fish are small 'rats', there are some bruisers in amongst them for anglers who fish with larger baits and lures.

Wide of these areas in 50 to 70 m of water excellent numbers of mako, blue, thresher and whaler sharks can be found through the summer months. Berleying with minced fish and using baits suspended under balloons is a great way to find action. Best of all, while waiting for a bite you can fish with baits, lures and jigs on the bottom for the plentiful arrow squid, big barracouta and some great flathead, along with the odd snapper and gummy shark.

The Boilers

The boilers of the steamship Orungal are just outside the Barwon River mouth to the left and provide good cover for many fish. In the sheltered area inshore from the boilers, anglers fishing on the drift with whitebait make good catches of pinkies. Access offshore here is via the Barwon River mouth.

This area is popular with anglers casting small soft plastics lures for the pinky snapper—a very effective way to target them. Its popularity is enhanced by the fact it is reachable in smaller boats.

Formby Reef

A few hundred metres out from the boilers is Formby Reef, which is a high point on the west bank that runs right along the front of Barwon Heads, providing good grounds for commercial cray fishermen and anglers.

Formby itself should be avoided with any swell running because it can break dangerously. Drifting the outer edges of the reef is popular for anglers targeting flathead with paternoster rigs. Ironically, it is also a popular location to catch gummy sharks which are often caught by surprise.

BARWON HEADS TO TORQUAY

THE BLUFF

Good catches of salmon are made regularly about 500 m out from the Bluff by anglers trolling with lures. Although hard body lures are effective, trolling small 3" white occy skirts will yield a better result.

Around to the right-hand side of the bluff, about 300 m out, is an excellent place to catch sweep, some of them of good size. Setting a berley trail of mashed pilchards will get them into a feeding frenzy. Unweighted baits can then be sent down the trail.

On a cautionary note, it is often dangerous to cut to the right in front of the Bluff when leaving the river mouth, because waves can break without warning here. Maintain your heading until well clear of the bluff.

CHARLEMONT REEF

About 1 km out from Thirteenth Beach is the highest point on the West Bank called Charlemont Reef. Charlemont breaks in any kind of a swell so should be avoided most days.

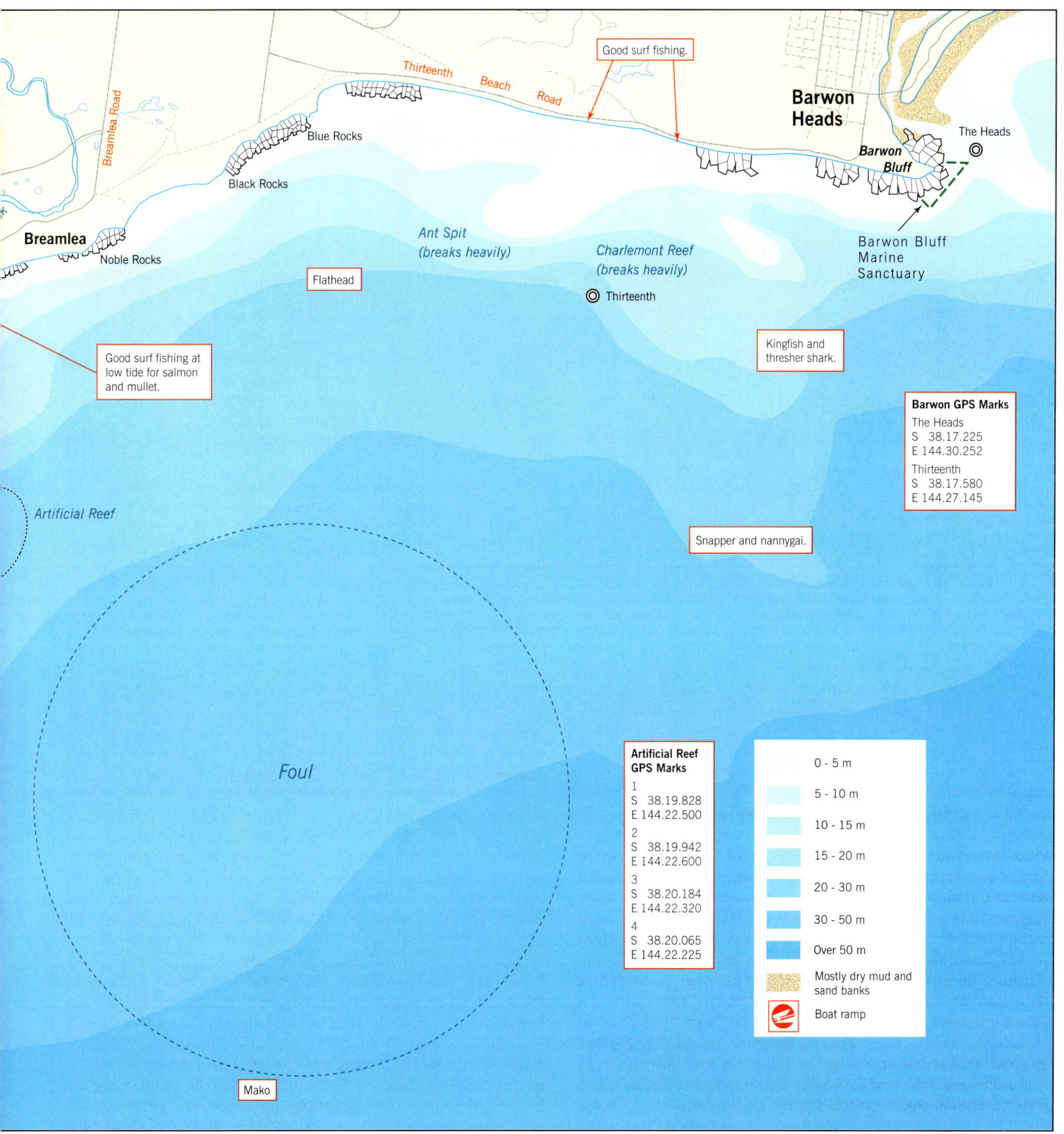

On a good day fish close to the reef to catch a wide variety of fish on both bait and lures. These include pike, snook, salmon and silver trevally. In recent times, kingfish have been making a huge comeback and this area has been producing fish to 15 kg. Trolling live baits such as calamari, salmon and yellow tail is effective. When the fish are on the surface, flicking soft plastics can be a lot of fun. If the kings are found down deep, anglers can use metal jigs in the 250 g to 200 g weight range which is also highly effective along the edges of the reef.

Thirteenth Beach

Thirteenth Beach runs west from The Bluff at Barwon Heads to the sewerage outfall at The Black Rocks and is so named because it begins under the thirteenth hole of the Barwon Heads golf course. It is popular with surfers during the day, but anglers can always find areas to fish.

The beach is interspersed with reef and the gutters adjacent provide the best opportunities for catching salmon, snapper and a good many others fish. Between the surf lifesaving club and the Barwon Heads Bluff, there are many small stretches of beach, interspersed with reef from where you can catch snapper in the evening, sometimes salmon as well.

This beach is very exposed making it hard to get out of the weather when it comes from the south however it does produce good fishing. As well as the gutters, the shallow washes hold great numbers of small mullet and juvenile salmon, all you need is a little berley in the form of tuna soaked pellets and small baits such as pilchard fillet, peeled prawn or pipi.

Larger baits fished in close proximity to some of the rock and reef often produce larger salmon, while at night anglers take a few gummy sharks along with the occasional mulloway, captures of which are kept very quiet.

At the Black Rock end, the sheltered bay adjacent to the first outcrop of black rocks fishes well after dark for pinkies and the occasional gummy shark. Access is from Ewing Blythe Drive, Barwon Heads and from either Bluestone School Road or Black Rock Road.

The Black Rocks (also called Black Rock)

The smell of this place, which is adjacent to the sewer outfall, is quite offensive, nevertheless it is a popular place from which to fish for snapper. Although the water is quite deep off the rocks, you have to cast a long way out to be successful.

The Black Rock Sewer Outfall has been a favourite place for anglers over many years. Access from Thirteenth Beach Road was cut when the Water Board cut a trench across the road. They also attempted the illegal closure of Black Rock Road, but had to reopen it when anglers protested.

The beach to the left, or east, of the rocks is sheltered and can be fished when most beaches along this part of the coast are washed out.

The sewer pipe platform produces good size whiting, small snapper and several other varieties as well. The majority of fish taken here are small, but in late winter and spring, you are likely to catch a better class of fish. Paternoster rigs tied from 15lb fluorocarbon and size #6 long shank hooks work best.

Sharks are also regularly caught from here. Both whalers and threshers have been caught from the outfall site. The best method is to use helium filled balloons which carry baits out into the deeper waters where the sharks frequent. In being successful in catching sharks, more specialised game fishing tackle is required.

The Wells

The right-hand side or west side of Black Rock is known as 'The Wells'. The water is deep here, but the ledges are somewhat precarious, particularly in any sort of a sea. You will get very wet here before things get dangerous.

Despite the deep water interface, best results on snapper are to be had casting well out. All you seem to get in close to the rocks is parrot fish. To improve success on snapper, try floating pilchards down a berley trail unweighted as this will keep the baits away from the bottom where the parrot fish reside.

Access is from Bancoora Beach and good fishing for large whiting and small snapper can be expected from the rocks here provided seas are favourable.

Bancoora Beach

Bancoora Beach is deepest adjacent to Black Rock and there is a protective outer reef that offers shelter from big seas, except when the tide is high. As the bottom is snaggy close to the rocks, it is better to move up the beach away from the visible reef before you begin fishing. The other end of Bancoora Beach is popular with swimmers and is protected by a sheltering reef that comes out from the shore. Small mulloway are sometimes caught from this beach after a hot day and mullet, salmon and trevally are caught from the east side of the sheltering reef by land based anglers.

The sheltering reef provides a modest platform from which to fish over a sandy bottom on the Bancoora side. Here you can catch mullet and small salmon in close to the rocks. Bigger salmon and trevally may be caught here if you can cast out to where the waves roll in past the end of the reef. A paternoster rig works will in this situation.

On the ocean side of this reef is a sand hole that produces very large whiting, but access is by boat only.

Breamlea

There is both estuary and surf fishing to be had at the small township of Bream Lea. Access is from Bream Lea Road from the Barwon Heads Road, or from Blackgate Road from the Torquay Road.

Thompson Creek runs past the houses and here you can catch mullet and salmon on the rising tide.

Upstream from the bridge on the Torquay Road (behind the site of the Bancoora Life Saving Club), good size bream can be caught in any of the several deep holes along the way up to the weir, which is within walking distance. These deep holes are popular with land based lure fishermen who often catch good numbers of big bream—they keep moving along the river casting at likely spots till fish are found rather than sitting in the one spot. Deep diving hard body lures work exceptionally well with metal vibes best offered.

The rock platforms at Bream Lea are modest; access is up Vagg Street and over the dune. Nevertheless, a variety of fish including sweep have been caught from here. The surf beach at Bream Lea is heavily interspersed with reef and is located over the dunes from Vagg Street. Large whiting, mullet and small salmon are the most common catch from the rock platforms and beach, but luderick and sweep have been taken from the rocks as well.

Buckleys Bay

The beach known as Buckleys Bay, between, Bream Lea and the mouth of the Thompson Creek, is usually covered with weed and very exposed to strong winds. The low tide, particularly on evening, allows the angler to walk out far enough to cast into productive water and a wide variety of fish can be caught from here. Small salmon and mullet are prolific at the mouth of the creek, which is usually open to the sea.

Access poses some difficulties the beach can sometimes be reached by wading across the mouth of Thompson Creek at Point Impossible.

Point Impossible

The road to Point Impossible is rough and carries a lot of surfing traffic, although not so much now that the road to Torquay has been closed from the Point Impossible end. This road gives access to the estuary of Thompson Creek where good catches of small salmon, silver trevally and mullet can be taken toward the top of the tide; particularly on evening when salmon up to half a kilogram occasionally come into the estuary.

The rocks to the left of the estuary mouth are not realistic fishing platforms, although there are areas where you could certainly fish with float setup at low tide. Using berley is also very effective and a float with a small piece of peeled prawn threaded onto a size #8 long shank hook will catch a variety of species including salmon, silver trevally and mullet.

Thompson Creek (also known as Bream Creek)

Bream Creek runs to sea at Point Impossible and where the creek runs alongside the road, anglers are often seen trying their luck for mullet and salmon. The tide runs fast here, and the amount of weed moving with it can make bait fishing almost impossible. A high tide during the late afternoon or evening often entices a good shoal of salmon into the creek and these provide top sport on lures cast from the bank.

Upstream from the Torquay Road, at the turn-off as you come into Bream Lea, the creek becomes deeper with some noticeably good holes upstream. There is an excellent population of bream in this section of the creek and some estuary perch also. (See Bream Lea).

Boat Ramp

The Torquay boat ramp is in front of the Torquay Bowling Club off the Esplanade. Unlike the beautifully designed slatted boat ramp it replaced the new ramp is solid concrete and collects so much sand it is often useless. Many of the anglers at Torquay use tractors to launch and retrieve their boats. During weekends and holidays the Torquay Motor Yacht and Angling Club, who charge a fee for its use, supervise it.

TORQUAY

Inshore Boat Fishing

Good fishing is to be had close in off Torquay. Whiting to more than 800 g are regularly caught less than 200 m from shore. One of the best baits for these is tenderised squid strips, but pilchard fillets, pipis and mussels will take fish as well. Whiting respond very well to berley and a paternoster rig with two droppers containing size #6 circle or long shank hooks.

Snapper are also caught out from Torquay, and in both directions along the coast. The biggest bags of fish are to be had close in, but you must be out early in the morning—sun-up could be too late to really get amongst them.

Snook can be caught on the drift and by trolling. They are mostly up and working over the weed beds on daybreak, but down deep during the day. Fishing with soft plastics lures or small metal slugs worked close to the bottom will have the snook fired up in the daylight hours. Trolling minnow type lures similar to that of Rapala x-wrap 10's and Yo-Zuri 120mm Hydro Magnums either at dawn or dusk is successful, however during the day you may need to find deeper running lures such as Tilsans and some of the deeper running Rapala lures. Otherwise, a "poor mans downrigger" sinker clip on the line will help to get the lure down deeper. Drifting over reef areas with baits of blue bait or whitebait or small garfish on gang hooks is also a sure fire way to catch snook.

The Flathead Grounds

About 4 km out from the boat ramp, the depth increases dramatically to about 30m over a flat bottom. The entire bottom is mostly sand in which an abundance of flathead call home. Here, good size flathead can be caught in large numbers on the drift.

Very early in the morning, you will get a much wider variety of fish including snapper, on these grounds, but barracouta can sometimes be a nuisance and sever rigs in seconds. In deeper waters, hooking flathead can be difficult due to the amount of line let out. In this situation, size 3/0 circle hooks will have the fish hook themselves without requiring the assistance of the angler.

While drifting for flathead in the summer months it can also be worth putting out a shark bait as quite often smallish mako sharks will chase up hooked flathead to the boat.

The Wide Grounds

Wider out still, in 40 to 60 m, barracouta are bigger and more plentiful. Slimy mackerel also shoal up near the surface and respond to berley and unweighted baits. These are sometimes more than a kilogram in weight and make excellent bait both live and dead. Catching slimies requires small hooks in the #12 and #14 short shank style.

Sharks are also more plentiful out here during summer through autumn, with the larger mako and blue sharks being evident in March and April. These can usually be berleyed up to the boat and tempted with fresh bait.

While drifting and berleying for sharks in the deeper water it is still worth fishing some smaller baits on the bottom as at times there are some very good sized flathead to be caught, along with the odd gummy shark and snapper. They say "activity creates activity" so where possible always continue to catch fish off the bottom to better your chances.

Spring Creek

Spring Creek is a favourite bream spot producing some good size fish. Bait fishing with live bass yabbies is effective on a running sinker rig and small size 1 or 2 ball sinker. Lure fishing is also productive with shallow diving lures and slow sinking stick baits working well.

The Torquay Road crosses Spring Creek, but access is from Bell Street to the left before the bridge. Another access point is from Duffields Road to the right about 2 km up the hill after the highway bridge.

Point Danger

At low tide it is possible to fish from the north side of Point Danger, the south side is more popular with swimmers. Access is across The Esplanade from the bottom of Bell Street where there is a toilet block and electric barbecues.

The beach in front of the toilet block is an excellent beach for pumping yabbies provided the tide is out far enough to expose their holes.

Yellow Bluff

At the bottom of Zeally Bay Road, Yellow Bluff is an unlikely fishing spot, but at low tide, both snapper and large whiting are within casting range. Unfortunately the bottom is snaggy and you are likely to lose a few rigs. If you do choose to fish here, insure you have a substantial back up of tackle.

Zeally Bay and Other Beaches

The beaches from Yellow Bluff, past the boat ramp, about halfway back to Point Impossible all produce reasonable inshore fishing for whiting and snapper along with mullet in the shore break. Sometimes gummy shark, larger snapper and mulloway are taken here as well.

The beach in the vicinity of the boat ramp is best fished on the high tide, particularly when this occurs in the evening or just after day break. The beach in the vicinity of Horseshoe Bend Road is best fished on the low tide when this occurs either in the morning or evening.

The Gap

Continuing along The Esplanade toward the municipal tip you will come to a distinct gap in the sand dunes where you can park and walk through to a very promising beach where large whiting

MAP 33 TORQUAY

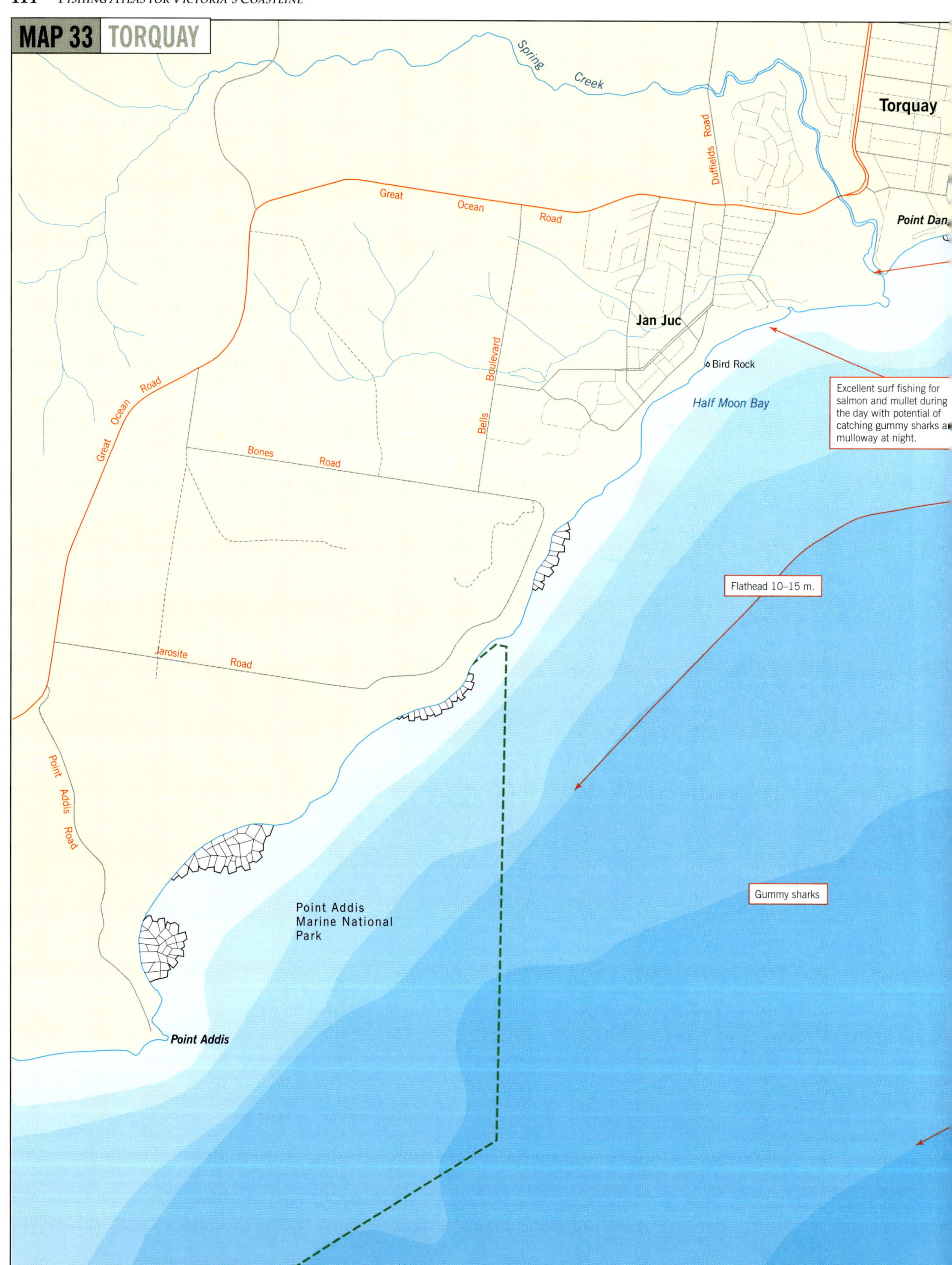

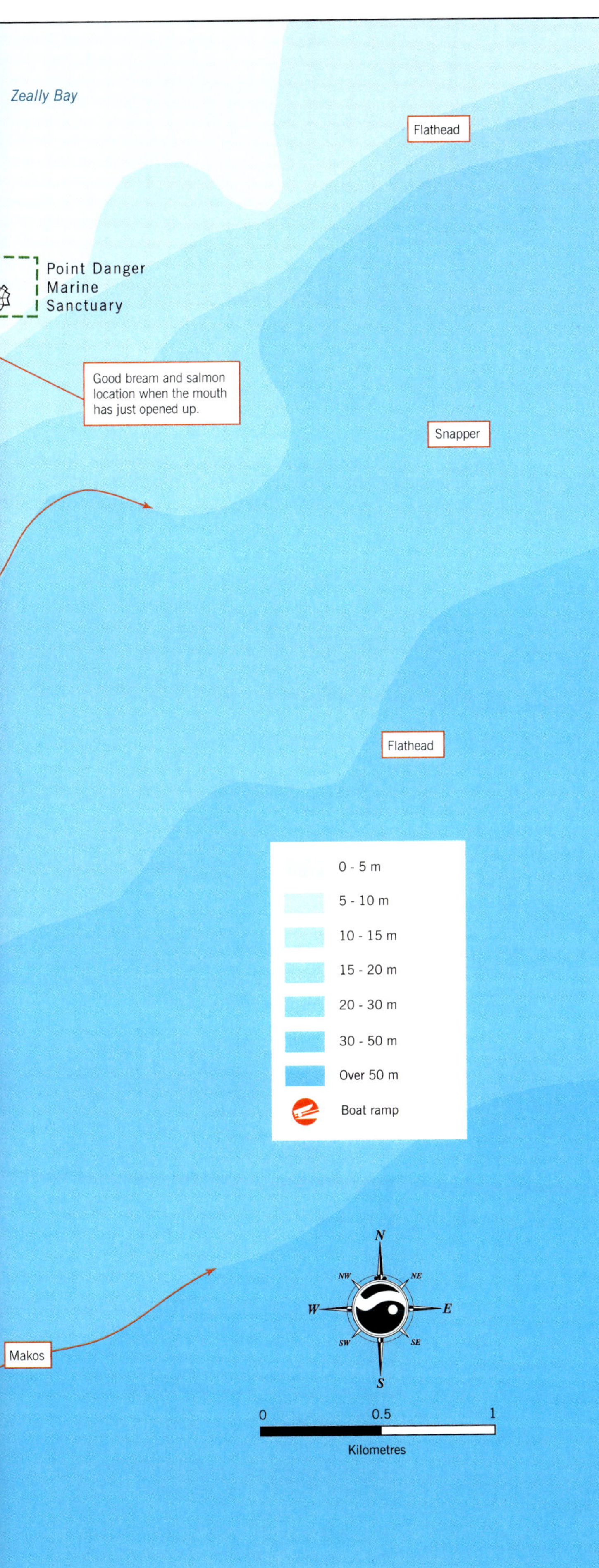

have been taken along with snapper and an occasional mulloway. Specialised rigs are required as to get the distance required to land the bait out wide. Long cast rigs will offer this chance and are sold at all good tackle stores.

WHITES BEACH

Continuing on past the tip, Whites Beach is on the right. You can park above the beach on a fairly rocky area that looks as though it has been graded at some time. The beach is heavily interspersed with reef and is a productive area to catch large whiting. Whites Beach is popular with 'free' bathers so avoid this area if nudity offends.

JAN JUC

The beach in front of the Torquay Golf Club at Jan Juc is a popular fishing beach producing salmon, flathead and occasionally mulloway and gummy shark. Access from the main road is via Hoylake Avenue then left past the toilet block and past the Life Saving Club.

A pronounced gutter formation here sometimes runs so close to the beach at the bottom of the tide that you need to be careful not to throw over it and onto the sandbar beyond. Establishing a berley trail will bring fish into your immediate area and providing you fish for baits on the right rigs intended for the target species, you'll find success.

HALF MOON BAY

Half Moon Bay is between the creek at Jan Juc and the rocks at the base of the cliff. The bottom seems to be weedy here and not as good as on the other side of the creek.

The rocks at the base of the cliff are sometimes fished for snapper, but you have to be careful to retreat when the tide begins coming in or you may be cut off. Access is from the stairs down the cliff below the Princes Terrace parking area.

TACKLE & GENERAL INFORMATION

Compleat Angler Geelong
205 Melbourne Road
North Geelong Vic 3215
Phone: (03) 5272 3201

Trelly's Tackle World Geelong
105 Shannon Avenue
Manifold Heights Vic 3218
Phone: (03) 5222 3257

Ray's Outdoors North Geelong
340 Melbourne Road
North Geelong Vic 3215
Phone: (03) 5278 7633

Pro Angler Geelong
22 Boundary Rd
East Geelong 3219
Phone (03) 5248 8338

Mario's Fresh Bait
11 Noel Road
Moolap Vic 3221
Phone: (03) 5248 5201

Outdoor Sportsman
19 Pakington Street
Geelong West Vic 3218
Phone: (03) 5221 5133

CHAPTER 10

MID WEST COAST

Anglesea to Apollo Bay

The coast from Anglesea to the Cape Otway area offers a wide range of fishing options—beach, rock, estuary and offshore fishing. The beaches produce mullet, whiting, Silver trevally, salmon, snapper and gummy sharks to name a few. The main surf beach at Anglesea is a popular place to fish, as are other beaches including The Cove, Hutt Gully, Moggs Creek beach and Wild Dog Creek beach.

Many rivers and creeks also exist in this area. The Anglesea River is among the clearest along this stretch of the coast and has good populations of bream, estuary perch, mullet, salmon and trevally. Other rivers and creeks include Painkalac Creek, Erskine River, St George River, Cumberland River, Wye River, Kennett River, Skenes Creek and Barham River to name a few. Available species include bream, salmon, trevally and mullet.

Rock platforms are also present along this section of the coast, with many species, including kingfish, available at different times of the year. There are also numerous well-known marks offshore from Apollo Bay which produce exceptional fishing at times.

BOAT RAMPS

LOCATION	BOAT SIZE	PARKING	BUILD
Anglesea	4.5 m	Poor	Concrete
Lorne	5 m	Good	Concrete
Apollo Bay	7 m	Excellent	Concrete

Due to this stretch of coastline being rugged and exposed, it offers few boat launching opportunities to access some of its rich offshore waters, the exception being Apollo Bay—here anglers chase big whiting, salmon and great numbers of school sized snapper.

Much of the fishing is around large reefs that also produce plenty of other prize species such as squid, sweep and other rock/reef dwelling species. This stretch of coastline also produces top class mako and thresher shark fishing during the warmer months.

ANGLESEA

The main surf beach at Anglesea is fairly shallow near the river mouth and produces mostly mullet for anglers using soft baits like pipis and worms, but whiting and salmon are also a possibility. Good results are to be had on evening with a high tide beginning to ebb.

During summer, this beach is worth fishing for snapper when the tide is low on evening, enabling you to walk out far enough to cast into productive water. The most productive section of beach is between the old boat ramp below the caravan park and the river.

To the right side of the river mouth, under the look-out and beyond, there is more side drift, and weed is often a problem. Adjacent to the visible reefs, the problem is alleviated to some extent.

THE COVE

The easiest access to this excellent beach is through the caravan park to the left just as you come into Anglesea, then via the old, disused concrete ramp to the beach. It is about a fifteen minute walk around the rocks to the left. The Cove is steep sided, very sheltered and fishing is good.

Considering there is no access at high tide, make sure that you time your trip to walk in before the tide comes in far enough to cut you off. Likewise, make sure you walk out before the incoming tide cuts off your retreat.

POINT ROADKNIGHT

Access from the main road past Anglesea is down Third and Eighth avenues. There is a boat ramp here, but although the point shelters it, locals frequently choose to launch from the beach.

Launching from this area is difficult, even on the ramp because of the accumulation of soft sand. Owners of 2WD vehicles are advised to carry a long rope in case the trailer has to be uncoupled and retrieved from where the vehicle can gain traction. Launching from the beach requires experience so either take an experienced beach launcher along with you or be prepared yourself and take your time.

There are good colonies of bass yabbies in the lee of Point Roadknight, and these can be pumped when the tide is out enough to expose their holes. Ensure you have a good bait bucket in which regular water changes can be made without having to run the risk of tipping out your prized bait. Regular water changes will keep your bait alive longer.

There is a rock platform at the tip of Roadknight giving access to deep water in conditions of low tide and small swell, but most of the time it is a good place to avoid.

BACK POINT

The Point Roadknight back beach is a beachcomber's delight because of the flotsam washed up here. Nowhere else will you find so many cuttlefish bones or pieces of driftwood and other debris around the area.

As you walk over the sand dune from the car park, you will see a dual drain running to sea at the west end of the reef below you. The beach immediately adjacent to this reef to the right is a productive spot for small snapper on evening, with salmon and whiting a good possibility as well.

Further up toward the point, there is a small bay area in the reef. Although you can fish both sides of the bay, the right hand side is most productive. Access is via Melba Parade then along the beach to where the sand finishes.

Care must be taken here, as with all rock fishing locations facing the ocean. Wearing waders is particularly dangerous and has contributed to the number of recorded fatalities from this area.

ANGLESEA RIVER

The Anglesea River is the clearest river on this part of the coast. It has good populations of bream, estuary perch, mullet, small salmon, silver trevally and eels.

Between April and August, the best fishing is to be had between the bridge and the river mouth. From September, better results are to be had upstream from the bridge. These are general rules to coincide with the movements of fish within the river.

Above the Great Ocean Road Bridge, there is vehicle access along the west bank of the river to Coogoorah Park and then you will have to walk. On the east bank you can go almost up to the island below the power station in your car, passing many convenient fishing locations along the way.

Many of these locations are along Bingley Parade in the township itself where one can fish the east bank of the river without moving very far from the car—this is particularly convenient in bad weather.

Below the bridge, access to the east bank is via the walking track that begins at the bridge and gives access to the whole of the east bank between the bridge and the mouth of the river.

Vehicular access is through the caravan park. To avoid any problems during the summer months when overcrowding is common, ask at the main office before entering.

The best times to fish the Anglesea River are early morning and from late afternoon through the evening and into the night; daylight fishing tends to be patchy.

Small fish and mosquitoes will both try your patience on the Anglesea River. The tougher baits like crabs and squirters will slow down the pickers, and Aeroguard the mosquitoes... but keep the two separate!

HUTT GULLY

The first easily accessible beach just out of Anglesea, Hutt Gully has long been a favourite beach for salmon, with some snapper being taken from the exposed reef at low tide. Silver trevally are another possibility.

This spot fish's best when there is a channel running off the right hand side of the reef. A high tide running off from evening through until dark is most productive. Winter is the best time of the year to catch salmon and trevally at Hutt Gully. Fishing techniques don't have to be anything special, just a simple paternoster rig will suffice. To enhance your success, a little berley can go a long way. Salmon and silver trevally are partial to a variety of baits but you can't go wrong with a bag of pipi's.

The stretch of beach between here and Urquharts Bluff is interspersed with reef and offers many opportunities for piscine prospecting. Good vehicular access with parking close to the beach.

URQUHARTS BLUFF

The most notable feature here is the deep hole and run-out to the left of the reef under the bluff. The beach is sheltered, which gives light tackle enthusiasts opportunities to catch garfish, mullet and salmon. The hole at the end of the reef is most productive for the latter. Full tide is usually productive during daylight with good garfish catches to be had in the lee of the reef when conditions are calm. Garfish are a mid to top water feeder whereby a float setup is favoured. When choosing a float, a waggler style or quill provides better bite detection than a conventional "bobby cork" type float. Garfish have only small mouths so opt for a light gauge offset hook such as the Mustad 4540 ½ model.

NATHANS POINT LEFT

Access to this ledge is from Urquharts Bluff car park. It is quite a long walk to the right to reach the far end of the reef. Snapper, whiting and salmon are the main species to be caught, and a low tide rising through dusk seems most productive. The bottom is lined with rock and sand and unfortunately you will lose sinkers and rigs so take some back up terminal tackle. If you can work out where the sand patches are, you'll be in the right spot for whiting. A paternoster rig with strips of tenderised strips of fresh calamari works really well. If you are looking for a snapper or salmon, flick out a big bait amongst the reef.

ELEPHANT ROCK

This distinctive formation, and other rock fishing platforms between Urquharts Bluff and Aireys Inlet, used to be accessible from the highway by a 4WD track that has now been closed. However, there is access through the housing estate.

AIREYS INLET TO APOLLO BAY

AIREYS INLET

Aireys Inlet is notable for the semi-detached headland known as Eagle Rock, which stands out from the cliffs under the lighthouse on Split Point and is visible for many miles along the coast. You can get out to the rock at low tide and fish from the lower ledge until the next low tide change. Unfortunately the ledge is narrow and doesn't give you very much room to cast. Care must be taken at all times. This location does fish quite well producing flathead, salmon snapper, wrasse and the occasionally whiting in season. it is quite reefy terrain and tackle lose is imminent so be prepared.

OFFSHORE

Approximately 1km out to sea from Split Point, there is an obvious drop-off directly in front of the lighthouse. This is a productive area for snapper in October and November.

Co-ordinates to locate this area are: The three chimneys on the lighthouse in line, and to the north-east or Anglesea side, the right hand corner of an obvious paddock with the car park. These co-ordinates should locate you at the outermost point of the bank. If the ocean swell is low, anchoring is effective over the reef but to find a variety of fish species, drifting is preferred.

BEACH FISHING

The beach to the right of the river mouth is quite a walk from where you can park your car but worth it should you fancy light tackle fishing in the surf for mullet and small salmon that are plentiful. Large salmon and gummy sharks sometimes move into the surf on dark. When targeting mullet and salmon, a berley trail of pellets placed into an onion bag and left to wash around in the shore break is highly effective. After dark, you might want to get out the heavier tackle and rig up a fresh salmon fillet on a running sinker rig and cast it out as far as you can. Fishing for gummy sharks is most productive during the lead up to a full moon.

Painkalac Creek

Bream are taken both above and below the bridge in sufficient quantity and size for this estuary to have a strong following of anglers. Other species found within this estuary include estuary perch, yellow-eye mullet, small salmon and trevally. The best times to fish are early morning and evening.

This estuary fishes best of all when the entrance is open and tidal. Access to the mouth of the river is by foot over gravel across from the hardware shop. Access to the sand dune side of the river is via the car park at the main road bridge.

Another popular place to fish for bream is where the road to Bambra runs alongside the river upstream from the town. Here the stream takes an abrupt bend and turns away from the road again almost at right angles. Upstream access to the heavily wooded section of the stream is by canoe or small rowing boat

Estuary perch are prolific throughout the Painkalac Creek but more difficult to catch than bream. A shrimp or bass yabby drifted down beside reeds or obvious snags is an excellent method of catching them. Estuary perch are more active in the summer months and respond well to surface poppers worked across the surface of weed beds on warm balmy evenings. During the day, soft plastics worked in the deer holes works well. Twitching suspending hard body lures amongst the snags and along the edges of the reeds is best.

Fairhaven

Although more popular with swimmers than with anglers, Fairhaven is a productive beach on evening and after dark, both for salmon and gummy sharks. The surf tends to be heavy on this beach when the tide is high.

Between the Fairhaven Surf Lifesaving Club and the Moggs Creek Bridge is a broken channel running parallel to the beach. Salmon feed here during the day, while gummy sharks and silver trevally move in on evening and after dark. Ensure you're ready for action if you're keen on catching a gummy shark. Due to the surf, heavy sinkers on a star pattern to 6oz may be required from time to time. Gummy sharks have a knack of busting anglers off in the shore break when an attempt is being made to land them. In this case, it is vital your using 80lb leader and a good 6/0 circle hook. Gummy sharks love fresh baits whereby calamari, salmon and silver trevally work extremely well. For your best chance, fish the lead up to full moons.

Moggs Creek Beach

The stretch of beach in front of Moggs Creek itself has a better reputation than other beaches in this area because it has produced a lot of salmon over the years. It's rare to find nobody fishing at Moggs should the weather be reasonable.

The best time of year for salmon along this section of beach would be from the beginning of May until the end of September. A full tide on dusk is well worth trying here. Fishing for salmon with just a simple bait in the water isn't really going to attract a hoard of fish to your area but with berley it will. Take a tin of home brand tuna cat food. Punch around 20 holes in it about half the size of a 5c coin. Through two of the holes, thread a sturdy piece of wire or 100lb leader line and crimp or tie off to create a loop. Then attach a rope to the loop, secure to a rod holder and toss into the water. The smell of the tuna and oils, will attract fish from far and wide.

Moggs Creek

Although the creek only has a short, overgrown estuary penetrating a few hundred metres above the road bridge, good size bream have been caught in here. Bait fishing methods are best used with a running sinker rig containing a live bass yabbie or piece of peeled prawn.

Eastern View (Great Ocean Road Sign)

Eastern View is a noted night fishing spot for salmon: They often come in very close here, particularly on a high tide in the early hours of the morning. When they do move in, you can see them clearly in the beam of a spotlight or powerful torch. Pipi, white bait and blue bait work extremely well and where possible thread on a blue/white coloured surf popper to the bottom dropper of your paternoster rig, salmon surely love them.

Beach anglers here sometimes take snapper. Low tide on evening during summer is ideal for snapper fishing in the surf at Eastern View because you can wade out far enough to cast into productive water. A good sand spike and pair of waders are recommended though.

Offshore Fishing

Fishing behind the breaker line along this section of coast can be productive—for whiting and snapper using bait, and for salmon with lures. If fishing behind the "breakers" of any beach, the skipper must pay particular attention to the ocean swells as unexpected waves can be unpredictable. Trolling lures is effective for salmon as well as pike and snook. Always ensure you put some knottable or single strand wire in front of your lure to prevent being bitten off.

Flathead are also a common catch by those tending to drift throughout the area. a paternoster rig with squid baits works best.

The headland at Grassy Creek, which is the first toward Lorne, is particularly productive for a wide variety of fish including those mentioned.

Moggs Ledge

Offshore from Moggs Creek there is a ledge dropping away fairly sharply into deep water. Co-ordinates to locate this drop-off are: To the north-east, line up the outer margin of the big rock in front of the Aireys Inlet lighthouse with the tip of the next headland.

To the north, the right hand side of the Moggs Creek Bridge with the gravel road behind it. The ledge or reef is about 600m long and runs parallel to the beach. It is a noted spot for snapper, producing the biggest specimens in November. Anglers targeting snapper both anchor in calm conditions and or drift. When at anchor, a berley trail of mashed pilchards through a berley pot will attract the fish, squid baits are preferred. When drifting a paternoster rig with half pilchards usually sees good results.

Spout Creek

Small aluminium boats are occasionally launched from the relatively sheltered beach to the left of the Spout Creek/Grassy Creek headland, but care should be taken because of the patch of shallow reef just out from the beach.

The rocks on the right-hand side produce a wide variety of fish, particularly on evening. These include mullet, garfish, whiting and salmon. Winter and spring seem two particularly productive times of the year to fish here.

Grassy Creek

The descent from the car park on the hill immediately past Spout Creek, down to Grassy, is well worthwhile if you enjoy rock fishing. The track to the left side of the hill goes down to the rocks at Spout Creek, and the track to the right leads down to Grassy Creek.

The mouth of the creek is fishable at high tide for mullet and small salmon, and the high rock sides of the mouth make safe platforms for the kids.

The cleft rock platform to the left of the river mouth has obvious access to deep water where you may catch sweep, leatherjackets, rock blackfish, zebra fish and others. The cunjevoi growing on the rocks is excellent bait.

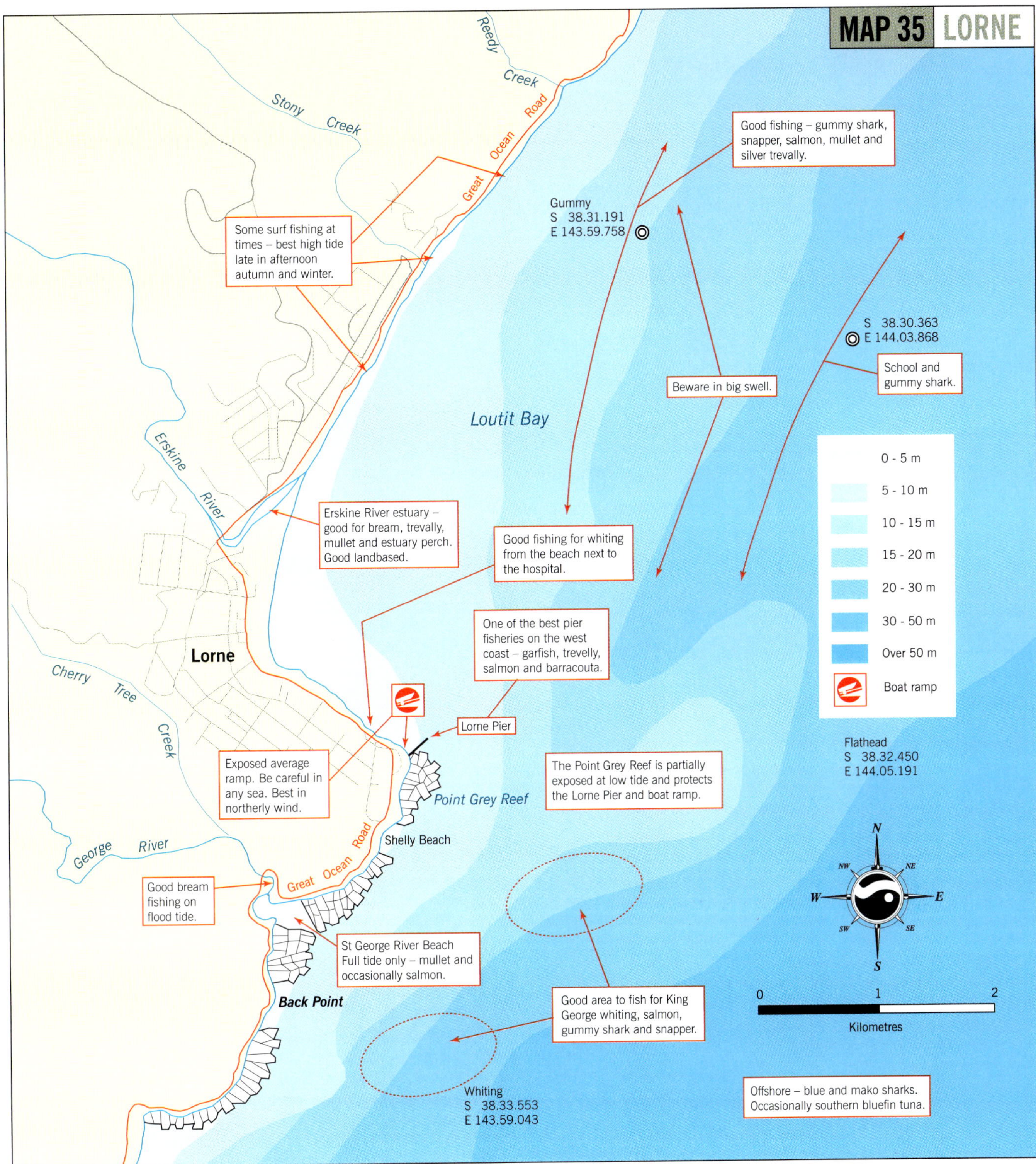

Good casting ability is required to reach snapper, whiting and salmon that seem to remain some distance out from the rocks. All three species bite most readily toward evening. Flathead are also a common catch as the bottom is predominantly sand apart from a few stray patches of reef. Paternoster rigs with squid strips used for bait cast as far as possible and then slowly retrieved yields a food result.

Good lure fishing for salmon is available from the rocks at times, on both sides of the creek, but long casts are required. Chromed metal lures in the appropriate weights for the tackle you are using, are most suitable here. When spinning for salmon, replace the treble hook on the metal lure for an inline single, this will prevent losing the fish when it jumps during battle.

CINEMA POINT

Access to the rocks under Cinema Point is by crossing the shallow waters of Grassy Creek. It is a leisurely 20 minute walk from the car park above Grassy Creek to the best spot.

Walking in from Grassy, you will see car remains of all vintages that have been stolen, stripped, and pushed over the cliff; a few comparatively recently, but most have been reduced to an engine block and a few shards of rusty metal.

The best ledge is a short distance after passing a large cave in the cliff face. It has little or no kelp growing in front of it, and although you would find it difficult to land a fish from the shelving platform, you can lead your catch into the sheltered rock pool or blind channel on the left side.

This ledge fishes well through spring and summer with November being possibly the most productive month. Evening is the best time of day to fish from here.

This ledge fishes well through spring and summer with November being possibly the most productive month. Evening is the best time of day to fish from here.

Big Hill Creek

Here is where the road returns to the coast after climbing through the hills. The rather exposed rock ledges make suitable spinning platforms for salmon, but the amount of kelp here would make bottom fishing rather expensive on tackle. An effective fishing technique in areas where the reef is thick is to cast out pilchards and or blue bait unweighted. Once it gets to the bottom, you can retrieve it and re-cast. This is particularly productive when you have an established berley trail and the fish have gathered in it.

Cathedral Rock

This platform has become increasingly popular with lure casting and garfish enthusiasts, probably as a consequence of the better known platforms situated closer to Lorne becoming more crowded. Snapper and whiting can also be caught on evening if conditions allow.

There are two productive points at Cathedral Rock. One is directly in front of the main car park. The second is to the right of the channel that runs out from the beach below the car park.

The remains of an old car sits on the rocks toward Reedy Creek from Cathedral Rock. To the left and right of this wreck, snapper and whiting have been caught on evening. The bottom of the tide and start of the flood have proven productive here.

Flat Rock

This platform is a short distance past Cathedral Rock where there is room to park your car at the side of the road. This platform fishes well on evening for a wide variety of fish including gummy shark, rock cod, snapper and the occasional whiting and salmon. Though the area is predominantly sand, there are some rocky patches in which you could become snagged on or busted off on. When targeting gummy sharks it pays to use 60lb and or 80lb leader to prevent this from happening.

Reedy Creek

Approaching Lorne there are passable rock platforms at both sides of Reedy Creek, giving access to sufficiently deep water at the creek mouth for good results on a variety of fish.

Bobby corking for mullet or lure casting for salmon is recommended here because the bottom is snaggy and you could lose quite a bit of gear.

Fishing on the bottom with a paternoster rig is also effective as there are some nice flathead which move into the area in the summer months. Strips of squid make great baits.

Lorne Rocks

Just before you get to Stony Creek on the outskirts of Lorne, are rock platforms that are dry in good weather and are probably among the best fishing platforms along the Great Ocean Road: Jump Rock would be the most popular of these.

In recent years, mullet have dominated catches from the rocks between Reedy and Stony creeks, and the most effective technique is bobby corking. In years gone by though, lure casting enthusiasts have taken good catches of barracouta and salmon here, particularly just on dark. Use wire as these two species are known for biting lures off.

Anglers fishing with bait on the bottom occasionally catch salmon. However, on evening, and in the marginal situation between a sloppy and dangerous sea, good catches of salmon, whiting and small snapper are commonplace from here. Big snapper are sometimes caught here in late spring as well.

Loutit Bay

Anglers fishing from the shores of this usually sheltered bay at Lorne seldom do well during the day, unless there is are good numbers of flathead close to shore. However, fishing improves toward dusk and continues after dark. Small sharks and the occasional snapper are the main quarry here, but salmon can also be caught at times.

The Pumping Station

Access to this rock ledge is via a walking track that begins at the main road across from Albert Street. This track takes you to the beach. Whiting can be caught anywhere between here and the pumping station to the right. The best time to fish is on evening with the high tide running off.

Good size whiting can be caught from the reef in front of the pumping station, which is a wet, but safe and a sheltered platform in reasonable weather. Long casts are not required here. As long as you clear the reef by 20 m or so you are likely to catch fish. Heavy tackle is not required. Try 3 kg tackle with a 15 g sinker and No 4 hook.

Boat Ramp

The Lorne boat ramp is situated on the left side of the Lorne Pier. It is not used as frequently as you might imagine because it is both a difficult and dangerous ramp from which to retrieve a boat when there is a swell running. The most common problem arises when anglers launch their boats early in the morning, at which time the sea is often fairly flat. Later in the day, with a swell running, retrieving becomes difficult, sometimes dangerous.

There is a smaller ramp beside the main ramp that belongs to the Lorne Aquatic and Angling Club. This ramp is for the use of members only.

On the other side of the pier, between Point Grey and the pier itself, there is a strip of sand between the rocks that is used in an emergency to launch and retrieve boats to 5.5 m, but only by 4WD vehicles.

Lorne Pier

This is probably the most productive man-made platform to fish from along the west coast. Long poles slung over the side are a common sight at the pier, and bobby corking close to the pier with soft baits like worms and pipis will sometimes produce mullet and gars.

The same baits fished deeper down will produce good catches of silver trevally when they are about. This same technique with fresh pilchards or whitebait on heavier tackle will sometimes produce salmon and barracouta after dark. Use ganged hooks on a wire trace for the latter.

Casting out from the pier with light or medium tackle produces a variety of fish, including salmon at times. Big whiting are often caught halfway up the pier on evening and big snapper are not uncommon. Lure casting from the pier may produce salmon and barracouta in the early morning and evening.

There are some anglers who eagerly seek squid, and good catches can be made from the pier at times, particularly at night. A baited jag suspended under a float works well but anglers tossing size 3.0 and 3.5 artificial jigs around the piers lights at night see most of the action. When looking for a place to make your cast, inspect the pier and where you notice a lot of ink splatter from past catches, make casts in these areas. This is a good indication that there is a weed bed out from the pier which might hold numbers of calamari. There is also a platform underneath the pier from where it is possible to catch leatherjackets and parrot fish. This spot is popular with young anglers.

Point Grey

You can fish toward the pier from the rocks at Point Grey, but only from the outside on a calm day—usually it is too rough. The inside, or sheltered side toward the pier is good for whiting and garfish when the tide is out, particularly on evening.

The ledge is a wet one with any swell at all, but relatively safe by rock fishing standards. Rock blackfish and zebra fish of good size can sometimes be caught in the lee of the reef using sandworms for bait.

Erskine River

The estuary of the Erskine lies between the beach and the Great Ocean Road bridge; it produces good catches of mullet, small silver trevally and the occasional small salmon to anglers using baits like pipis and sandworms.

Access to the east side of the estuary is through the caravan park on the main road near the Deans Marsh turn off. Access to the west side is through the caravan park on your left after crossing the bridge over the river, this is the same road that goes to the paddle boats.

More challenging species like bream and estuary perch respond to appropriate techniques in the evening and after dark. Bream bite well on the incoming tide when the mouth is open to the sea. Best bream fishing is right down near the mouth in winter and near the toilet block in summer. Lure casting enthusiasts will find plenty of scope in the estuary for perch. The most productive months for bream are May, June and October, and estuary perch from December until March or April, depending on salinity. Small trevally, salmon and mullet may be present at any time throughout the year.

St George River

The estuary of the St George River below the Great Ocean Road after leaving Lorne is shallow, but it produces good catches of mullet and small salmon when the tide is coming in toward full and again for the first hour or so of the ebb.

The obvious deep holes in the vicinity of, and upstream from the bridge may produce a bream or two in the evening. Bream will respond well to a variety of baits but freshwater yabbies are the top bait. Remember to remove the two front claws before casting. This will increase your chances.

St George River Rocks and Beach

The beach at the St George is also shallow but its proximity to the river mouth ensures that there are plenty of mullet waiting to be caught on soft baits like pipis.

The rock platforms adjacent to the river mouth sometimes produce good size whiting and occasionally a small snapper of an evening, but the bottom is snaggy. You only seem to catch parrot fish here of a day.

As you climb the hill away from the St George River, there is a spot to park your car near the 145 km post. The big rock just below is a reasonably safe platform in good conditions and produces sweep, parrot fish and the occasional rock blackfish.

St George River Back Point

The second car park on your left past the St George River gives access to the Back Point. It produces salmon, and trevally during winter with snapper and whiting as well during summer. Best results here are to be had in the evening.

There are two platforms. Access to the first is via the car park and directly below it. The second platform is about 100m from the first platform and accessible from a track down from the road 200m from the first car park past the river.

Offshore

The water offshore from the St George River is noted for good catches of whiting and snapper. The occasional good size gummy shark is also taken, particularly on moonlight nights.

Drifting the offshore waters is the most effective technique because you will cover a great deal of ground and encounter a wide variety of species. Ideally, a paternoster rig will be suitable for snapper while a running sinker rig is ideal for gummy sharks. When drifting offshore, it pays to use harder flesh baits such as tuna and squid.

Windy Point

Just before you descend the hill to the She Oak River entrance, you will see a concrete pole near a short guard rail. The car park above Windy Point is just past here.

The track winds down to the rocks from a culvert to the left of the car park, where there are three platforms from which to choose. Like other rock platforms in this area, it fishes best on evening, but this one is particularly dangerous with any swell running because the water is deep in close and the occasional larger wave brings green water pouring over the rocks.

She Oak River

The rock strata on the left side of the She Oak River mouth has been pushed up sharply forming steeply shelving platforms with deep water below, but it is difficult to fish from these ledges.

Salmon occasionally have bait cornered in the little bay here on dawn or dusk giving lure casting enthusiasts a chance to experience exciting fishing. Salmon have a knack of jumping off hooks so if your casting metal slugs, change the treble hook for a single inline hook.

On the right side of the river mouth, the rock ledges are flatter, making more comfortable fishing platforms. The best of these would be some distance around to the right from the mouth.

The Quarry Hole

Access is immediately below the second car park past the She Oak River, then over the boulders and stones down to the platform below. Be very careful of loose rocks on your descent.

This platform fishes best on an evening low tide and for the first hour or so of the flood tide. The platform is dangerous in a building swell. Target species are salmon, snapper and whiting. Never turn your back on the ocean while fishing from the rocks and always make sure you have the right foot attire such as rock boots.

The Ninety Mile Post

Another platform worth mentioning is at the old ninety mile post. Looking from the direction of the She Oak River, the platform is the furthest point toward the end of the reef before it turns into a small bay. The track from the car park takes you directly down to a platform from where you can fish.

This is a safer platform than some of the others mentioned because the rock is well out of the water. You will need good casting ability to do well because the reef where the fish are is almost a hundred metres out. Target species are salmon, whiting and snapper.

Cumberland River

The estuary of the Cumberland is a beautiful scenic spot with large rocky escarpments overlooking the estuary. Though small, it sometimes holds small mullet, salmon and brown trout. There is a camp ground along the Cumberland River which is run by the Cumberland River Holiday Park. To book a campsite or cabin, call 03 5289 1790.

Staying for a night or longer will allow you to really explore the area and river. Brown trout are a popular catch with anglers finding success using fly and lure spinning methods the most effective.

Cumberland River Beach

The beach at Cumberland River is fairly shallow, but in common with most estuary mouth beaches, it has good populations of salmon and mullet that take soft baits like pipis fished on light tackle. Bigger salmon are taken spasmodically from the month of May through until September.

The rock platforms on the right-hand side of the river mouth do not look all that attractive, but produce good catches of small snapper on evening, particularly on the early ebb tide. During the day, parrot fish seem to be most active with an outside chance at a salmon or small silver trevally.

Mount Defiance

It helps to have some mountain goat ancestry to get down the gully to the platforms on the Cumberland River side of the Howard Hitchcock Lookout at Mount Defiance. If you are experienced at rock fishing, the descent may be worthwhile.

Excellent catches of snapper have been taken from these ledges, and experimental attempts at live baiting with small mullet and salmon have produced yellowtail kingfish to four kilograms. Throughout the summer months, Kingfish frequent the entire coastline but you never know when they will show up. If you are fishing in this region between December and April you're in with a good chance. Occasional mulloway captures have also been reported.

If you intend to fish here, take some time to familiarise yourself with the behaviour of the sea. This is no spot for beginners.

Jamieson River

The rock platforms at the mouth of the Jamieson River attract anglers who catch salmon and other varieties of reef fish such as wrasse, Parrot fish, silver trevally and flathead. These platforms are overshadowed by those nearby at Artillery Rocks.

Artillery Rocks

As you climb the hill away from Jamieson River, you will see the sign marking Artillery Rocks where there is parking space for several cars.

The descent to the left-hand side of the rocks can be made quite easily, and the most popular platforms are just in front of you and to your left.

The obvious deep sand hole to the left as you walk out on the rocks produces mullet that respond to berley. Good size whiting have been taken here on evening and early morning as well. Casting to the east with bait or lures on surf fishing tackle, you are most likely to catch a good size salmon, with evening producing the best results.

Fishing from the front of the platform is dangerous with any sort of sea running, but a variety of fish are caught out here including salmon and the occasional big snapper or whiting. You need to cast at least 50 m to clear the rocks and kelp or you will be snagged repeatedly.

Walking some distance along the rocks to your right, you will reach a sloping ledge from which you can fish at low tide. The water is deep and produces a variety of fish including snapper. However, when waves begin washing up the ledge on the incoming tide then it is time to leave.

Further along still, you will come to a little rocky bay that produces some really big whiting. Weed and toadfish can both be a menace here, but persevere until you find where to cast and you may get some thumpers.

Boggaley Creek

There is plenty of room to park your car here, and an excellent protected channel between the rocks into which you can fish for garfish. But unless you get there early, the best spots most likely will be taken.

The outer reef at Boggaley on the far side of the channel can occasionally be fished when conditions are flat enough, but on most days it gets a fair bit of spray.

Separation Creek

The mouth of Separation Creek is a short distance before Wye River. It is a popular spot, with someone always fishing from the rocks or beach. Salmon and yellow-eye mullet are the main species caught here. A little berley goes a long way and will attract fish in good numbers.

Wye River

There is a hotel and shops here as well as camping facilities at the BIG 4 holiday park, but you will have to book early for the holiday season.

Bream are occasionally caught in the estuary, along with mullet, small salmon and brown trout in the upper reaches if you're prepared to go for a walk along the river bank. Flicking small hard body lures is very effective.

The rock platforms on the right-hand side of the river mouth sometimes produce a salmon or two and an occasional good bag of gars, particularly from the rounded boulder out from the rest known as 'Old Baldy'. When targeting garfish, use a float setup for best results.

Station Point

The rocky point under the Wye River Telecommunications Installation known variously as 'Station Point' or 'Radio Point' is popular with anglers. The descent is easy from where you can park your car and the water is deep within easy casting distance of the rocks. The high tide running off on dark is a productive time to fish for snapper here.

Although the best catches of snapper have been taken from the end of the point on dusk, you can always fish in the deep hole in the lee of the point if the sea is too rough to fish elsewhere. There is always the chance of catching a flathead, salmon, whiting or trevally from here.

Flat Rock

Leaving Wye River and traveling toward Apollo Bay, the road runs parallel to the beach before taking a left, followed by a right turn. Just before the right turn there is parking space for only two cars. Pull in here and you will find a track which leads down to a reasonable platform. The best results are to be had on a high tide ebbing through evening, but be careful because seas roll in heavily at times.

Kennett River

The beach is popular with surfboard riders, which usually confines angling to the evenings and early mornings.

The river mouth is well populated with small salmon, silver trevally and mullet on the ocean side of the bridge, and upstream from the bridge, small brown trout share the same water with bream and the species already mentioned. Good catches of bream have been taken in the vicinity of the bridge from October through until December. Fishing with small diving crank baits and soft plastics sees most of the action.

The beach on the Apollo Bay side of the bridge is a noted flathead spot. Casting out with whitebait, then beginning an immediate, slow retrieve will produce good catches of flathead, some of them quite large.

The rock platform on the right-hand side of the river mouth produces a variety of fish including large whiting, salmon, snapper and occasional kingfish. However, the bottom is snaggy with a great deal of kelp in close to the ledge, making this area very hard on tackle.

Fishing offshore from the reef, large yellowtail kingfish have been hooked fairly frequently but few have been landed due the amount of shallow reef in the vicinity. Heavy tackle is recommended when seeking these bruisers some of which have been estimated to be in excess of 20 kilograms.

Grey River

The reef on the right-hand side of the river is productive for snapper, whiting and salmon and fairly intensively fished because it is substantially sheltered from prevailing westerlies by Cape Patton. The bottom is snaggy and you usually lose a fair bit of tackle when fishing from here. Access is via the car park on the Apollo Bay side of the bridge.

APOLLO BAY

CAPE PATTON

Anglers have taken good catches of snapper from the ledges at the base of Cape Patton in calm seas, but regard these ledges as off limits unless you can find someone to show you the area. Most fish are taken from boats.

Drifting across the face of the cape in a boat is considered to be a most productive way of fishing. If you pick up no fish on your first drift, go in or out a short distance until you find the action. In summer the main target are snapper. Boat access to Cape Patton is from the port of Apollo Bay to the west.

CARISBROOK CREEK

Carisbrook Creek is clearly signposted on the Great Ocean Road just before Apollo Bay. To the right of the creek mouth, an excellent rock platform produces a variety of fish including sweep and garfish. Berley is required for the best results. Lure casting enthusiasts may also experience good sport with salmon here and possibly barracouta on evening.

WHITE CRESTS

The White Crests guesthouse is prominent on the Great Ocean Road between Carisbrook and Smythes Creek and the adjacent rock platforms are noted for producing excellent catches of garfish.

A particularly productive area is the gutter about 400 m back toward Geelong. Other anglers have reported good results from the rocks in front of White Crests in good weather.

Some anglers launch small boats from a sheltered gap in the reef near White Crests. This requires a 4WD vehicle and some caution.

Offshore from here there is a reef or ledge running parallel to the coast beginning in 10 fathoms and descending to fifteen. You will probably require a depth sounder to locate it but it is a highly productive feature, fishing well on the drift for snapper and trevally. Drifting over the sand will also produce some nice flathead.

WHALEBONE CREEK

This popular platform is found between White Crests and Petticoat Creek. The preferred spot, which produces whiting and snapper, is on the left point. Fish the bottom of the tide on evening for the best results.

VON MUELLER GULLY

There is a small car park at the side of the road where the Von Mueller Creek descends the steep gully to the sea. It is a fair climb down to the rocks below, but there is a reasonable fishing platform to the left.

Like many of the platforms along this part of the coast, a high tide running off on evening is the best time to fish.

PETTICOAT CREEK

The short beach between the rocks at Petticoat Creek shelves steeply and the water looks deep with waves breaking very close to shore. On evening, this beach is worth trying with fresh squid or whitebait in the hope of catching a salmon, snapper or whiting.

There is a passable rock platform right of the creek that is suitable for lure casting in good weather, but avoid it with any swell running.

SKENES CREEK

The beach at Skenes Creek is close to the car park at the bridge and very popular with anglers. The quarry here is most commonly mullet and salmon, although some good size silver trevally have been taken from the beach after dark. Throughout the day, spinning with metal lures is most effective for salmon and the odd barracouta.

WILD DOG CREEK

The beach between the Wild Dog Creek and Apollo Bay has been dependable over the past few years. Salmon are often caught here during the day, and silver trevally after dark. Pipis are good bait on this beach as is blue and white bait. A paternoster rig is recommended so to cast into the deeper water.

The road runs parallel to the beach for quite some distance and there are many spots from where you can fish without being too far from your vehicle.

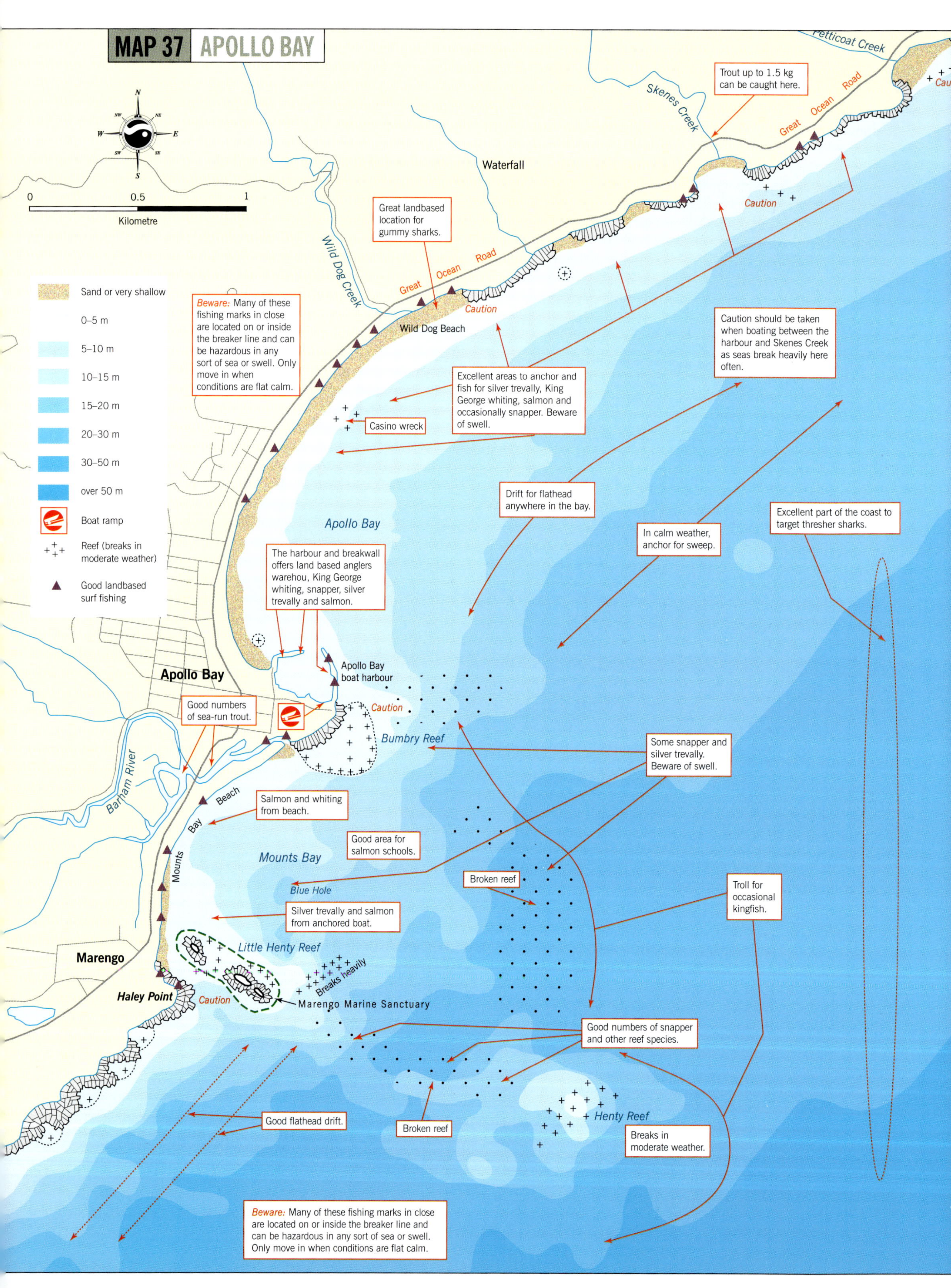
MAP 37 APOLLO BAY
0
0.5
1
Kilometre
Sand or very shallow
0–5 m
5–10 m
10–15 m
15–20 m
20–30 m
30–50 m
over 50 m
Boat ramp
Reef (breaks in moderate weather)
Good landbased surf fishing
Petticoat Creek
Skenes Creek
Trout up to 1.5 kg can be caught here.
Great Ocean Road
Caution
Waterfall
Great landbased location for gummy sharks.
Wild Dog Creek
Wild Dog Beach
Beware: Many of these fishing marks in close are located on or inside the breaker line and can be hazardous in any sort of sea or swell. Only move in when conditions are flat calm.
Caution should be taken when boating between the harbour and Skenes Creek as seas break heavily here often.
Excellent areas to anchor and fish for silver trevally, King George whiting, salmon and occasionally snapper. Beware of swell.
Casino wreck
Drift for flathead anywhere in the bay.
Excellent part of the coast to target thresher sharks.
In calm weather, anchor for sweep.
Apollo Bay
The harbour and breakwall offers land based anglers warehou, King George whiting, snapper, silver trevally and salmon.
Apollo Bay boat harbour
Good numbers of sea-run trout.
Bumbry Reef
Some snapper and silver trevally. Beware of swell.
Barham River
Beach
Bay
Mounts
Salmon and whiting from beach.
Good area for salmon schools.
Mounts Bay
Blue Hole
Broken reef
Troll for occasional kingfish.
Silver trevally and salmon from anchored boat.
Little Henty Reef
Breaks heavily
Marengo
Haley Point
Marengo Marine Sanctuary
Good numbers of snapper and other reef species.
Good flathead drift.
Broken reef
Henty Reef
Breaks in moderate weather.
Beware: Many of these fishing marks in close are located on or inside the breaker line and can be hazardous in any sort of sea or swell. Only move in when conditions are flat calm.

APOLLO BAY TO CAPE OTWAY

Apollo Bay Surf Beach

Hayley Reef shelters the beach at the mouth of the Barham River which can still be fished even when the weather is heavy enough to wipe out other locations.

One of the good things about this beach is that the kids can fish for mullet in the estuary while mum and dad fish in the surf. But if the bream are biting in the river, it's the kids who might bring home the prize catch. Running sinkers rigs work best here with peel prawns or live bass yabbies used for bait.

Mounts Bay

One and a half kilometres or so west of Apollo Bay is Mounts Bay. It fishes well on both the top and bottom of the tide; particularly should either coincide with evening.

When the tide is in, you can cast out from the shore into the surf, but when the tide is out, you will need to wade out into the shallow surge to be able to cast into productive water. In the latter case you will need waders and a good sand spike.

Marengo

A turbulent beach with many run-outs or rips. The whole beach is interspersed with reefs and channels, probably why it attracts so many fish. The outward or left-hand end, adjacent to the reef, is one of the best places to fish, especially early morning or evening.

Local anglers have caught whiting over 900 g from this beach, but report that it can be hard getting them in past the kelp.

The extreme left of Marengo, just at the beginning of the reef, is an excellent spot for salmon and silver trevally, but only in the very early morning or late evening.

Boat anglers launching from Apollo Bay fish for big whiting in the gap in Haley Reef offshore from Marengo. The direction of tide flow will determine on which side of the gap you will be able to fish.

The Rifle Butts

Another productive spot for catching garfish and sweep from the rocks is the Rifle Butts, an obviously good rock platform adjacent to the third little bay as you exit Marengo to the right or west, about 1.5 km past the caravan park.

The Barham River

The good thing about the Barham River is the wide variety of fishing options it offers close to the township. In the lower estuary, which runs parallel to the road between the mouth and the bridge, good catches of mullet can be taken on a variety of soft baits including pipis and prawns.

Bream are usually present in good numbers both below and above the bridge and can be taken on a variety of baits including both sea and freshwater shrimp, crabs, bass yabbies, scrub worms, and some packaged baits like prawns.

Estuary perch can be caught from the Barham. The estuary perch is noted for its lightning fast strike, and quick dash back to cover, which must be halted to avoid losing it among the snags. Both bream and perch respond well to lures with soft plastics really working well when worked around the snags.

Apollo Bay Harbour and Boat Ramp

You may need to go no further than the boat harbour for your holiday angling requirements at Apollo Bay, because a variety of fish including barracouta, salmon, trevally and big flathead can be taken from the harbour walls. The jetties within the harbour also fish well of an evening, and at night, producing trevally, warehou (sea bream), as well as mackerel and the occasional big barracouta.

The boat ramp is fairly well sheltered except from an easterly wind or swell, and gives access to numerous good spots around Apollo Bay. Even when it is too rough to fish in open water, you can still fish inside the harbour from your boat with some expectation of catching fish, particularly silver trevally.

The harbour has become very popular with lure fishermen as they get in and around the wharves casting small lures and soft plastics into the shadows for trevally. Try to stop the trevally from breaking you off on the poles— often this is easier said than done.

Elliot River

Access is via the Elliot River Road that runs off the Great Ocean Road approximately 4 or 5 km past Marengo. You must descend a steep walking track to get to the rock platform below, which is approximately 200m to the left of the track.

The exposed rock platform at the inlet is relatively safe in a light swell and good catches of whiting, salmon and snapper have been made here. Garfish are another possibility if it is really calm. The bottom is a mixture of reef and sand throughout the area. Unfortunately, due to the reef sinkers and tackle will be lost so ensure you have adequate tackle if you are going to fish here.

Parker River

Parker River is accessible from the track into Blanket Bay. Take the Cape Otway Lighthouse Road for approximately 400m to the left to reach the access track to the beach. Road access is to within 2km of the Parker River entrance.

There is little value fishing in the river, but the rock ledges on either side produce a wide variety of fish including King George whiting, salmon, small snapper and garfish.

Crayfish Bay

The turn off to Crayfish Bay is also from the Blanket Bay track approximately 100 m past the turn-off to Parker River. The best ledge is usually awash so take care. Excellent fishing opportunities occur when good weather coincides with calm seas.

OFFSHORE MARKS FROM APOLLO BAY

There are numerous well known marks offshore from Apollo Bay that produce excellent fishing, some are included here.

Cape Patton

Many of the really big catches of snapper taken from Apollo Bay come from the area between Cape Patton and Petticoat Creek. When in front of the Cape you will see a bare white cliff and it is from here you will travel offshore. The reef is approximately 1.5 km directly off the point of Cape Patton in 35 to 40 m of water. It runs north-east towards Lorne.

In order to get a good drift one needs a mild south-west wind and the tide coming up to the flood. If the snapper are on the bite you will almost certainly see other boats in the area.

Whalebone Creek Outlet

This area has produced large numbers of small snapper, both to anglers fishing from the beach and from boats. From a boat, this mark can only be fished on a dead calm sea because it is only about 100 m offshore!

From the water you will see the Sea Ranch Holiday Units on a hillside and the creek outlet is to the left of these. Looking up the outlet, you will see a house and a vineyard as well. Again make sure you only approach this mark in flat, calm seas.

THE WATERFALL

Offshore from this obvious landmark back toward the Wild Dog Creek is one spot where anglers have caught Apollo Bay's most famous fish, the silver trevally.

The productive ground is not far from shore, only about 300m, maybe less. When the big trevally are about, you will see other boats fishing there, so move within a discreet distance before anchoring.

Chunking is the technique most used for catching the biggest trevally. This means cutting fish, usually pilchards, into small pieces, and feeding the pieces over the side one by one rather than clouding the water with particles. Every so often a piece of bait is dropped over the side with a hook in it. If there is no result, it is retrieved, and the process is then repeated. Trevally have quite a soft mouth and anglers should take their time and not put too much pressure on initially. In an ideal world, anglers should use a high abrasive fluorocarbon leader ranging 12-16lb as well as a small hook, either a size 4 circle hook or 6 long shank hook. Once a silver is hooked, ensure the reels drag is set and take your time to bring it to the boat.

BRUMBY REEF

This reef is situated directly out from the big wall of the harbour and is very popular in the summer. Drifting is the best approach and you will notice distinct drop-offs on the sounder screen. Small snapper, whiting, silver trevally and flathead are common catches.

BIG HENTY REEF

About a kilometre out from the Apollo Bay inner reef, this feature attracts huge populations of fish including salmon, silver trevally and barracouta and many more species that don't respond to standard methods of fishing.

Trolling with lures on the surface, or on a leaded snook line are proven methods of getting good bags of fish here. On good days you can approach close enough to cast lures on light tackle into the wash around the reef.

Similarly, you can anchor up and fish with bait for snapper and trevally close to the reef when there is a low swell, but keep an eye out for any change in conditions that could increase the risk of breaking waves.

HALEY REEF

In rough conditions, anglers can fish in the lee of Hayley Reef with either bait or lures and expect to do well on salmon, snapper and silver trevally.

On each side of the gap in Hayley Reef—both the Marengo side and the ocean side—you may be successful at catching the big whiting this reef is noted for, but do not obstruct the passage through the reef because it carries a fair bit of boat traffic.

BALD HILL

On the ocean side of Hayley Reef are the flathead grounds where some excellent catches are made. The area out from Bald Hill is said to be particularly productive. Should the flathead be on the bite, and conditions permit, you will see other boats grouped in the area and fishing on the drift—approach discreetly.

This location is easily found by travelling south past Hayley Reef for about one and a half kilometres. Looking to land you will see a large, dark fern-coloured hill. Drift directly in front of this hill about a kilometre off shore. Caution must be exercised here in any sea conditions as it can frequently break.

BLANKET BAY

Blanket Bay is about 10 km down the coast by boat from Apollo Bay and is sheltered by the first major headland on the way down to Cape Otway. Blanket Bay is famous for excellent catches of snapper by offshore anglers. These are usually up to 2 kg with an occasional bigger fish among them.

Recent captures of yellowtail kingfish from here suggest anglers using appropriate methods could catch more of this species. Jigging with suitable lures in the deep water just off the reef is suggested.

Exceptional silver trevally are taken from Blanket Bay at times, usually by anglers fishing for snapper. By road, Blanket Bay is somewhat further, more than double the distance, but the trip is worth it. Turn off the Great Ocean Road on to the Cape Otway Lighthouse Road about 25 km past Apollo Bay, then turn left down the Blanket Bay Road to Point Lewis. It is about 6 km to Blanket Bay after crossing the Parker River Bridge.

There are camping facilities here and a small beach from where light boats can be launched and retrieved behind a sheltering reef. Fishing from both the rocks and beach is possible when weather and tide are suitable, and there are a variety of fish to be caught. On a cautionary note, the ascent from Blanket Bay to the main road is steep and the track is sometimes impassable after heavy rain, so keep this in mind when planning a trip.

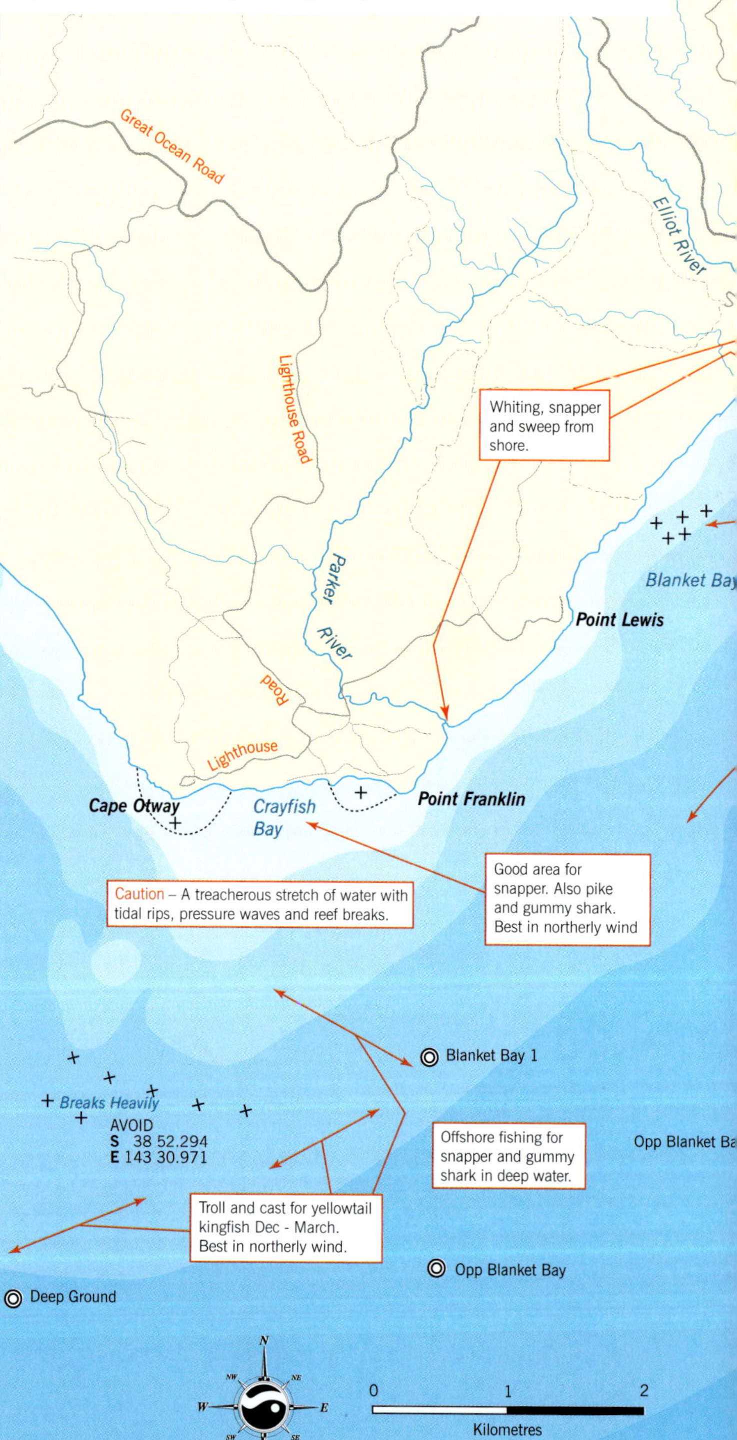

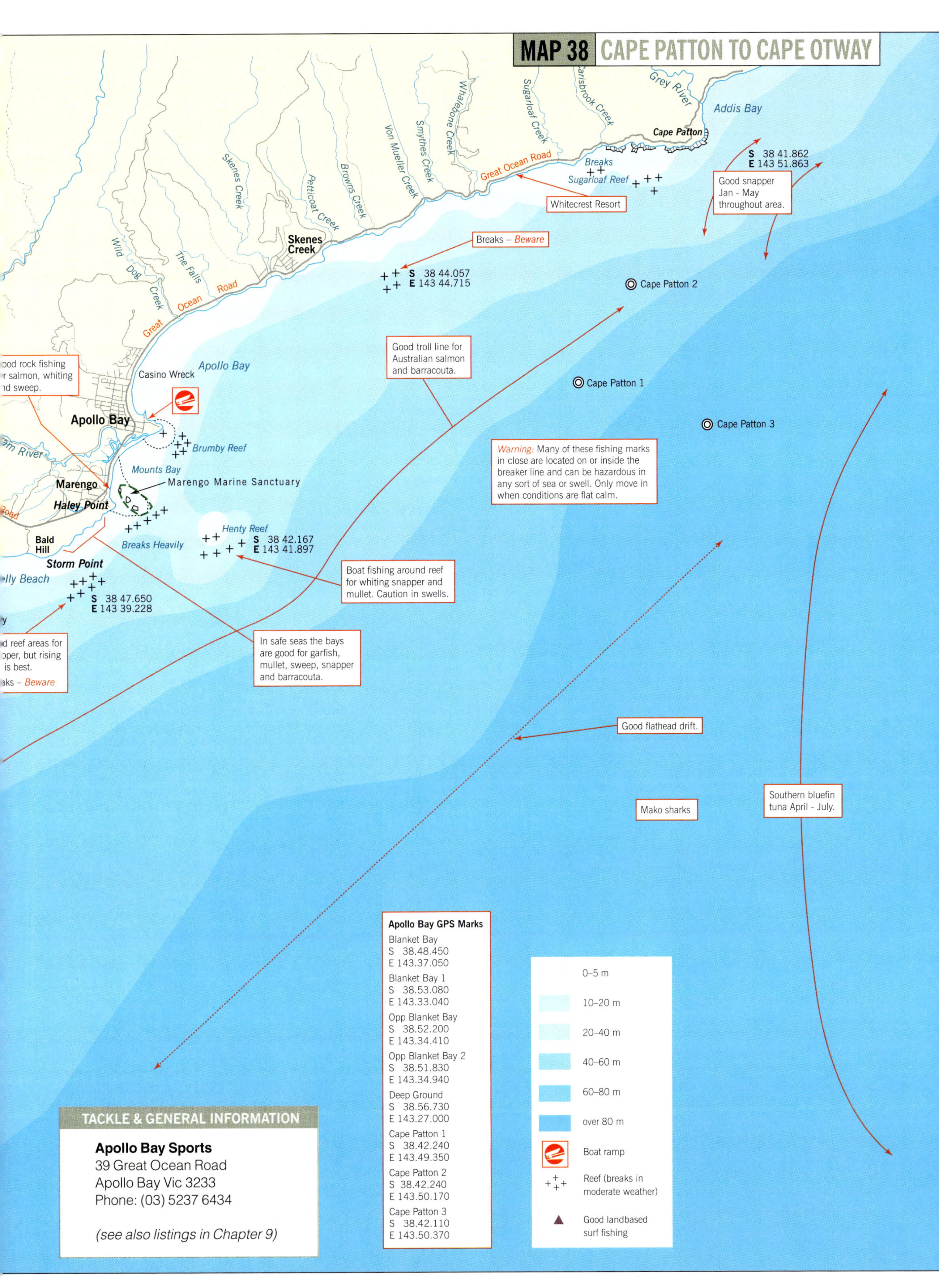
MAP 38 CAPE PATTON TO CAPE OTWAY
Grey River
Addis Bay
Cape Patton
Whalebone Creek
Sugarloaf Creek
Smythes Creek
Von Mueller Creek
Browns Creek
Petticoat Creek
Skenes Creek
The Falls
Wild Dog Creek
Great Ocean Road
Breaks
Sugarloaf Reef
Whitecrest Resort
S 38 41.862
E 143 51.863
Good snapper Jan - May throughout area.
Skenes Creek
Breaks – Beware
S 38 44.057
E 143 44.715
Cape Patton 2
Good troll line for Australian salmon and barracouta.
Cape Patton 1
Cape Patton 3
Casino Wreck
Apollo Bay
Apollo Bay
Brumby Reef
Mounts Bay
Marengo
Marengo Marine Sanctuary
Haley Point
Warning: Many of these fishing marks in close are located on or inside the breaker line and can be hazardous in any sort of sea or swell. Only move in when conditions are flat calm.
Henty Reef
S 38 42.167
E 143 41.897
Bald Hill
Breaks Heavily
Storm Point
S 38 47.650
E 143 39.228
Boat fishing around reef for whiting snapper and mullet. Caution in swells.
In safe seas the bays are good for garfish, mullet, sweep, snapper and barracouta.
Good flathead drift.
Mako sharks
Southern bluefin tuna April - July.
Apollo Bay GPS Marks
Blanket Bay
S 38.48.450
E 143.37.050
Blanket Bay 1
S 38.53.080
E 143.33.040
Opp Blanket Bay
S 38.52.200
E 143.34.410
Opp Blanket Bay 2
S 38.51.830
E 143.34.940
Deep Ground
S 38.56.730
E 143.27.000
Cape Patton 1
S 38.42.240
E 143.49.350
Cape Patton 2
S 38.42.240
E 143.50.170
Cape Patton 3
S 38.42.110
E 143.50.370
0–5 m
10–20 m
20–40 m
40–60 m
60–80 m
over 80 m
Boat ramp
Reef (breaks in moderate weather)
Good landbased surf fishing
TACKLE & GENERAL INFORMATION
Apollo Bay Sports
39 Great Ocean Road
Apollo Bay Vic 3233
Phone: (03) 5237 6434
(see also listings in Chapter 9)

CHAPTER 11

FAR WEST COAST
Cape Otway to Warrnambool

This stretch of coastline runs from Cape Otway to the South Australian border. While it does experiences some hostile weather and rough seas, it also produces some of the best fishing to be found along the Victorian coast.

Many of the west coast estuaries have always been favoured by anglers as they produce top class bream and estuary perch fishing—they've become only more popular with the growing band of anglers who chase these species with lures and flies.

Several of the west coast estuaries also produce mulloway, and while most are on the smallish side they are often available in good numbers, with none better or more famous than the Glenelg River at Nelson. If you are after a large mulloway then several beaches and offshore reefs produce huge fish.

The surf beaches produce not only great numbers of salmon, but many caught are of a far better size than those found further east. The beaches also produce good gummy and school sharks for anglers fishing at night. While most of these beaches are well known and offer good access such as Johanna, Logan's Levy's, East, Yambuk and Narrawong, there are also some lesser known ones that take more effort to get to, sometimes involving climbing down steep slippery tracks. However, the results can be well worth it.

When the swell is small there are several fine land based locations to fish where anglers can catch good numbers of snapper, whiting, snook, trevally and even kingfish.

Fishing from a boat in this part of the world can produces all sorts of great fishing. Close to shore anglers have opportunities to target big whiting, lots of school snapper, gummy and school sharks, snook, squid, trevally and some decent kingfish through the warmer months.

Fishing further offshore anglers can find bluefin tuna ranging from 10 to over 100 kilograms. Aside from the tuna there are mako, thresher and blue sharks, all of which are in good numbers for those who enjoy the challenge.

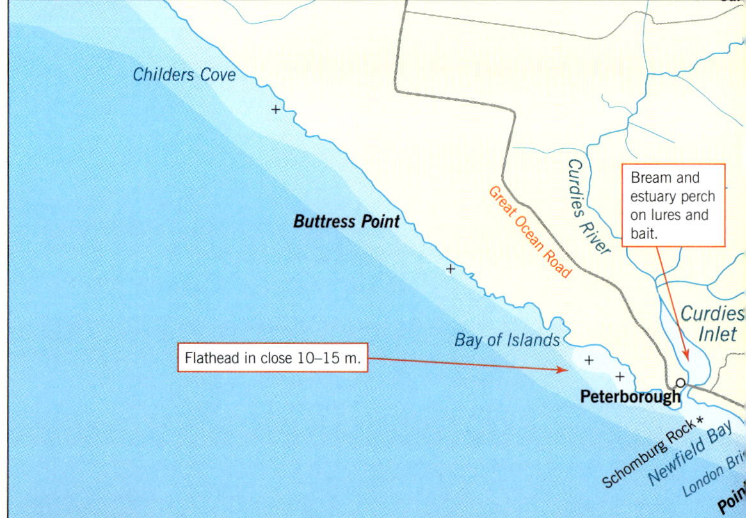

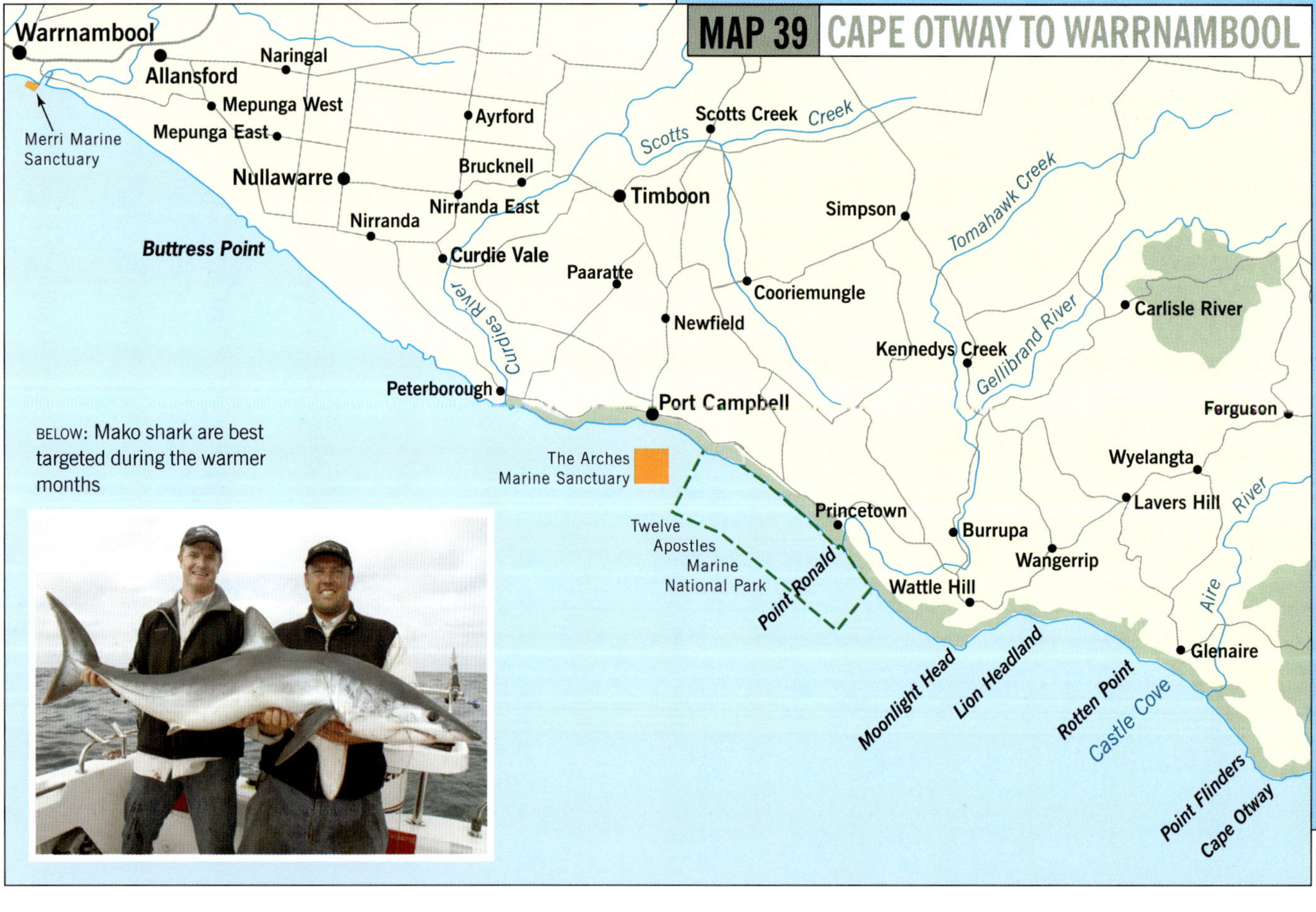

MAP 39 CAPE OTWAY TO WARRNAMBOOL

Warrnambool
Allansford
Naringal
Mepunga West
Mepunga East
Merri Marine Sanctuary
Ayrford
Scotts Creek
Nullawarre
Bucknell
Nirranda East
Nirranda
Timboon
Simpson
Tomahawk Creek
Buttress Point
Curdie Vale
Paaratte
Curdies River
Cooriemungle
Newfield
Kennedys Creek
Gellibrand River
Carlisle River
Peterborough
Port Campbell
Ferguson
The Arches Marine Sanctuary
Wyelangta
Lavers Hill
Twelve Apostles Marine National Park
Princetown
Burrupa
Wangerrip
Point Ronald
Wattle Hill
Aire River
Glenaire
Moonlight Head
Lion Headland
Rotten Point
Castle Cove
Point Flinders
Cape Otway

BELOW: Mako shark are best targeted during the warmer months

BOAT RAMPS

LOCATION	BOAT SIZE	PARKING	BUILD
Curdies River	6 m	Good	Concrete
Peterborough	5.5 m	Good	Timber
Bay of Islands	5.5 m	Average	Concrete
Hopkins River, Mahoneys Road	5 m	Average	Concrete
Hopkins River, Lyndock	5 m	Very good	Concrete
Hopkins River, Institute Ramp	5 m	Very good	Concrete
Warrnambool	8 m	Excellent	Concrete
Killarney	4.5 m	Poor	Sand
Port Fairy	7 m	Very good	Concrete
Yambuk	4.5 m	Average	Crushed rock
Portland	8 m	Excellent	Concrete
Nelson	7 m	Very good	Concrete
Simpsons	7 m	Very good	Concrete

AIRE RIVER TO CHILDERS COVE

Aire River

Take the Horden Vale turn-off from the Great Ocean Road approximately 6 km past Cape Otway to reach the lower Aire River estuary. Should you come via Lavers Hill, it is about 30 km after reaching the Great Ocean Road. Take the second turn-off to the right, which is approximately 6 km after leaving the Great Ocean Road. After travelling a further 1.5 km you will reach the river.

You may launch a small boat here or walk to your destination—the surf beach or the river up or downstream.Should you intend to fish upstream, cross the bridge and proceed along the east bank to where there is excellent bream fishing. When water levels are lower, such as when the river is open to the sea, it is possible to

MAP 40 AIRE RIVER TO CHILDERS COVE

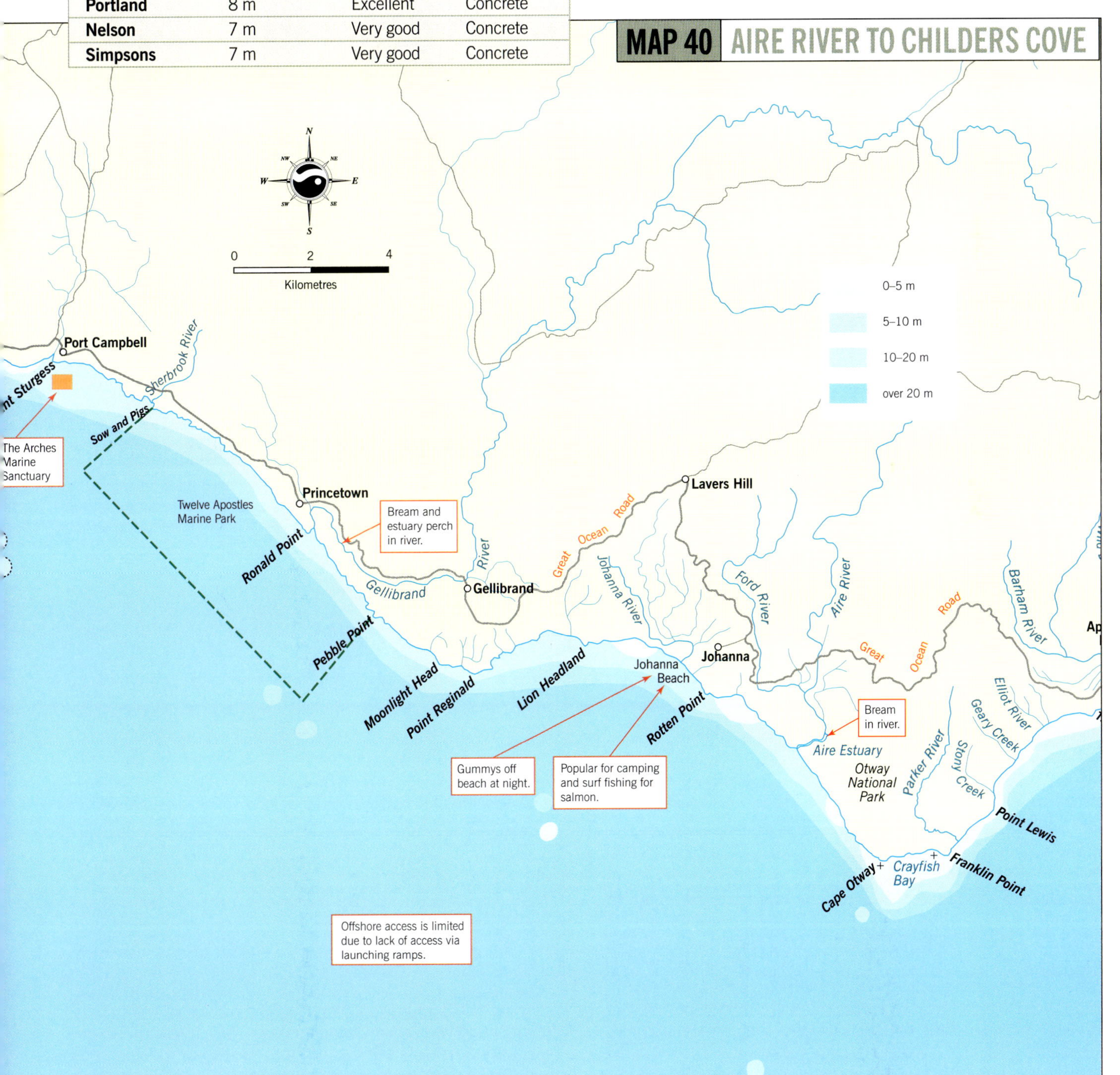

get small boats under the bridge.Bream can be caught fishing with shrimp on the edges or with prawns fished on the bottom. Lure fishing for bream is also very effective. The best bream fishing is usually in the lower reaches of the river during the weeks following the river mouth opening to the sea.

Up and downstream from the Great Ocean Road, the Aire River contains some very large brown trout as well as other estuarine species including the occasional mulloway, estuary perch, Australian salmon and yellow eye mullet. You will need to explore the area by day to find the holes you want to fish. Trolling or casting lures from a small boat is effective on trout; however, one of the best methods of targeting the larger fish is to fish from the bank with bait after dark on a moonless night. Live baits of minnow, shrimp, mudeye or black crickets are very effective. Big trout specialist, Stan Wright, advises anglers not to use a light of any kind because these big fish can spook very easily. The junction of the Ford River and Aire River downstream from the highway bridge is a popular spot to fish for trout. The Ford River is a smaller tributary of the Aire River and is also a popular trout fishery which carries a healthy population of brown trout.

Both the Aire and Ford Rivers downstream below the Great Ocean Road Bridge are exempt from the Victoria salmonid closed season regulations and trout fishing is permitted all year round. While not an overly popular waterway, the Aire does produce great fishing and is a favorite location for many local anglers, especially those who like to fish with lures. Camping is allowed near the old bridge, for bookings contact Parks Victoria on 13 1963.

Aire River Surf Beach

Should the surf beach be your destination, do not cross the bridge. It is about a 15 to 20 minute walk to the surf or about the same time in a small rowing boat. The beach on the east side of the river is one of the state's most productive surf fishing beaches, particularly at night when you will catch salmon without fail. Other species sometimes caught here include gummy shark, school shark, snapper an7d mulloway. Remember, fish at night with baits of octopus, squid or cured eel fillet for best results.

Castle Cove

Shortly after crossing the bridge, the road swings to the coast at Castle Cove where you can fish from the beach. The track down to the beach is very steep, and, although not quite as good as the beach at Aire River, the fishing is excellent. A variety of fish can be caught from here with whiting, salmon, trevally, flathead, pinky snapper, barracouta, pike and snook. Spinning with metal lures usually see's salmon, barracouta, pike and snook being caught while the rest tend to come from those soaking a bait on the sea floor. When fishing this location, stick to using squid baits, they are highly favoured by all listed species.

Moonlight Head

Although more popular with scuba divers seeking crayfish and abalone than with anglers, Moonlight Head does have suitable ledges dropping sharply into deep water from where a variety of species including sweep and snapper have been taken.

Anglers casting lures from this location do catch decent numbers of snook, salmon and some kingfish, best results usually come by also using berley to attract the smaller reef fish which then brings in larger predators.

It is a long, but reasonably safe climb down to the main ledge for anybody accustomed to rock fishing. However, this area should be avoided if physical fitness is in question.

Johanna Beach

The schooner Joanna went aground here in 1943 while travelling from Tasmania to Portland, and the beach has carried its misspelled name ever since. Access from the Great Ocean Road is down either Blue Johanna or Red Johanna Roads to a large clearing a few hundred metres from the water's edge.

A steep and turbulent beach interspersed with reef, Johanna produces salmon and a variety of other fish for surf anglers throughout the night and day. Night fishing is most productive for all species, but a visual inspection of the beach in daylight is necessary to ascertain where reefs and rips occur. While well-known as a salmon beach, this location produces some very large gummy sharks to 30 kg for anglers fishing at night. Try fishing on the top of the tide around the full moon with baits of fresh salmon fillet, octopus or cured eel for best results. Camping is allowed along the foreshore, for more information contact Parks Victoria on 13 1963.

Princetown

There is a general store at Princetown, a Football Club and not much else. But it is the nearest settlement to the Gellibrand River and Serpentine Creek. The junction of the Serpentine Creek with the Gellibrand River downstream from the Great Ocean Road, below Princetown, is a great spot for family fishing. Bream, estuary perch, yellow eye mullet and small Australian salmon are abundant throughout the estuary. Fishing downstream of the old bridge is very popular and there is plenty of bank access. You can even launch a small boat at the boat ramp on the south side of the bridge. Camping is allowed at the Princetown Recreation Reserve, situated on Old Coach Road (just off the Great Ocean Road).

Gellibrand River

The Gellibrand River is often closed to the sea, but has a healthy population of bream and estuary perch. School mulloway have also been caught from this estuary, as well as large brown trout. Large sea-run brown trout frequent the lower reaches of the estuary during the spring months and can reach over 4 kg in size. The Gellibrand River downstream of the Great Ocean Road Bridge is exempt from the Victorian salmonid closed season regulations and trout fishing is permitted all year round.

There is pedestrian access to the eastern side of the estuary near the mouth and the most promising looking spot to fish is the deep water close to the bank where the river takes a sharp bend. You can fish from the sand spit at the entrance when the mouth is open and the tide out, or from the reedy bank adjacent to where you can park your car. Snags and weed beds upstream do hold good numbers of estuary perch and big bream for anglers casting lures or un-weighted baits of shrimp or minnow. Trolling and casting lures from a small boat is a good way to target the larger sea-run brown trout.

Surf Beach

The Gellibrand River runs to sea (when the entrance is open), over a steeply shelving beach between two rocky headlands. This beach is well-known and popular with surf anglers. There are good angling prospects for Australian salmon, snapper, gummy sharks and the occasional mulloway on the beach on the eastern side of the river mouth. Walking further east, you will reach another excellent beach with some very obvious deep water within metres of the shore. Note that the Twelve Apostles Marine National Park covers a large expanse of the inshore waters in the area. Surf fishing from the beach is allowed in the 2km exclusion zone which runs 100m out from the high water mark southeast from Point Ronald near the Gellibrand river mouth to Rivernook. As with all surf fishing exploits, More information about Victoria's marine parks and sanctuaries can be found at www.parkweb.vic.gov.au.

Gibsons Steps

Approximately 4.5 km past Princetown, Gibson's Steps are clearly signposted, less than 100m from the highway.

The descent from the car park to the beach below is a demanding one, but nothing compared to the climb back up should you be fortunate enough to catch a few fish!

Clifton beach below Gibson's Steps is deep, with a reefy bottom and a good deal of weed. The best daytime prospects are at the base of the steps where whiting are an obvious target species from the sandy areas visible amongst the reef and weed. Australian salmon are regularly encountered on the beach but fishing on evening and after dark will produce gummy shark or snapper. Be careful climbing back up the cliff and make sure you take a torch.

This area is listed in the vicinity of the Twelve Apostles Marine National Park where fishing is not permitted; however there is an exclusion zone which runs 100m from the high water mark along the coast from Gibson Steps eastward to the end of Clifton beach where shore based angling is permitted. For more information about the Twelve Apostles Marine National Park visit www.parkweb.vic.gov.au

Port Campbell

The crayfishing fleet manages the Fisherman's Jetty on the Great Ocean Road at Port Campbell. It produces a wide variety of fish including silver trevally, whiting, squid and snapper. Night fishing may produce an occasional barracouta, and crayfish have also been caught from the jetty by anglers fishing flesh baits on ganged hooks on the bottom, and from the rock shelf either side of the jetty.

Campbell's Creek runs in at the back of the cove and is fishable for at least 1.5 km upstream. It occasionally produces some good size bream and mullet.

The rock ledges around Port Campbell are popular with dedicated sweep fishermen; however caution must be taken along this dangerous area of the coast. Snorkelling or diving for crayfish and abalone is popular when calm conditions allow.

Small aluminium boats may be launched and retrieved from the beach in the cove at Port Campbell, but there are no facilities to launch and retrieve larger boats except for the angler's crane on the pier.

Flathead and sharks are popular target species offshore, but local knowledge is required along this treacherous part of the 'Shipwreck Coast'.

Note that the Arches Marine Sanctuary (45 ha) is situated about 1.5 km offshore, south from the township of Port Campbell and fishing is not permitted in the sanctuary. For more information visit www.parkweb.vic.gov.au.

The Arch

There is some climbing involved to fish from the rock ledges either side of The Arch look-out, but rock fishing enthusiasts take some excellent sweep here and drop-netters catch the occasional good size crayfish.

London Bridge

Continuing towards Peterborough, there is easy access to the beach adjacent to London Bridge that fishes well for salmon in good weather.

Onshore winds make this beach unfishable most of the time because of the amount of weed that gets blown up on the beach.

Newfield Bay

Just before Peterborough, Newfield Bay is a favourite with anglers seeking Australian salmon, whiting and small snapper. There is a parking area towards Peterborough, from which it is only a short walk over the sand dunes to the beach.

The west end of the beach is usually clear of weed and produces good catches of salmon. While surf fishing with bait is popular at this location when the salmon are close to shore, casting metal lures can be very effective. The east end of the beach is rocky and difficult. However, this end of the bay, also known as 'The Blue Hole', produces a wider variety of fish including whiting, garfish and an occasional snapper.

Curdies Inlet

The Curdies Inlet at Peterborough is often closed to the sea, however the shallow inlet, and the much deeper Curdies River which feeds it, produces excellent fishing for several species. There are two boat ramps to access the river and inlet: one is behind the caravan park at Peterborough on the western side of the inlet, and the other much further upstream near the bridge at Boggy Creek.

The upper reaches of the Curdies offer some excellent lure and fly fishing for bream, and also carries good numbers of estuary perch. Both species frequently hold tight in the snaggy water so accurate casting will bring the best results.

From here down to the where the Curdies River runs into the inlet or 'lake' as it's sometimes called, the bream fishing can often be first class with not only plenty of fish, but also numbers of bigger specimens. Again, there is excellent lure and fly fishing and the banks become more open. There is good fishing from boat or bank, although shore access by vehicle is limited and requires some local knowledge. A range of baits will work from prawns and sandworms to scrub worms, spew worms and freshwater yabbies.

Good fishing occurs right down through the inlet to the mouth, although much of the inlet away from the main channel can be quite shallow. As well as the bream and perch, there are often reasonable salmon present in good numbers, plenty of mullet, and several other species show up at times. When the river mouth is open to the sea, King George whiting can sometimes be caught around the Great Ocean Road Bridge.

Peterborough

Peterborough is located at the mouth of the Curdies River. Small aluminium boats can be launched at Peterborough provided the ramp isn't sanded over. Salmon and mullet can be caught from the beaches around Peterborough, the best beach possibly being at the mouth of the Curdies. Park your car in the parking area on the east side of the bridge from where the beach is only a five minute walk or alternatively you can park on the western side near the point, but access to the beach is dictated by the river mouth channel being open or not. When the river mouth is open, large schools of Australian salmon sometimes frequent this beach and they can be targeted with bait or casting lures from the beach.

Bay of Martyrs

Clearly signposted west of Peterborough, the Bay of Martyrs is popular with anglers seeking mullet and salmon although drifting weed can be a problem. When fishing at this location it does pay to use heavier tackle. Rigs such as paternoster rigs should be tied from 15lb fluorocarbon leader or use a pre-tied rig purchased from any good tackle store.

Red Hill

Walking out of the Bay of Martyrs car park to the east you overlook a rocky point; this is known as 'Red Hill'. Although a difficult spot to fish, it has produced good bags of mullet along with sweep and salmon.

Crofts Bay

The Crofts Bay track is signposted from the highway past Peterborough. Although not a popular beach with anglers, it does produce good catches of salmon and mullet during the day and occasionally a good size whiting. Snapper and gummy shark may be taken on evening and after dark.

Crofts Bay seems to fish best of all on low tides when anglers can wade out far enough to cast into productive water, particularly when the low tide occurs on evening or after dark. This is a great place to dive for abalone and crayfish when the sea is calm.

Childers Cove

The turn-off to Childers Cove is very well marked, but the cove is more popular with divers who are after abalone and crayfish than with anglers. However, it is a good spot for a picnic with public toilets and barbecues. Small salmon and mullet may be caught from both the beach and rocks adjacent during calm weather. Due to the thick heavy reef, you will lose a lot of tackle so be well prepared if fishing here.

WARRNAMBOOL

HOPKINS RIVER

The lower Hopkins is probably the best-known and one of the most productive estuary systems on the whole west coast of Victoria. Despite being only a modest-sized estuary system, it produces excellent bream fishing as well as good numbers of estuary perch and at times good numbers of school sized mulloway. Small to medium sized salmon and mullet are often abundant.

The Hopkins was once best-known for its bait fishing, however it is very popular these days with lure and fly fishers, and for good reason. It produces first class fly and lure action for bream and perch, and the size and numbers of the fish caught are impressive.

The estuary itself is tidal for eight kilometers from the mouth, which closes and opens depending on rainfall and heavy seas.

There are four boat ramps along the river giving access to all sizes of craft. There's one on the west side of the river just upstream from the bridge at Lyndoch, next to Proudfoot's boatshed, the end of Mahoney's Road and another at Jubilee Park.

There is good fishing to be had along the whole river, although fish will at times be concentrated in some areas depending on time of year, river height, salinity and other factors. The mouth area produces good bream and at times large schools of perch are found at the road bridge and nearby weedbeds. The sandflats near the mouth are often a great place to pump bait such as sandworms and bass yabbies. Both are top baits in the Hopkins.

Heading upstream there are a variety of locations to fish, from sand flats, to reed banks and rock walls—one of the most famous of these being the Kings Head area. There are also plenty of weedbeds, all of which can produce fish on their day.

Further upstream, the Jubilee Park area is also well regarded. Further up still, is some deeper water, all of which holds good fish. The deep hole at the

Nelson
Lake Bong
Discovery Bay
Discovery Bay
Marine National
Park

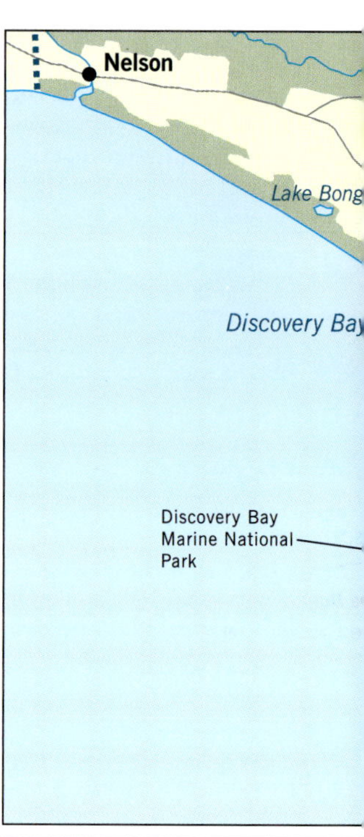

MAP 42 HOPKINS RIVER AND LADY BAY

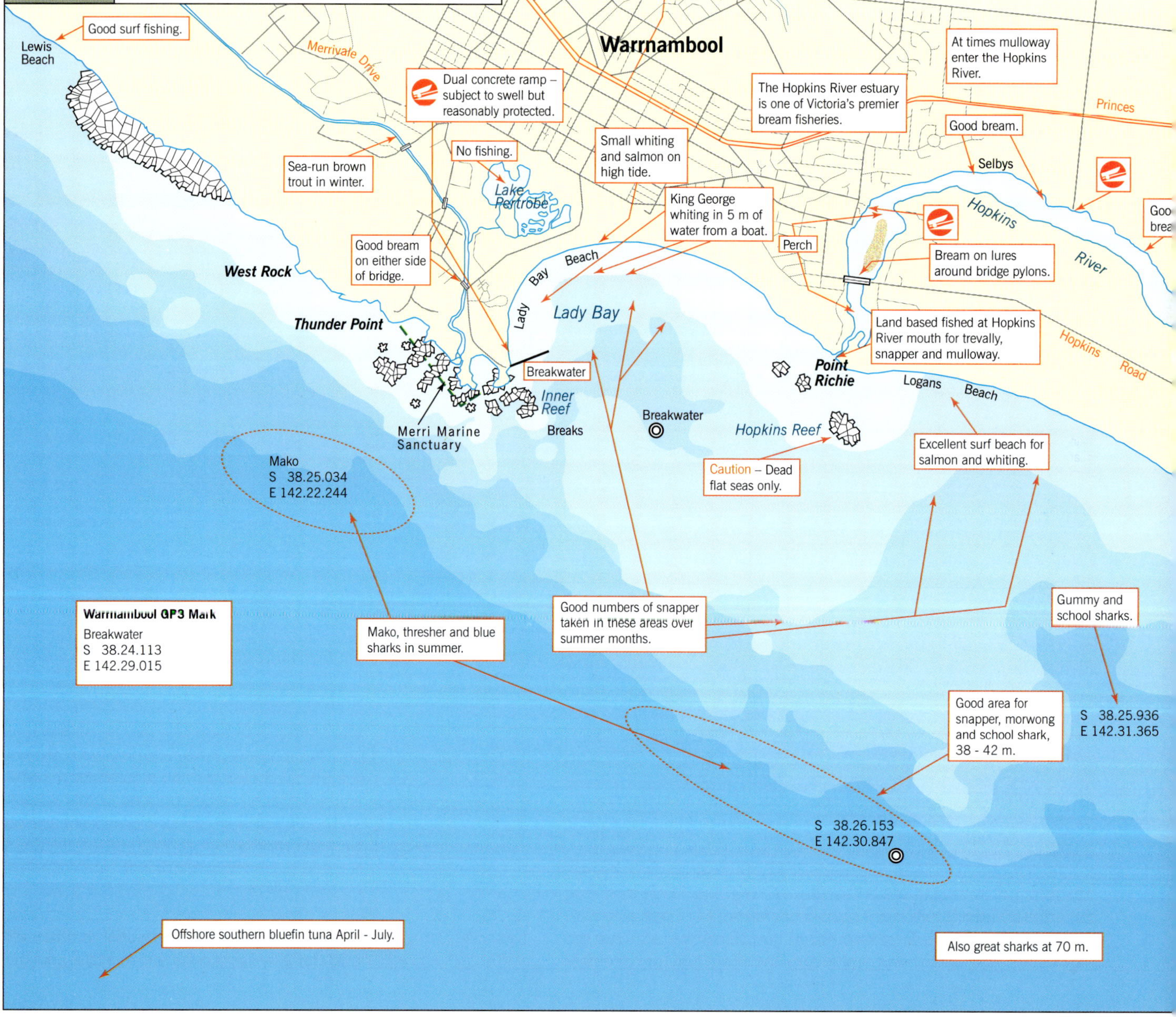

Good surf fishing.
Lewis Beach
Merrivale Drive
Warrnambool
Dual concrete ramp – subject to swell but reasonably protected.
The Hopkins River estuary is one of Victoria's premier bream fisheries.
At times mulloway enter the Hopkins River.
Princes
Good bream.
Selbys
Sea-run brown trout in winter.
No fishing.
Small whiting and salmon on high tide.
Lake Pertrobe
King George whiting in 5 m of water from a boat.
Hopkins
River
Good bream
Perch
Bream on lures around bridge pylons.
Good bream on either side of bridge.
West Rock
Lady Bay Beach
Lady Bay
Thunder Point
Land based fished at Hopkins River mouth for trevally, snapper and mulloway.
Hopkins Road
Breakwater
Point Richie
Logans Beach
Inner Reef
Merri Marine Sanctuary
Breaks
Breakwater
Hopkins Reef
Mako
S 38.25.034
E 142.22.244
Caution – Dead flat seas only.
Excellent surf beach for salmon and whiting.
Warrnambool GPS Mark
Breakwater
S 38.24.113
E 142.29.015
Mako, thresher and blue sharks in summer.
Good numbers of snapper taken in these areas over summer months.
Gummy and school sharks.
Good area for snapper, morwong and school shark, 38 - 42 m.
S 38.25.936
E 142.31.365
S 38.26.153
E 142.30.847
Offshore southern bluefin tuna April - July.
Also great sharks at 70 m.

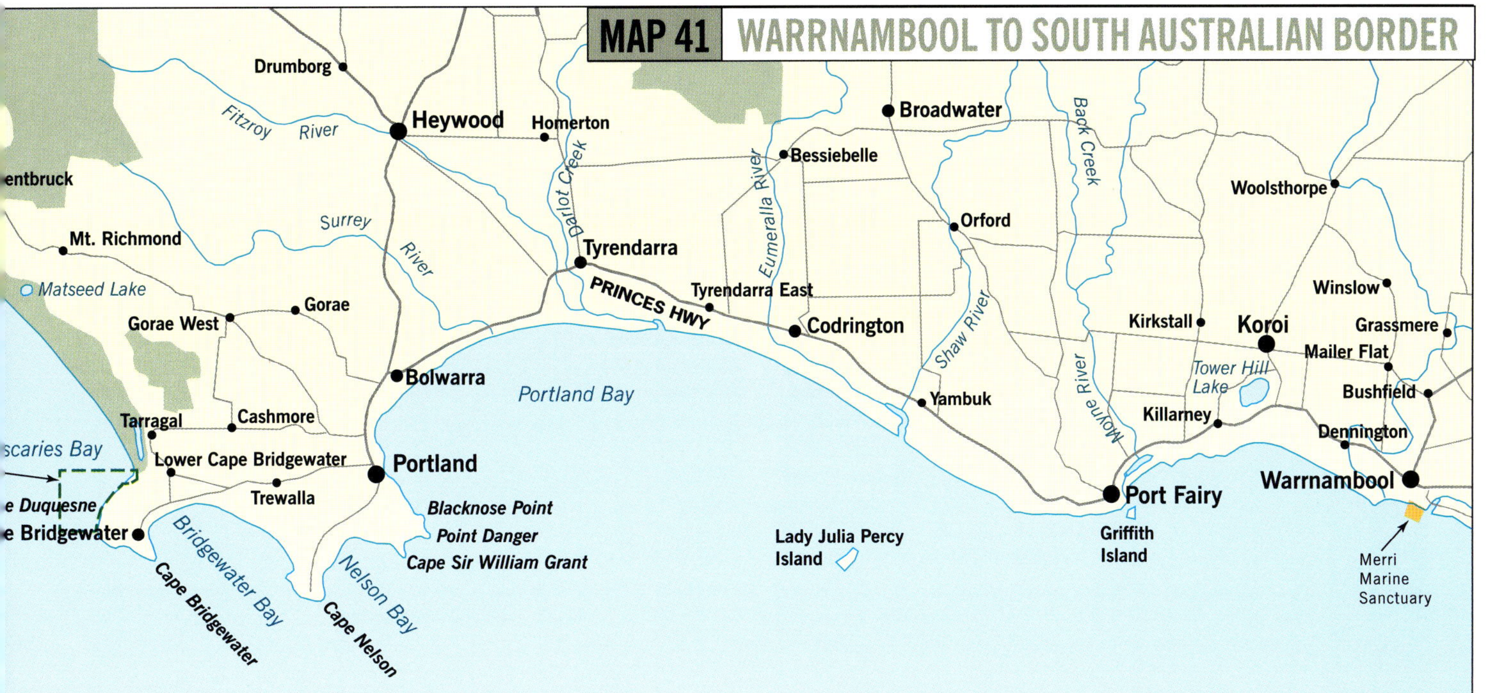

Tooram Stones (where the estuary ends) is also a known mulloway spot, while the reed beds that line this stretch offer excellent estuary perch fishing, especially with flies.

Boat operators should be wary of several shallow reef areas in the Hopkins River, some in unlikely spots. Keep speeds around 8 km/h, especially until you know the waterway.

Occasionally sea-run brown trout are also caught in the estuary. The lower Hopkins River is classified as a sea-run trout fishery and is exempt from the Victorian closed season regulations and is open to salmonid fishing below Hopkins Falls all year round. The river is stocked with 4000 yearling trout each year.

The Merri River

The estuarine section of the Merri River extends for several kilometres. It is famous for large brown trout, some of which appear to be genuine sea-runners. This water receives the largest riverine stocking of brown trout in Victoria with 7000 yearling brown trout stocked annually. These fish provide good wet fly and lure fishing, especially when the river is carrying a decent flow. Some sections of the river are suitable for small boats, but there is plenty of good, accessible bank fishing. The lower Merri River below the Bromfield Street Weir is classified as a sea-run trout fishery and is exempt from the Victorian salmonid closed season regulations, offering some of the State's best brown trout fishing with fish averaging 1.5 to 4kg commonly encountered by anglers.

Although not as well-known as a bream fishery, the Merri does produce good size bream, along with estuary perch, the occasional small mulloway, and plenty of mullet.

There is a boat ramp at the bottom of Drummond Street, just upstream from the Princes Highway at Dennington, and another area upstream at the end of Russell Street where small craft may be launched. The narrow 'Cutting' is difficult to navigate in all but the smallest craft. There is plenty of foot access including a bicycle track along this stretch of water on the north side of the river. The 'Cutting' produces large brown trout during the spring months when the river is flooded.

Be aware of the Merri Marine Sanctuary at the mouth of the Merri River. Fishing is prohibited downstream of the footbridge near the river mouth. For more information about the Merri Marine Sanctuary visit www.parkweb.vic.gov.au

Lady Bay

The breakwater on the west headland in Lady Bay receives most attention from anglers. The outside and end of the breakwater does produce the occasional good size whiting and snapper on evening, and barracouta are sometimes taken after dark. Squid too may be taken under the lights and are quite plentiful. Fishing for them is best with small artificial jigs in the 2.5 and 3.0 size.

Daytime fishing is poor, unless you happen to encounter a shoal of salmon moving around the end of the breakwater, however the inside of the breakwater does produce small sand whiting and mullet. Salmon are common but also hard to catch in any numbers. The best success comes to those using berley and casting unweighted fillets of pilchard into the trail.

The boat ramp in Lady Bay is just north of, and sheltered by, the breakwater and gives access to good snapper grounds within a kilometre or so of the headland. However, dawn and dusk are the best times to fish because catches are seldom spectacular during the day.

Anglers fish from the relatively sheltered beach inside Lady Bay with mixed results. The dominant catch would be mullet, but snapper and mulloway have been taken here as well.

Logans Beach

Of the several beaches around Warrnambool, Logans Beach would be the most popular. The pronounced gutter east of the Logans Beach car park and whale observation area is considered the most productive area to fish.

This is a well-regarded salmon beach, which regularly produces numbers of big fish especially early and late in the day.

ABOVE: Salmon are the main target species throughout winter and a lot of fun to catch from the beaches.

Fishing at night can produce good sized gummy sharks, the odd snapper and mulloway, and at times it offers great fishing for school and gummy sharks. The best way to catch any of the mentioned species at night is with fresh salmon or mullet fillets which can be collected from the nearby estuary. If small pinky snapper are stealing your bait, try using tougher bait like squid or octopus. There are also large numbers of seven gill sharks in this area and when they move in it's often a good idea to move locations. Heavy tackle is required when targeting any of these species and although many have teeth that can bite you off, your still best to stick with using 80lb leaders and 7/0 circle hooks.

Levy's Beach

Several kilometres west of the Merri River mouth, Levy's Beach is one of the most consistent salmon producing beaches along the coast. Although there is no guarantee you will be successful, your chances here are always good. A paternoster rig is best offered and salmon respond well to berley. Best baits are white bait, blue bait and pipi. Mullet are also caught in good numbers close in behind the wash.

Helens Rock

Approximately 1.5 to 2km offshore from the west end of Levy's Beach, Helens Rock is a pinnacle rising to within a few metres of the surface. The pinnacle is only visible in a sea heavy enough to be unfishable. In calm to moderate conditions you will have to locate the pinnacle with your sounder. Having located it, take shore marks or a GPS reading for future reference.

The pinnacle holds good populations of snapper, yellowtail kingfish, warehou or snotty trevally and thresher sharks have often been sighted in its vicinity.

Various fishing techniques can be used here. For snapper and warehou a paternoster rig will suit while for kingfish you can either troll diving lures, squid strips or live baits such as salmon and or calamari.

The Cutting

Almost directly in front of The Tower Hill Game Reserve on Armstrong Bay, The Cutting is accessible from Gorman's Road. The beach produces mullet, whiting and salmon all year as well as the occasional bronze whaler and gummy shark at night. Anglers fishing for large sharks do so with specialised tackle but a good 12ft surf rod can still do the job. Due to the sharks sharp teeth, a rig made from wire will prevent being bitten off.

The Basin

The Basin produces good catches of salmon, whiting and mullet on light tackle and snapper have been taken from the reef at the eastern tip of Basin Point.

Yellowtail kingfish have been taken offshore from Basin Point and anglers have occasionally been successful drifting a fresh squid or live salmon out from the rocks under a balloon. However, when the word is out that kingfish are about, most boats trolling this area disregard rigs floated out by anglers from the rocks. Kingfish have been caught in this vicinity by anglers trolling garfish, live salmon and squid in water less than 5 m deep. Make sure you choose your tackle accordingly as fish up to 15 kg can be encountered. The point at the end of the Basin is popular with divers targeting abalone and crayfish when the sea is calm.

Small boats can be launched from the beach when conditions allow, although a 4WD is essential for launching.

Killarney

Killarney is popular among whiting anglers and good catches are taken, both from the beach and from boats anchored inside the sheltering reef that is located approximately 250 m offshore.

The sheltered waters at times also offer some of the best salmon fishing imaginable, with big fish pushing bait into the area on a run in tide. Here anglers can cast, troll and even fly fish for them, often with light tackle as the offshore reef breaks the heavy swell, doing away with the need for traditional long, heavy rods and tackle.

Small aluminium boats may be launched on the east end of Killarney Beach, which is accessible from the Basin Track although a 4WD is essential for launching.

Warrnambool—Offshore

While not always easily accessible, the offshore waters here do produce good fishing for anglers in the know. It is advisable to obtain local information before heading out as there are several large shallow banks that can and do break heavily. The area produces great snapper fishing out on the various reefs that can be found in 30 to 60m of water, along with Queen snapper, gummy and school shark. The best way to target them is by either drifting, or anchoring and using berley. The best snapper fishing is during the warmer months, with fish as large as 10kg caught during the spring months.

Heading out deeper still, anglers will also find good numbers of blue and mako sharks during the warmer months. From February throughout to the end of winter, Southern blue fin tuna are a common catch. While many are school sized ranging 12 to 25 kg, some fish in excess of 150 kg have been caught trolling lures. The fish are often wide spread and to find them, your best to head out a look for any surface feeding activity from either the tuna and or birds diving into bait balls. Tuna are usually found from 70m depth to the Continental shelf.

PORT FAIRY TO PORTLAND

PORT FAIRY

When you reach a place with a name like Killarney you can bet there is a good deal more that is Irish. In 1810 Captain Wishart sailed into the Moyne River for shelter and named the place Port Fairy after his ship Fairy. The town was renamed Belfast but eventually was it was changed back to Port Fairy. During the 1830s, this town was second only to Sydney as a trading port, so times have certainly changed since then.

EAST BEACH

Sheltered from prevailing westerlies, East Beach can be a comfortable if somewhat unproductive area by day. Evening and after dark produce the best results with mulloway and gummy shark among the prize catches. Good salmon can be caught at dawn and dusk. Bream are also caught occasionally, particularly when the river is in flood.

Generally, the fishing improves as you move further away from the river with favourite locations past the Life Saving Club. One of the better spots is the north-east end of the beach at Mill's Reef where good catches of snapper and yellowtail kingfish are sometimes taken.

SOUTH BEACH

South Beach is a difficult, rocky area where good size whiting are sometimes caught. However, parrot fish are the main capture using bait. Those with patients and are happy to persist through the parrot fish do catch some nice whiting. Drop-netters catch crayfish here, and anglers casting lures take salmon although they are usually small. Summer time is the prime to be fishing this location.

MOYNE RIVER

Anglers fishing from the main breakwater of the Moyne catch a variety of fish including gummy and school shark, rock cod, salmon, small snapper and many others. Small salmon, silver trevally and mullet are often taken in the Moyne River while bream are a possibility, particularly in the shallower waters of Belfast Lough and upstream. In the winter months good sized silver trevally up to 2 kg move into the river. The best time to fish for them is during the evening and after dark.

The rock walls of the Moyne are a great source of shrimp for bream bait. A baited shrimp trap among the rocks will usually get you a good supply. Mulloway come into the Moyne at times, usually school fish, but a prize nevertheless for prepared anglers.

The Moyne River is also stocked with 2000 yearling brown trout annually and its lower reaches are classified as a sea-run trout fishery. The river below the Toolong Bridge is exempt from the Victorian salmonid closed season regulations and is open to fishing all year round. Trout can be taken using a number of techniques with those flicking small trout imitation hard body lures yield the best results.

BOAT FISHING

The boat ramp in the Moyne River is completely protected, giving anglers access to splendid fishing for whiting and snapper within a few kilometres radius of the harbour. Kingfish are also a possibility around the reefy point known as Mill's Reef at the eastern end of East Beach during the summer months.

Good snapper fishing, for relatively small fish, is to be had around Griffith Island on daybreak and dusk. There is good whiting fishing available in the lee of the breakwater, near Mill's Reef, and around the coast to Killarney. Labella Reef, approximately 400 m ESE of Griffith Island is one of the more productive areas for snapper, but it pays to be on the water at first light to have a reasonable chance of doing well

Birds working in Port Fairy Bay often betray shoals of salmon that take lures readily, and shark fishing enthusiast will find blue sharks, makos and threshers right along this stretch of coastline. Large great white sharks, a protected species, are also in this vicinity, particularly around Lady Julia Percy Island. Gummy shark, school shark and Queen snapper are also targeted by anglers either drifting or anchoring in 30 to 50 m of water off the Port Fairy Lighthouse. The larger snapper are also caught here during the spring months.

LADY JULIA PERCY ISLAND

A 25 km run from Port Fairy, Lady Julia Percy Island is to the west and offshore from Yambuk. The waters around the island produce a wide variety of fish including kingfish, sweep, Queen snapper, warehou or snotty trevalla, snook and many others.

Thunder Point, the southern-most headland of the island, is an excellent area to jig or live bait for kingfish provided the weather is not coming in hard from this quarter. Their characteristic habit of schooling vertically over prominent reef makes them easier to locate using a sounder than most fish.

Lady Julia's great white sharks are no myth, and berleying is very likely to bring a visitor. Retrieve your lines and enjoy the experience of seeing a predator of this stature at close quarters.

As the kingfish have come back in better numbers over the past years local anglers have also uncovered several patches of reef about half way to the island. These reefs hold big numbers of kings and snapper over the warmer months. There are a couple of techniques that work when trying to locate the schools of kings. The first is to anchor on the edge of the reef and berley, or secondly to troll diving minnow lures around the island until the fish are located.

Fishing wide of Julia Percy during autumn is a good way to find schools of bluefin tuna. In fact it was along the edge of the shelf wide of here in 2006 that some local anglers caught a huge bluefin tuna on a lure—the beginning of a run of massive fish that anglers had never seen or caught in Victoria before. Since this time, fish over 150 kg have been landed in water as shallow as 50 m, during the autumn months as the fish endure their annual migration. Trolling lures and cubing with pilchards are methods which have successfully taken these lager fish.

THE CRAGS

The Crags is more noteworthy for its impressive rock formations than for fishing. Access to the Crags is down Crags Road from the Princes Highway. There is limited beach access here where mullet, whiting and salmon are sometimes taken.

In calm weather, the rock formations offer marginal access to rock anglers who take good catches of sweep and a variety of reef fish. Large swells make this location dangerous.

YAMBUK LAKE

Approximately 16 km east of Port Fairy, Yambuk Lake is the combined coastal lagoon estuary of the Eumeralla and Shaw Rivers. Periodically open to the sea, the channel extends little more than a kilometre upstream from the boat ramp on the east side of the entrance.

Although a variety of fish including mullet are available, bream are the main target in Yambuk Lake. The best specimens are found in the shallow waters of the lagoon upstream from the entrance channel where a shallow draught boat will maximise your chances.

Weed is a nuisance throughout Yambuk, but fishing unweighted baits, or lures and flies, usually overcomes the problem. Bait anglers fishing from the bank have resorted to using partially filled bubble floats to give additional weight for casting, just like many trout anglers do in fresh water.

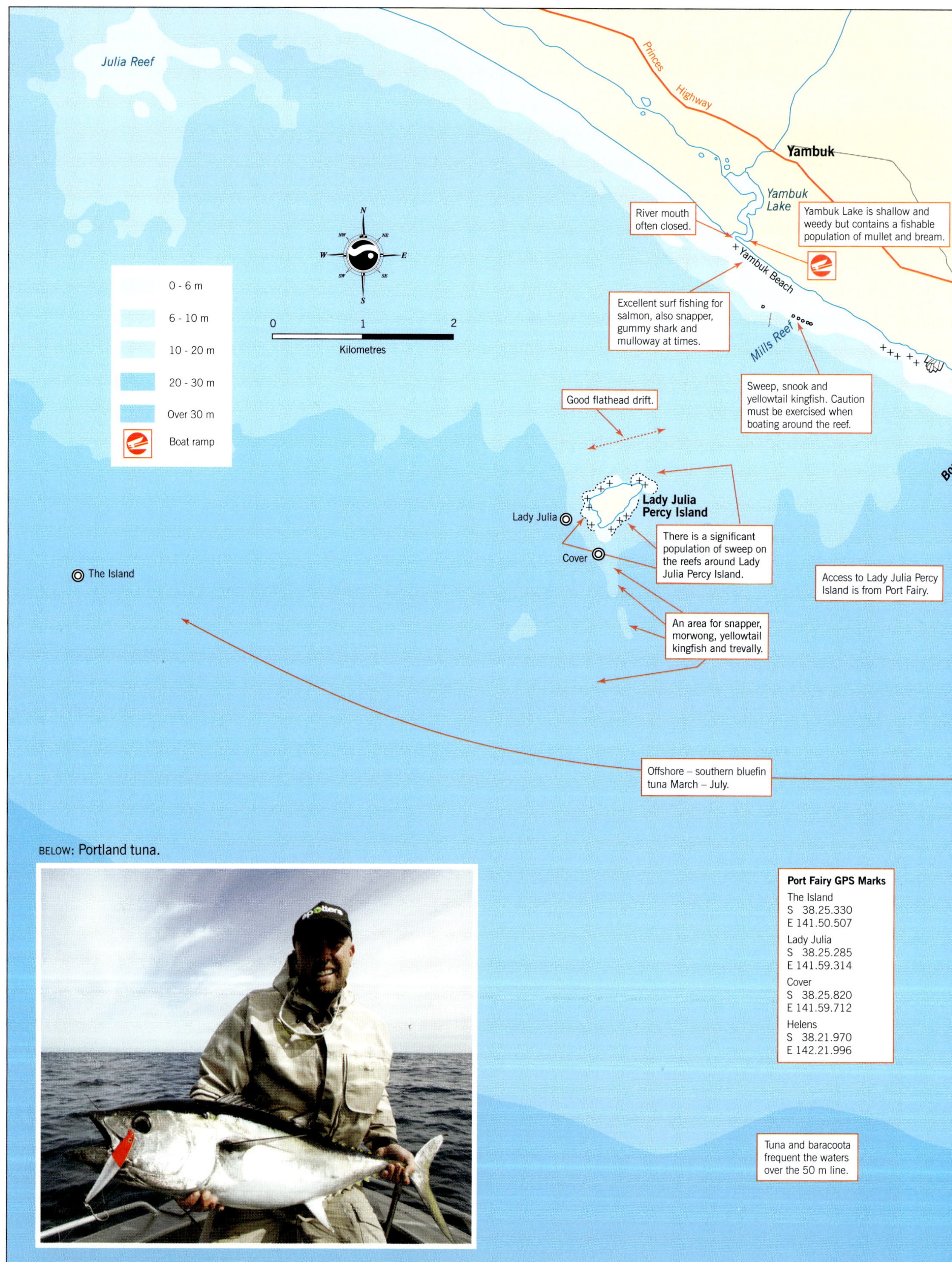

BELOW: Portland tuna.

MAP 43 HELEN ROCK TO YAMBUK

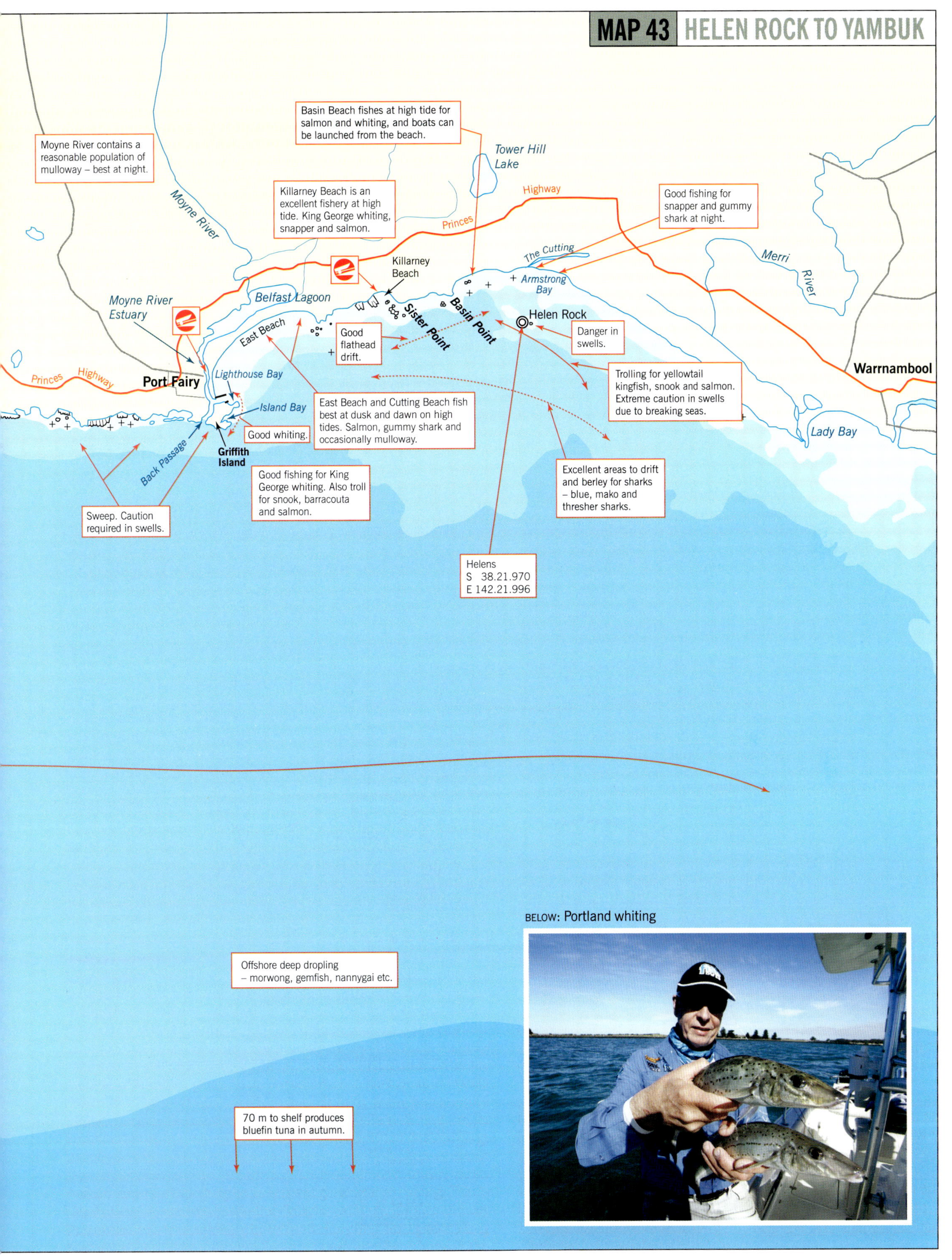

BELOW: Portland whiting

Bank access is limited at Yambuk with possibly the lower Eumeralla River—between the stone ford crossing downstream to the lake—offering the best chance of catching bream. Butcher's jetty and O'Brien's Point, approximately 500 m upstream from the boat ramp, are also popular spots with anglers. The new floating pontoon jetty at the boat ramp makes launching easy and provides a good platform to fish.

YAMBUK BEACH

The entrance beach of Yambuk Lake is among the more productive areas for surf anglers along the coast, producing a variety of fish including snapper, salmon and sharks. It is an easy walk from the car park to the beach. There is a camp ground situated not far from the beach on the edge of the lake and it is a great location for visiting anglers and families.

The beach on the west side of the entrance is best should you be prepared to wade across the shallow entrance and walk several hundred metres past the reef. Evening is the best time to fish here with salmon, snapper, gummy shark and the occasional mulloway. Mulloway to over 25 kg have been taken along this beach during the warmer months. Fishing at night using squid and fish fillet baits is the most productive time to fish with a run in tide.

FITZROY RIVER

Although it is not a noted estuary, both bream and estuary perch are caught in the Fitzroy River. There is a camping area at the Fitzroy River, but there are no facilities available other than toilets and fire-places.

Fitzroy River is better known for providing access to Narrawong Beach, which is one of the most productive surf beaches on Victoria's west coast (see below). The beach at the bottom of Thompsons Road is snaggy and difficult to fish but the river mouth is usually shallow enough to wade across. However, there is a log crossing 100 m upstream from the stormwater drain should the entrance prove difficult.

NARRAWONG

The township of Narrawong is about 19 km east of Portland on the Princes Highway. There is a caravan park and camping area and most requirements for anglers. Bream are sometimes taken in the Surrey River, but small fish are a nuisance. The bend upstream from the mouth is a productive spot toward evening. Bait fishing methods are best offered.

NARRAWONG BEACH

Narrawong Beach lies between the Fitzroy and Surrey rivers north-east of Portland. The beach has an excellent reputation for producing snapper from legal size to several kilograms, along with gummy sharks and mulloway.

Narrawong beach is not particularly deep; the key to success is to fish in the evenings and after dark. However, during the day, you will need to look for suitable gutter formations and deeper areas that should produce fish.

One area that regularly produces snapper to 3 kg and school mulloway, begins about 400 m north-east of the Surrey River mouth, but like all beaches, formations are changeable so you constantly need to re-assess where to fish. Narrawong Beach is a good option if you find the beaches further east are too rough to fish. The coastline of Portland reduces the impact of the south-west swell along this stretch.

PORTLAND TO GLENELG RIVER

PORTLAND BAY

Anglers fish at many spots in Portland Bay, both from the rocks and beaches, and from boats offshore. The boat ramp in Portland Bay gives boat access to this productive area. While the majority of anglers target the great whiting that can be taken here, there is also some the best fishing in Victoria for species such as snapper, squid, kingfish, salmon, gummy sharks and mulloway.

SNAPPER POINT

Snapper Point and the Beach to the east toward Church Camp include productive areas for beach anglers and anglers fishing offshore.

There are several shallow reefs in the area that produce good snapper after rough weather and the sand holes produce good sized whiting. While the water has a bit of colour to it, fishing at night with live baits and fresh squid, both of which can be caught nearby or in the Portland Harbour, can produce mulloway.

During the summer months when the water is clean and warm it is also a great area to find kingfish, many of which are taken by trolling squid strips and live baits. If you are fishing from a boat, try anchoring on the back of the reef in about 8 or 9 m of water off the abalone farm and fish with a live squid or salmon under a balloon on one rod and fish for snapper and whiting on the bottom with another rod. In recent times, casting surface for kingfish has been increasing in popularity. When the kings can be seen on the water's surface, that is the time, stick baits and popper should be cast about.

THE ROCK WALL

Landbased anglers seeking snapper will also find their quarry within casting distance of the rock wall along Dutton Way, both during and immediately after an onshore blow.

Although the snapper run does not get underway until November, as early as August, snapper have been caught along the rock wall under the conditions mentioned.

Other species often taken from the rock wall include salmon and some big whiting. Often the really big whiting are taken on baits such as whole pilchards and squid strips intended for bigger fish. Occasionally mulloway are taken just out from the small creek known as 'Maritemo Gates' along the western end of the rock wall during the spring and summer months. During the summer months, kingfish are also taken both on dead baits such as strips for squid fished on paternoster rigs and live baits by those ballooning them out into the deeper water. When targeting kingfish, heavy tackle is required.

Those fishing a running sinker on the bottom often come into contact with some large gummy sharks. Gummy sharks can be caught year round but tend to more abundance at night and during the lead up to a full moon. Fresh salmon or squid baits are a hot favourite.

NUNS BEACH

Just north of the Lee Breakwater large King George whiting can be caught from Nuns Beach from first light until an hour after sun up.

If the sea conditions are dead calm while chasing the whiting and if fishing near either end of the beach where there is some rock and reef, it can be worth having a baited squid jig out under a float. Some really big whiting of over a kilogram are caught here regularly during the summer months.

PORTLAND OFFSHORE

You would be hard pressed to find another location that produces more big fish each year than the offshore waters of Portland.

The reason this area fishes so well has something to do with the fact that the continental shelf runs past here, and although it is a long way offshore it brings nutrient-rich water and fish with it.

The area also has deep water close to shore and extensive reef systems that offer prime fish habitat. Combined with all this is a deep, safe harbour that allows boats of all sizes to be launched with

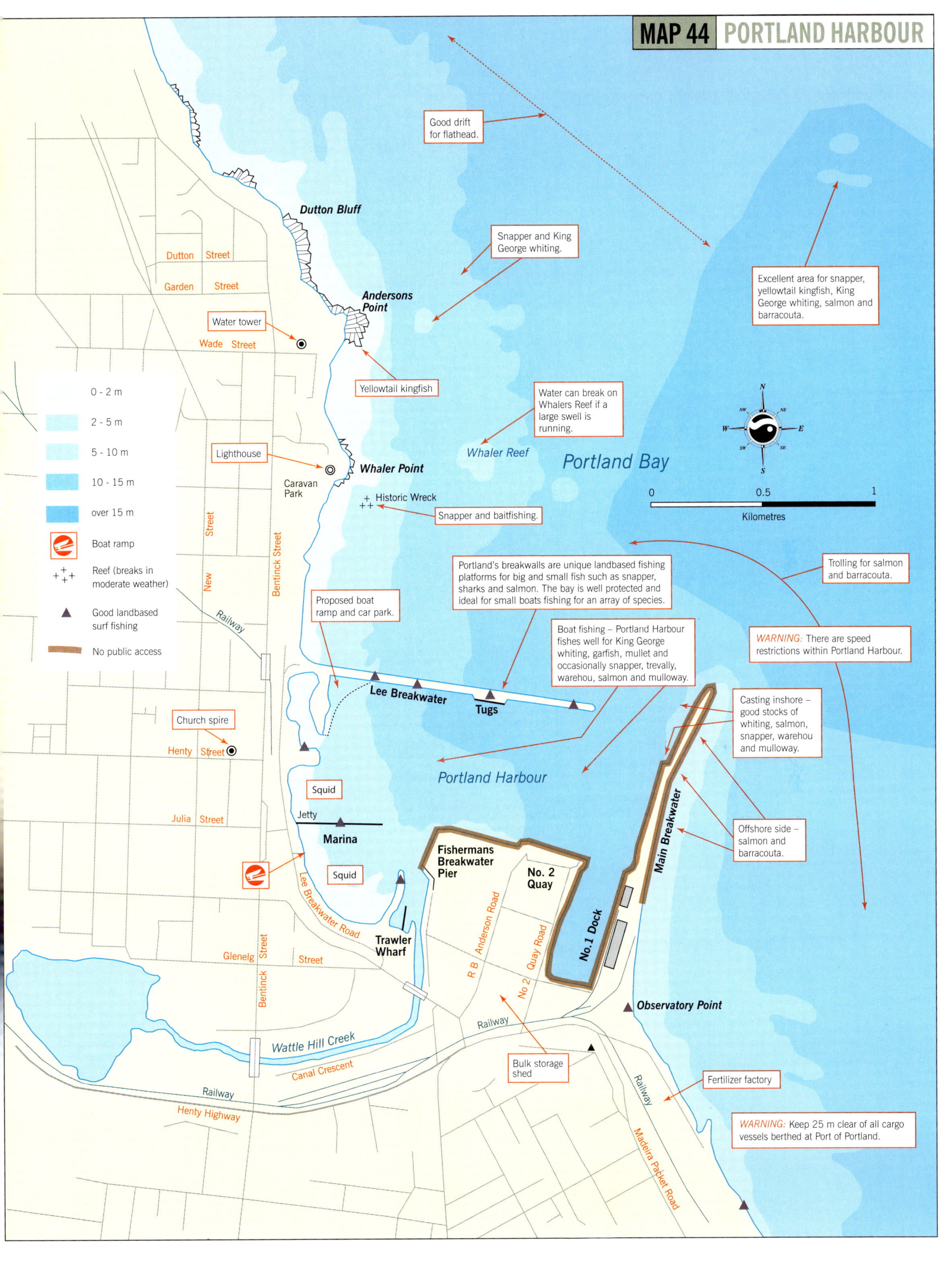

MAP 44 PORTLAND HARBOUR
Good drift for flathead.
Dutton Bluff
Snapper and King George whiting.
Andersons Point
Excellent area for snapper, yellowtail kingfish, King George whiting, salmon and barracouta.
Water tower
Wade Street
Dutton Street
Garden Street
Yellowtail kingfish
Water can break on Whalers Reef if a large swell is running.
Whaler Reef
Portland Bay
0 - 2 m
2 - 5 m
5 - 10 m
10 - 15 m
over 15 m
Boat ramp
Reef (breaks in moderate weather)
Good landbased surf fishing
No public access
Lighthouse
Whaler Point
Caravan Park
Historic Wreck
Snapper and baitfishing.
0
0.5
1
Kilometres
Trolling for salmon and barracouta.
Portland's breakwalls are unique landbased fishing platforms for big and small fish such as snapper, sharks and salmon. The bay is well protected and ideal for small boats fishing for an array of species.
Proposed boat ramp and car park.
Boat fishing – Portland Harbour fishes well for King George whiting, garfish, mullet and occasionally snapper, trevally, warehou, salmon and mulloway.
WARNING: There are speed restrictions within Portland Harbour.
New Street
Bentinck Street
Railway
Lee Breakwater
Tugs
Casting inshore – good stocks of whiting, salmon, snapper, warehou and mulloway.
Church spire
Henty Street
Portland Harbour
Squid
Jetty
Marina
Julia Street
Main Breakwater
Offshore side – salmon and barracouta.
Fishermans Breakwater Pier
No. 2 Quay
Squid
Lee Breakwater Road
Trawler Wharf
No.1 Dock
Anderson Road
R B
Quay Road
No 2
Glenelg Street
Street
Bentinck Street
Observatory Point
Railway
Wattle Hill Creek
Canal Crescent
Bulk storage shed
Railway
Henty Highway
Railway
Fertilizer factory
WARNING: Keep 25 m clear of all cargo vessels berthed at Port of Portland.
Madeira Packet Road

MAP 45 FITZROY RIVER TO PORTLAND AND DISCOVERY BAY

RIGHT: Port Fairy gummy shark.

ABOVE: Tuna of all sizes can be caught with the typical size averaging around 15 kilos.

ease, meaning anglers can venture out to target the species on offer at different times of the year.

It's the nearer reefs and rubble patches which offer some of the best snapper, whiting and flathead fishing on the coast, while trolling around Danger Point, Whaler Reef and out around the famous Lawrence Rock will nearly always produce some pike and snook. In season there are some great salmon to be found as well as good numbers of kingfish during the summer months.

Along the north shore area there are some shallow patches of reef to be found such as Minerva Reef and Julia Reef. These are known kingfish areas, and while they are very shallow with the best areas being about 5m deep, the kingfish often show up here in big numbers. The most productive way of targeting them seems to be by trolling squid strips or skipping garfish, however many anglers are now finding success using soft plastic lures fished on light tackle.

At night these reefs are also good spots to try for mulloway, which are best targeted with live baits such as mullet.

Heading further around the coast to the headlands of Cape Nelson and Bridgewater you will find similar species, and this area has some huge kingfish on offer for those who take the time to target them. Take note that when fishing these exposed headlands, you are in the Southern Ocean and the swells can be big and very powerful, so be careful how close you get to the rocks.

Gummy and school shark can be caught by drifting and anchoring whilst using berley in 30 to 100 m of water off Cape Nelson. Queen snapper are also regularly encountered when drifting over the reef patches.

Each autumn the waters here produce good bluefin tuna. The bluefin action differs from year to year, and it can depend on how close to shore they come whether anglers can catch them, and how big they are. In general the smaller school-sized tuna around the 20 kg mark tend to come within a few kilometers of shore, even if it is only for a short time on their migratory route. However as anglers start to head further offshore to the outer edge of the continental shelf (around 60 km out) some huge bluefin are being found with many anglers getting stretched by fish that can range in sizes from 60 to 130 kg and bigger. The area known as the 'Horseshoe' to the south-west is a popular place to start trolling. This is a popular area to find good numbers of albacore, some of which reach over 30 kilograms.

During the summer months the same waters produce first class shark fishing for blue and especially mako sharks, many of which are big ones, while the shallow reefs hold numbers of big thresher sharks. Mako sharks are also seasonally abundant off Cape Nelson in around 50 to 60 m of water when the tuna are around.

At the other end of the scale, whiting anglers have done well fishing inside the reef and indeed all the way from Portland to Narrawong Beach when the weather permits. Productive whiting marks in Portland Bay include 400m offshore from the Dutton Way caravan park.

Offshore from the creek in front of the historic homestead 'Maretimo', is popular with anglers who occasionally take whiting at dawn and dusk, and snapper.

Cod Splat

This productive snapper mark is a patch of light rubble some 3 to 4 km off the harbour entrance in line with Lady Julia Percy Island. Anglers blessed with favourable weather drift across this area until a snapper or flathead is hooked before putting down the anchor.

Portland Harbour

In this part of the world the weather is often far from kind, however with a harbour such as the one at Portland, a bit of bad weather is almost a good thing as it will encourage you to fish in this protected—and very productive— water.

Being very deep the harbour holds all types of fish. Anglers catch good numbers of whiting up to a kilo along with pinky snapper and the occasional bigger fish, as well as numbers of trevally that live around all the wharves.

It is also a great place to chase smaller fish, either for bait or fun with good numbers of mullet and garfish, and during the warmer months, slimy mackerel. Winter also sees schools of salmon enter the harbour. These tend to be caught by anglers trolling diving hard body lures as well as casting and retrieving metal slugs. Bait fishing will produce some nice fish on occasion.

Casting a squid jig around the rock walls and weed beds will also turn up squid, some of which are monsters usually from October to April. Still, they are a viable option for anglers all year.

In the harbour it's not just smaller bread-and-butter fish that are on offer. For those who want to try for something bigger, a larger bait can see you hooked up to a big snapper, or an occasional gummy shark or a mulloway, while during February and March anglers often hook kingfish which range in size from rats to hoodlums. To find if there are any kings around, berley up the garfish and mullet then put out one or two live. If the kings are nearby, you will see them sending baitfish everywhere.

Lee Breakwater

Possibly the most popular and famous part of the whole harbour, the breakwater offers land based anglers the chance to get amongst the great fishing. From here it is possible to catch all the mentioned species within the harbour, while casting larger baits on the outside of the rock wall sees you in with a great chance of snapper, gummy sharks, mulloway, salmon and kingfish. A smaller bait of pipi or squid puts you in the running for some huge whiting. This can all take place while sitting in or next to the comfort of your car.

As with most land based fishing, the best results come to anglers who fish first and last light and at night, and to those who use fresh baits, especially squid or garfish. Garfish and squid are plentiful in the harbour. These can be caught very easily and used immediately. If live baiting with garfish, pin them gently and suspend them under a bobby cork float or small balloon.

The Reclaimed Land

The reclaimed land in front of the convent beside the Lee Breakwater, is a popular spot for King George whiting, and catches of over half a dozen prime specimens are not uncommon during the warmer months. During the cooler months the area is usually invaded by silver trevally which can reach up to two kilograms. Various techniques can be used here but those using bait fishing methods tend to see the better results. A paternoster rig with two droppers each containing a size #6 circle hooks will suffice.

Bridgewater Bay

Bridgewater Bay lies between Cape Nelson and Cape Bridgewater. Shelly Beach, at the western end of the bay, is one of the few locations where snapper can occasionally be seen feeding close to shore at night. When they are schooled up and feeding here, a powerful torch may show their tails protruding from the water as they feed head down in the sand.

Depending on the sea, Bishops Rock and Flat Rock are productive fishing platforms but take care because anglers have been swept in from here.

Discovery Bay

Discovery Bay, between Cape Bridgewater and the mouth of the Glenelg River, is noted for big salmon, but snapper, gummy shark and the occasional mulloway have been taken along here as well. Fishing at night with fresh baits is the most productive time to fish, although salmon will bite throughout the day. At the eastern end (Cape Bridgewater end) of the bay is the Discovery Bay Marine National Park, where fishing is prohibited. For more information visit www.parkweb.vic.gov.au

Travelling toward Nelson, the first point of access is the road to Swan Lake camping and picnic area. From here there is a 1.5 km 4WD track to the beach, but it is not permitted to drive along the beach or through the sand dunes.

The next point of access is about 2 km further along the Portland-Nelson Road past the Winnap turn-off. This leads into a car park from where you can walk to the beach.

Discovery Bay terminates at the mouth of the Glenelg River. Access to Discovery Bay from Nelson on the Glenelg River is via a beach road followed by a walk of approximately one kilometre.

GLENELG RIVER

Situated very close to the South Australian border, the township of Nelson lies on the Glenelg River. This area is without doubt a favourite location to head away for a few days of low stress fishing in some of the best surroundings imaginable.

With huge limestone cliffs that wind their way along the river, mixed with rocky banks, snags, old boat sheds and cabins built over the water, and reed beds, it is bream heaven, offering an endless variety of locations for them to live in.

What also makes the Glenelg River so famous is the run of school mulloway that enter the river each year, often in huge numbers. While it may not produce the very large fish it used to (just head to the Nelson pub to see some pictures of massive jewies from years ago) the river continues to produce good fishing for school mulloway, with several fish up to 12 lb often being taken in a single session.

The preferred method for targeting the mulloway used by the locals is to tow live mullet behind old putter boats at slow speeds, however these days many anglers now fish the same way but with electric motors to move more silently along the river.

above: Glenelg River

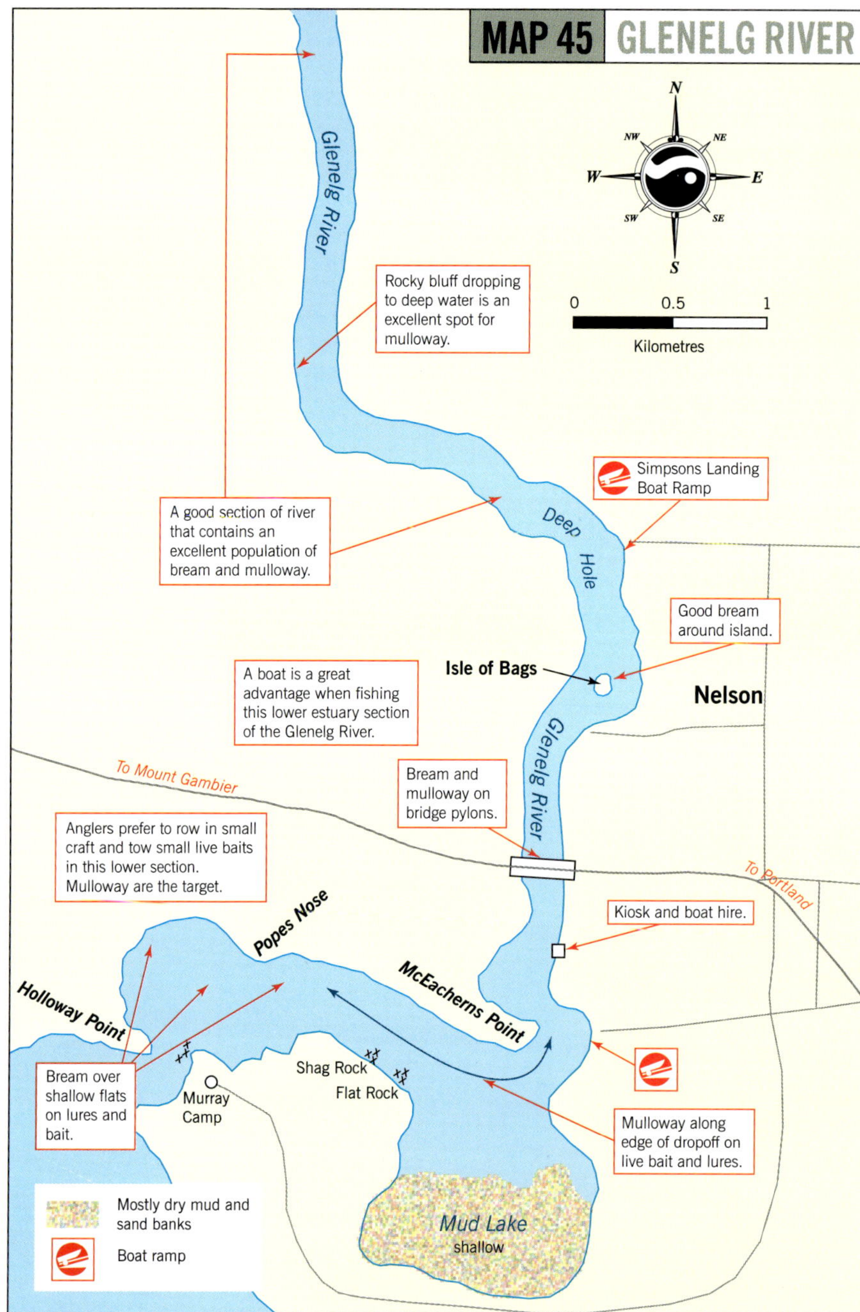

Known spots to target mulloway are the estuary at the mouth, the main highway bridge, Taylors Straight, Donovans, Dry Creek and Sapling Creek.

At times the mulloway also respond very well to trolled or cast diving minnow lures and anglers also do very well casting soft plastics along the rock walls and other drop-offs where they hold. While the river itself doesn't regularly produce big mulloway, the beach out of the Glenelg River does. It is very shallow and featureless, and does require you to wade out a fair way to get your bait into one of the distant gutters that can be spotted in daylight hours.

Aside from the mulloway, good bream fishing can be found along the entire river, although certain spots are better than others depending on time of year. The preferred technique is to either nose the boat into the bank casting baits of worm, prawn or similar out onto the bottom, or to use tow anchors holding the boat front and back, then cast baits of fresh caught crab towards the shaded rock walls—this is where the really big bream often live. Crabs can be easily gathered all along the rocky shoreline by placing a tin in the water with some fish in it. Leave it for a few hours before checking it and you should have some bait.

The whole river is also a great location to target bream on lures and flies—often the bream fishing in here can be so good it's hard to get past the small bream to get to the bigger ones.

Other species on offer in the river include estuary perch, most of which live in heavy snags from Sapling Creek and further upstream. There are plenty present, many of which are huge and hard to stop.

Down towards the mouth there are lots of mullet and small salmon, as well as the occasional small King George whiting. There has also been the odd gummy shark and elephant fish taken in the mouth area.

You can buy live mullet and other bait from the Nelson boat hire—there and the Nelson pub are the best places to get the local info on where to fish.

There are several boat ramps at Nelson on the Glenelg River; two below the highway bridge, one upstream at the island monument, and another upstream from that at Simpsons Landing.

The Glenelg River crosses the South Australia Border above Taylors Strait some 10 km from the mouth. The settlement of Donovans and Donovans Landing are in South Australia so South Australian regulations on boating and angling apply.

Above Donovans, the Glenelg River runs east back into Victoria once more past the Princess Margaret Rose Caves and Sandy Waterholes, where there is another boat launching ramp.

Access throughout the entire estuary is mainly by boat, however, there is limited upstream bank access from the Winnap Nelson Road and Wanwin Road.

TACKLE & GENERAL INFORMATION

Compleat Angler Portland
69 Bentiinck Street
Portland Vic 3305
Phone: (03) 5521 1844

Port Fairy Sports and Toys
64 Sackville St
Port Fairy Vic. 3284
Phone: (03) 5568 1788

Portland Bait & Tackle
111 Bentick Street
Portland Vic 3305
Phone: (03) 5523 5213

better boating VICTORIA

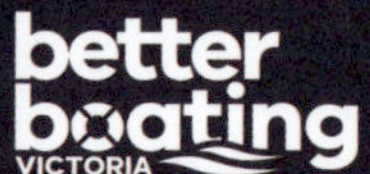

Better boat ramps at Inverloch

Boating access to Anderson Inlet is better than ever thanks to two projects funded by your boating licence and registration fees.

At Mahers Landing, there's a new two-lane ramp that provides great access to deep water.

A new jetty alongside has room for 8 boats to tie up and is complemented by 55 asphalt parking spaces for cars with trailers, plus a fish cleaning table and toilet block.

The $5.45 million project includes guard rails, rubber fenders on the jetty, and solar lighting to aid launching in the dark.

At the Inverloch ramp nearby, a second jetty has been built to provide more protection from tidal flow and increase the number of boats that can be tied up while trailers are retrieved from the car park.

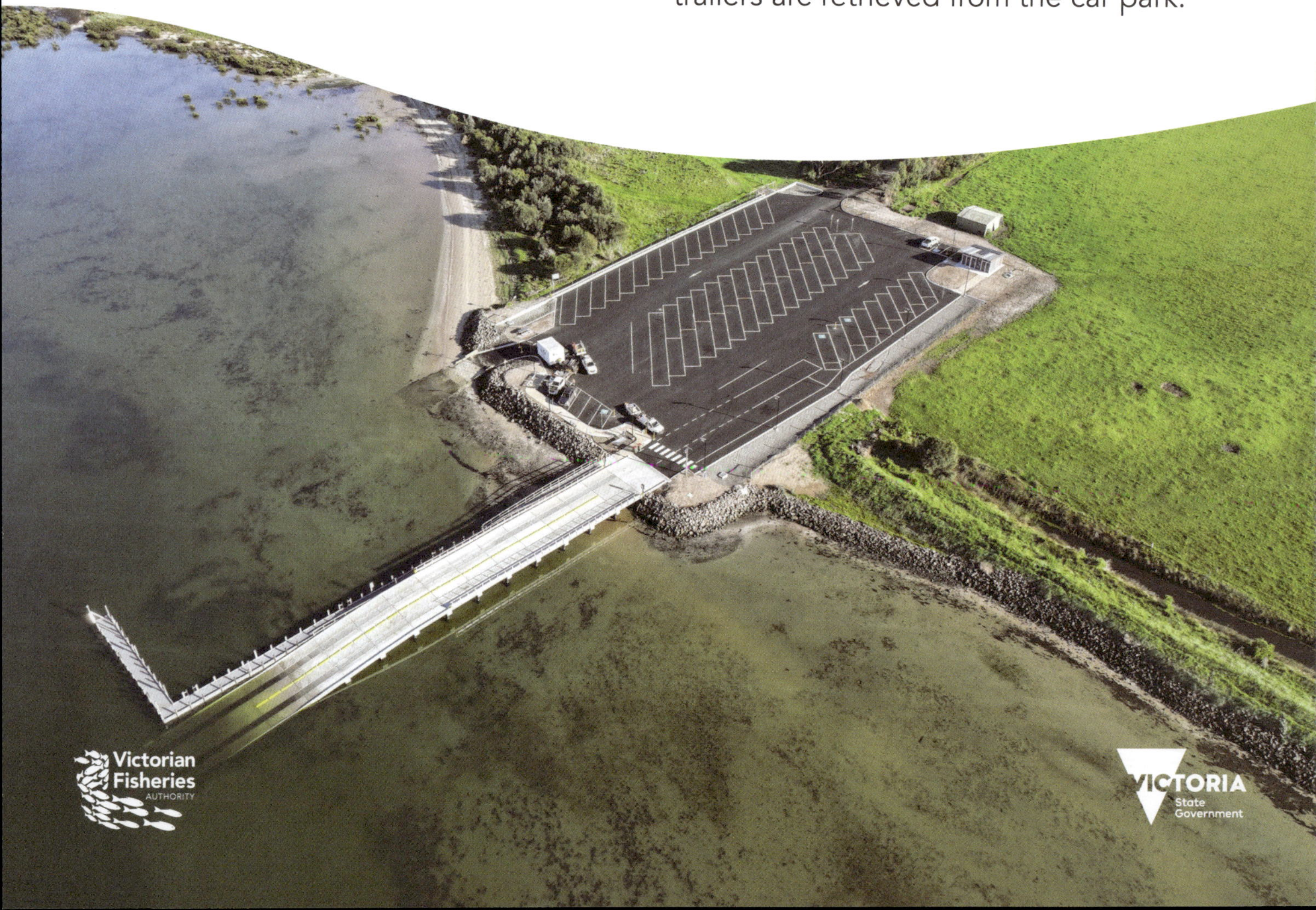

Victorian Fisheries AUTHORITY

VICTORIA State Government